A Revolution for Our Rights

A REVOLUTION
FOR OUR RIGHTS

Indigenous Struggles for Land
and Justice in Bolivia, 1880–1952

Laura Gotkowitz

DUKE UNIVERSITY PRESS
Durham & London 2007

© 2007 Duke University Press
All rights reserved
Printed in the United States of America
on acid-free paper ∞

Designed by Jennifer Hill
Typeset in Minion Pro by Keystone Typesetting, Inc.
Library of Congress Cataloging-in-Publication Data
appear on the last printed page of this book.

The author thanks the Institute for the Study of the Americas, University of London, for permission to reprint earlier versions of portions of chapters 7 and 8 and the conclusion, which appeared in Laura Gotkowitz, "Revisiting the Rural Roots of the Revolution," in Proclaiming Revolution: Bolivia in Comparative Perspective, *ed. by Merilee S. Grindle and Pilar Domingo (London: Institute of Latin American Studies, University of London; and Cambridge, Mass.: David Rockefeller Center for Latin American Studies, Harvard University, 2003). Earlier versions of chapters 7 and 8 also appeared in " 'Under the Dominion of the Indian': Rural Mobilization, the Law, and Revolutionary Nationalism in Bolivia in the 1940s,"* in Nils Jacobsen and Cristóbal Aljovín de Losada, eds., Political Cultures in the Andes, 1750–1950 *(Durham: Duke University Press, 2005).*

To the beautiful spirit of my sister Frances

In memory of my father, Joe

For my mother, Helen

CONTENTS

ILLUSTRATIONS

ACKNOWLEDGMENTS

It is a pleasure to thank the friends and colleagues whose help, support, and wisdom sustained and inspired me during the years that I worked on this book. My first debt is to the staff at the archives and libraries in Bolivia who generously facilitated my research. I would especially like to thank Froilan Pérez, former staff member at the Archivo de la Corte Superior de Justicia de Cochabamba; the judges and aides in the courts of Cliza and Punata; and the staff at the municipal archives of Punata and Quillacollo. All graciously allowed me to sort freely through the rich and largely uncatalogued documents in these repositories, lent corners of their offices and desks, and taught me about local history and legal systems. For their guidance and assistance, I am also grateful to the staff at Cochabamba's Archivo Histórico de la Prefectura, Biblioteca Municipal, Hemeroteca Municipal, and Archivo del Arzobispado, and to the staff at the Archivo Histórico del Honorable Congreso Nacional in La Paz, at the Archivo de La Paz, and at the Archivo y Biblioteca Nacionales in Sucre. I especially wish to thank the director of the Archivo Histórico Municipal de Cochabamba, Itala De Mamán, and successive directors of the Archivo de La Paz—Roberto Choque, Laura Escobari,

Ximena Medinaceli, and Rossana Barragán—for their generous assistance and advice.

Very special thanks are owed to my professors at the University of Chicago: John Coatsworth and Friedrich Katz. I can only say how much each has inspired me through his own work, and how much their teachings, incisive questions, encouragement, and generosity have meant to me. I thank them, too, for their ongoing support in the years since graduate school. My deep thanks also go to Tom Holt, whose comments and encouragement were critical to the development of this project.

Many friends and scholars have been crucial to the life of this project in myriad ways. It would take many pages to recount the specific ways that each one helped, but I would like to at least express my gratitude to Xavier Albó, Esther Aillón, Cristóbal Aljovín, Rossana Barragán, Kate Bjork, Katherine Bliss, Pamela Calla, Itala De Mamán, Robin Derby, Alison Dorsey, Bruce Dorsey, Roberto Fernández, José Gordillo, Mónica de Grigoriú, Guido Guzmán, Kevin Healy, Iván Hinojosa, Martha Hodes, Pieter Judson, Jennie Keith, María Lagos, Erick Langer, Brooke Larson, Kathryn Ledebur, Ana María Lema, Susy López Portillo, Agnes Lugo-Ortiz, Joanie Matlack, Ximena Medinaceli, Lucía Melgar, Zoila Mendoza, Fanor Meruvia, David Mercado, Diane Miliotes, Laurie Milner, Mercedes Niño-Murcia, Andy Orta, Michela Pentimalli, Seemin Qayum, José Antonio Rocha, Stuart Rockefeller, Gustavo Rodríguez, Wálter Sánchez, Sinclair Thomson, Esteban Ticona, Claudia Urquidi, Miriam Vargas, Chuck Walker, Rich Warren, Bob Weinberg, Sarah Willie, Eileen Willingham, and Ann Zulawski. My thanks go to all for their encouragement and intellectual support.

My gratitude also goes to many people who read and commented on versions of various chapters: Jeremy Adelman, Cristóbal Aljovín, David Arkush, Rossana Barragán, Joe Barton, John Coatsworth, Brodie Fischer, José Gordillo, Jeff Gould, Charlie R. Hale, Olivia Harris, Nils Jacobsen, Erick Langer, Brooke Larson, Debbie Poole, Hernán Pruden, Lara Putnam, Seemin Qayum, Cynthia Radding, Joanne Rappaport, Shira Robinson, Gustavo Rodríguez, Frank Safford, Shel Stromquist, Ann Zulawski, and Charles A. Hale—whose presence in Iowa City is much missed. I thank Charlie not only for his comments but also for being a wonderful colleague. I owe a special debt to Nils Jacobsen and Brooke Larson for their extensive comments and insightful suggestions on early versions of the entire manuscript, and to Sinclair Thomson for his tremendously stimulating feedback on a penultimate one. Michel Gobat commented on and discussed multiple drafts and contributed in every possible way to the final product. I would also like to thank Duke's anonymous readers for their extremely helpful comments and suggestions. For endlessly inspiring conversations about shared interests and passions, my deep thanks go to Rossana Barragán and Brooke Larson.

While carrying out the initial research, I was affiliated with the Centro de Estudios de la Realidad Económica y Social (CERES) in Cochabamba, and I wish to thank the researchers there for their guidance and support. Roberto Laserna, Rosario León, Alberto Rivera, and Juan Torrico all taught me much about contemporary Cochabamba and provided crucial assistance and advice. I am grateful to Roberto Laserna for helping me negotiate some tricky archival situations. I thank Rosario for her perceptive suggestions and questions, and Don Juan for his generous support for my research and for sharing his knowledge of the 1940s and 1950s. Conversations with Federico Sánchez de Losada, Dr. Raimundo Grigoriú, Eduardo Arze Loureiro, and Alcira Patiño further illuminated Cochabamba's past. I am grateful to all of them for sharing their insights and experiences with me. I owe a special debt to Susy López Portillo and to María Ana Cantuta for their assistance with research in Cochabamba and La Paz; and to David Gilbert for his help in the United States. My deep gratitude goes to Roger Mamani Siñani for his indispensable assistance tracking down and obtaining photos in La Paz; to Luis Antezana E. for generously allowing me to use photographs from his private collection; and to Sam Bryan for taking the time to show me the wonderful photos that his father, the filmmaker Julien Bryan, took in Bolivia in the 1940s, and for permitting me to include them in the book. I thank Todd Erickson at the University of Iowa Center for Media Production and Onno Brouwer and Heather Francisco at the University of Wisconsin, Madison, Cartography Lab for making the maps, and the staff at the map libraries at the University of Iowa, the University of Wisconsin, and the University of Chicago for helping me obtain the necessary raw material.

I would also like to express my thanks to the institutions that provided financial support for this project: Social Science Research Council/American Council of Learned Societies, Mellon/University of Chicago, and Harvard University's Graduate School of Arts and Sciences funded the bulk of the initial dissertation research and writing on which the book is based. A Fulbright-Hays Faculty Research Fellowship, American Historical Association Beveridge Research grant, Swarthmore College, and the University of

Iowa (College of Liberal Arts and Sciences, History Department, and Office of the Vice President for Research) supported subsequent research and writing. I thank Dieter Stadler, director of the Casa de los Tres Mundos in Granada, Nicaragua, for making available the palatial surroundings where the first pages were written, and Jay Semel, director of the Obermann Center for Advanced Studies at the University of Iowa, for providing a congenial space to work at a later phase. It has been a great pleasure to work with Valerie Millholland and Miriam Angress at Duke University Press, and I am grateful for their generous assistance and advice. I owe a special debt to Mark Mastromarino for guiding the manuscript through the production process and for his astute editorial eye. I thank Jo Butterfield and Alayna Cohen for some crucial assistance at the very end.

My heartfelt thanks go to Elizabeth and Ronald Méndez; Michela Pentimalli; Cristina de Lizarazu; Rossana Barragán and Ramiro Molina Rivero and family; and Jenny Luray and family for their warm hospitality, generosity, and the happy times shared in Cochabamba, La Paz, Boston, and Washington, D.C. A special thanks is also owed to Martha Benson and Susy López Portillo, who shared many experiences in Cochabamba and have remained a constant source of warmth and inspiration.

My deepest thanks go to the friends and family whose love and practical assistance make everything else possible: my sisters Carrie and Madeline, my cousins Eric, Sue, Judy, and Kenny, my brother-in-law Jim, and a fantastic network of friends in San Diego have supported me and my family in ways for which I am forever grateful. I thank cousin José for his interest and *cariño* from afar. My mother, Helen, my father, Joe, and my sister Frances were unflagging supporters of this project, and I thank them from the bottom of my heart. My nephews Ed and Spence made weekends in Madison "tremendous" fun. Daniel sent inspiring mail. Madeline's love, friendship, and sharp sense of humor have meant the world to me.

No one has done more than Michel Gobat. My thanks are impossible to sum up, but they are for everything from comments on innumerable drafts to unfathomable generosity, endless inspiration, and the love of every day.

"[We demand] that government authorities comply with the law, faithfully and legally, without special treatment for anyone, and within the boundaries of equality." Thus declared Guillermo Cruz, the respected leader of a Quechua-speaking Indian community of Cantón Vacas (Cochabamba) in a 1927 petition to Bolivia's minister of war.[1] For generations, Cruz's family had cultivated land in this remote area of small lakes and arid plains about fifty miles southeast of Cochabamba city; the territory posed little interest to outsiders. Cruz's situation changed in the early 1910s, when a long-awaited railroad line neared completion. Hopeful about markets the railroad would open up, *hacendados* (estate owners) began to encroach on the community's land. In 1917 one such hacendado evicted Guillermo Cruz from his home and had the defiant *comunario* (Indian community member) imprisoned for nine months. Fearful of reprisals, Cruz avoided Vacas after his release. He made his way to the national capital, La Paz, in Bolivia's Aymara heartland—probably after traveling on foot for more than a week. In La Paz, Cruz took up work as a poorly paid porter, melded into the emerging neighborhoods of rural migrants, and became connected with an extraordinary network of Aymara and Quechua Indian community leaders from throughout Bolivia.

Guillermo Cruz's predicament mirrored the experience of thousands of comunarios whose land was usurped during a turn-of-the-century wave of communal land expropriation—the most damaging assault against the Indian community since the seventeenth-century era of colonial hacienda expansion. Over a period of almost two decades, Cruz and hundreds of other community activists deluged public officials with petitions demanding the return of stolen land, equal "protection and guarantees" (*amparo y garantías*), and armed force to shield the community from abuse by landlords and local state officials. Their relentless campaign stands out for an extraordinary degree of coordination: Cruz's grievance against the abusive landowner was just one piece of a transregional campaign for land, justice, and local power.

Almost thirty years after Guillermo Cruz joined the national network of Indian community leaders, a similar insistence on the powers of the law continued to mark indigenous political practice. Much had changed since Cruz faded from the historical record in about 1931. The repression and social dislocation caused by the devastating war between Bolivia and Paraguay—the Chaco War of 1932–35—debilitated the earlier movements of community-based leaders. A new generation of rural leaders nevertheless emerged in the war's aftermath. Heightened labor oppression on rural estates and continued abuse by local officials led these activists to lobby government authorities for labor rights and land. Their organizing drives culminated in the Indigenous Congress of May 1945. This was an extraordinary gathering that brought together comunarios and *colonos* (dependent estate laborers) from throughout Bolivia to air grievances and discuss proposed reforms. It was one of the first such national Indigenous Congresses to take place in Latin America. On the concluding day of the congress, the Bolivian president, Col. Gualberto Villarroel, announced a series of historic decrees to end hacienda servitude. The unfulfilled promises of these laws, together with the president's brutal death in 1946, triggered what were arguably Bolivia's largest rural uprisings of the twentieth century, the so-called 1947 cycle of rebellion or unrest.[2]

In the course of the 1947 strikes and uprisings, Indian and peasant rebels envisioned and in some cases enacted a revolutionary transformation of society that augured the end of a state perceived to be ruled by landlords. They claimed their own law, generated alternative visions of the nation, and in some cases replaced local state officials with their own appointees. A communiqué from one of the rebel leaders declared that colonos in one region were waging a "revolution against exploitation and misery . . . [and] abuses"—a "revolution in defense of our rights."[3] Despite brutal repression of the 1947 rebels, rural mobilization for land and justice persisted and helped pave the path for Bolivia's 1952 Revolution. How this hidden revolution before the revolution came to be, and what it meant, is the story this book tells.

✳ The Forces of the Law

The vitality and continuous force of indigenous social movements are a peculiarity of modern Bolivia. Today more than ever, international attention is being drawn to the country's powerful currents of mobilization by Aymara, Quechua, and Guarani Indians and peasants. But the history of indigenous political action and imagination stretches back at least to the massive anticolonial rebellions of the late eighteenth century, and it played a formidable role in the formation of Bolivia's modern state after independence in 1825. The period spanning the late-nineteenth-century export boom until the 1952 revolution was an especially tumultuous time, one that was riven by a sequence of major rebellions. Three of those revolts (in 1899, 1927, and 1947) encompassed multiple regions, involved thousands of people, and culminated in acts of state repression. Not just insurrection defined rural political action in Bolivia during the first half of the twentieth century, however. Revolts coincided with petition drives, rural labor strikes, political assemblies, and congressional lobbying. The two most remarkable instances of such legal political engagement were the transregional networks of Indian community leaders of the 1910s–20s, and the 1945 national Indigenous Congress. Rarely in early-twentieth-century Latin America did Indian and peasant activists sustain such highly coordinated national political networks.[4]

A Revolution for Our Rights puts this long history of Indian and peasant mobilization at the center of Latin America's least-studied social revolution, the 1952 revolution led by the Movimiento Nacionalista Revolucionario (MNR; Nationalist Revolutionary Movement). Typically the Bolivian revolution is associated with class-based movements that accompanied the rise of peasant leagues, mineworker unions, and reformist political projects after the Chaco War.[5] This book instead roots the revolution in a deeper history of rural mobilization that was itself closely linked with labor organizations, urban reform movements, and the politics of state making.[6]

While the book explores rural struggles for land and justice from the rise of a liberal oligarchic order in the late nineteenth century until the 1952 revolution, it puts special emphasis on the formative but little-studied period of 1940s military populism. Above all, it traces the making and unmaking of a tense pact between populist politicians and Indian and peasant activists in the decade before 1952. This fateful alliance built on a longer history of struggles to control the meaning and the power of laws.

Acute contests over the law not only shaped the legal campaigns that Indians and peasants pursued in the 1910s and the 1920s; such disputes also influenced the rural strikes and rebellions of the 1940s military populist era. In both contexts, local officials' abuse of power and disregard for the law were fundamental grievances. Likewise, Indian and peasant activists of the two eras appealed to and insisted on the law's force. Their pleas for rights were motivated by specific histories of violence and the state's repeated failures to apply the law equally. Throughout this period, indigenous leaders demanded equal protection and guarantees while insisting on difference: they demanded individual and collective rights as *indígenas* (Indians). Time and again, they seized the rights that successive constitutions afforded to all "men," "persons," or "Bolivians." They appealed to the actual terms of those rights, as guarantees to political association, property, and personal security. They also widened the meanings of the guarantees by associating them with rights to collective representation, local self-government, and communal landholding. Finally, colonos and comunarios of both eras not only appropriated favorable decrees but distributed duplicates of laws and proposed laws among their own constituencies. As they insisted that local authorities comply with the law and developed their own interpretations of it, Indian and peasant leaders challenged experts' and authorities' monopoly on legal knowledge. They did not just use the law instrumentally, as a tool for other ends. They also claimed the right to determine the law's meaning and how it would be applied. Ultimately they became the bearers of their own law.[7]

In appealing to state authorities, colonos and comunarios selectively appropriated aspects of colonial and republican legislation, all the while expressing—and enacting—a different vision of justice and law. Two legal terms stand out in the documents they produced: *amparo* (protection) and *garantía* (guarantee). The concept of "amparo" is somewhat similar to habeas corpus but implies a much wider sense of protection: it entails the defense of constitutional rights when those rights are violated by the state or private persons. Sometimes known as "recurso de amparo" or "derecho de amparo," amparo did not become an explicit constitutional provision in Bolivia until 1967. Other kinds of laws nevertheless affirmed some rights of amparo early on, for example, by obliging departmental authorities to "protect people and property from attacks."[8] Garantía was used in a looser and more fluid manner by indigenous activists. It could refer to the security of rights (much like amparo), as well as to rights themselves. Guarantees, in addition, had a kind of materiality that amparo lacked. For example, rural leaders talked about the papers of guarantee they obtained from this office or from that person, or about the guarantees a hacienda administrator had confiscated. Guarantees were sought by rural petitioners throughout the entire period studied. They acquired special meaning in the 1940s, however, when they were produced and distributed not only by state authorities but by sympathetic lawyers and social movement leaders. Indian and peasant activists imbued guarantees with great legal and symbolic significance. They viewed them as official papers that high authorities of the state endorsed and confirmed. Sometimes they also saw them as a kind of symbol of future promises or hopes. Although colonos and comunarios repeatedly condemned local authorities' disregard for the law, and denounced the law's futility, they did not discount the powers of the law. Instead they insisted on its enforcement. A struggle over the law and over the power to determine the law's meaning was at the center of pre-revolutionary rural social movements. That struggle fused appeals for equal protection of Indians under Bolivian law with demands for a radical reconfiguration of political power, landholding, and rights.[9]

✳ The Revolution before the Revolution

If significant continuity marked rural social movements of the 1920s and the 1940s, those movements were also transformed by the social and political changes unleashed by the Great Depression, the Chaco War, and the rise of military populism. The multifaceted process of change involved heightened hacienda oppression in a context of deepening economic crisis; renewed waves of rural–urban migration; changes in the internal organization of hacienda laborers; closer ties between burgeoning labor organizations and rural indigenous activists; and government ratification of pro-Indian reforms. Pre–Chaco War governments certainly faced political pressures in the countryside. But it was only after the war that the Bolivian state confronted a truly revolutionary crisis.

The groundbreaking period was the rise of Villarroel-MNR rule (1943–

46) and its violent unwinding in 1946–47. Four factors made these years a revolutionary time.[10] First, Bolivia experienced widespread social discontent: urban workers, mineworkers, Indians, peasants, and the middle class all rallied against social and economic inequities and state violence. Second, their battles drew strength from an ever-widening process of political mobilization, which was best evidenced by the emergence of a national labor federation, broad-based women's organizations, regional and national indigenous congresses, and assemblies to rewrite the Constitution. Equally important, the early 1940s saw the rise of reformist and revolutionary parties that vied for worker, peasant, and middle-class support. A third critical element in Bolivia's unfolding revolutionary conjuncture was the vision of a viable alternative; this came in the form of Villarroel's populist project, which inadvertently strengthened rural movements. Emboldened by their own radical readings of the president's rural reforms, hacienda colonos who had long sought to enforce negotiated labor agreements now aimed in some places to expel the landowners altogether. As sit-down strikes escalated in the final months of Villarroel's presidency, and wide-scale rebellions broke out a year after his death, a fourth factor took shape: a crisis of legitimacy. Conflicts between peasants and landlords, peasants and local authorities, landlords and other landlords, and among contiguous Indian communities spiraled out of control. In this tumultuous context, a crisis of state authority deepened in the countryside. Indians had long complained about local authorities' disregard for the law. In 1947 townspeople and landlords also began to question those officials' legitimacy. The unrest of 1946 and 1947 exposed a growing political vacuum in the countryside, and ironically it was the president's contentious attempt to expand the state's reach that widened the gaping hole. When the MNR's urban revolution triumphed in 1952, another revolution—a rural indigenous revolution—was already unfolding.

Two ironies of Bolivian state making help explain the genesis and significance of the widespread rural insurgency that shaped the coming of the 1952 revolution. The first has to do with the inadvertent ways that late-nineteenth-century liberal land laws bestowed tools for the resurgence of Indian communities. Convinced that private property would secure the nation's advance, Bolivian statesmen abolished the Indian community in 1874 and created procedures to partition and privatize communal land. As lawmakers declared in the so-called Disentailment Law: "No individual or group of individuals may take the name of community or ayllu, nor appear for such an entity before any authority."[11] Although the statesmen hoped to extinguish communal property by these means, their efforts to implement the law instead triggered a lengthy struggle over the community's legal status and the political power of its representatives. In the end, the late-nineteenth-century privatization drive helped engender a new form of indigenous leadership that would wage a national campaign for land, local power, and rights. Tacitly state authorities even came to recognize these indigenous leaders as legitimate delegates of Indian communities—despite the fact that the communities had been outlawed by the 1874 Disentailment Law.

The second irony of state making was the unintended impact of military populist attempts to institutionalize state power in the 1930s and the 1940s by taking the law to what was often considered a lawless countryside. Like the modernizing governments that preceded them, the military populist regimes sought to root out local corruption and expand state power in the nation's rural hinterland. Ideally they wished to implant law-abiding, non-Indian officials. Instead the military populists inadvertently empowered Indians and peasants to be the government's agents of order and the law. During the brief period of Villarroel-MNR rule, a national campaign against hacienda servitude took hold, a crisis of state power deepened in the countryside, and a populist president made indigenous leaders his representatives and bearers of favorable laws. In fact, Villarroel bestowed the law directly to Indians at a national indigenous congress that was fiercely contested by landlords. Escalating rural unrest in the months just after this May 1945 assembly exposed the state's utter inability to control colonos' use of the president's contentious edicts. In the turbulent and highly polarized atmosphere that followed Villarroel's brutal overthrow, hacienda colonos transported the president's decrees to their own communities, delivered them to local officials, and insisted that they were the ones who would determine their meaning. In waging a revolution for their rights, they turned the legal hierarchy on its head.

✳ Region and Nation

The large-scale struggles for land and justice that Indians and peasants pursued at key historical junctures were not isolated movements. Like their Mexican counterparts, Bolivian peasants intervened decisively in national political upheavals, usually in pursuit of autonomous agendas.[12] Several

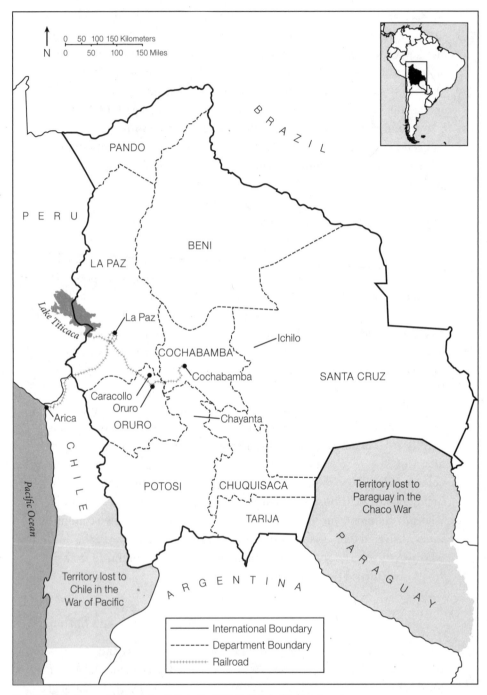

Map 1   Political map of present-day Bolivia (in 1900, Bolivia had 8 departments; Pando was established in 1938)

recent works explore the strategic alliances that Indians and peasants forged with elite politicians in Bolivia during the period of oligarchic rule (ca. 1870s–1920s).[13] Contrary to conventional wisdom, this book shows that rural indigenous movements also engaged with and shaped the populist pacts that marked the decades leading up to the 1952 Revolution.[14]

To explore the course of Indian-state relations and indigenous political projects from the rise of a liberal oligarchic order to the 1952 revolution, the book combines an emphasis on national legislative debates and congresses with a fine-grained focus on Indian communities and large estates in the department of Cochabamba (see map 1). At first glance, this might seem an odd choice, for the region is generally associated with a smallholding mestizo peasantry, not Indian communities.[15] And in fact, although about 70 percent of Bolivia's indigenous population lived in Indian communities at the time of independence, only a small number of those communities were located in Cochabamba.[16] It is precisely the limited presence—but political force—of Cochabamba's Indian communities, and the pioneering significance of its peasant unions, that make this region a propitious vantage point for exploring contests over competing national visions and the origins of the revolutionary project. During the 1940s, the Cochabamba countryside stood out as one of two principal centers of unrest. The book endeavors to trace the changing scope of this rural conflict across diverse local environments by combining research in provincial, departmental, and national archives. This multi-leveled approach at the same time permits an exploration of the dynamic associations that Cochabamba colonos and comunarios established with Indians, peasants, and workers in other Bolivian regions. Cochabamba's rural social movements not only underscore the continuous force of Indian and peasant mobilization but its close connections with urban labor movements and the state.

Cochabamba's diverse population inhabited an ecologically varied zone that spans tropical, valley, and highland areas ranging from sea level to altitudes as high as 4,500 meters (about 14,760 feet).[17] The region is best known for its fertile central valleys. Quechua-speaking colonos, smallholders, artisans, and merchants drove the flourishing commercial economy that developed in this area of the department. The valleys were also home to a landowning class that included medium and large propertyowners who were often bilingual (Quechua-Spanish) and who were identified variously by local inhabitants as "cholo," "mestizo," or "white."[18] The department's three central valleys are situated at an average 2,700 meters (about 8,860 feet) above sea level. They encompass the well-irrigated zones of the Valle Bajo, where maize and other crops thrive year-round, and the drier, densely populated Valle Alto, which is known for its pastureland and somewhat less intensive potato and maize cultivation. The third valley, the Sacaba, is smaller than the other two. It juts out from the northeastern end of Cochabamba city, which lies within the Valle Bajo. Founded in 1574, the departmental capital grew from a population of 22,000 in 1900 to 81,000 in 1950. Until recently, it was Bolivia's second largest city.[19] In the late nineteenth century and the early twentieth, these three central valleys saw the expansion of a smallholding economy that thrived on the production of maize and *chicha* (maize beer).

To the west of its capital, Cochabamba department climbs upward to the highland provinces of Arque and Tapacarí. It was here that owners of large estates vied for land with Indian communities (Quechua and Quechua-Aymara).[20] Bordering on Oruro and Potosí, Cochabamba's western provinces served in the colonial period and the nineteenth century as a critical trade route that connected the valleys' large- and small-scale agricultural producers to highland markets. While Indian communities in these provinces historically held an important economic place as producers of wheat, late-nineteenth-century liberal reforms threw the commercial circuits they controlled into crisis and unleashed new cycles of poverty. In the early twentieth century, better-endowed valley peasants viewed the highland comunarios disparagingly as *laris* (insult for "highland Indian").

Essentially reduced to a corner of the department and occupying marginal land, Cochabamba's Indian communities have generally been considered the most fragmented in all Bolivia. When Spain conquered the Andes in the 1530s, Cochabamba was already one of the region's most ethnically diverse areas. It was populated by a mix of ethnic groups both native to it and brought from other areas, including the Sipesipes, Cotas, Chuyes, Charcas, Caracaras, Soras, Quillacas, Carangas, and Urus. Spanish colonization further fragmented these native groups by cutting them off from their highland communities and placing them under the authority of *encomenderos* (Spanish colonizers) and local *kurakas* (Andean ethnic lords), who were selected by Spaniards. When colonial authorities undertook a major resettlement policy in the sixteenth century, those ethnic groups were further "reduced" from dozens of dispersed hamlets to a small number of villages where the state could more easily control them. Indians relocated to such villages (*reducción* communities) nevertheless took flight to towns, cities, other Indian villages, and private estates. In Cochabamba, the hacienda had expanded early and forcefully, and it competed with Andean villages for indigenous laborers while providing a haven from tribute (Indian head tax) and *mita* (rotating turns of draft labor, especially in the Potosí mines). As a result, Cochabamba in the colonial era became the area of greatest out-migration from the original community, and one of the places most touched by the process of *mestizaje*.[21] To escape the burdens of tribute, colonial authorities complained, Indians pretended to be mestizos by altering the outward cultural signs that served to mark such colonial identities as Indian, cholo, and mestizo. Authorities were particularly perplexed by the porous boundary between the cholos—who they defined as one-quarter Spanish and subjected to tribute obligations—and the mestizos, who they classified as one-half Spanish and exempted from the onerous tax. Ultimately it was impossible for colonial authorities to control native peoples' movements and the process and politics of ethnic change.[22]

Given this early fragmentation and sociocultural transformation of Cochabamba's Indian communities, it is all the more striking that leaders such as Guillermo Cruz reclaimed communal territory and authority in the early twentieth century. The campaign pursued by Cruz and hundreds of other Quechua and Aymara leaders testifies to a process of ethnic revitalization that encompassed not just Indian communities but eventually some of Cochabamba's most entrenched haciendas. Unleashed by an early-twentieth-century process of hacienda expansion that threatened Indians' longstanding control of extensive territory, this process of community revival was nurtured not by the communities' isolation or purity, but by their engagement with transregional social and political processes. Migration between the Cochabamba countryside and the capital city, La Paz; continuous contact with highland indigenous leaders and a labor movement that defended communal land and authority; pro-Indian laws and populist discourses, all these things helped revitalize Cochabamba's Indian communities and even the communities that colonos forged within long-established haciendas.

An exploration of ethnic revitalization in Cochabamba thus widens our understanding of rural mobilization in modern Bolivia. It also calls attention to the relationship between regionalism and racial ideologies. Many recent works recognize the political weight of indigenous movements and visions in the formation of Bolivia's modern nation-state, yet the force of that mobilization is almost always associated with the Aymara people of the La Paz altiplano. Cochabamba, in turn, tends to be associated with unionization, mestizaje, and private not communal property. Indeed the history of Cochabamba and the ethnic ideologies associated with the region conjure up powerful relationships between concepts of race and place.[23] In response to post-1899 government policies that privileged La Paz, Cochabamba's local intellectuals used images of mestizo patriotism and enterprise to demand a fair share for their region. Taking the central valleys as the department's cultural and political essence, they deemed Cochabamba Bolivia's most mestizo and unified region. In the 1940s, Bolivia's populist military regimes elevated this regionalist view to the level of state ceremony: they identified the market women who defended Cochabamba city from Spanish forces during the early-nineteenth-century wars of independence —the mestiza heroines—as the soul of the nation. After 1952, the revolutionary party's official history privileged the village of Ucureña (central valley), where hacienda colonos had established in 1936 Bolivia's first agrarian union and eventually transformed themselves into "mestizo" smallholders. Partly because the revolutionary leaders took Ucureña's smallholding tradition as a symbol of the national culture, they announced the 1953 agrarian reform in this locale.

Rather than charting the formation of the mestizo image that diverse historical actors mapped onto a profoundly varied place, this book instead emphasizes the multi-variegated realities beneath that surface. Certainly the Cochabamba region exhibits some striking features: "acceptance" of the liberal reforms, an influential class of smallholders, mestizaje, and rural unions all figured prominently here. Yet while these attributes took particular force in this region, they were not its singular qualities; nor were these things entirely absent from other Bolivian regions. Just as notable as Cochabamba's apparent peculiarities are its connections in the pre-revolutionary era with national indigenous movements that called for the union of peasants and workers, comunarios and colonos, the Aymara and the Quechua. By tracing the making and unmaking of a multiethnic movement for communal land, local power, and rights from the lens of a region rarely associated with such projects, the book shows both the force and the fragility of a national indigenous network in pre-revolutionary Bolivia.

✳ The Politics of Language

Any study dealing with ethnic mobilization and racial discourse confronts the powers and problems of language.[24] The term "Indian" bears the traces of a history of colonial and neocolonial domination and the struggles against it. As elsewhere in the empire, Spanish colonizers in the sixteenth century homogenized Cochabamba's diverse ethnic groups by assigning them to this uniform category. The act of naming was a powerful sign of cultural and racial domination, one of colonialism's defining features. After independence in 1825, the term Indian followed a complicated course. Up to a point it continued to define distinct obligations and—to a lesser degree—distinct rights, but it did so side by side with new notions of juridical equality. In specific economic and political contexts of the late nineteenth and early twentieth centuries, as the process of land privatization further reduced and impoverished Indian communities, elite politicians and intellectuals further imbued "Indian" with notions of poverty, ignorance, or savagery and in either case with the idea of intrinsic inferiority.[25]

In Cochabamba as elsewhere in Bolivia, then, state officials did not strictly tie the category "Indian" to membership in an Indian community. Instead a series of social and cultural markers such as language, dress, and economic status largely determined who would count, officially, as indigenous.[26] A 1921 law concerning the marriage of indígenas illustrates the standard approach. It defined as Indian those people of the "aymara, quechua or guarani race" who lived in the countryside or worked the land, that is to say, Indian community members, hacienda colonos, and often also smallholders. This particular law in addition classified some urban inhabitants as Indian, depending on their clothing and "domestic habits"—but many state authorities essentially equated Indian with rural.[27] The underlying criteria nevertheless shifted over time. The 1900 census, which apparently equated Indian with tribute payer, labeled a large proportion of the department's Quechua speakers mestizos and concluded that just 23 percent of its population was Indian. In contrast, Bolivia's 1950 census took native language use as the primary mark of Indianness and consequently regarded Indians as Cochabamba's majority (75.2 percent).[28]

State authorities and politicians of varied ideological hue used a variety of terms in this period to describe the colonos and comunarios who lived and labored in the countryside; in addition to *colono, comunario,* and *indio*, they used the words *indígena, clase indígena* (indigenous class), *raza indígena* (indigenous race), *campesino* (peasant), and *labriego* (farm-worker). In petitions, manifestos, and other written records, colonos and comunarios often referred to themselves and members of their communities with the very same words. Even though *indio* was a disparaging term, in certain highly politicized contexts indigenous leaders nevertheless used it to denounce discrimination, claim rights, and convoke broad constituencies. Government authorities in turn tried to undercut such acts by asserting that indigenous leaders were "really" mestizos.

The meanings of "Indian" and "indígena" changed over time, in specific face-to-face situations, and depending on whether the context was rural or urban. But these were also rigid categories that some people used to label and fix other people to a subordinate social, political, and economic position. Without presuming a set ascription, or belying the often fluid and contested nature of categories such as mestizo/a, Indian, and indigenous, I use these terms because they were the ones that historical actors employed to identify themselves and others. To illustrate the complexities of such acts of labeling, the tensions entailed, and the changes that took place, I sometimes use more than one term simultaneously—such as Indian and peasant. Where possible, I also discuss the political controversies that raged over the meanings of the categories. It was precisely in the 1940s—as delegates congregated in the capital for a national indigenous congress, and rural rebels dreamed up revolutionary laws—that the contest about who would speak legitimately for "Indians" and who indeed counted as an Indian became the focus of open political debate. Although populist politicians valorized assimilation, feared indigenous mobilization, and lauded the "civilizing" potentials of education and agricultural modernization, they did not automatically substitute the term "peasant" for Indian, as scholars often assume. Where turn-of-the-century liberal ideologues forecast the indigenous population's demise, anti-oligarchic politicians reluctantly recognized Indians as Bolivia's irrevocable majority.

✳ Organization

The book first considers the experience and perspectives of Indian community leaders in their myriad encounters with authorities of the oligarchic state (ca. 1880s–1920s). Chapter 1 lays the groundwork for this discussion by tracing the persisting tensions between ideals of national unity and the colonial caste order in late-nineteenth-century Bolivia. Although liberal legislators vowed to abolish communal land and political authority, ironically they bestowed legal tools for the resurgence of Indian communities. The next two chapters explore how indigenous leaders viewed, appropriated, and challenged the liberal project. Chapter 2 maps out the origins of the national political network that Indian community leaders maintained in the 1910s and the 1920s. The chapter looks closely at the congressional debates and policy proposals of these decades, which raised community leaders' expectations for protective legislation and the return of usurped land. Narrowing the focus to the region of Cochabamba, chapter 3 delves more deeply into indigenous leaders' perspectives on the law; it also considers how their political activism influenced—and was influenced by—national legislative debates. Although the principal demand for an inspection of communal landholdings was never carried out, Indians' tenacious lobbying set hurdles for the process of privatization and helped compel government authorities to reform the liberal project.

The second half of the book shows how Bolivia's devastating defeat in the Chaco War triggered the rise of a new generation of Indian and peasant leaders who forged tentative alliances with populist state authorities. Chapter 4 outlines the political dilemmas that preoccupied post–Chaco War reformist politicians by looking in depth at the 1938 National Convention, which produced Bolivia's first major constitutional change since 1880. Ultimately the convention did not significantly reconceptualize the place of Indians in the nation, but it did outlaw rural servitude and it bestowed expansive social rights to workers, women, and children. Looking closely at the protests waged by hacienda colonos, chapter 5 then explores how these constitutional reforms helped trigger renewed waves of rural mobilization in the late 1930s and the early 1940s. The petitions and sit-down strikes analyzed in this chapter reveal that claims regarding land and "community" did not diminish after the Chaco War, as often thought, but remained vital to rural mobilization. Chapter 6 in turn considers how the Villarroel-MNR government fashioned a particular vision of national unity that valorized mestizos and mestizaje, just as it was seeking to control the indigenous majority that was pressing its demands on the state. As the military populist governments of the post–Chaco War era aimed to build a stronger, "mestizo" nation, they also made gender norms and family life issues of public preoccupation. The family, like Indians, became a target of state protection.

The last two chapters show how the populist vision of a mestizo nation was challenged and reshaped by another groundswell of rural mobilization. Chapter 7, which explores Bolivia's 1945 Indigenous Congress, details the Villarroel regime's attempt to control this local indigenous initiative. The government above all sought to use the congress to create a legal order in the countryside. Rather than resolving a perceived crisis of the law, the Indigenous Congress instead exacerbated the turmoil by empowering the delegates to be agents of the law. Chapter 8 considers the role that this process of legal empowerment played in the 1947 cycle of unrest. These largely unexplored uprisings were arguably the most extensive rural revolts in Bolivia's twentieth century. Although haciendas composed a central theater of the disturbances, comunarios also intervened in actions to recuperate usurped land, expel corrupt authorities, and end discrimination and abuse. Focusing on the two main areas of conflict, Cochabamba and La Paz, the chapter shows that the 1947 rebels not only appropriated and redefined the populist state's ambiguous rhetoric about indigenous rights and guarantees, but enacted their own vision of justice and the law. Their protests were violently suppressed by state and private forces. While the repression struck a powerful blow, it did not fully suppress indigenous political movements, as often thought. Outright rebellion diminished, but rural mobilization persisted until the revolutionary triumph of 1952.

The conclusion-epilogue considers the implications of this history of mobilization for the 1952 revolution, and reads critically the suppression of the revolution's rural indigenous roots by both the revolutionary regime and much scholarship on 1952. Although it is impossible to say that the revolution would not have triumphed if not for the Indian and peasant movements of the 1940s, it can—and should—be said that another revolution, a rural revolution, was already in process when the MNR's urban-based movement defeated the national army in 1952. In the aftermath of the revolutionary triumph, the MNR state struggled to contain this revolution before the revolution. Tension between support and restraint of indigenous political participation was a defining feature and a lasting legacy of the 1952 revolution.

CHAPTER ONE

THE PECULIAR PATHS OF
THE LIBERAL PROJECT

Three months after Bolivia's long wars of independence ended in April 1825, the victors convened a general assembly to deliberate the fate of the liberated territory. The forty-eight deputies assembled in Sucre, the nation's new capital, overwhelmingly agreed to proclaim Bolivia an independent state. They made "the Liberator," Simón Bolívar, its first president. Bolívar and his associates viewed the founding of the republic as a fundamental break with colonialism. Once installed in the presidency in August 1825, Bolívar set about applying the force of the law to that break. He announced a rapid succession of decrees on all the most urgent aspects of the country's political and economic organization.[1]

A fundamental subset of the new laws aimed to free Indians from the discrimination of the colonial past. Embracing ideals of liberty and equality, and proclaiming an end to all taxes "degrading to the dignity of citizens," Bolívar ended tribute, the colonial-era head tax imposed on Indian men between the ages of eighteen and fifty.[2] He also abolished the position of the *cacique* (Spanish term for *kuraka* or *mallku*, ethnic lord) and declared Indians owners of the land in their possession. Fiscal and administrative shortcomings quickly derailed Bolívar's liberal dream: just one year after tribute was abolished, his successor, President José Antonio de Sucre, reinstated the discriminatory charge.[3] Rather than giving Indians the "dignity of citizens," Bolivia's first generation of liberal statesmen partially revived the "degrading" obligations of the colonial past.

In the 1860s and 1870s, as international demand for Bolivian raw materials surged, a second generation of free-trade liberal reformers took power.[4] They emerged in the wake of the silver-mining industry's recovery, which diminished the state's reliance on income from tribute. Thanks to this revival, mine owners and landed elites pushed through plans to ease free trade, privatize corporate entities, liberalize land and capital markets, and construct an export-oriented railroad network. Inspired by Bolívar's liberalism, the second generation of reformers also sought to eliminate discriminatory legacies of colonial rule: tribute, caste, the cacique, and even the Indian community itself. Although their efforts to eradicate communal landholding ultimately proved unsuccessful, the second wave of reforms would have more enduring, and damaging, effects on Indian communities than those of Bolívar. Most notably, the late-nineteenth-century reform process dramatically reduced the amount of land controlled by communities and exacerbated divisions within them. Inadvertently, it also engendered a new form of indigenous leadership that would wage a national campaign to recover usurped land. Rather than abolishing the Indian community, the reforms unleashed a lengthy struggle over its legal status and the political power of community authorities.

Bolivia's late-nineteenth-century attempt to privatize communal land was hardly unique: it was a hallmark of liberalism throughout much of Latin America. Yet the Bolivian reforms stand out in two ways. First, Bolivia's laws followed an exceptionally aggressive path, for the state intervened directly in one of the region's most brutal privatization campaigns. Second, the reform process initially proved markedly unsuccessful. The first two significant attempts to privatize the land not only resulted in major legal concessions but in wide-scale rebellion. President Melgarejo's attempt to disentail communal property concluded with his overthrow in 1870 and the restoration of usurped land. A decade later, another privatization law sparked legal protests that first extracted from the government provisions for collective tenure and ultimately resulted in the 1899 rebellion for Indian self-rule. These attempts at disentailment also provoked disputes among politicians over the rights of Indians. After the 1870 defeat of Melgarejo, some statesmen acknowledged Indians' contribution to the removal of the dictator and offered a form of gradual citizenship. But this potentially more inclusionary strand of liberalism withered with the 1899 Indian rebellion, which led rival elites to unify around racist images of Indians as a "barbaric" and allegedly antinational force. After 1899, most elite politicians would deem Indians unqualified for citizenship.[5]

The tensions between inclusion and exclusion that marked Bolivia's liberal project were neither simply intrinsic to liberalism nor purely traces of the colonial past.[6] Above all they sprang from a history of conflict over attempts to abolish the Indian community. Late-nineteenth-century ideas about rights, obligations, property, and "race" were shaped and reshaped by what happened on the ground when the government intruded on Indian communities with titles, fees, and survey teams. Although politicians vowed to eliminate communal landholding and the Indian community itself, time and again they had to admit publicly that they could not.

✴ Melgarejo's 1860s Assault against the Indian Community

The nemesis of Latin American liberals was the military strongman or caudillo, who embodied the most stubborn obstacle to national order, growth, and progress. Mariano Melgarejo (1820–71), a Cochabamba general of lower-class origins, played that role in Bolivia from 1864, when he took power in a coup, to 1871, when a popular uprising overthrew him with the collaboration of an estimated 40,000 Indians. Vilified by late-nineteenth-century politicians, Melgarejo became an enduring symbol of lawlessness, tyranny, and transgression.[7] For generations of liberals, his regime epitomized the antiliberal practices that stymied the formation of a modern nation.

If Bolivian liberals differentiated their "enlightened" program from Melgarejo's darker age, their economic and anti-Indian policies nevertheless sprang from the dictator's attempt to construct a liberal order. The Melgarejo regime advanced the first concerted attack against protectionism, ending tariffs on imports from Argentina and Brazil and a government monopoly on purchases of silver, Bolivia's main export product. The cancellation of the monopoly allowed Bolivia's large silver companies to sell overseas freely. Melgarejo also unleashed the first major attempt to dismantle the Indian corporate community since President Sucre had suspended Simón Bolívar's early-nineteenth-century decrees.[8] With an 1866 decree,

Melgarejo ordered Indians to purchase individual titles within sixty days or forfeit land for auction by the state.[9] His government deliberately tried to keep Indians from obtaining those titles by requiring a substantial size and cost for all sales.[10] Two years later, a second decree stipulated that communal land was state property.[11] Since approximately half of all farmland was still in communal hands, the measures had devastating implications.[12]

Melgarejo's policies engendered an unprecedented process of communal land expropriation. Between 1866 and 1869, government auctioneers sold the land of 356 communities to private bidders.[13] Three hundred twenty-one of them were located in the department of La Paz, primarily in its most densely populated provinces (Omasuyos, Pacajes, Ingavi, Sicasica [present-day Aroma], and Muñecas).[14] The land sales sparked a series of indigenous uprisings in 1869 and 1870, largely in La Paz but also in the Potosí region.[15] Since most of the communal territory accrued to parvenus closely linked to the state bureaucracy and the army, the sales also antagonized traditional landholding elites.[16] Indeed the underlying logic of the sales was Melgarejo's need to pay off loyal relatives or clients and subsidize costly military activities. In numerous instances, medium-scale producers, merchants, townspeople, and former indigenous authorities benefited from the auctions.[17] The nonelite origin of these buyers is key to understanding traditional elites' outcry against Melgarejo, for the land sales enabled upwardly aspiring sectors to gain a foothold in local and regional power structures.[18] The anti-Melgarejo sentiments culminated in a massive uprising in 1870 that deposed the regime and expelled the dictator across the Bolivia-Peru border. Under a torrent of stones, so the story goes, Melgarejo was sent packing.[19]

The 1870 revolt against Melgarejo marked a fundamental watershed, for it was the first such political alliance between Indians and non-Indians in postindependence Bolivia.[20] Indians, however, pursued their own objectives, pressuring for the return of communal land and in effect reoccupying usurped territory.[21] Traditional elites risked this pact because they were angered by Melgarejo's disregard for the law and by his favoritism for cronies, the army, and aspiring new middle sectors. They also opposed the extensive concessions foreigners received on southern land rich in guano and nitrates.[22] But anger quickly turned to fear. Reflecting on the uprising, anti-Melgarejo elites recalled the massive Indian rebellions of the 1780s and the 1811 siege of La Paz; one congressional deputy insisted that the future of the nation would be jeopardized if the government again threatened Indian communities by permitting the usurpation of their land.[23] Indian participation in the 1870-71 revolt not only sealed Melgarejo's fate. It cast an ineffaceable shadow over the legislative debates about land, tribute, and nationhood that ensued once the "barbarous caudillo" was expelled.

✳ Small Communal Properties

Immediately after Melgarejo's overthrow, political elites clamored to define a new legal order in the 1871 Constituent Assembly.[24] Not coincidentally, the question of communal landholding overwhelmingly colored the legislative debates. After allowing a public reckoning on the effects of Melgarejo's assault against Indian communities, the 1871 assembly unanimously ratified indigenous rights to all the land they possessed, including the so-called *sobrantes* (common land considered vacant because cultivated on rotating cycles).[25]

The 1871 assembly's confirmation of communal landholding, at a time when plans to privatize it were gaining ground, could not be more striking. Yet ratification did not necessarily equal approval. The assembly restored the land largely because its members feared Indian uprisings. And its members intertwined anxious utterances about Indian political power with praise for private property. Indeed their resolve to restore usurped land was only temporary. Both within Congress and beyond its halls, politicians voiced support for the privatization of communal land over the long term.

Hand in hand with the 1871 assembly, political elites fiercely debated in the press and in pamphlets the particular form that the privatization of communal property should eventually take. One group of statesmen who defended Melgarejo's sales advocated the rapid incorporation of communal land into haciendas and the transformation of Indian *comunarios* into dependent estate laborers (*colonos*). An opposing cluster of politicians instead heralded a nation of independent smallholders.[26] Since the participants linked the ability to own and manage property with the capacity to exercise political rights, their debate also touched on questions of citizenship. The discussion broke down between those who viewed Indians as servile laborers and noncitizens (i.e., as inherently lacking the very quality on which citizenship was based), and those who considered them productive proprietors and therefore potential citizens.

To back its position, each side traced a distinct history of property regimes back to the Inca empire. The participants then raised a series of questions about land tenure. Did Indians own property in the past? Did they own it now? Could they exercise the "full and absolute rights of dominion"? Their answers drew on a mix of imported ideas; inexact reflections on colonialism; political and fiscal exigencies; and the demands and virtues of myriad arrangements of communal and private property.[27] Because the arguments of the smallholding faction left the most visible stamp on subsequent legislation, the following pages focus on its vision of property, "civilization," and rights. The pro-smallholder views also shed light on the underlying contradictions of Bolivia's liberal project. Although this bloc favored small private property, some of its members expressed hesitant praise for Indian communities.

The smallholding faction's contradictory perspective is best exemplified by the views of its principal spokesperson, José María Santivañez, a Cochabamba estate owner and congressional delegate. In a widely circulated 1871 pamphlet, Santivañez lauded Indian communities while referring to them as "small communal properties."[28] For social, economic, and political reasons "of vital importance to the republic," Santivañez maintained, communal property could not be subsumed by latifundios.[29] When opponents disparaged his desire to preserve Indian communities intact, Santivañez clarified his position: "comunarios" should be declared "owners of their lands." It was because Indian communities were already subdivided, he implied, that such ownership was both viable and just.[30]

Surely Santivañez viewed Indian communities as a cluster of small properties because he was inspired by a particular geographic backdrop, his native Cochabamba. In contrast to the resistance that community members in La Paz waged against the 1860s land sales, comunarios of Cochabamba's productive Valle Bajo (Santivañez's principal reference point) purchased title to their own parcels when Melgarejo put their land up for sale.[31] In lauding these "small communal properties," however, Santivañez not only spoke about Cochabamba's present, but about the colonial and Inca past. He never acknowledged that smallholding within Indian communities might be an anomaly of Cochabamba. Instead he took the region's fragmented communities as a universal pattern of the nation's agrarian history—and as a model for its future. The import of the smallholding argument thus resides not only in its anti-hacienda position, but in the way its proponents connected ideas about property, justice, and rights with a specific vision of the past.

In advancing his peculiar view of the Indian community, Santiváñez labored to refute the pro-hacienda faction's claims that Indians under Inca rule were not property owners but merely held use rights to state-controlled land. To prove that Indians were in fact proprietors, Santiváñez made predictable allusions to republican legislation such as the early-nineteenth-century decree in which Simón Bolívar called indígenas "natural and absolute owners of the land that they inherited from their fathers."[32] But Santiváñez did not rely just on republican laws. He grounded the republican restoration of Indians' "small communal properties" in colonial as well as precolonial land tenure systems. Drawing on works by the nineteenth-century U.S. historian William H. Prescott and the eighteenth-century Scottish historian William Robertson, as well as Garcilaso de la Vega's sixteenth-century account, Santiváñez first maintained that the Inca empire had itself promulgated private property.[33] After denouncing the devastation of the conquest, he then praised the Spanish Crown for creating an even more efficient system of land tenure. The concessions in land that Spain gave Indians, Santiváñez said, were equal to the private grants that immigrants received in the nineteenth-century United States.[34]

To sustain this point, Santiváñez and other proponents of smallholding selectively conceptualized pre-Hispanic and colonial communities as collections of private plots. They highlighted particular characteristics of Indian communities and ignored others, and, above all, overlooked the fundamental fact that Andean property rights were based on kinship ties and multilayered exchanges of labor. First, they failed to note that access to land and other resources was organized by kinship groups (*ayllus*) that traced their origins to a common ancestor. Second, they ignored the fact that usufruct rights were obtained via exchanges of labor among families of a particular ayllu as well as with higher-level ethnic groupings. Under Spanish colonialism, Andean territory became the property of the Crown, which granted Indian communities usufruct rights. Indigenous rights and obligations thus continued to be mediated by the community just as the Crown theoretically protected the possession of land worked.[35] Santiváñez focused principally on families' rotating usufruct plots, which he misread as individual property. As such, his argument reduced complex social and cultural ties to the simple use of the land.

Although Santiváñez and other prominent spokespersons for smallholding were men from Cochabamba—where smallholding was pronounced—regionalism was not the primary motor of their argument. Proponents of smallholding also came from Potosí, Chuquisaca, and even from La Paz, the department where elites most strongly supported hacienda expansion.[36] And they all expressed similar views about the internal structure of Indian communities and about their potential political power. Consider the case of La Paz congressional deputy Bernardino Sanjinés, whose oblique defense of the Indian community was partly based on his views of smallholding systems in the Yungas province of La Paz, then Bolivia's most important coca-producing region. Like Santiváñez, Sanjinés claimed that land cultivated by "small property-owners" was more productive than land worked by forced laborers (i.e., hacienda colonos).[37] To sustain these claims, Sanjinés did not simply offer praise for smallholders but lauded the agricultural expertise and productive capacity of Indian communities. "Under equivalent circumstances, and with equal proportions of land," he claimed, "communities produce the double of haciendas."[38] Mine owners and landowners from northern Potosí, where powerful ayllus encircled haciendas, echoed Sanjinés's view. For example, the silver magnate José Avelino Aramayo lauded the dedicated labor of communities, which he too viewed as agglomerations of small parcels. The obstacle to greater agricultural output was not Indian communities, he maintained, but the hefty taxes that reduced the communities' capacity to produce.[39]

A striking ambiguity about the Indian community thus marked the pro-smallholding position: proponents expressed real admiration for Indian communities just as those communities might have been extinguished. Certainly their views were driven by the simple need to persuade; they praised the communities' efficiency in order to challenge the pro-hacienda faction, which claimed that Indians' failure to produce made large estates an imperative. Praise for communities was also a logical product of the economic realities of the time. Before the liberalization of trade and the construction of railroads allowed foreigners at the turn of the century to flood Bolivian markets with cheap imports, Indian *arrieros* (muleteers) transported the nation's goods and Indian agriculturalists sustained its inhabitants. The smallholding camp remained acutely aware that non-Indians needed Indian communities to survive.

Survival was not only an economic matter but also a political one. As the future president of Bolivia Narciso Campero recognized, the 1871 restoration of communal land merely confirmed what had already been approved "by the triumph of arms, by the cry of 40,000 Indians."[40] Advocates of smallholding thus defended Indian land rights because they feared a rebellion like the one unleashed by Melgarejo's policies. For example, San-jinés insisted that additional confiscations of communal land would spark a "general uprising of Indians: a revolution by one half of Bolivia against the other half." His solution was to incorporate Indians into the nation as "free men" (who could buy and sell property), but only gradually, without attacking their rights.[41] To ward off unrest and promote productivity and "progress," Santivañez similarly presented Indians as potential members of the nation. He stated that the initial wave of resistance to Melgarejo was the effort of Indians' duly defending their rights in a "national battle" between justice and tyranny. Santivañez's universal rhetoric evoked a much greater contest than a mere uprising: when "all rights, all interests were violated—everyone should demand their restoration."[42]

Indian participation in the overthrow of Melgarejo not only convinced statesmen to restore usurped land; it also drove them to "civilize" Indi-ans. To this end, the pro-hacienda bloc backed tutelage by landlords, who would facilitate Indians' controlled contact with cities and "civilized men."[43] Those opposed to hacienda expansion, in contrast, looked to in-struction and the state for protection and civilization. For example, San-tivañez considered the central obstacle to Bolivian "progress" the "igno-rance" of the "indigenous race." All Indian men and women between the ages of twelve and twenty-five, he proposed, should be declared "absolute proprietors and owners" of their land only upon the completion of pri-mary instruction. In turn the "humiliated race . . . would be raised to the level of a citizen worthy of the Republic."[44] If the pro-hacienda group situated Indians completely outside the national fabric, the smallholding faction included them in an inferior status: Indians' transformation into "free men" was contingent on the prior improvement of their status via access to "civilization."[45] Like nineteenth-century European colonizers of Africa and the Caribbean, the smallholding faction made citizen status dependent on education and a civilizing process that could only occur in steps and had no guarantees.[46]

Ultimately the smallholding contingent resumed what Melgarejo had started. Just three years after his overthrow, the 1874 Ley de Exvinculación (Disentailment Law) unleashed a more enduring process of expropriation. Although this law granted indígenas the "right of absolute property in their respective possessions," it explicitly abolished the Indian community: "Once property tiles are conferred, the law will not recognize communities."[47] Commissions (*mesas de revisita*) appointed by departmental prefects would measure and partition the land among community members, who were required to purchase titles for two bolivianos. Once the process was complete, the plots could be sold in departmental capitals under the supervision of public prosecutors.[48] The sobrantes (i.e., common land considered vacant because cultivated on rotating cycles) would revert to the state.

The Disentailment Law, with its allusions to an 1824 Bolivarian decree, essentially signaled the triumph of a smallholding vision similar to Santivañez's (but without his ambivalent praise for Indian communities and his stipulations for education and only gradual immersion in the market). In reality, however, pro-hacienda advocates also influenced the 1874 edict by accelerating the process of legal change and influencing the way it would be implemented.[49] A compromise of sorts, the law's fundamental goal was clear: it aimed to eliminate Indian communities.

The ambiguous claims about the powers and positive traits of Indian communities that buttressed the 1871 restoration of communal land were submerged in the unequivocal terms of the 1874 abolition. But the peculiar logic that Santivañez and other statesmen used to make their case about property rights mattered as much as the conclusion. The contradictory historical vision that marked lawmakers' 1871 dispute presaged dilemmas that political elites would face in subsequent struggles to extinguish the Indian community. After the Melgarejo episode, the desire to privatize land held by Indian communities was laden with the idea that it was a dangerous endeavor.

✳ "This Anomalous Republic"

The 1874 Disentailment Law sought to "unchain" the land. It also aimed to free Indians from discriminatory duties and the presumed oppression of their own authorities. Repeating the main terms of an 1824 decree by Bolívar, the law "exempted indígenas in the whole Republic from forced personal services required by political, military, and church authorities." It did not, however, outlaw such obligations on haciendas, and in practice both types of service persisted and even increased.[50] Announced just three years after Melgarejo's ouster, the Disentailment Law ushered in a second phase of communal land privatization and protest. In Cochabamba the process commenced in 1878; in most other regions, the Disentailment Law did not begin to be implemented until additional regulations were passed in December 1880. The spark for this procedural legislation was the outbreak of the War of the Pacific (1879–83), which set Chile against Bolivia and Peru in a conflict revolving around coastal lands rich in guano and nitrates. The War of the Pacific also triggered disputes among political elites about national sovereignty, economic progress, and the meanings of citizenship.

Bolivia's defeat in the war with Chile profoundly affected the course of its liberal project. Although Bolivia exited the conflict in 1880 and was spared a Chilean invasion of its heartland like the one that devastated Peru, it suffered the complete loss of its coastal territory. Not surprisingly, the political controversies engendered by the military defeat added new layers to the corpus of liberal laws and discourse. If communal land dominated reflections on the "Indian question" after Melgarejo's overthrow, tribute and rights took precedence against the backdrop of the war. Champions of the Disentailment Law argued that its implementation could be used to raise funds for continued combat with Chile. They also insisted that ending tribute and privatizing the land would make Indians "citizens."

No one better embodies this new emphasis on Indian rights than the politician and writer Nataniel Aguirre, the minister of war during the War of the Pacific and later the chief of Cochabamba's Liberal Party branch. As president of the 1871 assembly, Aguirre had been a leading proponent of smallholding in that year's legislative debates. Already in 1871, Aguirre insisted that Indians become citizens. "It's not sufficient, Señores Deputies," he declared, "to return [the Indian] to his hut and his plot of land, so he can vegetate in ignorance and humiliation. . . . Let's make the poor Indian, who until now has served . . . the State, the Church, and the landlord, a citizen like us."[51] Later, during Bolivia's 1880 National Convention, Aguirre spearheaded the campaign to implement the 1874 law and abolish tribute. In his speeches against tribute, he once again invoked a contrast between servitude and citizenship. "Independence," Aguirre said, "should have conferred complete equality to all inhabitants of the Republic. . . . This marked and oppressive difference . . . between the white and the Indian [should] not exist. . . . The Indian [should not be] the servant of the State or of private parties. . . . Let's give the Indian his rights."[52]

Aguirre's association of citizenship and rights with autonomy and liberty conjures up a basic principle of Bolivian suffrage rules. The Bolivian

Constitution defined citizenship as the right to vote and be elected. In Bolivia, as elsewhere in Latin America, these rights expanded unevenly over the course of the nineteenth century.[53] A variety of socioeconomic and cultural factors defined the boundaries of the select male population that cast ballots.[54] Along with assets and education, a fundamental concern with men's "independence" determined who would vote. Bolivia's nineteenth-century constitutions consistently required of all voters ownership of property or income from activities other than domestic service. They also stipulated the loss of citizenship for particular kinds of addiction or dependency: habitual drunkenness, gambling, or begging.[55] "Race" was never explicit grounds for exclusion, but scholars generally agree that the requirements for literacy and property or income barred most Indians from participating in elections.[56]

As Aguirre's comments reveal, Bolivia's late-nineteenth-century statesmen did not, however, limit the meaning of citizenship to suffrage. Their use of the term also conjured up a more figurative sense of national devotion or belonging. For Aguirre in particular, citizenship most immediately signified a deeply patriotic investment in the nation. In his post–War of the Pacific literary forays, Aguirre expressed passionate regret about the absence of nationalistic sentiments. He suggested that all men should be "citizens"—loyal soldier-citizens—but he also privileged the political role and will of a lettered elite over that of the indigenous and mestizo masses. The lower classes would achieve only limited levels of education, and they would be steered clear from positions of political leadership.[57] When it came to citizenship, the pressing issue in Aguirre's view was not political participation at all but the lack of national cohesion in the face of foreign invasion.

In ongoing debates about the Indian community, Aguirre and other deputies also linked citizenship with the problem of tribute and the notions of dependence and racial discrimination on which tribute was based. Aguirre called Bolivia an "anomalous republic" because it was the only nation in which tribute and "servitude" remained.[58] And he charged hyperbolically that Bolivia and the "race of ants" were the only societies structured by "this difference of castes." The best thing, he said, would be "to make the Indian a great citizen."[59] The goal, he also declared, is to "make all Bolivians equal."[60] Like early-nineteenth-century liberals, Aguirre and his cohort explicitly distinguished the "dignity" of the citizen from the "degradation" of the tributary. Our "grand objective," another deputy declared, is to "emancipate the Indian from his special tribute and put him on the same level as all other citizens."[61] One more echoed Aguirre's claim that the abrogation of tribute would "make the Indian a great citizen."[62] Although the deputies attributed varied meanings to the word *citizen*, their comments repeatedly invoked the link between citizenship and economic autonomy. And tribute, more than anything else, obstructed the independent condition that epitomized the citizen.

It is not surprising that tribute in the late nineteenth century was such a patent symbol of colonialism and caste difference, for the tax lasted longer in Bolivia than in any other Latin American nation.[63] Because mining and commerce collapsed after independence, tribute in the nineteenth century made up an even more important share of revenue than it did during the colonial era. Until the 1850s it represented the republican state's largest and most important single source of income.[64] Led by Aguirre, the commission responsible for drafting the 1880 bill to implement the 1874 Disentailment Law finally called for tribute's abolition and advocated a substitute tax. Land titles would be distributed to Indians as per the 1874 law, but now they would be exchanged for a one-time fee five times the amount of tribute, which would in turn compensate for the loss of the old tax.[65] With this drastic proposal, Aguirre sought to finance Bolivia's continued involvement in the war with Chile.

No amount of lobbying could secure approval for Aguirre's motion, however, for some congressional delegates defended the colonial tax even at this late date. They feared that replacing tribute with a one-time fee for land titles would enrage Indians and cause a "race war." Tribute's defenders also insisted that "incorporation" could be accomplished only through the tutelage ensured by that very tax. Rather than a sign of "civil degradation," its supporters maintained, tribute brought Indians into the nation as "contributors"; it also provided a system to govern, educate, and "civilize" them.[66]

Still the current was clearly moving against the colonial tax. Or at least it seemed to be. In 1882, tribute was formally abolished. The release took effect gradually, however, and Indians who possessed land would be subject to the "contribución territorial de indígenas."[67] In practice, this new tax essentially replicated the old tribute.[68] The government postponed the 1880 law that had called for full-scale shift to the *catastro*, a Napoleonic-inspired procedure designed to equalize levies on all rural property owners in line with annual production.[69] And so tribute may have been abolished, but it disappeared very slowly. In many regions, it remained the most important element of the departmental budget well into the twentieth century.[70] Indeed Aguirre's campaign to end tribute and make Indians "citizens" coated in palatable language a plan to increase their financial burden.

Ultimately Aguirre and his followers could not escape the contradictions of nineteenth-century liberalism. They strove to make Indians economically independent without altering the rules that restricted their political participation.[71] In a time of war, the abolition of tribute opened space for discussion about discrimination, but it did not produce substantive social or political change.

✳ Titles, Fees, and Survey Teams

Post–War of the Pacific governments could not fully eliminate the head tax, but they did commence wide-scale implementation of the 1874 Disentailment Law and the land privatization process. The mechanism they employed was the *revisita*, or land survey. The colonial revisita consisted of periodic assessments of Indian tributaries that were designed to recalibrate tribute quotas. It used population figures collected by Indians and local authorities; higher-level colonial officials conducted their own inspections only in places where conflict arose.[72] Late-nineteenth-century revisitas differed dramatically from their colonial namesake. They authorized an army of bureaucrats—whose earnings were tied to the number of land titles sold—to penetrate, interrogate, and literally divide up the land of Indian communities. With the assistance of a judge (often a local resident and according to law named directly by the president), a secretary, and an aid, the surveyor measured the land, determined the productive capacity of each plot, and dispensed titles.[73]

While the Disentailment Law ratified Indians' "absolute" rights to their "respective possessions," it also declared the sobrantes property of the state and thus available for immediate purchase. This provision allowed outsiders to grab a community's territorial foundation, making it easier to dispossess individual families of their rotating usufruct plots.[74] Before an 1881 decree amended the initial terms of the 1874 edict, recipients of individual titles were also obliged to pay tribute in the new bolivianos rather than in the old pesos. This requirement increased comunarios' tax burden by a full 25 percent.[75] All told, the 1874 law paved the way for the most devastating assault against communal property since the seventeenth century, when the Potosí mining boom triggered a rapid expansion of the hacienda.[76] In 1880, Indian communities held approximately half of Bolivia's farmland; by 1930, the communities' holdings had been diminished to less than a third.[77]

Bolivia's communal land sales entailed exceptional levels of external violence and fraud.[78] Government reports confirm that community members were threatened and compelled to sell land at low prices.[79] Forced debt, false representatives, the designation of areas as *tierras baldías* (so-called vacant lands), and outright coercion were just a few of the tactics employed to wrench territory from Indian communities. In some places, comunarios' houses were burnt down.[80] Elsewhere, buyers misled Indians by erroneously presenting bills of sale as rental contracts. Authorities sometimes used false accusations of rebellion to justify the confiscation of land.[81]

The process of disentailment was also shaped by pressures internal to Indian communities that had to do with class, generation, and gender differences. Over the course of the nineteenth century, Bolivia's Indian communities had become increasingly stratified due to heightened pressures to provide labor, tribute, and agricultural goods.[82] Prosperous community members took advantage of the late-nineteenth-century sales, particularly in Cochabamba. Throughout Bolivia, internal stratification, power relations, and factionalism undoubtedly played a role in the protracted attempt to privatize communal land. Nuts-and-bolts procedures must have also shaped local outcomes. A great deal nevertheless remains to be learned about how the actual course of measurement, titling, and sale proceeded in specific places.[83] Why did some community members sell their land, while others refused? How were communities transformed internally by the uneven process of privatization? What kinds of negotiations led some communities to insist on a collective deed, while others accepted individual titles? How were the different titles perceived?

Although the internal dynamics remain somewhat obscure, we know with certainty that the revisita process and its effects differed markedly from one area of the country to the next. External pressure and violence unquestionably reached extremes in the department of La Paz, yet even here internal divisions and pressures undoubtedly played a role.[84] The revival of silver mining in the 1860s and 1870s spurred population growth in La Paz and other highland towns and cities, which in turn increased the demand for foodstuffs.[85] During the first wave of land sales, in the 1880s, elite *paceños* (residents of La Paz) found acreage in the provinces of Omasuyos, Pacajes, and Cercado particularly attractive for commercial agriculture or as collateral for loans to finance nonagricultural activities. Land investments in these provinces were either close to the expanding capital, situated near the fertile shores of Lake Titicaca, or adjacent to the department's major roads. During a second, more virulent wave of sales in the early twentieth century, leaders of the ruling Liberal Party figured as major beneficiaries, although less prominent elites, including many women, also filled the ranks of the largely absentee owners.[86] If the revisitas sometimes resulted in the sale of entire communities at once, such cases were rare even in this department. In general, the process of disentailment proceeded in stages. The sale of land by some community members essentially forced others to follow suit, as the gradual depletion of the community's holdings left little land for reallocation and impoverished those holding out. By the end of both phases, as much as one-fourth of all community lands in this department had been sold to non-Indians.[87]

The land surveys also affected Indian communities in Chuquisaca, a southern department diverse in land tenure systems and with an economy closely tied to the fate of Potosí silver mining. Although revisitas commenced in 1881, resistance waged by Indian communities helped prevent inspections from being completed in much of this department until the 1890s and into the twentieth century. On the whole, communities in districts close to the departmental capital and having obvious commercial prospects suffered more than those occupying marginal land. Communities with access to multiple ecological tiers or possessing llama and alpaca herds also proved less vulnerable. Elites and townspeople purchased the majority of the land, but some shares were acquired by one ayllu member from another.[88] Here, and quite likely elsewhere, indebtedness and court costs drove comunarios to sell their land.[89] The surveyors' failure to respect local custom also contributed to dispossession. Land of ayllu members who died without heirs generally reverted to the community, but the commissions ignored this practice, declaring such territory vacant and available for rental or sale to outsiders. Over time, many community members were compelled to relinquish their possessions. Compared to La Paz, however, it was extremely rare for *all* members of a community in Chuquisaca to sell land. Some communities in this region even managed to shelter their entire holdings from the survey teams.[90]

Resistance to land sales ultimately had the greatest impact in northern Potosí, where Indian communities controlled one of Bolivia's most important wheat-producing areas before the late-nineteenth-century liberalization of trade.[91] When the revisitas commenced in the early 1880s, the ayllus of Chayanta immediately rose up in opposition. Following repeated conflicts over attempts to measure land and raise taxes, the communities definitively blocked the surveyors' access to their territory in 1901. Uniquely in this region, Indian communities also replaced state-appointed tax men with their own collectors.[92]

If opposition peaked in Chayanta, "acceptance" reached a high point in Cochabamba. Initial outcomes of the land sales in this region coincided most closely with lawmakers' intentions, for many Indians in the department's central valleys willingly received private titles. Results varied markedly by subregion, but Cochabamba most vividly reveals that peasants could benefit from the privatization policies. In the Valle Alto (Cliza, Tarata, and Punata), where Indian communities no longer survived, the reforms weakened local landlords and accelerated a process of hacienda division with roots stretching back to the late colonial era.[93] Rather than encouraging the expansion of large estates, the reforms promoted a smallholding peasantry and new middle sectors. Even in some areas of the department where Indian communities still prevailed, smallholding took hold. In Capinota—an exceptionally fertile grain- and alfalfa-growing province southwest of Cochabamba city—communal land was subdivided in the late nineteenth century; former community members and outsiders acquired small plots. The revisitas had a more variegated outcome in the provinces of the Valle Bajo, a well-irrigated zone for fruit, vegetable, and grain cultivation and one of Cochabamba's highest-yielding areas. While traditional hacendados acquired some communal land in Sipesipe, El Paso, Tiquipaya, and Colcapirhua, smallholders, artisans, and comunarios themselves often purchased parcels in these places.[94]

Smallholding did not come to prevail everywhere in Cochabamba, however. Attempts to impose the 1874 law on Indian communities in the department's highland areas (Tapacarí, Arque, and Vacas) met with a mix of acceptance and resistance. In the bulk of these places, comunarios' complaints ultimately left the land surveys incomplete. Details of the resistance remain unclear, but we know that a member of a survey team was killed in Arque in 1897. In Vacas (Arani highlands), inspectors managed to finish their work, but Indians forced them to grant larger extensions of land than the government had authorized.[95] Despite this opposition, communities in Vacas, Tapacarí, and Arque ultimately lost considerable land to outsiders, just like Indian communities in other regions.

While communities throughout Bolivia forced suspensions of the surveys, in the end they could not permanently derail the process. Almost everywhere, a new stream of surveyors followed the ones community members had expelled. These successive and uncoordinated attempts to measure land added layers of confusion and conflict as consecutive surveyors distributed additional—and sometimes duplicate—titles.[96] It is worth remembering, however, that the acceptance of individual titles did not necessarily equal the recognition of private property; nor did it always imply the dissolution of community. In Cochabamba, as we will see in chapter 3, some comunarios who had accepted private titles rose up in defense of communal territory and authority when external incursion threatened their still extensive holdings in the early twentieth century. Rather than extinguishing communal forms of governance, or replacing collective rights with individual ones, private titles could matter in some cases because they substantiated the legality of comunarios' use of the land.[97] If Bolivia's late-nineteenth-century liberals took Indian communities of Cochabamba as simple collections of small plots, some of the region's "smallholders" instead showed that private property fit with and sustained a cultural and political community.

* The Rise of Indigenous Apoderados

Although most Indian communities could not halt the late-nineteenth-century revisitas, their resistance compelled two important modifications of the law early on. An 1881 presidential resolution authorized *proindiviso* (undivided) titles for communities that unanimously opted for them. In 1883 a second law gave communities another loophole. This measure exempted from the revisitas *terrenos de origen* (land held by Indian communities) that had been consolidated during the colonial era via *cédulas de composición* (titles examined and certified by colonial officials); according to the law, such land was the "property of its possessors."[98] In effect, both measures allowed communities to maintain collective land rights.[99] Almost as quickly as the surveys began, community resistance forced lawmakers to grant significant concessions.

Given late-nineteenth-century liberals' valorization of private property, and their resolve to break with the colonial past, both laws are remarkable developments. Still the lawmakers' ultimate aims did not completely change. Neither law rescinded the 1874 provision that denied communities a legal persona. The one concerning proindiviso titles allowed a type of collective land claim, but it did not restore the juridical status of Indian communities.[100] Nor did the ruling prevent surveyors from intruding on communities that opted for the shared title. Sometimes the surveyors repeated inspections precisely in those places where proindiviso titles were granted, since they believed that the titles thwarted the very objective of the reform.[101]

Bolivia's liberal legislators could not control the practical significance of the concessions they made, however. In practice the favorable decrees further fueled a concerted campaign against the land surveys by Indian communities of La Paz, Oruro, and Potosí.[102] With the initiation of the revisitas in 1881, Indian *apoderados*, who served as legal representatives for broad groupings of ayllus or communities, forged networks to block inspections of communal land. The apoderados also defended the interests of their communities in provincial and sometimes departmental courts.[103] They used the 1881 and 1883 decrees to bolster their claims. Ironically their actions also found justification in the very law that had eradicated the Indian community. Article 7 of the 1874 Disentailment Law declared that "no individual or group of individuals may take the name of community or ayllu, nor appear for such an entity before any authority."[104] The same clause stipulated that "indígenas" should thenceforth "take care of their own affairs or be represented by authorized agents [apoderados]."[105] But the law never stipulated that these apoderados could not be Indians. The indigenous apoderados who took advantage of this law were often individuals who held positions of authority within their ayllus (as *hilacatas* or *segundas*); sometimes they obtained legal counsel from non-Indian lawyers who resided in provincial towns. In large part the collective body of Apoderados Generales they formed was an Aymara movement based in the La Paz altiplano; however, it also included indigenous legal delegates from Potosí and Oruro.[106]

During the 1880s and 1890s mounting Indian resistance to the revisitas in all three departments dovetailed with rising discontent inside the nascent Liberal Party. Shortly after the bulk of the land surveys commenced, Liberals—who were repeatedly prevented from taking power by ruling Conservatives—began to wage their own series of revolts. Together these events produced an unlikely series of alliances between Liberal Party leaders and Indian authorities. The escalating process of conflict and mobilization eventually culminated in Bolivia's 1899 civil war.[107]

That the Liberal–Conservative conflict could spawn such a devastating battle seems at first glance surprising, for both parties essentially adhered to the same principles. The two parties were forged out of the crucible of the War of the Pacific, and the war itself was the main element that distinguished them. The Conservative Party was founded around 1884 under the leadership of Sucre-based silver-mine owners who advocated peace with Chile. Because these mine owners believed the war was damaging the national economy, they backed a peace treaty to protect their interests in mining and to preserve their ties to Chilean industrialists. The Liberal Party was in turn created in 1883 by a rising group of La Paz–based tin mine owners and urban professionals who called for continued combat against Chile in alliance with Peru. When the war was over, politicians from both parties embraced similar positions on most essential questions: Liberals and Conservatives diverged with respect to the church, but both parties backed civilian-dominated government, national unification, the development of mining and transportation, economic modernization, and the abolition of Indian communities.[108] Indeed the ruling Conservatives initiated the communal land sales in the 1880s.

Despite their shared ideological positions, the two parties could look very different on the ground. The Liberal Party program was vague enough, and its membership sufficiently heterogeneous, that this political organization could be disassociated from its oligarchic origins. As the Liberal–Conservative struggle for power deepened in the 1890s, the Liberal Party articulated an explicitly pro-Indian discourse and successfully gained Indian adherents to the anti-Conservative cause.[109] Specifically, Liberals pledged to return communal land that had been seized during the revisitas and to abolish the *contribución indigenal* and other taxes that weighed heavily on Indians.[110] At the same time, Liberals promised regional elites they would establish a decentralized form of government and address local economic interests. Before the civil war, then, the Liberal program could be associated with popular ideals and regional demands.[111]

Traditionally the conflict that culminated in the 1899 war has been viewed as a struggle between the regional oligarchies of silver (Sucre) and tin (La Paz). Yet the war was also shaped by an autonomous indigenous movement even more extensive than the one directed against Melgarejo. Its two principal leaders—Pablo Zárate Willka and Juan Lero—mobilized indigenous armies in La Paz, Oruro, and Tapacarí (Cochabamba).[112] Their project has sometimes been viewed as a plan to take national power and eliminate whites. In reality it revolved around the defense of communal

1   Indigenous troops led by Feliciano Condori Willka, a high minister in Zárate Willka's army
and government, 1899. General Condori Willka led the forces in Cochabamba's western
highlands. *Courtesy of the Archive of La Paz.*

land and a program for Quechua-Aymara federalism based on Indian self-
government in local and regional spheres.[113] Many of the leaders—probably
even Zárate Willka—were former apoderados who had been involved in the
legal campaigns of the 1880s (see figure 1).[114] As designated representatives
of other Indians and legally recognized *apoderados generales* of sometimes
broad territorial jurisdictions, they gained extensive knowledge of the law
and government institutions. The political program indigenous rebels espoused was nevertheless driven by their own vision of justice.[115]

The events of the 1899 war and rebellion ultimately ruptured Indians'
fragile alliance with the Liberal Party. In the course of the conflict, Aymara
forces in Mohoza (Inquisivi, La Paz) killed a contingent of Liberal soldiers. The killings were carried out in reprisal for abuses that Conservative
and Liberal armies alike routinely committed against Indian communities.
They were also motivated by enmities between town families whose struggles for local power had been caught up in the partisan conflict: members
of one feuding family deceived Indians of the area into thinking the Liberal
soldiers were instead Conservatives. Above all, the incident revealed the
indigenous forces' growing autonomy from the Liberal Party. After killing

all members of the Liberal squadron, indigenous rebels established their own government in Mohoza.[116] When the Liberal army chief José Manuel Pando learned that Indians had turned against him and his troops, he tried to reach an accord with the Conservative army. Conservatives declined the offer. Knowing that he needed Indians to win the war, Pando waited to punish them for the killings until the Liberal Party emerged victorious in April 1899. The Liberal chief momentarily celebrated the war's end with Zárate Willka, and then ordered his and the other indigenous leaders' arrest.[117]

Once La Paz Liberals had triumphed over Conservatives and their own indigenous allies, they transferred the nation's political capital to the highland city, set about laying railroad tracks, and began to create stronger state institutions.[118] After Pando took power as Bolivia's first post–Civil War president in October 1899, authorities executed Zárate Willka and thirty-one other Indian prisoners. Dozens more were punished with lengthy terms of forced labor; still more had already died in detention before sentences could be imposed. The defendants were branded "savage" (or child-like) traitors to the Liberal cause, and deemed incapable of elaborating a politically motivated plan.[119] United in their fear of a "race war," many Conservatives put their differences aside and joined the Liberal Party.[120]

The course of the 1899 war, then, kindled deeply polarized views of race that could now be buttressed by elite unity and an alliance of bureaucratic and ethnographic intervention.[121] In the aftermath of the national revolt against Melgarejo, proponents of smallholding, such as Santivañez, viewed Indians as potential citizens so long as they passed through a civilizing process. After the Mohoza massacre, liberalism's racialized logic showed increasingly rigid exclusivity: liberal elites more uniformly believed that Indians innately lacked the attributes that could make them eligible for citizenship.[122] For their participation in the 1899 war, the Aymara in particular became objects of a more virulent racism: they were viewed as enemies of the nation.[123]

After the Liberal Party took power, its leaders renounced the oaths they made as a party in opposition. They embraced the centralist mold of their Conservative predecessors, and launched a third major assault against the Indian community. When land sales and seizures commenced again in 1905, and with them new forms of resistance, the state would have an easier time deploying more powerful contingents of repressive force.[124] After Melgarejo's overthrow in 1871, legislators so feared the Indian communities surrounding Bolivia's largest city that they unanimously restored usurped land. Elite politicians' second major alliance with Indians in 1899 had the opposite outcome. With the confidence gleaned from science, railroads, industry, and arms, the triumphant new government unleashed the most extensive process of communal land seizure yet.[125]

✳ Conclusion

The post-1860s assault against Bolivia's Indian communities stands out in the broader Latin American context. Throughout the continent, late-nineteenth-century liberal elites privileged private property, but they did not everywhere take action to deliberately undermine or eliminate Indian corporate communities. A variety of factors could foster reticence: strategic political concerns; recognition of the communities' productive capacity and utility; or an awareness that Indian communities occupied land unsuited for the cultivation of particular export crops. Moreover, although liberal ideologues throughout Latin America viewed Indian communities as an obstacle to "progress," they sometimes recognized that the communities did not actually block the pursuit of liberal economic agendas. Rather than the law itself, structural socioeconomic forces such as population growth, urbanization, and the market posed a greater threat to Indian communities. In particular places, coercive labor drafts caused the most destruction.[126]

If liberalism in theory was anticommunal, in practice liberal laws meant enormously diverse things for land tenure and ethnic relations across nations and regions. Among the Andean countries alone, the course of the liberal reforms diverged considerably. In Colombia, liberals sought to privatize *resguardos* (communal landholding entities) during the early post-independence period, but their objectives were thwarted in many regions by legal and technical factors or by indigenous resistance. In the end, privatization in Colombia was a piecemeal process that required significant concessions to Indians.[127] In Peru, liberal anticommunity campaigns ultimately had rather minor implications largely due to elite and regional divisions.[128] At the moment when liberal ideology had greatest currency in Peru (1850s–70s), government authorities took few actions that actually threatened to disintegrate Indian communities. Instead communities lost the most land precisely at the point when political liberalism had declined (1890s–1910s) but the wool export economy was booming.[129] Peru's liberal governments never outlawed the Indian community, nor did they wage a full-scale anticommunity crusade like Melgarejo's. In Ecuador, lawmakers coupled land privatization policy and attempts to regulate rural servitude with ongoing recognition of Indian communities.[130] Since most Ecuadorian Indians no longer lived in autonomous communities but instead worked as tenant laborers on an extensive array of haciendas, this was a minor concession, yet it confirms that support for privatization did not necessarily entail state-led anticommunity campaigns.[131]

Bolivia's liberal reform process more closely followed the path of Mesoamerica's nineteenth-century states, which waged more direct legal attacks against communal landholding than the bulk of the Andean countries. In Nicaragua and El Salvador, liberal regimes explicitly abolished the Indian community. Still, indigenous resistance in Nicaragua impeded the successive abolitions of the late nineteenth century and the early twentieth.[132] And even in El Salvador, the law did not automatically result in widespread communal land loss.[133] Guatemala's liberal creed undoubtedly represents one of the continent's most violently anti-Indian projects, yet Guatemalan liberals did not outlaw the Indian community or wage a direct assault against it.[134] Coffee exports, the *mandamiento* (forced labor drafts), and population growth devastated communal landholding by other means.[135] Mexico's 1856 Ley Lerdo, which was incorporated into the 1857 Constitution, perhaps most fully parallels Bolivia's 1874 law, but its underlying logic differed. While the Bolivian legislation uniformly targeted Indian communities, Mexico's liberal reform law instead approached communal land in connection with other forms of "corporate privilege"; its most immediate target was the wealth and property of the church.[136] Passage of the law did not itself lead to the massive expropriation of land. Rather than the simple outcome of state policy, the privatization of communal land in Mexico during the late nineteenth century may have been largely driven from below, by economic processes internal to landholding communities and in part by the landholders themselves.[137]

Within Latin America, Bolivia stands out for an enduring, state-led anticommunity campaign that was covered in legal trappings. Here too, the process of privatization was protracted and shaped by economic and social factors. The heightened stratification that came to characterize Indian communities in parts of the country during the nineteenth century undoubtedly played a significant role in the eventual process of disentailment. Still, the law had particular force in this case. Nowhere else was the gap between passage and implementation of the legislation so short. Between the 1874 Law of Disentailment and the first revisita (1878), a mere four years went by. Moreover, state representatives played a significant role in the privatization process once the law took hold. Even though Conservatives initiated the bulk of the process in the early 1880s, the most damaging effects were wrought after 1900 under Liberal rule. The connection between the law, the Liberal Party, the Indian community, and the violence cannot be unraveled in this case. State authorities directly attacked not just a particular form of landholding but a juridical and political entity.[138]

If the link between legality and coercion typified Bolivia's privatization process, so did constant retrenchment. The first major attempt to abolish the Indian community in the 1860s ended in an unprecedented alliance of Indians and non-Indians, a massive rebellion, and the return of communal land. And while those liberal politicians who favored restoration were partly motivated by the fear of Indian uprisings, the arguments they made recognized Indians' historic land rights and their contributions to the battle against a corrupt dictator. The 1874 abolition of communal landholding later negated the 1871 reinstatement, but the 1871 act would serve Indian community leaders as a political tool against expropriation in struggles to come.

The second major attempt to eliminate the Indian community in the 1880s resulted almost immediately in significant legal concessions and ultimately in another wide-scale uprising that began as an alliance between the Liberal Party and indigenous leaders. Although the government did not restore the community's legal standing when it reauthorized forms of collective tenure in the early 1880s, in practice this is precisely what occurred, for the two things could not be easily disentangled. Community leaders—the apoderados generales—used colonial composition titles not only to defend corporate land rights but to forge a broad-based movement that affirmed the community's legal standing and its right to collective representation. Eventually they would do this even in places such as Cochabamba, where Indian communities had already suffered great fragmentation.

Whether in stages or all at once, Bolivia's post-1874 liberal land laws envisioned the end of the Indian community. But the actual path that the policies followed belied that vision. Rather than extinguishing the Indian community or removing the category "Indian" from the law, the liberal reforms unleashed a long-lasting struggle over the community's juridical status and its powers of representation. As we will see in the next two chapters, against the backdrop of weak state institutions, divided elites, and nationally coordinated indigenous movements, early-twentieth-century governments not only failed to abolish the Indian community; they were compelled to call on indigenous authorities to help carry out the state's "civilizing" mission. And that too would prove dangerous.

CHAPTER TWO

INDIGENISTA STATECRAFT
AND THE RISE OF THE CACIQUES
APODERADOS

After prevailing in the 1899 civil war, La Paz–based Liberal Party governments set about constructing a strong central state founded on three pillars of "progress": railroads, private property, and schools. National authorities were anxious to prevent renewed protest in the aftermath of the Zárate Willka rebellion. They were also eager to portray the state as a force of civilization and progress. To heighten the state's repressive capacity and promote economic development, they created new duties such as universal military service and obligatory road work (*prestación vial*). Although the prestación vial law applied to all men over the age of eighteen "regardless of their class and condition," the service seems to have weighed most heavily on Indians.[1] Liberal Party governments were also intent on buttressing frontier regions via foreign immigration and colonization. And they launched a full-scale campaign against the church's remaining power by sponsoring laws to confiscate church property, abolish clerical privileges, and secularize schooling, marriage, and cemeteries. Of all its many state-building projects, the Liberal Party's hallmark reform was the education of Indians.

In the decade after the civil war, Bolivian political elites pursued these modernizing plans with a rare if fragile sense of unity. Surely the post-1900 union was linked with the traumas of the conflict itself. It also had much to do with the profits of the booming tin mines, which allowed Liberal Party governments to expand the state administration and placate dissident elites with economic incentives. Elite rifts nevertheless reemerged in the 1910s, largely due to the Liberal Party's refusal to relinquish the presidency.[2] In April 1914, dissident politicians took the first steps toward establishing the Unión Republicana on the initiative of the well-known lawyer-politician Bautista Saavedra. In 1920, Saavedra and the Republican Party came to power via a coup. Like Liberal Party governments, Republican-led regimes of the 1920s sought to "civilize" Indians via education. But Republican Party projects to expand the state and advance the nation were also premised on equally significant experiments in justice and the law.[3] Members of the Republican Party would prove to be the chief architects of Bolivia's little-known early-twentieth-century corpus of indigenista laws and legislative initiatives.

In the most general terms, *indigenismo* constitutes a field of dispute over national identity, regional power, and rights that places "Indians" at the center of politics, jurisprudence, social policy, or study. A fundamental element concerns the granting of special status to Indians or Indian communities, but such recognition has no univocal meaning. At its heyday (c. 1910s–40s), indigenismo throughout Latin America was marked by a diversity of political positions and modes of racial thinking.[4] In Bolivia, indigenismo did not become the basis of a specific political movement or party, as it did in Mexico and Peru.[5] An important cohort of Republican Party politicians nevertheless championed indigenista policy initiatives, especially in congressional sessions of the 1920s. The most influential indigenistas sidestepped the question of the land and instead centered their attention on education and the law.

As Bolivia's indigenista legislators drafted policies regarding schools, courts, and taxes, they entangled nineteenth-century notions of individual rights and equality with overt proposals for "special" justice (*leyes de excepción*). In the decades after independence, lawmakers enshrined the individual rights of (male) citizens in Bolivian constitutions and rejected a separate legal framework for Indians. Via minor laws and decrees, nineteenth-century policymakers nevertheless included Indian rights and restrictions in the modern legal corpus. And in subtle ways, these secondary laws revived colonial caste to perpetuate a hierarchical status quo.[6] In the 1920s, Bolivia's indigenista legislators did much more: they crafted overt proposals for separate institutions of justice. Congress debated a flurry of such initiatives for special laws, Indian courts, and Patronatos Indígenas (state agencies for Indian affairs) during the years of Republican Party rule (1920–34).[7]

In the end, Bolivia's early-twentieth-century lawmakers never created a separate legal code for Indians. Nor did they establish a *patronato* or indigenous tribunal. But they did not cease to promote such schemes. Their legislative disputes projected a paradox: Indians were considered equal before the law, but they were also viewed as inferior subjects of a neocolonial administration who needed to be protected and "civilized." To be sure, legislators sponsored these plans to quell a new cycle of rural conflict that was triggered by the reinitiation of the communal land sales and by the abuse that local authorities perpetrated against Indians. The laws were not, however, straightforward instruments of control. Some advocates of the special laws overtly backed indigenous demands to reform corrupt judicial institutions, expand education, and discipline local representatives of the state.

This chapter and the following chapter explore the trajectory of state policy on Indian education and justice, the rise of a new cohort of indigenous leaders, and those leaders' uses of the law. Chapter 2 traces these issues at the national level, while chapter 3 focuses on the department of Cochabamba. Post-1900 indigenous leaders never merged with the Republican Party nor with any other political party or state agency. Still, they intervened continuously in national political arenas. In doing so, they influenced—and were influenced by—legislative debates of the 1910s and the 1920s. Time and again, Indian community leaders shrewdly exploited the ambiguous status of 1920s legislative initiatives to press their demands for land, education, and justice. The law, they would show, could be an instrument of struggle as well as a a tool of domination.[8] Eventually, national authorities came to view the law itself—in educated Indians' hands—as a subversive weapon.

✳ The Origins of the Caciques Apoderados

The Liberal Party politicians who took power after 1900 set out to finish what their Conservative predecessors had started: they built an intricate system of rails linking Bolivia to its exterior (see map 1). Completion of these lines increased land values in outlying areas, sparking a second wave of communal land sales and seizures between 1905 and 1915. Unlike the late-nineteenth-century period of appropriation, which focused in cantons where haciendas already existed, the second phase entailed incursions into areas where communities remained strong. And although the most devastating effects once again transpired in the La Paz altiplano, communities in regions previously sheltered from hacienda expansion suddenly began to experience its results.[9]

With the reinitiation of the land sales, the countryside—and also now the city—became the site of renewed Indian community mobilization. Building on the experience of the late-nineteenth-century apoderados, a new generation of indigenous leaders known as *caciques apoderados* forged a broad-based legal movement to reclaim usurped land.[10] By 1917, their networks had acquired an unequivocally national stature. Quechua and Aymara men affiliated with the movement came from five Bolivian departments: they were active in nearly every province of La Paz, Cochabamba's highland areas, the western part of Oruro, northern Potosí, and particular valleys in Chuquisaca, where altiplano ayllus still possessed land.[11] Nowhere else in the Andes would early-twentieth-century indigenous movements achieve such exceptional levels of national coordination.[12]

Over the course of almost two decades, the caciques apoderados waged campaigns for land, education, and rights largely by submitting petitions to state authorities. In and of itself, such petitioning was a common convention that stretched back to the colonial era. The practice pursued by apoderados of the 1910s and the 1920s stands out for an unusual degree of collaboration. From the capital city, La Paz, caciques apoderados from many regions effected a highly coordinated diffusion of grievances throughout all levels of government, sympathetic newspapers, and their own bulletins. Although some of the caciques apoderados were implicated in major rebellions, their political practice above all centered on the law.

What accounts for the rise of this extraordinary movement of caciques and caciques apoderados? And how did they establish and maintain a highly coordinated national network? By all accounts, a 1914 land conflict in the La Paz province of Pacajes (today Gualberto Villarroel) constitutes a kind of founding moment for the caciques apoderados.[13] With the completion of a railroad line in 1913 that linked remote highland areas with the Pacific coast, territory in Pacajes and other relatively protected areas became vulnerable to encroachment by outsiders.[14] When a neighboring

2 Sagárnaga Street, in the
Indian quarter of La Paz,
circa 1902. *Courtesy of the
U.S. Library of Congress,
Prints and Photographs
Division, Stereograph Collec-
tion (44805-Bolivia-11541).*

hacienda owner began to intrude on the land of ayllu Ilata, the Indian originario Martín Vásquez set off for Lima, Peru, in search of colonial composition titles to confirm the community's land rights in line with the 1883 law. When Vásquez returned to La Paz in March 1914, he convened an assembly on Sagárnaga Street in the center of La Paz's Indian quarter (see figure 2). The assembly, a space reserved for collective reflection and decision making, was an important element of Indian community politics and a longstanding strategy of Andean social movements.[15] On this particular occasion, 100 delegates from La Paz, Potosí, Sucre, and Cochabamba came together to deliberate the contents of the manuscripts Vásquez had retrieved.[16]

Although he was not an established community leader, Vásquez enjoyed the support of apoderados who had been associated with Zárate Willka, leader of the 1899 rebellion. He also recruited Indian community authorities—*hilacatas* and *alcaldes*—to the direction of the movement. At a 1914 assembly in the Pacajes canton Callapa, these indigenous authorities designated Vásquez apoderado general of the *ex-comunarios.*[17] Vásquez relied in addition on assistance from non-Indians. The lawyer Eusebio Monroy accompanied Vásquez to Lima and reportedly helped organize the assembly on Sagárnaga Street. Monroy likely belonged to the Republican Party, which had pledged to help Indians recuperate usurped land.[18]

Vásquez's initiative in defense of communal land quickly acquired a sweeping, multiregional scope.[19] To recruit delegates to the assembly, emissaries from La Paz traveled to Cochabamba, Oruro, and Potosí. Although Vásquez's movement favored legal tactics, the evidence suggests that his supporters also contemplated other forms of pressure. In fact, several revolts took place around the time of the Sagárnaga Street assembly. A 1914 uprising in Vásquez's native province of Pacajes called for dramatic changes, including the return of usurped land; administration of cantons and vice-cantons by Indians named among themselves; election of indigenous representatives to Congress; exemption of young men from military service; an end to forced labor and taxation; and "new" laws.[20] Shortly after the uprising, Vásquez and other leaders were arrested on charges of sedition. The case was dropped for lack of evidence, but Vásquez himself eventually disappeared from the movement; because he had forged close ties with duplicitous non-Indian allies, his followers began to doubt his authority.[21]

Before exiting the movement, Vásquez named Santos Marka T'ula as his successor. Marka T'ula hailed from the same community as Vásquez and claimed to be a descendent of the colonial caciques mentioned in the documents the latter had recovered in Lima. The legal campaigns forged under Marka T'ula's leadership would be punctuated by two major uprisings: Jesús de Machaqa (La Paz) in 1921 and Chayanta (northern Potosí) in 1927. In Jesús de Machaqa, the catalyst of the revolt was an abusive local official who victimized Indian community members; in Chayanta, not only comunarios but also colonos rose up against abuse and communal land usurpation. Although the rebellions differed in scope and strategy, both evinced the caciques apoderados' demands for land, schools, and local power.[22]

In addition to the network led by Santos Marka T'ula, a second group of apoderados emerged in the 1920s under the leadership of the Aymara educator Eduardo Leandro Nina Qhispi. Up to a point, the visions and strategies of the two leaders overlapped in ways that typified indigenous political projects of the era. Both Marka T'ula and Nina Qhispi labored unremittingly for the restoration of communal territory via the call for a general inspection of land boundaries. They also demanded particular rights embodied in the corpus of republican legislation, such as protection against abuse.[23] Although both leaders established roots in the capital, they journeyed frequently to the countryside to publicize favorable legislation or promote *deslindes* (demarcation of land boundaries) and schools. Their demands for territorial restitution, as historian Carlos Mamani has shown, were also projects for political self-determination.[24]

If they shared essential political convictions, important differences separated the two leaders. Santos Marka T'ula, who was born in about 1879 in Curahuara (Pacajes), was one of the first of the Indian apoderados to claim kinship with the colonial *caciques de sangre* (descendents of the Andean nobility). Although his energies centered on the defense and recuperation of communal land, Marka T'ula did not restrict his activities to the countryside. He maintained close ties with the Federación Obrera Local (Local Labor Federation, FOL), an anarchist organization based in La Paz, and championed an inclusive political identity that encompassed rural and urban Indians.[25] Eduardo Leandro Nina Qhispi in turn hailed from Taraqu (Ingavi), an area of exceptionally fertile land closer to Lake Titicaca. Like Marka T'ula's community, the one where Nina Qhispi lived essentially escaped the effects of hacienda expansion throughout the colonial era. Nina Qhispi's community was also sheltered from the late-nineteenth-century land sales. But it was grabbed up whole during the surveys that took place between 1905 and 1915. When the ex-comunarios (now hacienda colonos) tried to retake communal land in 1920, Nina Qhispi fled to La Paz to escape police repression. Although he traveled to the countryside to set up schools and promote deslindes, Nina Qhispi established solid urban roots by immersing himself in labor organizations and the field of education.

Nina Qhispi's extraordinary engagement with education and literacy distinguished his political persona from Marka T'ula's public figure. Although Nina Qhispi never received formal schooling, he engaged personally in the promotion of rural and urban schools and served as an instructor. After teaching himself to read, he turned his home into a makeshift school for children of the *matarifes* (slaughter men), who formed one of the most important Indian guilds in La Paz. The subsequent years evince Nina Qhispi's ever-increasing dedication to the field of education. In May 1930, he convened an Indigenous Congress in La Paz to discuss pedagogical issues.[26] In the same year, he created the Sociedad Centro Educativo "Kollasuyo," also in La Paz. The sociedad established schools in rural communities and haciendas, and worked to defend communities whose land had been threatened or already seized by hacendados.[27] Nina Qhispi identified himself as the apoderado general and founder of the Sociedad Kollasuyo; he never claimed the title of the cacique.

To be sure, Marka T'ula promoted schools: in 1928 he founded the

Centro Bartolomé de las Casas, an educational institute in La Paz that established affiliated schools in rural communities.[28] But Marka T'ula was not fully literate, and he never worked as a teacher. To craft written appeals to local and national authorities, he relied on scribes, nephews, and his own extraordinary capacity to memorize texts. The distinct experience of the two leaders helps illuminate how hundreds of other apoderados mastered and manipulated manuscripts, laws, and land titles.[29]

If Nina Qhispi's and Marka T'ula's connection to written words differed, so did their public style and rhetoric. In contrast to Marka T'ula's political practice, that of Nina Qhispi was marked by an explicit, almost self-conscious recognition of republican rituals and institutions. The Aymara educator, for example, organized children from his La Paz neighborhood to march in a civic parade and praised the efforts of Bolivia's Colegio Militar de Ejército (military academy).[30] And even as Marka T'ula identified with a pacifist position during the Chaco War (1932–35), Nina Qhispi expressed his support. In a note to President Daniel Salamanca, probably written in 1932, he pledged to "inculcate in the indigenous schools the duty to sacrifice ourselves for our beautiful flag and our beloved country." Marching in civic parades and offering support for the nation's war-torn honor were forms of public presentation that made Nina Qhispi and other Indians appear as loyal "members of the nation."[31]

Nina Qhispi's concern with patriotism, "civilization," and "progress" were not just masks for subversive ends, however. Instead he suggested that the recognition of indigenous territory and autonomy could be the basis for the nation's advance, the means to "regenerate" a country mired in conflict and violence. Through its promotion of deslindes, the Sociedad Kollasuyo also vowed to build harmony among Indians: "[Let] there be no conflicts among indígenas," a document creating an affiliate society in Pucarani reads. "All are brothers of the same race . . . and the same language." The Sociedad Kollasuyo, in short, spoke to the inter- and intracommunity tensions unleashed by the land sales, just as it addressed the confrontations between communities and landlords. Through its petitions and political practice, the association linked indigenous solidarity with a vision of intercultural harmony.[32]

Perhaps the distinction between Nina Qhispi and Marka T'ula is best expressed as a contrasting approach to history and the law. Leandro Condori Chura, an Aymara scribe who knew both men well, characterized the difference as a division between *caciques*, who identified with Marka T'ula, and *apoderados*, who associated with Nina Qhispi. Although lines between the two groups were not fixed, Condori suggested that Marka T'ula and his followers respected the "ancient laws of the Spanish Crown," while Nina Qhispi, as an apoderado, rooted his work in "recent laws," in the laws of the Republic.[33] Indeed the caciques' fascination with early times contrasts sharply with the apoderado Nina Qhispi's rendition of a more modern character that valued *renovación* (renewal). Nina Qhispi not only mastered the written word but fashioned an identity around literacy, legal expertise, and his own professional status as an educator.

However much they differed in language and political style, Nina Qhispi and Marka T'ula ultimately pursued comparable objectives. Both stood out for their attention to the law and persistent intervention in the public sphere.[34] The two leaders submitted petitions to all levels of government, published articles in national newspapers, printed their own bulletins, distributed laws, met with government officials, and created civic institutions. For approximately two decades, they focused unremittingly on issues of land, education, discrimination, and local power. Finally, although Santos Marka T'ula identified as a cacique, both leaders were apoderados, legal agents. Whether they drew on colonial or republican language, Nina Qhispi and Marka T'ula shared one essential trait: they studied, preserved, and conveyed land titles, "books of grievances," petitions, and laws.[35] Not just the content of the law was at stake, but who would have knowledge of the law—and where it would be conveyed.

✳ From Colonial Cacique to Republican Cacique Apoderado

The movements forged by Nina Qhispi, Marka T'ula, and hundreds of lesser-known Quechua and Aymara community leaders built upon the late-nineteenth-century networks of apoderados. But the second generation of legal representatives differed in significant respects. During the 1910s and 1920s, Indian apoderados forged a much wider network that drew on extensive transregional and multilingual ties (see figure 3).[36] And although the twentieth-century apoderados took counsel from non-Indian lawyers, the new cohort eventually relied on its own scribes. The twentieth-century apoderados not only sought to ward off encroachments on communal land but to recuperate territory that was occupied by long-established haciendas.[37] Finally, while the nineteenth-century apoderados served as legal

3 Caciques apoderados, 1920s. The man kneeling in the center of the first row and
wearing a cross is most likely Santos Marka T'ula. *Credit: Julio Cordero. Courtesy of the
Cordero Family Archive*.

delegates for broad groupings of ayllus or communities, only the twentieth-
century apoderados revived the colonial-era cacique title. Indeed indigenous petitioners from Cochabamba rarely used the term *apoderado* at all.
Instead they generally referred to themselves as "caciques," "caciques principales," "orijinarios principales," or "casiques originarios."[38] In response
to the deepening assault against Indian communities in the early twentieth century—with its economic, cultural, and political ramifications—
community leaders looked to the colonial past to revive the maximum
authority of the cacique. But they credited that figure with very different
meanings.

In colonial times, the cacique or kuraka (Quechua term for "ethnic
lord") was the highest-level delegate of an extensive lineage of ayllus and
official representative of the community before the state. Put most simply,
cacique signified Indian community governor. Although the colonial state
associated caciques with the subordinate "Republic of Indians," authorities
granted caciques the honors and privileges of noblemen; the caciques
became Hispanicized native lords. These favored state agents were also
beholden to Indian communities. And from the local perspective, caciques
were not just managers but defenders of community resources. When
judicial action was required to preserve territory, caciques took community matters to court. They were also keepers of the community archive, a

sacred source of information about possessions, obligations, and the community's past.[39] Women sometimes served as *cacicas*, but the colonial caciques were usually men.[40]

Shortly after independence, Simón Bolívar abolished the office of the colonial cacique.[41] In many parts of Bolivia, however, the legal abolition merely formalized a state of affairs already come to be. During the second half of the eighteenth century, the *cacicazgo* entered into crisis, largely due to the political conflicts that were unleashed by the *reparto* (forced distribution of goods by cantonal officials).[42] In La Paz, this crumbling of cacique legitimacy caused political authority to shift away from the ethnic elite as power became vested in a local religious and political hierarchy that rotated among members of the community.[43] In Potosí, caciques remained an important force, but the eighteenth-century crisis produced a new standard of political legitimacy. As the native aristocracy lost status and authority in the eyes of community members, communities rejected the principle of hereditary power; instead they asserted the right to choose caciques on the basis of their ability to safeguard the social and economic life of the ayllu.[44] The colonial caciques of Cochabamba, in contrast, rooted their authority in both ancestry and personal wealth: they claimed that their affluence made them efficient collectors of tribute. In eighteenth-century Tapacarí, the caciques became so gripped by their own prosperity that they lost their communities' respect.[45]

During the nineteenth century, caciques became private landlords or *corregidores* in much of the Andes.[46] Bourbon reformers had eliminated the *corregidor* post (state-appointed provincial official) after the 1780s Indian rebellions, but postindependence governments revived the position at a lower level. The corregidor was now appointed head of a canton by the subprefect, and replaced the cacique as the party responsible for tribute collection.[47] In an effort to maintain power in the new republican context, the caciques of old—who no longer held legal power—sought to establish a foothold in the emerging local bureaucracy. They also labored to retain their rights to "lands of the caciques" via appeals to an 1831 law that proclaimed caciques de sangre and their offspring "owners of the lands they possess."[48]

In some areas—Chuquisaca and Potosí—caciques or kurakas persisted in name after independence, but they were no longer maximum leaders. Instead they became the rough equivalent of colonial *hilacatas*, leaders of local ayllus. Hilacatas themselves lasted into republican times as representatives of an ayllu, yet their functions became more limited. For example, corregidores used the hilacatas to round up laborers for public and private works.[49] Hilacatas also adjudicated conflicts among community members, assisted with tribute collection, and preserved the community's papers and its information about land boundaries. Another important position of authority within Indian communities, in both colonial and republican times, was that of the alcalde. Like hilacatas, the alcaldes played a key role in the administration of local justice; they were also central to the twentieth-century caciques apoderados movement.[50] Although the terms *cacique* and *kuraka* occasionally appear in nineteenth- and even twentieth-century documentation from Cochabamba and other regions, these sporadic appearances did not hold colonial-era connotations. The term now referred to a community authority with locally circumscribed duties, or to a *major-domo* (hacienda foreman), or sometimes even to a local upstart.[51] The demise of the ethnic lords, in short, followed varied regional trajectories. But the high-level, state-sanctioned community leader receded everywhere after independence.[52]

Given the delegitimation of the caciques over the course of the late eighteenth century, and the transformation of many caciques into private landlords in the nineteenth, it is striking that Indian communities reclaimed the title in the first decades of the twentieth century. Community leaders recovered the cacique title only by investing it with new significance. As one group of petitioners stated in a 1924 appeal, "legally, our customs have been abolished, casicazgos, etc., nevertheless we maintain these among ourselves."[53] This poignant claim points to a process of recreation; it conjures up a leader very different from the colonial cacique, one with roots in the community, who is maintained "among ourselves." To be sure, twentieth-century caciques often claimed descent from lineages of the traditional caciques de sangre, who appeared in the documents they culled from distant archives. But these men were not actually caciques de sangre. Most likely, the twentieth-century caciques were comunarios who held important communal posts (as alcaldes or hilacatas), had experience, and were trustworthy. They emerged from and were beholden to the base of their communities.[54] It is even possible that the cacique post rotated among community members, just like the position of alcalde or hilacata. Men who presented themselves as caciques of communities, provinces, and departments first appeared in petitions to government authorities as *indios originarios* or *comunarios*. After spearheading major appeals, they might reappear as simple signatories to a subsequent cacique's text.[55]

Because the caciques apoderados were designated by the community rather than the state, they did not constitute official intermediaries. Indian communities nevertheless revived this colonial figure in the early twentieth century precisely because it offered the much needed prospect of external mediation.[56] Moreover, the caciques apoderados repeatedly requested government recognition of their powers to represent local Indian communities, broad groupings of communities, or even the Indians of an entire department. Whether and how the caciques apoderados established real authority over such extensive territories remains unclear. Archival and oral historical sources confirm that they enjoyed local respect and legitimacy, but their legitimacy was not necessarily complete or unchanging. Some of the caciques were named by their communities or by the community's body of hilacatas.[57] For example, the caciques who presented a 1925 plea to the minister of government and justice claimed that their titles had been conferred by the alcaldes of various ayllus and by "the originarios and comunarios of the same ayllus."[58] Other caciques may have been appointed by their predecessors, but this did not mean that they lacked local authority. The leadership of Santos Marka T'ula, apoderado of the ayllu Condo, commenced when Martín Vásquez named him his successor in 1914. Marka T'ula enjoyed such great legitimacy that he soon became "apoderado and cacique" of the precolonial jurisdiction of Callapa, Curahuara, and Ulloma (the area that traversed the provinces of Pacajes and Sicasica, present-day Aroma). In 1919, Isidro Kanki entrusted to Marka T'ula a higher position as "representative and apoderado of the ayllus of La Paz."[59]

Even though the twentieth-century caciques apoderados were not direct descendents of the colonial caciques de sangre, they often made such claims to lineage. Marka T'ula was the first leader to assert that his ancestors were colonial caciques de sangre. Many other apoderados followed suit.[60] Since the caciques apoderados' activities centered on the discovery and close reading of colonial documents, the emphasis on descent is not surprising. A crucial characteristic of the caciques de sangre was itself an ardent interest in history and historical sources. And colonial-era regulations not only encouraged concern with "blood" origins but also inspired a fixation with male forebears.[61] The twentieth-century caciques discovered these traits in the documents and mimicked them. Female cacicas also appear in the colonial record, and they played important roles in the 1780s indigenous uprisings, but during the early twentieth century men alone occupied the cacique apoderado post.[62] Women nevertheless held a critical place in the twentieth-century networks as *yatiris* (ritual specialists) who officiated over ceremonies to purify the documents and land titles that the caciques apoderados conveyed. They also performed rites to protect the apoderados in their encounters with officials and courts of the non-Indian world.[63]

To legitimize their power, caciques apoderados sometimes drew on republican as well as colonial legal provisions. For example, a group of caciques apoderados from Cochabamba sought to validate their position by citing a July 1825 resolution by Simón Bolívar. It is ironic that they referenced this particular decree, since it extinguished the "title and authority of caciques." Ignoring the law's overarching purpose, the petitioners quoted article 3, which stipulated that "the venerable caciques should be treated by the authorities of the Republic as citizens worthy of consideration, in all that does not prejudice the rights and interests of other citizens."[64] The caciques apoderados also elaborated novel forms of legitimacy. Consider a 1924 petition from Tapacarí in which a group of indigenous petitioners asked the president to recognize Manuel Ramos as the "cacique principal and representative of the indigenous class of Cochabamba." Rather than noting Ramos's lineage or privilege, the comunarios cited his good deeds and honorable character. They described him as an "honorable man" who worked in a "disinterested manner" for the "benefit of the indígenas of the entire Republic" and for the "good of the nation [patria]."[65]

No matter the language, law, or history employed to validate the caciques' position, their legitimacy ultimately relied on visible deeds: recovering documents, distributing laws, promoting deslindes, and obtaining authorizations for schools.[66] These legal dealings required extensive contact with the city and the state, and over time the caciques apoderados forged a community apart in the capital, even as they honored ongoing ties to their communities with reciprocal acts and duties. Migration and new forms of ethnogenesis made it possible to create transregional networks, yet urbanization could also take a toll on the caciques and their family members, who faced new hardships.[67] A group of caciques principales from Cochabamba recounted the isolation and hunger they experienced in La Paz: "Not even our fellow comunarios remember us," they wrote.[68] Their recovery of laws and titles could refurbish organizational structures where they were weak, or exacerbate divisions in places threatened with dispossession or violence (see chapter 3). The divergent experience of Nina Qhispi and Marka T'ula confirms that the revival of the cacique was neither an inevitable discovery nor an accidental one. Twentieth-century networks of apoderados and caciques apoderados drew inspiration from colonial documents and ancestors, but they forged new kinds of leaders.

* Caciques Apoderados and the State

As much as Indian communities' creative response to the land sales shaped the cacique apoderado networks, the movement was also bound up with intra-elite conflict and the politics of state making. The year Martín Vásquez set out for the archive in Lima (1914) stands out for the demise of a fragile elite unity that was cobbled together after the 1899 civil war. The reemergence of elite rifts in turn opened space for subaltern sectors as increasingly splintered political parties vied for clients. Under the direction of Bautista Saavedra, dissident politicians created the Unión Republicana in April 1914. Republican Party members would prove to be important interlocutors, though fleeting allies, of the caciques apoderados. The caciques apoderados would also draw strategic support from members of Bolivia's nascent Left.

Labor federations, leftist political parties, and radical student movements emerged in Bolivia in the 1920s. These activist organizations not only championed the rights of workers but announced pro-Indian agendas. The Partido Socialista, founded in 1921, called for the abolition of *pongueaje* (colonos' unpaid domestic service for landlords); legal recognition of Indian communities; and armed revolution by workers, soldiers, and peasants.[69] And Bolivian university students endorsed a resolution backing the distribution of land to Indians at their first national congress.[70] But the chief support for indigenous activists came from Bolivia's most celebrated leftist, Tristán Marof (1896–1979), and his associates. In 1927, Marof and other exiled non-Indian intellectuals established the "Grupo Tupac Amaru," which endorsed the "distribution of latifundios to . . . the indigenous class . . . and freedom for the indigenous class to organize and establish agricultural communities."[71] Although Marof repeatedly invoked a proletariat vanguard, he also claimed that Bolivia's enduring colonial legacies could be extinguished only by Indians themselves, in alliance with urban artisans, students, and mineworkers. Marof hailed a national indigenous movement rooted in community institutions, and called on Indians "of the north and those of the south," the Quechua and the Aymara," to elect representatives to Workers' Congresses.[72] The vanguard he envisioned included educated Indians.

Throughout the 1920s, Marof and other non-Indian leftists established direct contact with the caciques apoderados; they also offered support for the 1927 indigenous uprising in Chayanta.[73] In his influential essay *La tragedia del altiplano* (1934), Marof even campaigned for Santos Marka T'ula and "his comrades," who were languishing in jail "with no one to lobby for them."[74] But the connections forged between non-Indian politicians and the caciques apoderados did not follow the same trajectory in every region. In Chuquisaca, the caciques established especially close ties with the Socialist Party.[75] Petitions from Cochabamba and La Paz point to a tacit dialogue with leftist leaders, but caciques apoderados from these departments conversed more directly with Republican Party members. Their principal interlocutor was Bautista Saavedra, even though—or paradoxically because—Saavedra considered the Indian community a "reactionary" institution.[76]

Born in La Paz in 1871, Bautista Saavedra was one of the most influential politicians of the pre–Chaco War era. He not only authored numerous works in law and sociology but held a number of government positions ranging from minister of public instruction to senator and deputy to the national congress. Saavedra also spearheaded the Republican Party's July 1920 "revolution" and served as Bolivian president from 1921 to 1925. He could be called a caudillo, a sociologist, a lawyer, landowner, politician, veteran of the civil war, criminologist of sorts, and even somewhat of a historian.[77]

At first glance, Saavedra's position on the "Indian question" is rather inscrutable: his political life was exemplified by swings between reformist initiatives and brutal anti-Indian repression. In his 1901 "defense" of the Indian insurgents tried at Mohoza, Saavedra inscribed the "savage" nature of the Aymara. His 1903 study *El ayllu* in turn depicted the Indian community as a backward institution that should be eradicated. After the 1921 uprising in Jesús de Machaqa, Saavedra used similar arguments to justify his government's brutal repression of the rebels.[78]

Notwithstanding his open contempt for Indian communities, Saavedra provided logistical support to the caciques apoderados who, of course, sought to sustain those communities. In 1916 and 1917, Saavedra together with his brother Abdón Saavedra and brother-in-law Max Bustillos offered legal council to Santos Marka T'ula and other caciques regarding criminal charges and land registration.[79] In 1919, he sponsored a law to protect Indians from fraudulent dispossession and to exempt those who possessed communal land from the new tax on agricultural production (catastro). Saavedra even may have helped elaborate a 1919 petition in which Santos Marka T'ula and fifty other caciques requested a comprehensive "inspection of boundaries."[80] With the 1920 revolt that brought Saavedra to the presidency, expectations heightened that this revisita would finally be carried out.

Saavedra and other Republican Party members offered tentative support for indigenous land struggles partly to attack the political power of their principal rivals, the leaders of the Liberal Party. In the areas where the second major wave of sales took its greatest toll on Indian communities, a good number of the buyers were in fact Liberals. Two of the most avid purchasers were José Manuel Pando and Ismael Montes, who served as president between 1899–1904 and 1904–9/1913–17, respectively. It is no coincidence that dissident elites affiliated with the Republican Party forged clientelistic ties with Indians in the very region where leading Liberals were prominent landowners.[81]

When the Republican Party was first established in 1914, its contestatory tone carried considerable weight in political debate.[82] The party initially championed an ambiguously antioligarchic position, and its ranks included oligarchs who were shut out of the ruling Liberal Party as well as members of the emerging Left, such as Tristán Marof and Fernando Siñani. After the fall of the Liberal Party, with which most La Paz landlords were affiliated, hacienda colonos refused to work in several altiplano locales; in Nina Qhispi's Taraqu, they briefly managed to replace hacienda administrators with their own hilacatas. There is even evidence that leaders of the Jesús de Machaqa uprising thought that President Saavedra would recognize the indigenous government established there in 1920. When pressed, however, the president's class and race prejudice clearly outweighed his party loyalties: after Indians rose up in Jesús de Machaqa, Saavedra gave ready assistance to landowners affiliated with the Liberal Party.[83]

Still, Saavedra did not fully abandon his populist posture after becoming president in 1921. Besieged by elite opposition and seeking new allies among workers and the middle class, Saavedra sponsored Bolivia's first protective labor legislation.[84] He also approved the requests for schools that Indian communities submitted to his government. He even continued to meet frequently with caciques, who referred to him as a protective figure, as a "true father who would save this nation like no other."[85] In 1920, Saavedra decreed that land possessed by Indians could not be sold or transferred without the intervention of a judge or because of debts. According to the order, such "protective measures" were "essential to shield the indigenous race from the plunder of their lands . . . due to their debility and ignorance."[86] This decree, together with a 1916 decree that rigidly controlled the appropriation of Indian lands, contributed to ending the decades-long alienation of territory.[87] But land conflicts did not vanish with these executive orders. Cacique apoderado petitions from the 1920s (see chapter 3) show that encroachments and fraudulent sales persisted even after the two decrees virtually ended the official revisita process. If Saavedra offered a modicum of redress, he stopped short of approving the caciques' fundamental demand for a general inspection of land boundaries; in 1923 Saavedra concluded that such an assessment would violate the rights of others who "legally" possessed communal land.[88] The Republican Party nevertheless gained a reputation for backing indigenous land rights. In the countryside, Saavedra's party was known as the "Cacique Party" because it supported Indian authorities' claims.[89] As late as 1935 one besieged landlord complained of being the victim of the 1920 Republican "revolution," which had promised Indians their lands would be returned.[90]

Despite these lasting connotations, Republican support for the caciques apoderados was only tentative. In their post-1921 petitions, caciques apoderados sometimes appealed directly to Saavedra for support, but they no longer harbored expectations that his government would initiate radical change. Saavedra in turn abandoned pro-Indian policies at particular junctures not simply because he no longer needed to curry electoral favor, but because he could not control rising social movements with ameliorative gestures alone.[91] The seemingly incongruous images of protection and terror that his presidency conjured up were not random couplings: they defined Saavedra's political practice.[92]

If intra-elite conflicts led Republicans to hesitantly support cacique apoderado land claims, the indigenous movements were also caught up in a deeper struggle between national and provincial elites over the expansion of the central state. Political elites engaged in disputes about a variety of issues ranging from taxation, education, and local autonomy, to law, order, visions of progress, ideas about race, and images of the nation. Saavedra's guarded association with the caciques apoderados was also rooted in this deeper problematic.

In Bolivia as elsewhere in Latin America, the making of states and nations both shaped and was shaped by historically specific concepts of race.[93]

And Saavedra's views about race overlapped to some degree with those espoused by other Latin American elites. Following Lamarckian tendencies, turn-of-the-century Latin American intellectuals tended to emphasize the role of environmental factors in biological evolution. Still, they did not necessarily dismiss biology or phenotype. Their racialized views of peoples, regions, and nations were rooted in culturally specific understandings of biology, and in biologized visions of culture. Nationalism and anti-imperialism were key factors in this particular genealogy of racial thinking. As they rejected images from the United States and Europe that portrayed Latin Americans as degenerate, prominent intellectuals began to reconceptualize race mixture in positive terms. In turn they suggested that "superior" race was an achievable state that could be accomplished through education or other forms of social intervention.[94]

Saavedra's ideas coincided with these characteristic trends, but he stopped short of championing race mixture. In the early twentieth century, Bolivia's intellectual elites generally valorized "pure" races—"Indians" and "whites"—and denigrated "mixed" ones, which were said to pose social, political, and moral dangers.[95] Saavedra, though closely identified with the "mestizo-cholo" plebe and even considered a kind of defender of "cholos," was no exception.[96] Along with immigration from Europe or the United States, Saavedra urged a certain level of cultural incorporation of Indians that he referred to as "cholification."[97] The Aymara scribe Leandro Condori Chura, for example, indicates that Saavedra urged caciques to civilize or "cholify" themselves by learning to read and write and literally abandon rural attire.[98] While such ideas never translated into national laws, local elites in some places did pass regulations; for example, a 1928 municipal ordinance in Oruro required Indians to discard indigenous dress for European clothing, or "the modern dress of civilized peoples."[99]

Saavedra also took an incorporative stance with regard to education: as minister of justice and public instruction in 1910, he identified instruction in the "general language" (Spanish) as the primary goal of Indian education, and sought to ban instructional materials in Aymara.[100] At the level of work and public space, however, Saavedra openly endorsed a segregationist logic that was driven by specific images of colonization. In the 1901 "La criminalidad aymara en el proceso Mohoza," Saavedra said that what had to be done "with the indigenous race" was to "impose on it a civilizing . . . colonization [and] subject it to an autochthonous legislation, just like the British did in India." He believed that the state should "lift [the indigenous race] from its humiliating condition," protect it from "the depredation of the mestizo and the white," and "enlist it in the army and industries."[101]

Even though Saavedra named contemporary British colonialism as his model in the aftermath of 1898, he later passed laws that evoked the spatial vision of Bolivia's own Spanish colonial past. On the occasion of the country's 1925 centennial, Saavedra proclaimed a "Supreme Decree" that prohibited Indians from entering La Paz's main plaza and seat of government, the Plaza Murillo. The law also barred Indians from using sidewalks.[102] With this measure, the president and his cohort sought to inscribe in the urban landscape what industry and the army would instill in the body and the mind, an internal colonial geography that mapped power, occupation, and space in relation to perceived racial differences.[103] Saavedra passed the law to "avoid bringing shame on the nation," as recalled by the Aymara scribe Leandro Condori Chura.[104] Certainly, the president worried about the international gaze, but the law may have also been driven by anxieties about Indian political activity. Perhaps it targeted the caciques apoderados, to keep them from calling on government offices. Whatever the case, Saavedra clearly sought to "civilize" without assimilating, to "improve" Indians while keeping them in a racial—menial and apolitical—place.[105]

Like all "scientific" explanations of "race," Saavedra's own concoctions doubled back on illogic as they advanced.[106] But his attention to acculturation and differentiation, reform and repression, also points to a more general dilemma of colonial—and neocolonial—domination. The formation of Bolivia's modern state was based not so much on the assimilation of indigenous peoples as on the destruction of distinct societies and the creation of cultural differences. The post-1900 exclusionary political project, in short, both destroyed and sustained Indianness: modernizing elites promised to efface difference, but they repeatedly postponed its erasure.[107]

✳ Separate Schools, Special Laws

The colonial tendencies that marked Saavedra's writings and political practice left their most glaring mark on legislative plans for indigenous education and justice. With rural schools to "fit the race" and "special" courts for Indians, Saavedra and other legislators aimed to create a docile agricultural labor force and limit Indians' independent judicial action. But laws and legislative debates did not translate easily into effective forms of rule; in the end, the state established few new institutions. The reforms considered under Republican Party governments—as we will see in chapter 3—nevertheless created a political opening that fueled the caciques' expectations for schools, "new laws," and an "effective measure of protection."[108]

Shortly after the Liberal Party took power in 1899, the Ministry of Education began to create "mobile schools" (*escuelas ambulantes*) and teacher training institutes (normal schools) in particular rural areas. With the enactment of compulsory military service in 1907, President Montes's Liberal government also established obligatory literacy classes for new indigenous recruits.[109] These early educational experiments were not straightforward "civilizing" tools. Although proponents first privileged non-Indian teachers, ultimately they were compelled to train Indians to be teachers and "agents for the regeneration of their race."[110] The experience of Nina Qhispi and Marka T'ula shows that apoderados and caciques apoderados developed their own vernacular forms of literacy. But state-sponsored rural education also became important training ground, and provided legitimacy, for the new generation of apoderados. During the 1910s, several indigenous normal schools were created to train indigenous preceptors. Partly as a result of such programs, the caciques apoderados eventually counted on their own preceptors and scribes.[111]

Over the course of the first two decades of the twentieth century, educational policy underwent significant experimentation, debate, and change. In the years just after the 1899 war, Ministry of Education officials endorsed assimilationist policies to promote literacy and Hispanicization.[112] Eventually, they pronounced this kind of instruction politically dangerous. The policymakers' fears are well illustrated by the minister of education's negative assessment of normal schools for indigenous preceptors as places that "pull him [the Indian] out of his environment." They "give us," he stated, "that semi-literate being who aspires to be an extortionist corregidor, [an] enslaver of his own race."[113] To counter these perceived risks, one influential cohort argued that rural education should shift away from literacy to focus on agricultural development and the capacity for manual labor. A 1919 decree to convert rural normal schools into vocational schools made this growing preference national policy, for government officials eventually agreed that the change would keep rural communities intact and prevent Indians from being politicized.[114] Although such schools would be tailored to "each race and each region," they would pursue the same goal: the "adaptation of the Indian to a life of manual labor and agriculture and, . . . his incorporation into the social organism of the Republic as a citizen."[115]

"Citizen" in this context did not mean a politically active person with voting rights; the term was used figuratively to connote a patriotic worker and taxpayer.

However much national politicians acclaimed education as a source of civilization and progress, its expansion to rural areas was no simple feat. Provincial elites opposed the idea because it implied an assault on their autonomy and posed perceived political risks. And so despite the state's mandate for education as a means to "improve" Indians and develop the nation, local opposition stymied the expansion of schools beyond provincial capitals.[116]

To address this problem, and in line with the new emphasis on technical education, Bautista Saavedra sponsored a legislative proposal in 1919 that obliged not just haciendas but also estancias and ayllus to establish and maintain schools.[117] Saavedra and other legislators argued that the proposed law would eliminate Indians' need to "abandon their labors."[118] In the aftermath of the Jesús de Machaqa uprising, Saavedra had vowed to extinguish the Indian community, claiming that it "impede[d] all attempts at reform and progress."[119] Yet here he admitted the community as a site of instruction. The likeness that Saavedra posited between haciendas and communities in the proposed decree is striking: he and his colleagues viewed these distinct institutions as equivalent sites of labor mobilization, agricultural production, and civilizing missions that owed the same duties to the state. It might even be said that these politicians sought to use educational expansion as a means to recolonize the Indian community. Eight years after the ministry of education adopted the policy on agriculturally oriented instruction, the minister of education openly used colonial metaphors to make much the same case. He observed in a report that "the indígenas currently live in much worse conditions than they did under the *Spanish tyranny.*" "We need to bring Viceroy Toledo back to life," the minister wrote, for Toledo was "wise enough . . . to harmonize Inca and Spanish laws and traditions."[120] In line with new Hispanicist trends of the 1920s, it was no longer necessary to identify the British as Bolivia's colonial ideal, as Saavedra had done in 1901. Now some Bolivian authorities openly praised the Spanish past as a model to govern, protect, and civilize Indians.

Like Liberal Party politicians, then, Republican leaders deemed education central to state-building and civilizing missions. But the Republican proposals to manage Indian communities were also premised on little-known innovations in justice and the law. An important difference set the

Republican initiatives for juridical reform apart from their plans for education: while the ministry of education settled around 1919 on separate forms of instruction for Indians and non-Indians, in the realm of justice government authorities vacillated endlessly between universal rights and special protection.

In fundamental ways, Republican proposals for special laws were a reaction to the 1921 uprising in Jesús de Machaqa. The army's massacre of the rebels laid bare the violent, anti-Indian tenor of the Saavedra government. But the turn to repression did not obviate protective legislation. In the eyes of many congressional delegates, the events of 1921 made it impossible to rule by repression alone. One deputy warned that indigenous victims of injustice, languishing in prison on false charges of conspiracy, would take their revenge. "There [would] be no constitution or laws to control them," he concluded ominously.[121] And so as the paceño intellectual and landlord Alcides Arguedas observed in 1936, "First the Chamber [of Deputies], later the Senate, then the government, and finally the clergy and the press became embroiled in [the great theme of race] . . . and . . . from 1923 to 1926 there was a . . . flurry of plans, newspaper articles, [and] conferences."[122] The big stir included projects for special tribunals, Patronatos Indígenas (agencies for Indian affairs), and a wealth of proposed laws that offered "protection" and "guarantees."

Bolivia's first Patronato de Indígenas, which was sponsored by Rigoberto Paredes and like-minded Republican deputies in 1921, drew from contradictory impulses.[123] On the one hand, the proposal for this agency echoed an alternative indigenista tendency associated with provincial intellectuals who backed community land claims against expansive landowners.[124] On the other hand, it ascribed a subordinate status to Indians and contained insidious tutelary objectives; the proposed institute aimed to survey, control, and incorporate autonomous action under state management. A three-page plan outlined its overall purpose: to regulate and enforce guarantees and privileges that the law granted Indians, while promoting their education, "incorporation," and "civilization." Labor needs figured centrally. If Indians were "extinguished," the sponsors noted, the "cruelty of the altiplano climate" would make it impossible to replace them with foreign immigrants.

According to its sponsors, the proposed patronato would be supervised by the Ministry of Instruction as well as prefects, and staffed by interdisciplinary teams with offices in the departmental capitals of La Paz,

Oruro, and Potosí. Through practical forms of education, the institute would preserve Indians as the national labor force, diffuse modern tools and instruments, promote new habits, and make Indians conscious of their civic duties, especially military service. The patronato not only defined Indians as a population in need of specific social and cultural remolding; it proposed to make "Indian" a special juridical category. True, its sponsors did not call for a separate legal code. Yet they gave the patronato's lawyer responsibilty for developing proposals for "special civil and penal laws"; the lawyer would also provide Indians with free legal assistance. "Incorporation," from this perspective, signified many things: fulfillment of obligations to the state, affinity with "modern" tools and technologies, "improvement" of customs, access to justice, and understanding of the concept of nationhood (*patria*).[125]

It may be difficult to understand why the Saavedra government endorsed full-scale initiatives for "protection" just after perpetrating a bloodbath in Jesús de Machaqa. His government backed the schemes precisely because they were not simple ameliorative gestures: they were modes of discipline bound up with beliefs about the perceived deficiencies of the state. For Saavedra, a focus on "protection" dovetailed with the need to build a moral image and enhance the state's legitimacy. The president's concerns about local officials' misconduct are well captured in a circular he sent to all prefects. Worried that the corregidor and subprefect posts were merely a means of self-enrichment, the president advised prefects that these local delegates of the state must truly serve as vehicles of government and the law. In a memo to subprefects, the prefect of La Paz (Saavedra's brother) similarly railed against corregidores and other local authorities who required the "indigenous class" to perform legally abolished services for no pay. Underlying the memo is a concern about the "idea" of the state: if abuse persisted, the prefect feared, "the indígena" would not see cantonal authorities as representatives of a government that worked "by all means possible toward their true and real incorporation into the nation but only as a parasite of their race." Any authority caught demanding unremunerated services, gifts, or garments from the "indigenous class" would be removed from office.[126]

In the end, the Patronato Indígena never fully crystallized. Still, legislative sessions of the 1920s repeatedly debated proposals for special laws, special courts, protection, and guarantees. Legislators even approved some of the more limited initiatives. For example, the Chamber of Deputies took *juicios de indígenas* (lawsuits by Indians) out of the hands of *jueces parroquiales* in 1923. These lowest-level judges were blamed for the most serious infractions of Indian rights.[127] The deputies who backed such proposals generally blamed landlords, local authorities, and priests for mistreatment and concomitant unrest, and called for the appointment of moral, law-abiding officials.[128] After another major indigenous uprising—the 1927 Chayanta revolt—legislators and national authorities became even more concerned about the consequences of abusive treatment.[129] But Congress never reached a consensus for protective laws. One central point of contention centered on the constitutionality of special courts or laws. Legislators against a proposed tribunal for Indians argued that it violated the proscription against judgment by "special commissions."[130] Or they objected that such courts would disregard the principle of neutrality by automatically favoring Indians. Those in favor assumed that a court for Indians could be fully rooted in the "common" laws of the republic, that it fit within existing legal codes. Legislators also disagreed about whether provisions specifically for Indians contradicted or encompassed the principle of equality before the law. Would Indians benefit from common rights, codes, and courts? Or should they be the subjects of separate laws? Ultimately legislators left the dilemmas they posed unresolved.

* Conclusion

The debate over special laws and courts closed down suddenly when the Chaco War broke out in 1932. But it would resurface more forcefully in the turbulent postwar period, when landlords and state authorities once again faced rising rural mobilization (see chapter 7). Such legislative disputes displayed an underlying contradiction of Bolivia's republican polity: it was simultaneously premised on the possibility of equal rights and on the racialization of subjects who were not considered worthy of those rights.[131] Republican Party governments of the 1920s not only endorsed techniques such as instruction; justice and the law were also constitutive elements of their civilizing projects. With schools for Indians, government authorities aimed to create a docile labor force that would be tied to the land. Legislative proposals for special laws and courts similarly inscribed a subordinate status upon Indians, and may have concealed a more insidious objective: to survey and control autonomous action under state management.[132] Yet even if the debates about protective measures were couched in paternalistic terms, and imbued with regulatory intentions, congressional proponents of those measures expressed powerful critiques of rural injustice. Several congressional delegates noted many of the same things that the caciques apoderados denounced in the petitions discussed in the following chapter: they deplored the exaggerated fees, bribes, intimidation, fraud, and routinely perjured testimony that skewed the courts in landlords' favor.[133]

Ultimately Bolivia's 1920s indigenista lawmakers failed to create a "special" legal code for Indians; nor did they establish a patronato or indigenous tribunal. Still, they did not cease to promote such initiatives. As one deputy noted in 1923, Congress was favorably disposed toward indigenous protection and guarantees.[134] The 1920s legislative contests over instruction and justice left fundamental questions unresolved. Would special protection reign, or juridical equality? Some deputies promised both, but the government delivered neither. As we will see in the next chapter, the caciques apoderados not only exposed this contradiction. They demanded that the government fulfill the two promises.

CHAPTER THREE

"IN OUR PROVINCES THERE IS NO JUSTICE"

Caciques Apoderados and the Crisis
of the Liberal Project

On 21 November 1917, Mariano Rosa, "cacique principal of the community of Vacas," submitted a petition to the minister of finance protesting attempts by the city of Cochabamba to lease the immense latifundio in Cantón Vacas (see map 2). Rosa accused the city of usurping communal property "without title or precedent" and requested an administrative review of land boundaries based on colonial titles. He also claimed that the 1874 Disentailment Law, which had abolished the Indian corporate community, actually guaranteed the community's "absolute rights" to all of the land it possessed.[1] After winding its way through repeated bureaucratic postponements, Rosa's petition finally reached the desks of subprefects in Arani and Totora (provinces of Cochabamba). Arani's subprefect sent back a dismissive reply: there were no Indian communities in his province because the communal land (*tierras de origen*) had already been distributed on the basis of the 1874 law.[2] Totora's subprefect, for his part, claimed that Rosa and one cosigner were simply landholding Indians, not caciques. He flatly denied that there had ever been any Indian communities in his jurisdiction.[3] The caciques apoderados' relentless lobbying opened up a dispute. Would Indians have the

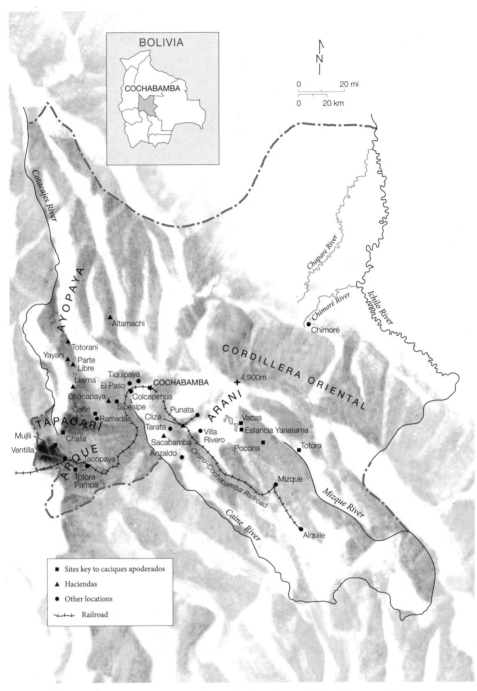

Map 2   Topographic map of Cochabamba, showing sites of cacique apoderado activity

right to collective land rights and representation? Did the 1874 law and the revisitas it authorized truly extinguish Indian communities and authorities, or did they retain a legal status?

From about 1914 to the eve of the Chaco War (1932–35), Mariano Rosa and his successors in the Cochabamba region lodged petitions with local and national authorities demanding the return of communal territory and an end to "400 years" of abuse. Their movement gradually stretched from Vacas, Totora, and Pocona in the southeastern section of the department all the way to Arque and Tapacarí in its southwestern corner. The Cochabamba caciques did not organize in isolation but coordinated their campaign with the national networks of Aymara and Quechua apoderados and caciques apoderados led by Santos Marka T'ula and Eduardo Leandro Nina Qhispi. Together these far-flung leaders filed petitions, circulated laws, recuperated unauthorized authorities, and claimed expansive territorial domains that challenged the elite project to delimit and dominate the national space.[4] The organizations they established mirrored levels of Bolivian state authority, with their own representatives of cantons, provinces, and departments. The caciques apoderados, in short, assumed a parallel structure of government: the effort to recuperate land went hand in hand with the struggle for local power.

As they campaigned for territory and autonomy, Cochabamba caciques and caciques apoderados simultaneously appealed to colonial titles *and* demanded specific republican rights. They insisted on "absolute" rights to communal land, protection from abuse, and freedom from forced services. Their copious appeals are a vantage point for exploring how indigenous leaders viewed, used, and challenged the liberal project. To contest legacies of colonial oppression, the Cochabamba caciques deployed republican laws. But they also used colonial laws to argue eloquently against republican injustice. Community leaders from Cochabamba and other regions disclosed the falsity of "equality" and the inconsistencies of citizenship in their relentless denunciations of abuse and discrimination. Through selective engagement with national legislators, republican laws, and the colonial past, they exposed the underlying contradictions of the liberal project—and uncovered its roots in colonialism.

✳ Petitions, Sedition, and the
"Absolute Rights of Property"

In July 1916, a Cochabamba municipal commission set out for the highest point of Arani Province to measure and mark the limits of the municipally owned hacienda called Vacas. Situated at about 3,200 meters (approximately 10,500 feet) above sea level, the area is known for its small lakes, cold climate, and the intensive cultivation of an enormous variety of potatoes and other tubers. During the colonial era, Vacas was occupied by Indians from neighboring communities with little interference from the state.[5] Following the late-eighteenth-century indigenous rebellions, colonial authorities distributed *hilos* (plots) to landless forasteros in the area.[6] Bolivia's first republican governments later reclassified Vacas's extensive remaining territory—its so-called vacant lands or sobrantes—as state property; in theory the land would be administered by the city of Cochabamba to benefit public education.[7] The resulting municipal latifundio consisted of thirteen separate estancias, or hamlets, that together spanned almost 7,500 hectares and were inhabited by more than two thousand colonos. It was one of the largest properties in the department.[8]

The official designation of the Vacas estancias as municipal property had little immediate import, for the territory essentially remained in Indian hands until the late 1860s, when outside renters began to take an interest in it. On the basis of an 1878 revisita, Indians accepted titles to hilos of approximately eight hectares, but the community also lost nearly three-quarters of its land to the municipal hacienda.[9] While some Indians held on to their hilos, many of the new *hilatarios* (smallholders) sold parcels to hacendados and mestizos who resided in the town of Vacas; they became colonos on their own former properties.[10] When the state once again distributed so-called excess land to community members in the 1880s, some of the hilatarios acquired more terrain. Since those distributions were not always equal, they led to greater social differentiation within the Vacas estancias and in some cases engendered disputes among community members. To complicate matters further, some of the hilatarios who acquired private titles remained colonos with obligations to a landlord. In exchange for grazing rights, even hilatarios who were not colonos could owe labor to neighboring landlords or to administrators of the municipal property.[11]

Although the rhythms of life and labor began to change in Vacas during the late nineteenth century, Indians' control of a significant land base was not truly challenged until the long-awaited Oruro-Cochabamba Railroad neared completion in 1916 (see map 2). As the tracks came into view, elites in the depressed Cochabamba region expected to gain access to highland markets, and land values rose.[12] In this changing context, interactions grew increasingly contentious between hilatarios, the city, and owners of contiguous properties who resided in Vacas or Cochabamba. Conflicts over violations of customary labor arrangements eventually became entwined with disputes about the land.[13]

The arrival of the municipal commission in July 1916 to measure and mark the land provoked what all parties agreed was a brutal encounter. In response to complaints about encroachments on hacienda land in Vacas, Cochabamba's Municipal Council had passed a law in December 1915 calling for a *deslinde general* (demarcation of land boundaries) in all Cochabamba provinces with land owned by the city.[14] The law aimed to clarify the boundaries of the city's property and to evict "intruders," Indian and non-Indian alike. The July inspection carried out on the basis of this law constituted the first major challenge to community land rights. When the inspectors commenced their work in Vacas, Rosa and his associates responded by trying to recuperate the entire latifundio—which they claimed was communal property.

Differently situated actors recounted sharply divergent narratives about the 1916 deslinde and its aftermath. Government authorities reported that attempts to survey the land provoked violent confrontations between government troops and the *indiada* (Indian inhabitants).[15] In lengthy reports on the unfolding events, the prefect of Cochabamba and the subprefects of Totora and Arani drew on several extensively circulated stereotypes of Indian resistance.[16] The local authorities referred to the Indians as *sublevados* (rebels), and insisted that their protest was directed against the law. But they also portrayed the Indians as innocent victims who had been tricked or forced to revolt by "outsiders" and non-Indians. For example, the Totora subprefect noted that one of the leaders, Feliciano Salazar, was actually a "mestizo" or "cholo"—a colono—who used his rudimentary writing skills to mobilize the "indiada" for "truly subversive movements."[17] The subprefect claimed further that "troublemakers" with contacts in La Paz had demanded contributions and persuaded other Indians in the region that "they had won or were about to win a big lawsuit and that they were going to recuperate the lands . . . that corresponded to them as descendents of the Inca . . . and that possession by whites . . . constituted an illegal dispossession."[18] The message conveyed in these official reports was a dual one: Indians were either a threatening presence or innocent victims of outsiders.

To refute the accusations, the indigenous petitioners detailed their own victimization by the individuals who were then renting the property from the city. They suggested, moreover, that the cause of attacks against them was not rebellion but their legal initiative to retain the land on the basis of their own legitimate titles. Mariano Rosa led the caciques in this campaign against the city's attempt to rent the territory to outsiders. At the time, Rosa was both a hilatario and a colono on the municipal hacienda; in repeated petitions, he described himself as Vacas's "cacique principal." For Rosa and his associates, the city's attempt to lease the land amounted to the usurpation of the "community's exclusive control."[19] Their appeal to the minister of government appeared in *La Reacción Social*, a Left-leaning La Paz daily. Although this particular petition was not signed by caciques apoderados from other regions, the national exposure confirms that Cochabamba caciques began to forge external connections even at this early stage.

In the ensuing dispute over ownership, the cacique Rosa was joined by Mariano Vásquez and Feliciano Salazar, who identified themselves as "originarios caciques" from the neighboring districts of Pocona and Totora. The three men called on the Ministry of Hacienda to declare null and void the revisitas that had been carried out in Arani and Totora in the 1870s; they asked, instead, for a "new demarcation of boundaries [*deslinde renovación administrativa*] in line with" their "colonial titles."[20] As per the 1874 Disentailment Law, the revisita measured land possessed or cultivated and dispensed private titles. The deslinde instead involved the demarcation of boundaries; from the state's perspective, it meant the demarcation of administrative boundaries, those between cantons, provinces, or departments. The caciques of Vacas requested a deslinde of a particular kind: they asked state authorities to delineate communal land boundaries in accordance with their colonial titles, precisely in order to prevent the division and expropriation of land that was historically possessed by Indian communities. Yet while Rosa and other litigants of the 1910s rejected the late-nineteenth-century revisitas and appealed to colonial rights, they also rooted their claim in the 1874 anticommunal legislation: "The laws disentailing communal lands of 5 October 1874 and 1 October 1880, which ratified the law of 31 July 1871, recognized the indígenas' absolute property rights to the lands they possess . . . [and called for] revisitas . . . in each of the Republic's provinces. . . . In cases where the lands had already been divided according to custom or previous land distributions, [the land commissions] would distribute plots of equal proportion; and in cases where division was not possible, they were authorized to give *proindiviso* [undivided] concessions."[21]

The preceding plea is just one of numerous exchanges in which caciques apoderados used elements of the liberal laws to defend community land rights. Here and elsewhere they rooted the 1874 declaration of "absolute property rights" in the 1871 law that confirmed *indígenas comunarios* (indigenous community members) as owners of communities and *terrenos de origen*. The 1874 measure of course made a devastating distinction between lands actually "possessed" and so-called vacant lands, or sobrantes. Theoretically, the 1871 edict instead restored *all* expropriated land, including the sobrantes.[22]

No doubt the caciques made highly selective references to the 1874 Disentailment Law, as the city's lawyer, Guillermo Urquidi, hastened to point out. Urquidi was both a member of Cochabamba's Municipal Council and a large landowner. When the Indians of Vacas used the 1874 law to claim absolute rights to the land, the renowned lawyer observed, they failed to mention the section that said the law no longer recognized communities.[23] "No individual or group of individuals will be able to take the name of *community* or *ayllu*, nor appear for such an entity before any authority," Urquidi noted, quoting the unstated passage. In sum, he said, Vacas's cacique (Rosa) had no power to represent anyone.[24]

What Urquidi considered a miscomprehension of the law, the caciques of Vacas instead perceived as a continuum. In essence they merged the 1874 declaration of absolute property rights with the 1871 restoration of community, suggesting a logical sequence that amounted to "absolute" property rights. It did not matter whether they possessed the land as individuals or as a corporation: their rights were absolute.[25] It is impossible to say with certainty whether Rosa and his associates failed to understand that the 1874 law negated the one of 1871, as Urquidi suggested, or engaged in strategic interpretation. But it does seem that the caciques astutely hedged several bets at once. Even though Rosa appealed to particular aspects of the Disentailment Law, he sometimes called for a deslinde based on "our ancient titles" or on titles granted by the "King of Spain."[26] Ultimately it made little difference whether Rosa used colonial or republican legal reasoning. His persistent point was Indians' inviolable possession of communal land.

From the city's perspective, the caciques' very allusion to "community" was the crux of the problem. According to Urquidi, Rosa had titled himself a "cacique of a community that no longer exists."[27] For Rosa and his followers, on the other hand, acceptance of private titles had not vanquished the Vacas community. Right up to the arrival of the municipal commission, the community in effect continued to control much of the "surplus" land that had been adjudicated to the city.

Was there an Indian uprising in Vacas in 1917? The evidence is not definitive, but Cochabamba's Superior Court ruled in favor of the jailed Indians, citing insufficient proof. According to Rosa, the Vacas renters imagined the revolt: "The leaseholders with absolute contempt for their victims . . . concoct imaginary riots and uprisings, which they use as a . . . pretext for excessive force."[28] In this violent context, the practice of submitting petitions mattered as much as their content, and the manuscripts prepared by caciques such as Rosa were more than a means to convey demands. Petitioning government officials was itself a ritualized political routine that allowed Indians to demonstrate the legality of their actions and to distinguish them from "truly subversive movements."

And so the very discourse of *indios sublevados* in part shaped the Vacas land boundary conflict, as it shaped other such conflicts. The subprefect of Arani advised his superiors that there were no Indian communities in the area and explicitly refuted the legality of the caciques' claims; he suggested that their submission of such briefs—the constitutional right of any individual residing in Bolivia, as Rosa pointed out in a 1917 petition—was the same as subversion.[29] "All the privileges and titles invoked by the petitioners," the subprefect said, "serve only as a pretext to engender new uprisings."[30] One key question the documentation from both sides posed was whether or not the contest had been waged within the arena of the law.

The caciques of Vacas who ambiguously invoked the Disentailment Law to defend communal property neither fully accepted nor fully rejected Bolivia's late-nineteenth-century liberal land laws. Instead they engaged in an interpretative battle over the meaning of the reforms and claimed the right to openly contest their practical efficacy. For these community delegates, the 1874 Disentailment Law guaranteed absolute rights to communal property that was already certified by "ancient titles." The fact that Cochabamba's municipal council felt compelled to publicly challenge the Indians' interpretation a full ten years after the events not only suggests that matters in Vacas were difficult to resolve.[31] It shows that Rosa and other caciques persuasively advanced an image of themselves as legal subjects and legitimate representatives of other Indians—just as the authorities insisted they lived outside the law, were too simple to comprehend it, or simply did not exist.

✳ Undoing the Revisitas

Following the 1916 confrontation, caciques of Vacas and other Cocha-bamba provinces—together with caciques from several additional depart-ments—waged a ten-year campaign to undo the late-nineteenth-century land surveys (revisitas). To justify their demands, Mariano Rosa and his successors pursued two distinct but intersecting lines of argument. One mode of reasoning merged republican legislation with colonial precedents under the rubric of absolute rights. Republican legislation, the caciques argued, validated Indians' "original"—colonial or even preconquest—land rights. A second logic rooted rights to communal territory in "ancient titles" bestowed by the Spanish Crown. Petitions making this case generally overlooked republican legislation altogether and instead noted that In-dians still paid the *contribución* (tribute) to the state.[32] Some such appeals to ancient titles included direct or indirect requests to annul the 1874 law. In a 1925 petition, caciques apoderados from several Cochabamba prov-inces thus demanded that authorities prohibit the rental or sale of commu-nal land.[33] In another plea, caciques said that the "insults, abuses, humilia-tions, and encroachments" afflicting them had all been caused by the "law that authorized the sale of tierras de origen."[34]

On the face of things, the two arguments could not be more different. From one perspective, the 1874 law served as a guarantee; from the other it was a menace. Yet the distinct approaches to property overlapped signifi-cantly, for the crux of the matter in both cases was Indians' uninterrupted possession. The positive interpretation of the 1874 law falsely associated that measure with colonial principles: the petitioners did not invoke the Disentailment Law on its own but suggested that it validated their "origi-nal" ownership. Finally, whether appropriating aspects of the 1874 law or rejecting it entirely, the petitioners demanded that the government repeal the late-nineteenth-century revisitas.[35]

Although the caciques apoderados clearly identified the ill effects and persistent dangers of the 1874 edict, it is not surprising that they tried to use the law in some cases to their own advantage. To advance claims within the republican framework, caciques apoderados logically identified themselves as property owners. But they assumed that notion while rejecting a market in land. In doing so, they exposed the internal as well as external affronts that endangered their territory. For the caciques not only underscored the intimidation, violence, and fraud that outsiders used to take their terrain; they also condemned other Indians for selling communal land. A 1923 document from Tapacarí specifically named Indians who put their land on the market: "José Manuel Choque Santos [and] Flores Agustín Choque . . . [are] indígenas with evil intentions who sold our land without our permission, thus causing us to become embroiled in huge lawsuits that cost us considerable money."[36] To prevent such "malicious actions," caciques apoderados sometimes called on the state to help impose tighter discipline within Indian communities.[37] One such request cited a sixteenth-century Toledan rule that imposed fines or whipping on caciques who sold or rented land. A 1923 letter to the president in the name of "all the indígenas of the Departments of Cochabamba, La Paz, Oruro, Potosí, Sucre, and others" similarly demanded "severe punishments" for indígenas who sold their land, "because they are the ones guilty of causing us so much harm."[38]

When they summoned their rights as property owners, Mariano Rosa and other caciques apoderados do not seem to have been promoting their own private accumulation.[39] Instead they used the language of absolute property rights to defend the community's land base from external and internal appropriation. The Vacas caciques' designation of themselves as *comunarios-propietarios* aptly captures this sense of community possession. Their language also testifies to a striking process of ethnogenesis: although a form of private property (hilos) took hold in Vacas during the nineteenth century, it did not extinguish community. Instead privatization gave way to new kinds of communities that were based on overlapping arrangements as smallholders, comunarios, and colonos.[40]

Over time, the caciques apoderados' struggles to recuperate land could pit communities from one locale against those from another. But the revival of extinguished forms of representation also revitalized Indian communities in places where state authorities insisted that the process of privatization had effaced them. Like their counterparts in La Paz and other regions, Cochabamba caciques appealed to the 1881 resolution that allowed proindiviso land tenure, as well as to the 1883 law that excluded from the revisitas land consolidated during the colonial era via composition titles. But they were doing much more than this in all regions. As we will see in the following sections, when caciques of Cochabamba and other regions combined colonial titles with the republican promise of absolute property, they did not just request collective tenure. They also demanded recognition of their communities' legal status and of their own cacique titles.

* Justice, Instruction, and "Civilization"

For reasons that remain unclear, Guillermo Cruz (from Vacas) and Manuel Ramos (of Tapacarí) replaced Mariano Rosa after 1917 as primary spokespersons for Indian communities of the Cochabamba region. Although the revisita or deslinde remained a fundamental concern, their petitions contain more general references to colonial and republican abuses and rights. The caciques' powers of representation, the legality of their actions, and their very identities would continue to be challenged by landlords and local officials. But the president, members of Congress, and the minister of justice in some cases affirmed their petitions by providing much-coveted protection and guarantees (amparo y garantías). Although the request for a new revisita or deslinde was never approved, the caciques' exchanges with state authorities intensified an ongoing contest over the legal status of Indian communities and authorities. In the end, their rights remained ambiguous. The government neither fully affirmed the caciques apoderados' requests nor completely discounted them. Tacitly, government authorities recognized the caciques as legitimate representatives of Indian communities.

Petitions signed by Rosa's immediate successor, Guillermo Cruz, vividly reveal how Cochabamba caciques became increasingly integrated into the La Paz–based network over the course of the 1920s. In a series of appeals, Cruz identified himself as the cacique principal of Yanatama, one of the thirteen Vacas estancias. As a result of the 1870s revisita, Yanatama's communal territory had been transformed into numerous small- and medium-sized parcels and a large city-owned estancia that occupied almost 70 percent of the community's former land.[41] Like Rosa, Cruz occupied an ambiguous social place. Both men had seen their land seized and their houses destroyed by the individuals who took possession of Vacas in the 1910s.[42] At that time, Cruz was probably a hilatario with a good-sized plot of land; when outsiders got hold of the territory, he became a hacienda colono. A 1917 confrontation with a Vacas landlord resulted in nine months of jail time for Cruz. After his release, the evicted leader eventually made

4 *Cargadores* (haulers) in La Paz, 1920s. *Courtesy of the U.S. Library of Congress, Prints and Photographs Division, Frank and Frances Carpenter Collection (LC-11356–26).*

his way to La Paz. In a 1926 petition, Cruz underscored his own distressing predicament: "This declaration for all those abuses would end up being more than thirty pages if not for . . . the lack of money; as I make my living only from hauling things and other humble services" (see figure 4).[43] The violence and dispossession that Cruz described occurred approximately ten years before he signed the petition. Much of this time must have been spent living in the capital, but the evidence suggests that Cruz journeyed to Cochabamba at least occasionally and maintained ties with Indians in Yanatama and the other Vacas estancias.

In the course of delineating his arguments, Cruz declared that his power to pursue the comunarios' claims had been bestowed by the *alcalde segundo* (Indian community authority) and the Cochabamba notary.[44] He also provided what can only have been an invented version of his own genealogy. Cruz said he was the "*Cacique nieto sangre* [grandson of a cacique de sangre] who inherited a *sayaña de originario* [land of an ayllu member] called Yanatama" from his father, grandfather, and great-grandfather, "Cacique principal y Gobernador" [principal cacique and governor] of the province of Arani.[45] Since Arani Province was not established until 1914, it is difficult to see how Cruz's great-grandfather could have been its cacique. Furthermore, although Cruz was a leader of the Yanatama estancia, the authority he held beyond this small settlement is unclear. Caciques from only a few of the thirteen Vacas estancias signed his petitions.

If Cruz's social and political situation essentially paralleled Rosa's, his claims diverged sharply. Most of the petitions Rosa signed were presented exclusively by people from Vacas and neighboring areas. Cruz, in contrast, usually submitted petitions with caciques from other provinces and departments.[46] And he staked out a much more extensive territorial claim. When Rosa linked the Vacas community with land in neighboring Totora and Pocona, he certainly asserted rights to an expansive domain. But Cruz's pleas encompassed an ever greater proportion of the Cochabamba department. Cruz even connected Vacas with land in the valleys of Cliza and Punata—where there were no longer Indian corporate communities.[47] He was claiming lost territory the caciques had discovered in colonial documents, in valley lands where highland ethnic groups had sent colonists (*mitimaes*) before the Spanish invasion.[48]

Over the course of two decades, Cruz established an especially close association with Manuel Ramos, a cacique apoderado who hailed from Tapacarí (a province far west of Vacas; see map 2). Ramos himself was a close collaborator of both Santos Marka T'ula and Eduardo Leandro Nina Qhispi. During Marka T'ula's 1923–26 imprisonment, he became de facto leader of the national cacique network.[49] This high-level involvement made Ramos a critical link between the La Paz–based network and Cochabamba caciques such as Cruz. Although Ramos occupied a prominent place, his personal background unfortunately remains obscure. The petitions identify him as an *originario* (ayllu member) of Moyapampa, an estancia or ayllu in Cantón Calliri (Tapacarí).[50] We know little more about the cacique's personal history, but it is clear that he possessed considerable authority. From *indígena originario* of Moyapampa, he became a provincial and eventually department-wide leader of Indian communities. In 1924, caciques of Tapacarí asked the president to confirm Manuel Ramos as "principal Cacique and representative of the indigenous class of Cochabamba."[51] Since he came from a bilingual Quechua-Aymara area, it is likely that Ramos spoke both languages and served as a bridge between caciques of both groups.

It is no surprise that Tapacarí held a prominent place in the national network of caciques apoderados. The province lies far west of Vacas at altitudes as high as 4,500 meters (about 14,760 feet) above sea level; it borders on Arque and Ayopaya provinces and the department of Oruro. In the late nineteenth century, Tapacarí stood out as the Cochabamba province with the greatest concentration of Indian communities. Of all the areas in the department that affiliated with the twentieth-century cacique networks, Tapacarí was the only one designated by the colonial state as a *pueblo real*, or reducción town. These official Indian communities were designed to reduce dispersed indigenous settlement patterns and facilitate mita obligations and tribute payments.[52] After independence, Tapacarí's two leading colonial cacique families remained dominant social forces in the region. Even though the caciques lost state sanction as rulers of the pueblo real, they took advantage of the liberal reforms to expand their own landholdings or to profit from sales to outsiders. Like former caciques in other regions, these local power brokers essentially transformed themselves into hacendados.

The caciques apoderados who emerged from Tapacarí represented a diverse constituency, for the late-nineteenth-century land surveys had followed two distinct trajectories in this former hub of interregional transport and trade. In Cantón Tapacarí, which sits on the irrigated lands of Tapacarí's river valley along the trade route between Cochabamba and the altiplano, about a third of communal land was lost to outsiders at the turn of the century.[53] In Cantón Challa, a cold and jagged environment of little interest to non-Indians, community members instead retained control of most of their territory. Tensions nevertheless emerged between comunarios and local landlords in this canton, and it was here that Tapacarí's caciques apoderados first emerged in 1916 under the guidance of José María Victoria. Although the comunarios of Challa received proindiviso title to communal territory in 1881, they lost land and goods to townspeople whose unlawful incursions were overlooked—or even backed—by corregidores and other local officials.

The illegal acts that local authorities perpetrated in Tapacarí, Vacas, and other Cochabamba provinces occupied a central place in cacique apoderado petitions of the 1920s. Land certainly remained a fundamental concern, but the appeals also began to center on questions of abuse, representation, and power. In 1923, Cruz and Ramos lodged the striking request for a commission or authority to review abuse.[54] Specifically, they called for a salaried official to visit "all departments, provinces, and cantons"; collect information; and create a registry of violence against Indians. They insisted that the government punish the perpetrators as stipulated by law, and demanded that national authorities order local ones to give them "guarantees."[55] Ramos, Cruz, and their many associates even offered to pay for the investigation of abuse if Congress denied funds.[56]

Up to a point, the caciques apoderados used the request for vigilance against mistreatment to pursue their longstanding struggles to recuperate territory. When authorities refused to approve the demand for a new revisita, the caciques refocused their grievances on abuse. This was a strategic choice, for cruel treatment was a problem that national authorities more readily entertained. Some indigenous claimants made the connection explicitly; they called those accused of committing abuses "land usurpers," or described the brutal tactics that typified land transactions.[57]

But the caciques did not just denounce cruelty in order to recover usurped land; their 1920s petitions also focused on the underlying problem of injustice. In 1927, Manuel Ramos and others from Cochabamba and La Paz decried the prohibitive fees lawyers charged for assisting with legal procedures.[58] In addition, they denounced a much-despised landlord in Tapacarí for removing the *alcalde de campo* (agent of the corregidor and the police) from his post with the subprefect's consent. Their complaint highlighted the limits of representation in the countryside: "We truly need indigenous authorities," the petitioners wrote.[59] Ramos, Cruz, and other caciques also protested the harassment they suffered at the hands of landlords and the police when they solicited *ramas* from other community members. These contributions, in money or in kind, were secretly collected by Indians in colonial times to cover expenses necessary to protect communal land; they were a fundamental element of the system of obligations and rights that defined community membership.[60] In the republican era, ramas remained a crucial resource that leaders such as Ramos used to finance collective judicial action. For example, the ramas funded leaders' costly journeys to archives and government offices. Republican authorities labeled the mandatory contributions coercion or fraud. Their efforts to block the tradition directly affected Indians' perceived right to remove conflicts from local arenas and pursue justice at higher levels. In 1918, the district attorney of Totora ordered the arrest of anyone caught contributing ramas. To defend the longstanding practice, Guillermo Cruz and others later explained to the minister of government that "the comunarios" made these "personal donations" to cover the costs of locating the "true titles" to their "tierras de origen" in the Archivo General de la Nación. "No law prohibits us from making such payments," they reminded the minister.[61]

The independent access to national authorities that ramas facilitated was absolutely critical to the caciques apoderados, for justice could not be attained at the local level. Whether the caciques protested land seizures, undue imprisonment, or other forms of abuse, their petitions almost always included complaints about the impunity of local officials. "As a result of continuous abuses, exactions, encroachments, [and] unjust expulsions," caciques from all departments together wrote to the minister of government, "we have come to this City to request guarantees because in our provinces there is no justice. . . . We ask that you send a memo to all departments and provinces because those that have been sent . . . have not been heeded."[62] The originarios of Totora complained, similarly, that the subprefect of Arque not only refused to carry out the president's order to guard them from a landlord's abuse and eviction, but threw the highest authority's "order of protection" (decreto de amparo) on the ground. "No one could force him to carry out the order," he told the Indians.[63] As the caciques apoderados described such mistreatment, they also noted the webs of power and kinship that joined authorities and landowners in oppressive blocks: "Since everyone in the cantons is related to each other or has mutual interests that align them, we can never attain even the most minimal compensation for the damages we have suffered."[64]

Who were these local authorities? In many cases corregidores and sub-prefects were themselves owners of medium-sized properties. In Cocha-bamba, they were often also embroiled in the business of chicha.[65] But they were not always simple associates of landlord power. Take the above-mentioned case of the originarios from Totora.[66] After they filed their grievance against Arque's subprefect for throwing the president's order on the ground, that lower authority was compelled to defend his reputation as a man above local interests and as a servant of the law. In a letter to the prefect, the subprefect maintained that he had provided the Indians with an administrative order to protect them from the landlords' abuse. The landowners (the Bustos family), he complained, objected to his inter-ference and took their own grievance to Arque's judicial authorities, who ruled against the beleaguered local official. The subprefect then found himself besieged in the press from all sides, on the one hand by the owners —who celebrated the vindication of their reputations—and on the other hand by the Indians—who published an article in a Cochabamba news-paper deploring the denial of justice. In conclusion, the lower official assured the department's executive that he had never tossed the president's document (*escrito*) on the ground. The subprefect's gloomy narrative not only indicates that Indians in isolated places could obtain support in high places. In the end it also confirms the confluence of local interests. The landlords' public denunciation of the subprefect was rooted in assumptions about an implicit pact: he was there to back their interests.

Whether or not local officials were corrupt guardians of landlord power, the cacique apoderado petitions publicized just such an image. By cataloging the very abuse they called on the government to suppress, the caciques revealed their own perceptions of the state. In the countryside, they insisted, state institutions and authorities had no legitimacy; no moral facade hid their coercive interior. For the colonos and comunarios who breathed daily the violence and corruption exercised by local officials and landlords, it was impossible to perceive the "effects" of the state, impossible to recognize any difference between hacendados and local state officials.[67] Where caciques apoderados should have perceived a state, they saw instead landlords using force, corregidores stealing cattle, subprefects disregarding laws, and courts ignoring procedure.

Even as the caciques of Cochabamba exposed the state's illegitimate local face, so did they express affinity with national authorities' civilizing aims: if cantonal officials blocked the spread of justice and "civilization," the caciques would help those things advance. The caciques' 1920s request for a full-scale investigation of abuse thus linked up closely with a second central demand for "instruction." Requests for schools had appeared occasionally in petitions of the 1910s, but they became ever more pronounced in the aftermath of the Saavedra government's violent suppression of the 1921 Jesús de Machaqa uprising. In a climate of heightened repression, caciques used the call for schools to profess their loyalty to the state. A petition submitted to the Ministry of Government and Justice by Ramos, Cruz, and others for example reads: "Since we have already suffered for a hundred years, we wish to be left in tranquility. We want to dedicate ourselves to the education of our children so they will be useful to the nation [*patria*]."[68] Here and elsewhere the caciques apoderados presented themselves as devoted patriots who helped the nation advance.

But the community leaders did not simply parrot the state's civilizing discourse: just as they professed loyalty, the caciques apoderados worked actively to set up their own schools. In a 1928 document to the Ministry of Education, Cruz and other indigenous authorities from Vacas and Pocona detailed the struggle to promote education.[69] Their petition first

denounces local authorities for confiscating school supplies the ministry had itself provided to them. Then it advised the minister that there
were never lacking "in any place, town, or City those enemies of the Indian [and] of his Civilization." It was those people, the petitioners said,
who tried by "any means possible" to hinder "the free operation of . . .
schools."[70] In a second document, Cruz revealed that he had established
schools in six of Vacas's thirteen estancias. The schools had functioned for
five weeks "correctly equipped with their respective Professors," at which
point the corregidor confiscated the instructional materials, presumably
because the schools hurt the interests of the landlords and renters.[71]

Cruz's appeal to the Ministry of Education depicted the corregidor and
the subprefect as authorities who were disconnected from the national
state and instead owed their allegiance to local landowners. Just as he
denounced the subprefect, however, Cruz also revealed that the ministry
was not the only institution that authorized community schools. Post-1900
governments advocated the expansion of education to rural areas and
approved dozens if not hundreds of requests for schools from Indian communities.[72] Cruz himself had received the ministry's authorization. A clue
at the end of the 1928 petition nevertheless suggests that Cruz's enterprise
was also approved by the Aymara educator Eduardo Leandro Nina Qhispi.
A legalized copy of the list of instructional materials delivered to Cruz by
the ministry is attached to Cruz's 1928 petition, but that document is
followed by a memo from Nina Qhispi dated about two years later. The
handwriting is difficult to decipher, but the message has something to do
with the delivery of a package to La Paz and Cochabamba. The title contained in the seal beneath Nina Qhispi's signature identifies him as the
"Director Indígena, Escuela Normal Rural" (Indigenous Director, Rural
Normal School).[73] As far as we know, Nina Qhispi never directed such an
institution; in fact, the name of the institution sounds like a government
office. Nina Qhispi's use of his own stamp is also noteworthy. Unlike
the caciques apoderados, who submitted petitions on the proper paper
with government-approved seals, the apoderado Nina Qhispi used his own
stamp.[74] By these means he presented his own educational endeavor as an
independent but authorized enterprise.

Although schools like the ones that Cruz founded in Vacas were often
sanctioned by the state, they were also separate from it. Government officials certainly meant to control the schools, but because the state could not
recruit preceptors or marshal sufficient administrative capacity, the au-

thorities had to rely on community initiative.[75] Indeed most of Bolivia's pre-revolutionary rural schools were sustained by community members: they were known as "pittance schools" because Indians paid the teachers themselves.[76] It is unclear who staffed the institutes in many cases, but the caciques apoderados specifically meant for Indians to teach in their own communities; men who had learned to read and write while performing military duty were instructors in certain instances.[77] Finally, although Cochabamba's caciques apoderados requested the state's authorization, they also demanded the right to create schools wherever Indians deemed fitting —without the ministry's permission.[78] The demand for education was a means to express loyalty and conformity at a time of great adversity. But the schools were not simple extensions of state institutions. The hundreds of schools that Indian communities established in the 1910s and 1920s were an expression of the struggle for local power.

✳ Incorporation into the Nation

Just as the caciques apoderados created their own institutions, and sought official recognition of their titles, they also insisted on "incorporation" into the nation. A word much used in the 1920s proposals for patronatos and special laws, *incorporation* conjured up modes of submission to the state. For government officials, it referred to dutiful performance of military service and prompt payment of taxes. It could also mean the acquisition of new customs or consumption patterns. The 1921 legislative proposal for a Patronato Indígena in addition linked incorporation with evenhanded treatment by judicial institutions. The caciques apoderados referenced this particular aspect of the word in their petitions. For Ramos and Cruz, incorporation above all meant recognition of their Bolivian nationality and their rights to communal land and political autonomy. Rather than emphasizing individual rights, their petitions focused on concepts of state protection. Repeatedly the caciques asked for protection and guarantees (amparo y garantías).

Up to a point, the protection and guarantees the caciques apoderados demanded were those already contained in republican constitutions and administrative codes, in laws offering universal protection to all men or persons regardless of citizenship or nationality. In the face of land usurpation, beatings, and calumnious charges of rebellion, caciques might for example refer to articles 4 and 5 of the Constitution, which guaranteed the freedoms of association and petition, and protection against arrest without warrant. They cited these articles so that, as one 1918 plea put it, they could enjoy "in peace [their] rights as comunarios."[79] Indigenous petitioners might also emphasize the obligations of law enforcement agents by referencing the 1886 police bylaws or the 1903 Reglamento de la Ley de Organización Política of 1888 (rules concerning the law on political organization).[80] When the caciques apoderados invoked existing republican legislation, they were demanding protection and guarantees not only in defense against their immediate tormentors but from the authorities' unfair application of force and the law.

In addition to these universal safeguards, the caciques apoderados took hold of the proposals for special rights, that is, the protections for Indians contained in the legislative initiatives discussed in chapter 2. In a 1925 petition to Congress, Manuel Yapiticona, Manuel Ramos, and others wrote: "[We] expect passage of the laws of protection favoring . . . the indígenas."[81] In another plea, caciques of Cochabamba demanded that "the proposed law to protect the aborigine be carried out."[82] In one more, Ramos and sixty-two other caciques asked the minister of government and justice for an "effective measure of protection" to safeguard them from ever increasing exactions against the "Indigenous race":

> Our race . . . lives in the same [state of] ignorance and slavery as it did in the colonial era, the only thing that has changed is the names of our duties; we continue to be pariahs in our own land. . . . We beseech you, Mr. Minister, to consider for a moment the hardships our race suffers, despite the great contribution it has made to the Nation's Progress, so that you may take pity and pass an effective measure to protect us. . . . Today there is a new way to punish us when we try to obtain guarantees. We are accused of being rebels, and with nothing more than our persecutors' assertions, the judges order us to appear in court for crimes we have never even contemplated, and imprison us, and persecute us endlessly. That is to say, the inflexibility of the law only exists when our enemies use it. This inequality has its origins in having legislated in the same way for the whites as for the indios. We do not know how to read nor do we know the language in which the country's legislation is written, and yet we must submit to it. Legally our customs, cacicazgos, etc., are considered abolished, and yet we maintain them amongst ourselves. And what is worse, law and custom are adhered to only when they do not favor us; for example, in Cochabamba the hacendados cling to colonial customs and insist that they cannot be changed under any circumstances.[83]

This remarkable passage neatly illuminates the caciques apoderados' views of rights and the law. First, the punishment the plaintiffs protested was inflicted in reprisal for a petition demanding guarantees. Second, they objected that the judges were swayed by their persecutors' mere assertions. In other words, the caciques identified and condemned the absence of a legal order: their appeals to legal procedures stood for subversion, while evidence, due process, and judicial independence did not exist at all. The passage also named something the caciques apoderados deemed a fundamental defect of the law itself: Bolivian lawmakers had legislated in the same way for Indians as for whites. This striking conclusion fit with the demand—expressed here and in other petitions—for congressional approval of the proposed laws that specifically protected Indians. But the caciques gave those protective measures different meanings. Where Congress had been unable to resolve the conundrum of juridical equality and special protection, the caciques apoderados readily linked corporate rights with full equality.

This essential connection between protection and equality is most evident in the caciques apoderados' demands for incorporation into the Bolivian nation. Incorporation was not an abstract concern: not being considered Bolivian carried tangible consequences. In a 1924 petition to the president, Ramos and sixty-two other caciques requested incorporation precisely as they protested the confiscation of goods by border guards who alleged they were Peruvians, not Bolivians.[84] They pleaded for an end to these arbitrary seizures and demanded "a regulation that [would] be the beginning of a new era for the autochthonous race, that [would] mean our true incorporation into the Bolivian Nationality and the recognition of our rights."[85] In this context, *incorporation* signified access to public institutions and equal protection before the law. It also meant the right to cross borders and engage in long-distance trade without any interference.

A 1927 petition from Cruz and others to the minister of war further underscored the relationship between incorporation and rights. They asked the minister for "protection and guarantees for their property and persons" and for "armed men to warn all those who commit abuses."[86] The petition explicitly called on the state to ensure the rights of Indians "within the boundaries of equality." Cruz and his associates wrote: "The stability . . . of public institutions . . . [depends on] government authorities' . . . compliance with the law, faithfully and legally, without special treatment for anyone, and within the boundaries of equality. . . . Each citizen, just like each indígena, [must] be protected and guaranteed in his personal rights as well as in his property rights, as our . . . Constitution stipulates."[87]

The phrase "each citizen just like each indígena" evokes a dual sensibility that differentiates "Indians" from "citizens" yet insists on the same protections and guarantees for all Bolivians. The law conceptualized the relationship between the "citizen" and the "Bolivian" in hierarchical terms.[88] Citizenship, which meant the right to vote and be elected, was exceedingly difficult to attain and its loss could have devastating consequences: citizens convicted of particular crimes were punished with "infamy," which entailed not only the loss of political rights but also the removal of civil rights.[89] Bolivianness, in contrast, could be acquired fairly easily: it was attained by birth, or by blood, or by blood mixed with residence. Theoretically, all Bolivians benefited equally from civil rights, even if they lacked the political rights of citizens. In practice, however, nationality, just like citizenship, could be an exclusionary category. Bolivia's civil and penal codes marked differences not only between citizens and Bolivians but also among Bolivians, along lines of gender, generation, birth status, honor, and reputation.[90] In theory and in practice, then, *citizen* evoked a special status in pre-revolutionary Bolivia. The law associated it with literate, propertied, and "independent" men. Quotidian usage, likewise, infused the word with inequality and social status.[91]

And so when the caciques apoderados occasionally deployed the concept of citizenship, they did not use it to refer to electoral participation. Instead they took the term to highlight a set of civil rights that the state guaranteed in theory to all Bolivians. They meant, above all, the protection of person and property. In practice, the caciques alleged, those civil rights were enjoyed only by "citizens," by men with a particular political standing. As they drew this link between civil rights and citizens, the caciques apoderados not only underscored the discrimination they suffered but also conjured up a notion of citizenship different from the one contained in Bolivian laws. Instead of associating citizenship with political rights, they related it to the civil rights that landowners and government officials repeatedly denied to them. Ultimately, the caciques apoderados underscored their own identity as indígenas while proposing an equivalency: when they wrote "each citizen, just like each indígena," they seem to have meant recipients of the same protections and guarantees.

In a 1927 petition, Ramos and others established a similar connection between the "indigenous race" and a more inclusive category that linked the citizen with the Bolivian, the "Bolivian Citizen." This particular appeal implored the president of the republic to establish a general commission to review abuses "in compliance with the laws of the constitution, [which stipulated] that every Bolivian Citizen should have the benefit of guarantees and that no one can oppress the indigenous race, which suffers in the remote cantons." It also praised the government for embarking on a plan to "give broad and effective guarantees to all the citizens of Bolivia, and especially to the indigenous race, constant victim of the wealthy people who take advantage of the indígenas' ignorance to amass colossal fortunes."[92] Both phrases are ambiguous, but the authors apparently included the "indigenous race" in the grouping of Bolivian citizens, just as they also separated it from that cluster: the guarantees should benefit all Bolivian citizens, but they should especially benefit Indians. Rather than making an abstract request for universal rights, Cruz and others demanded equality as indígenas.[93] But their pleas for "protection and guarantees" were not only about rights; they were also about enforcement. More than anything else, the caciques apoderados demanded that indígenas benefit equally from the force of the law.

* Powers of the Law

Petitions from Cruz, Ramos, and other Cochabamba caciques coupled comments on the deficits of existing laws with requests for new ones. Even more important, the Cochabamba caciques insisted on a broader dissemination of the law. For while laws might be conveyed to local authorities, the caciques repeatedly protested, they went unheeded.[94] Ramos and his associates especially stressed local officials' sense of themselves as individuals above the law: they "throw our grievances back in our face, saying they're useless."[95] Some functionaries, Ramos reported, even said that "in their jurisdiction, they were the only ones who gave orders." Others tossed "guarantees" in the trash.[96] Faced with these outright refusals, caciques apoderados demanded "strict compliance with everything stipulated by the high authorities of the Nation." And they asked for an official letter (*oficio*) in which the authorities pledged to observe "all the measures decreed in favor of the indigenous race of Cochabamba."[97] They also requested an official proclamation of the law in all cantons and provinces (*que se publique por bando*), so that it would be known "by all."[98] Finally, they demanded legalized copies (*testimonio*) of every "guarantee passed by presidential decree and other regulations in favor of the indigenous race," including the circulars passed between government agencies. We want it all "crystal clear in bold letters," the caciques said.[99] And then they worked to broadcast those circulars, memos, and decrees themselves.

Sometimes the audience the caciques sought to reach was the very congressional deputies who debated and potentially approved the law. For example, they might incorporate copies of laws and proposed laws into their own petitions—not only to buttress their claims but to remind or educate the authorities. Sometimes the intended audience was instead their own communities or a broader public whose sympathy the caciques cultivated via the press.[100] They were also quite simply compiling their own record of the law. But the caciques apoderados did not just preserve legal documents; apparently they sought to give circulars, memos, and decrees the status of laws by obtaining legalized copies from notaries.

If Cruz, Ramos, and other caciques condemned the authorities for failing to enforce the law, Cochabamba landlords instead protested a government they believed privileged Indians' legal rights above their own. And they viewed the caciques' conveyance of laws as a dangerous intrusion. As we have seen, landowners and local officials often accused Indians of real and imagined uprisings. They were also disturbed by Indians' transmission of the law and by national authorities' perceived willingness to dole out "protection and guarantees." The risks that landlords could associate with the law are encapsulated in a 1924 case in which legal representatives for the landlord Martín Bustos refuted caciques' claims to Totora, a community-turned-*finca* (estate) in Arque (not to be confused with the province of Totora). In a nutshell, the lawyers maintained that "public powers," including Congress, "swayed by passionate pro-Indian sentiments," had misled Indians into believing that any grievance they filed would be affirmed with offers of "protection."[101]

Arque figured prominently in the caciques' campaign for good reason. The Indian communities in this southwestern province, like those of neighboring Tapacarí, held a prominent economic place from the colonial era to the mid-nineteenth century (see map 2). In the eighteenth century and the nineteenth, Arque's Indian communities controlled one of Bolivia's most important grain markets, one that reached as far as Oruro and La Paz. With the construction of roads and railroads connecting Bolivia to the Pacific by the beginning of the twentieth century, an influx of cheap Chilean flour ruined Arque's trade. As a result, the region's cash-crop cultivators were transformed into subsistence producers.[102] Although communal lands in this province were not highly coveted by outsiders, a degree of external incursion followed the 1880s revisitas in Quirquiavi, a canton of Arque. The city of Cochabamba rented out so-called surplus land in parts of Arque, as it did in Vacas and Tapacarí, and this too was a source of dispute.[103] Finally, some communal territory was also lost to "insiders," as former community members—individuals enriched by commercial ventures—purchased shares of land from other ayllu members and became private landowners.[104]

Totora was one of Arque's largest and most disputed properties in the early twentieth century. Resident Indians called the land a community, but the hacendado Martín Bustos considered it his estate. When Indians of Totora initiated legal proceedings against Bustos with support from caciques apoderados of other regions, Bustos's lawyers published a pamphlet defending their client's ownership. The angry tract accused Guillermo Cruz, Manuel Ramos, and several other caciques from Arque and La Paz of creating a consortium of Indian "governors" and "generals" that not only threatened the rights of the owners of Totora but aimed to recuperate all the nation's land.[105] Its central points were conveyed in the title: *Cuestión social jurídica. Indios semi-instruidos atentan la propiedad privada. Las autoridades condescienden en sus pretensiones atentatorias* (Social Juridical Question. Semi-educated Indians Jeopardize Private Property. Authorities Acquiesce to Their Threatening Intentions).

When the Arque landlord called the caciques apoderados "semi-educated," he conjured up a specific notion. As discussed in chapter 2, the first phase of Bolivia's rural education programs centered on the "civilizing" potentials of literacy. Critics of this project in turn brandished the image of the "semicivilized" or "semiliterate" Indian: someone pulled from the countryside who became an "exploiter" of "his own race" following exposure to letters, politics, and cities. For the authors of *Cuestión Social Jurídica*, the dangers of "semi-education" centered not simply on literacy but on contact with laws. Rather than expelling the "erroneous" idea that the land belonged to Indians since time "immemorial," the authors declared, the laws and guarantees national authorities doled out made Indians' "ancestral ideas" grow stronger.[106] When Indians led by Mariano Rosa first claimed communal land in Vacas in 1916, authorities blamed an invading Peruvian or Aymara army. The culprit landlords now named was the Bolivian government and the law.

The powerful impression of a national government that constantly dispensed protection and guarantees was a vital outcome of the caciques' painstaking petitioning. But the image was not completely accurate. Although the caciques apoderados did benefit from the rhetorical support of higher powers, they received amparo only under specific circumstances. Those conditions were not accidental. Instead they illuminate how rights were distributed in practice, and show how the allocation of rights depended on the way they were "culturally elaborated in social interaction."[107] Not the law alone determined who received constitutional guarantees. The caciques' "successful" petitions reveal something about whom they had to approach, and about how they had to express their claims.

A close look at authorities' reactions to the petitions shows that the manuscripts followed a particular path through legal channels and elicited predictable replies. The Senate usually denied the caciques' claims. The Chamber of Deputies, on the other hand, tended to concur with their demands while deferring to other authorities for action. The 1920 response of the Deputies' Commission on Petitions to a bundle of appeals from diverse locales illustrates the standard reply. The commission's report explained that Congress—without doubting "the justice that attends their petitions"—generally referred indigenous claimants to the appropriate civil courts. It then noted that Indians' adversaries either influenced the outcome of such cases, or that the "extravagant costs" left the plaintiffs with nothing but the "record of their complaints." "The lawsuit in which the aborigine triumphs over the white must be very rare," the Deputies wrote. The commission then noted that Indians were the most "honest and reliable" taxpayers in the nation, and asked the executive branch to approve "effective measures designed to protect the indigenous race."[108] For, although congressional representatives often affirmed caciques' claims, they were not equipped to provide guarantees; those were only dispensed by the president or the minister of government and justice.

The caciques who ultimately succeeded in receiving such guarantees not only approached the right office; they elaborated claims that conformed to uncodified rules. Their petitions condemned the persistence of slavery and ignorance while appealing to the civilizing discourse espoused by national authorities.[109] The caciques might thus ask for the end of slavery. Or they might say, "We need to give our children access to civilization via education."[110] They might also state that national harmony depended on compliance with laws.[111] Or they might describe landlords and local officials as "absolute owners" who dismissed the law and higher authorities. Successful petitioners, in short, condemned lawlessness, solicited state involvement in local affairs, and pleaded for education and "civilization." With all the expected humility, they seconded the state's agenda in the countryside, especially its scrutiny of local corruption and disorder.

The petitions approved by state authorities were not just appeasing statements of loyalty or conformity, however. One crucial characteristic marks the missives that obtained guarantees: in addition to describing themselves as "ignorant" members of a "destitute race" that needed the state's enlightenment and aid, indigenous petitioners identified themselves as caciques. Indeed they requested official recognition of their own authority as caciques of the various entities they represented. To be sure, the law allowed Indians to serve as "apoderados"; these were authorized legal agents. The indigenous petitioners nevertheless asked for recognition not only as apoderados but specifically as caciques apoderados and in many cases simply as caciques. Their pleas often commenced with references to the caciques' own power to represent communities or ayllus, or with requests for official recognition of such power.[112] For example, the caciques who presented a 1925 appeal to the minister of government and justice claimed that their titles were recognized by the "Supreme Government."[113] Sometimes caciques also noted the authority their comunarios or alcaldes had already bestowed to them. "Our comunarios have granted us license and power" to represent them, one such petition reads.[114]

Why would a minister of government provide protection and guarantees to caciques, who possessed no legal right to represent Indian communities, which had, moreover, been denied a juridical status? In any specific instance, it is impossible to say whether government authorities overlooked the law or simply did not find it unusual for caciques to represent communities. Whatever the case, tacit acceptance of these outlawed delegates points to a deeper problematic of state making in the early twentieth century. Put most simply, the government relied on community-based indigenous authorities to assist with aspects of local administration, even as it sought to rule via non-Indian authorities who were appointed directly by the central state.

Nothing more accurately captures this predicament than a 1926 decree that prohibited "meetings of indígenas."[115] Surely the government edict was motivated by the caciques apoderados' activities, by the convocation of local and regional assemblies at which the caciques apoderados' powers were confirmed and petitions were crafted and copied over many times. But the particular terms of the law are curious testimony to state authorities' double bind. The government not only ordered subprefects and provincial authorities to enforce the rule but called on them to advise "kurakas, caciques, alcaldes and hilacatas of communities [and] haciendas" to ensure that no such meetings were convened. Local officials, in short, not only used indigenous authorities to organize public works but called on them to help impose order. From the government's perspective, community authorities were an integral component of the system of rule.[116]

As the 1926 law suggests, state authorities viewed caciques as the equivalent of alcaldes, as enforcers of the law who were tied to the state and one locale. The cacique network articulated something very different: the caciques apoderados were maximum leaders with roots not only in discrete communities but also in transregional ones. Their understanding of the law also differed from the state's design. Rather than obedient law enforcers, the caciques were mobile agents who acquired knowledge of laws. Indeed they broadcast the law themselves in order to defend community interests. Although state authorities did not share their definition, tacitly some officials not only admitted that caciques and Indian communities survived but viewed the caciques as authorized agents of communities.

And so just as they pledged to help build and belong to the nation, quietly the caciques apoderados constructed vital elements of their own state within the state. They appointed cantonal and departmental authorities, established schools, and promulgated laws. The caciques not only created clandestine schools—largely beyond the purview of the state—but mimicked the structure, seals, and orders of the Ministry of Instruction. And they did not simply circulate laws; in a sense they fashioned their own legal codes. An eleven-page bulletin published by Nina Qhispi in 1932 carefully ordered a diversity of documents, including Indian petitions, government responses (approvals, semiapprovals, and outright refusals), Nina Qhispi's correspondence with the president and elite intellectuals, and letters praising the Sociedad Kollasuyo's efforts to promote Indian education.[117] In more artisanal fashion, Ramos and Cruz assembled collections of laws and proposed laws, replete with excerpted commentary from their own and other caciques' petitions. Their resistance was forged not outside of but in relation to the sphere of the state—it centered on schools, laws, and political representation.[118] Yet the caciques apoderados did not simply operate within the state: they performed equivalent acts of government.[119] In their pleas for "protection and guarantees," caciques referenced the constitutional right to the security of person and property. But they insisted time and again that the efficacy of those guarantees hinged on the state's recognition of their own authority. They demanded individual rights only within the framework of community. For the caciques apoderados, the struggle for republican rights was at once a struggle for community government and for their own vision of the law.

✳ Conclusion

What was the fate of the caciques apoderados network in Cochabamba? After 1931, Cruz and Ramos faded from the documentation. By then, Ramos's broad influence had also diminished. Once the delegate of Cochabamba and even of *los indígenas* of all departments, Ramos was now scrambling for authority in the Cochabamba highlands. In their archival searchings, Ramos and others discovered that Tapacarí's colonial cacique held deeds to sobrantes in the Totora community of Arque. Their claims to the cacique's land eventually pitted Ramos and his associates against the comunarios of Arque, and both groups against a private landowner who also asserted ownership. In turn, the land conflict sparked a second dispute over political authority: against the objections of some comunarios, Ramos and his supporters insisted that they were the "true" representatives of Arque's Indian communities. Surely Cochabamba's broad-based network was put to the test when historical sources led one community to claim what another now possessed.[120] Conflicts among comunarios emerged in other regions, but internal contests seem to have been especially pronounced in Cochabamba. A marked combination of acceptance and resistance to the revisitas in this region deepened social differences within communities and gave way to factionalist strife.

Another principal cause of the caciques apoderados' decline, in Cochabamba and elsewhere, was the social dislocation and violence associated with the Chaco War. As discussed in the next chapter, the war triggered a dramatic wave of domestic political persecution that was directed against indigenous movements, labor, and the Left. The repression dealt a great blow to the caciques apoderados: it fragmented their networks, drove many leaders underground, and forced others to the war's front. Some leaders resurfaced when the conflict ended, but they would not recapture the same transregional space.

And so the impact of this two-decade-long struggle was mixed. There was neither a clear triumph nor full-scale suppression. As for the deslinde, the Senate called the request "alien to all juridical principles" and informed petitioners that only departmental authorities had the power to organize inspections of administrative boundaries.[121] Congress never fully agreed to the general review, either. But it did not categorically reject this demand, which Manuel Ramos and other Cochabamba caciques considered a "matter of life and death for the indígenas."[122] Although the Senate denied the request outright, the Chamber of Deputies on several occasions approved it before finally reneging because funds were scarce.[123] The ambiguity provoked frustrated pleas but it also raised, and sustained, indigenous leaders' expectations well beyond the Chaco War's end.

In the meantime, the caciques apoderados quietly restocked the shelves of local notarial offices, creating an evidentiary base for future claims. When the functionaries were compliant, they deposited notarized copies of colonial titles culled from distant archives. When the functionaries were not compliant, they clamored for the reinstatement of accommodating ones, not a "supporter of the landlords" but "the competent gentleman [who] carried out this job with complete probity and the confidence of the indígenas."[124] Safeguarding multiple copies was absolutely critical, for the caciques' papers could be lost by careless personnel or stolen by individuals who coveted communal land.[125] Finally, the early-twentieth-century caciques forced effective changes in the law: legal concessions from the 1880s to the 1920s legitimized and even encouraged corporate claims. Although none of those measures cancelled the 1874 abolition of community and cacique, in effect caciques and communities presented themselves as authorized agents and entities. In legal dealings, if not by law, communities did exist. Ultimately, the caciques fashioned a competing culture of legality.[126]

But how do we know that these multiauthored petitions genuinely embodied the caciques' vision of justice and the law? The manuscripts bear the traces of a complicated method of production. The wealth of detail about labor conditions, individual experience, and nominating procedures in specific locales makes each document uniquely grounded in the history of a particular place. Many of the petitions also seem like patchworked collections of variously authored texts, sometimes originals, sometimes obvious copies of laws, proposed laws, or manuscripts previously submitted by other community leaders. We know in general that non-Indian lawyers and indigenous scribes helped the caciques elaborate the manuscripts. In La Paz, disillusion with lawyers eventually led the caciques apoderados to depend almost wholly on their own scribes. Cochabamba caciques similarly protested the deception and excessive fees associated with legal professionals, but the lawyers' influence persisted in this region. The language of some appeals even resonates directly with the legislative debates discussed in chapter 2. Ricardo Soruco Ipiña, a socialist congressional deputy for Arque and Capinota who backed the proposals for special laws, denounced in much the same terms as the caciques apoderados the 400 years of oppression Indians had suffered, and the farce of equality.[127] Who influenced whom? Undoubtedly the documents bear the hand of a collective and continuously evolving authorship, with each petition one piece of a longer history of rapprochements and refusals. Beyond the specific content of the petitions, what mattered most was the caciques' own involvement in the compilation, preservation, and circulation of legal documents.

Up to a point, the caciques apoderados' demands for "protection and guarantees" fit with national lawmakers' concern to impose honorable, law-abiding authorities in the nation's hinterlands, to create a moral image of the state in the countryside. For a period of almost ten years, members of Congress raised caciques' expectations for revisitas and an "effective measure of support" by acknowledging the validity of their demands. But the window would not last. With the turn to war and stepped-up surveillance of political dissent, carrying laws—Eduardo Leandro Nina Qhispi and other Indians regrettably learned—would become a crime. In 1934, Nina Qhispi was sentenced to six years in prison for attempting to create a separate republic under his own presidency. What facts did the government use to make its case? The evidence was twofold. Nina Qhispi was discovered with "communist" propaganda, but he was also carrying something that authorities newly considered dangerous: an "imperfect catalogue of all the legal dispositions passed in favor of the indigenous class."[128]

Caciques apoderados were persecuted not only for presumed participation in violent uprisings but for their legal dealings. How they understood, used, and challenged the law nevertheless shaped the outcomes of the late-nineteenth-century liberal project. Of course the stagnation of Bolivia's national economy, which began to set in during the 1920s, played a primary role in essentially halting this period of hacienda expansion.[129] But Indian communities' struggles to recuperate land also put landlords on the defensive well before the wide-scale hacienda colono unrest of the late 1930s and early 1940s. Even in Cochabamba, where communities often "accepted" the revisitas, intermittent cycles of resistance made it troublesome for landlords to maintain their estates. In 1926, the attorney general angrily identified Indians' tenacious lobbying and violent uprisings as the most important obstacle to successful implementation of the surveys. It was impossible for non-Indians to purchase communal land, he said. And for all the attempts at reform, Bolivia's "anomalous" territorial system, "in conflict with the scientific principles of modern law," had persisted.[130] Just two years earlier, an Arque landowner published a treatise complaining that private property was utterly besieged in Bolivia; he blamed this state of affairs on Indians with knowledge of the law. About a decade later, a delegate to the 1938 constitutional convention commented that landowners had many court cases pending against comunarios in the Altiplano; for fear of bordering communities' predisposition toward "territorial expansion," estate owners had stopped buying communal land.[131] Seven years after that, another congressional delegate frankly stated that "the Disentailment Law had not been able to destroy the Indian community"; the community "maintain[ed] itself as an organic whole."[132] And here lies another outcome of the cacique apoderado networks: their traffic in laws compelled a new generation of politicians to view the late-nineteenth-century liberal reforms as a failure, as a project that needed to be "renovated."

CHAPTER FOUR

THE PROBLEM OF NATIONAL UNITY

From the Chaco War to the 1938 Constitutional Convention

Following Bolivia's devastating defeat in the Chaco War, a new generation of reform-minded politicians sought to wrench the nation from crisis and propel it toward a future of progress and unity. Driven by the momentum of a general strike, a group of young military officers took control of the government in May 1936. These self-proclaimed "military socialists" championed new visions of citizenship and the nation. Although they relied for political support on urban workers and the veterans who flooded Bolivian cities after the war, the reform-minded leaders did not ignore the country's rural inhabitants. As one outstanding military socialist leader put it, Bolivia's most pressing problem was the poverty and misery of the "indigenous race."

During and after the war, leftist groups circulated damaging critiques of the military, the oligarchy, and the nation's marked social divisions. But the most influential expression of Bolivia's emerging populist project was a legislative forum: the 1938 National Convention. In the course of this six-month constitutional convention, 122 specially elected delegates drafted a corporatist constitution, Bolivia's first major constitutional change since 1880.[1] The new constitution marked a sharp turn toward social protection rooted in new forms of state intervention; with its ratification, areas of life previously considered matters for civil law entered the constitutional arena. The corporatist provisions did not, however, imply a total break with liberalism. Bolivia's new charter embodied a mix of individual and collective rights—civil, political, and social.[2]

The convention delegates, who ranged in their political sympathies from the Left to the Right, identified competing causes and symptoms of the nation's crisis. But they agreed on one thing: the loss to Paraguay symbolized the failings of Bolivian society, and it created an urgent need to forge a more cohesive nation. Their debates focused on two key signs of weakness. The war not only revealed the dangers of ethnic and linguistic diversity; it also threatened the stability of family life and a gendered social order. Partly in response to pressures from women's organizations and the labor movement, the delegates made children and family well-being privileged issues of state concern. Like their oligarchic predecessors, however, the post–Chaco War legislators deemed the "Indian question" the nation's primary concern. In the end, the convention did not significantly reconceptualize the place of Indians in the nation. By providing valuable legal tools, it nevertheless opened up political space for Indians and peasants.

Bolivia's corporatist turn mirrors patterns of social reform and state making that were common throughout Latin America in the 1930s and 1940s. These populist projects, which encompassed diverse ideologies, stood out for their multiclass coalitions, charismatic leaders, social welfare policies, and nationalist campaigns against various forms of imperialism. Latin American populists—most notably Brazil's Getulio Vargas and Argentina's Juan Perón—typically forged pacts with urban workers. Indeed Latin American populism has generally been considered synonymous with urbanization and industrialization.[3] Bolivia's military socialism shows that populism was not simply urban based but could be a powerful phenomenon in the countryside.[4]

Populist regimes elsewhere in Latin America certainly convened constitutional conventions and approved socially oriented charters. The origins and ethos of Bolivia's 1938 Constitution nevertheless differed considerably from those of other such constitutions. Revolutionary conflict shaped the constitutional reform process in Mexico (1917), Cuba (1940), and Guatemala (1945); the catastrophe of war instead drove Bolivia's reform. And although Bolivia's convention approved similar changes, its overall philosophy differed sharply from the democratic discourse of the other assemblies. In Cuba and Guatemala the specific convergence of global and local factors led delegates to approve wide-ranging antidiscrimination statements.[5] Bolivia's new charter, in contrast, did not openly address class, gender, or racial prejudice.[6]

The delegates to the 1938 constitutional convention pondered who should belong to the nation, who deserved political and social rights, and on what basis. Their proposals broached controversial questions, ranging from agrarian reform to a more inclusive citizenship. Although the delegates endorsed a certain expansion of rights, they also insisted on the limits of equality. They grappled, further, with questions of representation: how would sectors of the new corporatist state be defined and differentiated—as classes, "races," or ethnocultural regions? Would women have representation, or just men, and what kind of women or men? Would Indians be citizens? The delegates did not fully resolve the questions they posed, but their negotiations highlight the dilemmas of citizenship, equality, and nationhood in the tumultuous post–Chaco War era. The 1938 constitutional convention embodied an essential tension of Bolivian populism: while expanding social rights for workers, mothers, and children, the new Constitution underscored equality's limits.

✴ The Chaco War and the Pacification of the Countryside

The Chaco War marks a major turning point in Bolivian history. In popular lore, the conflict comprised a dispute over oil lands that had been instigated by foreign oil companies: the U.S.-owned Standard Oil and the British-owned Royal Dutch Shell. In reality, most of the fighting occurred far from Bolivian oil fields; petroleum was an issue only at the end of the war, when Paraguayan troops came close to the Andean foothills of Tarija, Chuquisaca, and Santa Cruz. This oil-driven version of events nevertheless circulated widely during the war, and it galvanized the nationalist claims of post–Chaco War reformist and revolutionary movements.

At base, the war was propelled by the aggressive military exploration and settlement policies of the beleaguered Salamanca government (1931–34), which hoped to deflect social tensions caused by the 1929 depression.[7] The main goal of the president's exploration plan was to occupy and "stand firm" in the vast, uninhabited terrain near the border with Paraguay. What commenced with road construction and fort building quickly escalated into military hostilities. In June 1932, Bolivian troops occupied an abandoned fort in Paraguay. After Paraguayan troops regained control of the garrison, and against the opposition of his own military advisers, President Salamanca ordered the army to attack two other Paraguayan forts. Thus commenced a three-year conflict that would end in a devastating loss of lives and territory. Never before did the Bolivian army mobilize so many troops. More than 65,000 Bolivian soldiers—25 percent of the country's forces—were killed or died in detention. Scores more returned to their families crippled or seriously wounded. Approximately 36,000 Paraguayan soldiers died in the course of the combat. Not by chance did the war's theater become known as a "green hell," for it was fought in a remote environment plagued by insects, disease, and extremes of climate. To make matters worse, the soldiers often lacked sufficient food and supplies. Hunger, illness, and dehydration killed more Bolivian men than did armed conflict. This was the longest international war in twentieth-century Latin America and one of the bloodiest ever waged in the continent.[8]

With a total population of approximately 2 million, Bolivia's fatalities in per capita terms equaled Europe's World War I casualities.[9] But there was a difference: Aymara and Quechua Indians and peasants filled the army's rank and file and prevailed in the long lists of dead and wounded. Middle- and upper-class men obtained easy exemptions from frontline duty or even from military service altogether; those who did serve were generally rear-guard officers or doctors.[10] Occasionally, Indians rose to become non-commissioned officers of frontline troops, but they were excluded from the officer corps.[11] Non-Indians controlled all rear-guard positions and command posts. With the exception of men the government labeled communists, non-Indians did not serve at the front. The equation between indigenous and frontline was virtually absolute.[12]

A continual scarcity of soldiers also made Indians perpetual victims of violence in their own communities. When the war commenced, the government zealously sought volunteer recruits. Since peasants and workers often ignored these calls, the military formed bands to track them down.[13] And rather than pursuing urban draft evaders, the patrols tended to focus their round-ups in rural areas. Comunarios were wrenched from their homes, "rounded up like llamas," and shipped off to military barracks.[14] The violent procedures used by draft enforcers reduced the population of many Indian communities almost exclusively to women, children, and the elderly.[15] To top it off, draft commissions demanded contributions of food from rural producers, and sometimes waited on the edge of towns to seize the goods that indigenous merchants traveled immense distances to sell. Corregidores undertook their own forced collections of agricultural products, using the soldiers' needs as a pretext.[16] Finally, the government gave landowners another repressive arm by essentially granting them the right to choose which colonos would fill an official quota of conscripts. Although hacendados often hid resident workers from the draft to protect their access to labor, they also used this provision selectively to evict the ones they considered rebellious or insolent. Hacienda colonos and urban workers were critical components of frontline forces, but members of Indian communities in all likelihood formed the largest contingent of the Chaco War army.[17]

An internal war thus shadowed the international conflict, and the brutality of both centered on Indian communities.[18] Family members hid their men and sometimes directly confronted military recruiters.[19] Brutal acts of repression followed such attempts to block conscription.[20] And there was not only the draft. The war also intensified tax and labor obligations, as state authorities added surcharges to the customary contribución territorial and imposed turns of work on road projects.[21] The exigencies of the war made that public labor all the more demanding. In the war zone and the rear guard, wartime workers had to open new roads and keep existing ones clear.[22]

The war also gave rise to new waves of communal land expropriation. Before the fighting commenced, hacienda expansion had come to a halt in the altiplano as a result of the economic and political crises triggered by the Great Depression.[23] But the conflict with Paraguay revived conflicts between communities and haciendas. Landlords tried to compensate for draft-induced labor shortages by incorporating comunarios into the hacienda labor force. They also took advantage of colonos' absence to dispossess their families of usufruct plots. In general, landlords sharpened labor demands and service obligations to meet the crisis.[24] For the comunarios of Jesús de Machaqa, these unscrupulous landlords were "exemplary imitators of the Paraguayans, who want to take what doesn't belong to them by force, without . . . right or reason."[25]

Finally, the war gave way to domestic political repression. During the years of combat, Salamanca's government zealously sought to suppress labor unions, the Left, and indigenous movements. In 1933, the president decreed a ban on unions: only mutual and benevolent aid societies would persist. On the basis of this law, the government gradually dismantled worker federations in the nation's major cities. Some prominent intellectuals, labor leaders, and radical politicians suffered exile or confinement in remote locations; many others were conscripted and dispatched to front lines.[26] Just as the government pursued labor activists, it also harassed rural indigenous leaders. The police detained the influential apoderado Eduardo Leandro Nina Qhispi on charges of subversion, as discussed in chapter 3. Dozens of other apoderados were jailed or forced underground on the eve of the war, and in 1933 a military tribunal accused Santos Marka T'ula of inciting unrest among hacienda colonos.[27] The caciques apoderados were targeted not only because they demanded the return of their land, but because they openly opposed the war. Salamanca branded their claims for autonomy, land, and legal protection a communist, antinational plot.

During the first two years of conflict the president was hard pressed to control unrest in the countryside, but rebellion gradually ceded to repression.[28] In Pucarani (La Paz), government forces massacred rebels who tried to recover land, and jailed dozens of community leaders.[29] Because the military was deployed for combat, the government sought to quell the confrontations via private guards such as the newly formed Legión Cívica, a paramilitary institution with branches in major cities and provincial towns.[30] Eventually hacendados and town residents (*vecinos de pueblos*) formed their own patrols, sometimes with the aid of colonos and comunarios who did not join the rebellions. By mid-1934, the combined strength of state forces and private armies put a temporary end to the uprisings.[31] Although the caciques apoderados would continue to present petitions, the war's domestic aggression fragmented their networks. Rural political mobilization on the whole was suppressed.

The Chaco War finally ended with a peace treaty that was signed in the Argentine capital, Buenos Aires, on 14 June 1935. By that point President Salamanca had already been forced by the military to resign.[32] Coupled with the losses incurred in previous wars, Bolivia's 1935 defeat left the country with less than half the land it held at independence (see map 1).[33] The consequences of the war greatly exceeded this loss of territory. No sector of Bolivian society escaped from the conflict unaffected by it. The war did not, however, mark an absolute hiatus in political terms, as often thought. If the Chaco War provoked the repression of activists in the cities and the countryside, the war's aftermath witnessed the resurgence of social movements and labor organizations that had arisen in the decades before the battle with Paraguay. To be sure, the war itself fostered new political associations and projects, but these were partly rooted in the prewar movements. The rural indigenous networks of the 1910s and 1920s—weakened by repression and the war—could not directly influence the outcomes of the 1938 constitutional convention. The specter of unrest in the countryside nevertheless shaped the legislative debates and Bolivia's postwar populist turn.

✳ Social Mobilization after the War

Long before the war commenced, Bolivia's oligarchic political system faced significant contest and dispute. In addition to rural indigenous networks, labor federations and radical political groupings emerged in the decade before the international conflict. Although this prewar Left suffered persecution and expulsion, it resurfaced even before the war ended. Via a plethora of social realist novels and other forms of publicity, leftist intellectuals condemned the army and the oligarchy.[34] But the most influential critiques were voiced by male and female workers and the countless veterans who inundated Bolivia's major cities demanding work, housing, and a public accounting of the military leaders' egregious conduct.

Three years of conflict had caused enormous social dislocation. When the war drew to a close, multitudes of veterans bypassed their rural origins to take up precarious roots in the city. The population of Bolivia's urban centers, especially La Paz and Cochabamba, grew by at least 30 percent after the war, and the new migrants were mostly veterans.[35] Unprecedented flows of urban arrivals aggravated tensions in the war-torn economy, putting pressure on tight labor and housing markets. Organized labor reacted with hostility to the teems of unskilled migrants, and in 1936 the government approved an obligatory work decree that required "vagrants" to return to the countryside or "join industry."[36]

Postwar governments also had to deal with a mounting public outcry over health conditions in the nation's rapidly expanding cities. In La Paz, elite families blamed domestic servants—many of them recent migrants—for the spread of disease; they insisted (unsuccessfully) that the servants undergo medical exams and carry certificates of good health.[37] Legislators in turn proposed an expansion of medical services and approved the creation of a new Ministry of Public Health and Hygiene. But the resource-poor state was unable to significantly expand services or regulate public hygiene.[38] The postwar years, in short, witnessed great tension and anxiety around urban work, health, and housing. Veterans and recent migrants simultaneously bore the brunt of the regulatory policies and led the struggle for expanded services.

Women workers occupied a prominent place in the urban protests, and their involvement helped make gender central to postwar debates about citizenship and nationhood (see below and chapter 6). Like their male counterparts, female vendors, merchants, and artisans forged unions and mutual aid associations during the turbulent twenties (see figure 5). The conflict with Paraguay transformed those women into a more vocal political constituency, for the war made women's "honest" labor indispensable to the nation. Bolivia's workforce had always included women, but the war expanded the scope of female employment. War-related tasks, such as the production of clothes and food for the army, quickly became women's domain. Women also took up work in construction, previously an all-male sphere. And since many working-class and peasant women lost male partners in combat, the war not only boosted the numbers of women in the workforce but made more of them household heads.[39]

During and after the conflict, working women demanded official recognition of their patriotic efforts—and by patriotism they meant not only the sacrifices of husbands and sons but their own contributions of work. So they pressured for benefits as working women "alone with children."[40] On the basis of such pleas, food vendors escaped the closure of humble locales. And would-be merchants obtained licenses for small-scale businesses where they could eke out a living selling food, coal, or kerosene. Still other women demanded improved treatment from the authorities, or lower municipal taxes on ambulant vegetable- and meat-vending businesses. Together their sometimes desperate pleas advanced images of patriotic, tax-paying, hardworking mothers protecting their children from hunger and misery.[41] A 1933 petition to the Senate from an informal grouping of *chicheras* (chicha producers) exemplifies the wartime predicaments. Since their husbands, sons, and brothers were dying in battle, the chicheras explained, they were compelled to toil in the "only industry of the people." They asked the government to exempt them from taxes on chicha distribution and sale.[42] Finally, women protested the war itself. In 1935, 120 rural indigenous women led by Santos Marka T'ula demonstrated in the capital to demand the return of their husbands and sons from the front. In the name of those men's sacrifices, they also pleaded for the restoration of usurped land.[43] The war, it seems, feminized not just the workforce but also political networks previously made up of men.

5 The caption of this photograph reads, "A chola
cook in La Paz, 1920." She is wearing the bowler
hat typically used by "cholas" of this region.
*Courtesy of the U.S. Library of Congress, Prints
and Photographs Division, Frank and Frances
Carpenter Collection (LC-11356–26).*

Women's expanding workforce participation was matched by an accelerated process of unionization. With the creation of the anarchist and FOL-
affiliated Federación Obrera Femenina (Federation of Women Workers,
FOF) in 1927, women had already acquired a significant profile within
Bolivia's nascent labor movement.[44] La Paz–based women's unions dis-
banded during the war, but they regrouped with greater force when the
conflict ended. In 1936 the Union of Culinary Workers submitted a list of
demands to the government calling for an eight-hour day for domestic
workers, equal pay for women and men, and an end to the "certificate of
good health" that municipal officials had imposed on domestic workers.[45]

Middle- and upper-class women also contributed to the war effort with
moral and material support for soldiers and their families. And they too
expressed political claims on the basis of those contributions when the
conflict with Paraguay ended.[46] After the war, the Legión Femenina de
Educación Popular América, a national organization connected with international feminists, continued to promote charitable and educational work
as well as women's civil and political rights. Rising rates of illegitimacy,
child abandonment, prostitution, and poverty motivated the group's activism. To address these allegedly war-related concerns, the Legión Femenina

endorsed measures of critical significance to the 1938 constitutional convention, such as state support for single mothers.[47] The organization also backed working women's rights to severance pay, child-care centers in factories, and paid maternity leave. Although female delegates did not join the 1938 convention, elite and working women's groups intervened forcefully in the debates via newspapers, petitions, and public protest.

Bolivia's staggering defeat in the war gave these longstanding social movements new significance. When the hostilities ended in June 1935, streets were filled with protesting male and female workers, cafés were abuzz with talk about social reform and justice, and men steeped in the 1920s student movements created a slew of new political associations, both moderate and revolutionary.[48] In December 1934, with support from exile groups in Chile and Peru, Tristán Marof created the Partido Obrero Revolucionario (Revolutionary Workers Party, POR), the first of the post–Chaco War antioligarchic political parties. Eventually the POR gained significant inroads among mineworkers, but it did not achieve national influence until the 1940s.[49] Of all the new political tendencies, the moderate Confederación Socialista Boliviana (Bolivian Socialist Confederation, CSB) had the most sway in the postwar scene. This organization was established in 1935 by former members of Hernando Siles's Partido Nacionalista and future leaders of the Movimiento Nacionalista Revolucionario (Nationalist Revolutionary Movement, MNR).

The CSB's founding program provided a rough blueprint for the 1938 convention debates. Its November 1935 agenda privileged the demands of male and female workers and the middle class: it called for price controls, public housing, salary adjustments, and the improvement of public services. The program also demanded the investigation and judgment of "individual and collective responsibilities for the war."[50] In a more official plan promulgated in December of the same year, the CSB endorsed an even more extensive slate of reforms: state intervention in the economy, including the nationalization of oil fields owned by Standard Oil; a labor code; new ministries of labor and public health; full civil rights for women and illegitimate children; family maintenance allowances; and a long list of social laws focused on women, children, and the family. The party's second agenda in addition backed change in the countryside by endorsing an end to pongueaje and the discriminatory taxes that weighed on Indians. Yet it made no mention of land reform.[51] Inspired by corporatist principles and ideals of moral uplift common throughout the continent, the program promised extensive protection to already endowed workers and the middle class. It also placed gender and family life at the center of the social agenda.[52] Joined by every other new political entity in Bolivia, the CSB, finally, called for a convention to rewrite the Constitution.

In addition to new political parties, the Chaco War gave way to a second major political force: the *excombatientes*. For the first time in Bolivian history, large sectors of society had been mobilized into the army. Almost immediately after Bolivia signed the truce with Paraguay, the veterans established organizations in towns and cities throughout the country. Soon they created departmental and national councils, gained government recognition, and pressured for social protections and aid to veterans, their families, and their widows. Only men who had served at the front were allowed to join this Legión de Excombatientes (Legion of Ex-combatants, LEC).[53] Although the veterans left the ranks of the army when the combat ended, they maintained a strong connection with the war and valued their own experience as soldiers. Some even claimed a special status as devoted ex-combatants who defended the nation's honor.[54] As ex-combatants, the rank-and-file soldiers were in fact eligible for specific entitlements: every combat soldier or soldier's family was granted remuneration. The state also gave ex-soldiers or their relatives preferential consideration in public employment, and allotted pensions to the wounded and disabled. Deserters and draft dodgers (*omisos* and *remisos*), on the other hand, lost certain rights and were punished with turns of work in rural colonization schemes, school construction, or the mines.[55] The state's failure to deliver to the veterans what it promised in turn became a central source of protest. What was not provided in material terms, government authorities compensated for with symbols: the congressional record testifies to the unending commemorations of fallen and living soldiers.

✳ The Rise of the Military Socialists

Along with organized labor, the ex-combatants played a central role in the rise of Bolivia's reformist military regimes. In 1936, a massive strike precipitated the collapse of the José Luis Tejada Sorzano interim government (1934–36) and paved the way for the military socialists. Since the work stoppage affected virtually all industries, it was an obvious measure of labor's organizational strength. It also confirmed the importance of the veterans' movement, for ex-combatants were a core component of the striking workers. They were led by Waldo Alvarez of the Sindicato Gráfico (Printers' Union) and the newly organized La Paz branch of the Federación Obrera del Trabajo (Workers' Labor Federation, FOT). Their principal demands heeded the concerns of the veterans and their families. The strikers called for cuts in the cost of primary goods; salary increases; prohibition of night work for women and children; freedom of press and association; social legislation and employment for ex-combatants; and additional benefits for individuals crippled or made orphans by the war.[56] With the strike's increasing momentum, the government eventually collapsed and the army took control. On 20 May 1936, Colonel David Toro created a military junta and named Waldo Alvarez head of the new Ministry of Labor and Social Security, making this the first time a worker held a cabinet position in Bolivia.[57] The designation of Alvarez not only signaled the close alliance the military socialists sought to forge with organized labor. It was also a worthy sign of the regime's political ideals: the military socialists wanted to channel political participation through unions, and they viewed work as the primary condition for citizenship.[58]

Since the tragedies of the Chaco War provoked virulent antimilitary sentiments, especially against the officer corps, it is ironic that Bolivia's populist regimes were spearheaded by the army. The military's rising political place was a product of the peculiar postwar conjuncture: although the war had weakened the army, it remained the most viable institution of the old order. Prewar Left and labor movements did resurface, but these groups could not forge a solid political alternative to the withering traditional parties. As a result, labor and the Left looked to the army as a potential ally. Alarmed by rising social mobilization, the old conservative forces also turned to the military, hoping it would curb the radical momentum. Finally, the crisis of the war made the army itself worry about its own institutional survival. In this tense context, even conservative officers concluded that a slate of social reforms was the only way to demobilize the Left, pacify the ex-combatants, and counter elements of society who wanted to put the military on trial.[59]

Once in power, the military socialist presidents—first Colonel David Toro (1936–37), then Colonel Germán Busch (1937–39)—led the country through a brief period of rapid political transformation. Their approach combined progressive state labor policy with the emulation of European fascism. Toro had visited Mussolini's Italy and may have aspired to replicate aspects of its fascist state.[60] In his efforts to create a corporatist regime based on functional representation, the new president issued a decree that made work and union membership obligatory. The law required all men and women who worked to form unions, and called for a two-tiered structure of organizations, one made up of employers and another of men and women engaged in physical or intellectual labor. Another law obliged unemployed people to enlist in the army. This was a massive, albeit never realized plan for political and social management. According to the Toro government, the law on obligatory unionization heralded a "new system for the exercise of citizenship": political rights would be grounded in union membership and productive activity. Those without union cards would not vote.[61] As Toro promoted state-sponsored unions, he also endeavored to control the existing labor movement by creating an umbrella organization that linked labor groups with government institutions.[62] His regime tried to exert the same control over the political organizations that sprang up after the Chaco War. On both counts, military socialism failed.

Rather than restraining the labor movement, obligatory unionization resulted in new unions that the state never managed to control.[63] Moreover, Bolivia's two principal labor federations—the Federación Obrera Local (FOL) and the Federación Obrera del Trabajo (FOT)—established their own consortium to counter the regime's attempt to co-opt and subordinate them.[64] In 1936, the FOL and the FOT created the Confederación Sindical de Trabajadores de Bolivia (Bolivian Confederation of Labor Unions, CSTB), the most important labor federation of the era. Although this national federation was beset by internal divisions, it managed to retain its autonomy from both the Toro and Busch governments.[65] Finally, the more radical of the first two military socialists, Germán Busch, passed a far-reaching labor code in 1939. The code would serve as a tool of mineworker strikes in the 1940s.[66]

As much as the military socialists centered their attention on urban inhabitants, they did not ignore the rural populace. For example, Toro's 1936 public education statute called for schools that would make "the Indian" a "new factor of national progress" by improving health, hygiene, and agricultural production.[67] The government launched a network of sixteen "nuclear schools" on the basis of this decree; the two most celebrated institutes were those in Warisata (La Paz, near Achacachi) and Vacas (Cochabamba). These vocational boarding schools, it was thought, would spread knowledge and new habits to outlying schools and villages.[68] When Busch replaced Toro, he charged ahead with the rural schools and the ideal of Indian "rehabilitation." The boarding schools, he believed, would keep Indians "close to the land" and rescue them from the so-called antieducational influences of "indigenous culture" (*ambiente indígena*).[69] Noting in a 1939 speech that Indians represented 70 percent of the population, Busch called "the economic poverty and cultural misery of the indigenous race . . . the most serious problem facing the nation."[70] With rural schools, the military socialists would train Indians as agricultural technicians and "reincorporate" them into "the national life."[71]

Because Busch and Toro could not control the practical effects of their pedagogical experiments, the indigenous schools instead became sites of struggle for communal land restoration and peasant syndicalism.[72] And gradually the military socialists were pressed to accept some of the demands advanced by those peasant movements. Up to a point, they recognized peasant land claims. In November 1936, Toro signed a resolution allowing colonos to rent land owned by the Monastery of Santa Clara in Ucureña (Cochabamba). In January 1937, he announced a second, more general decree that required municipalities and religious institutions to give preference in rental contracts to Indians organized in unions. Yet the law carefully avoided any mention of privately owned haciendas, the bulk of Bolivia's landed estates.[73] On the basis of this decree, and following Ucureña's 1936 lead, Indians from Vacas and a number of other places—primarily in the department of Cochabamba—organized unions and petitioned the government to authorize rental agreements. Eventually Busch even endorsed the Ucureña union's request to purchase land the colonos had leased. This was a pioneering experiment with important implications for the 1952 revolution and 1953 agrarian reform. It also underscores the limits of military socialism in the countryside: the peasants of Ucureña were successful because they made effective use of an extended network of well-connected patrons.[74] Still, it was partly because Busch and Toro did not develop an overarching project of reform that their social laws eventually fostered the rise of autonomous rural movements (see chapter 5). And so rather than restraining urban and rural sectors via state-regulated political institutions, military socialism did the opposite: it sparked new forms of unrest that brought workers and peasants closer together.

✳ The 1938 Constitutional Convention

Despite the military socialists' efforts to manage change from above, post–Chaco War social movements effectively pressed for a wider reform of the nation's legal system. As soon as the first military socialist government took power, reform parties and student groups pressured officials to summon a constitutional assembly. Toro finally gave in, but the meeting was not convened until May 1938, after he had been replaced by Busch (in July 1937). The inauguration of the 1938 convention was a momentous occasion, for the country had not seen Congress convene for a full three years.[75] Although the elected slate of male delegates included some staunch conservatives, labor and the Left gained disproportionate representation.[76] Government pressure at the special March 1938 election ensured the imbalance: moderate and leftist groups created a short-term electoral alliance with labor (CSTB) and the ex-combatant association (LEC), which were both allowed to run their own candidates as if they were regular parties. This Sole Socialist Front (Frente Unico Socialista) then figured as the party of the Busch regime. Outraged, many candidates of the oligarchic parties withdrew from the elections.[77] With strong backing from Left and labor delegates, the CSTB managed to float radical proposals regarding the "agrarian system," the "social system," and "the family." The convention ultimately rejected many of these items, but women's movements, veterans associations, and organized labor clearly influenced the debates. Rural indigenous leaders did not have the same sway: just one "campesino" deputy held a seat, and he did not represent an organized movement.[78]

Once the convention was under way, it became a deeply contested event. Members of Bolivia's traditional political parties held few seats; however, they exerted great influence via the press. And the small but influential right-wing bloc voted to the convention—including most of the deputies from the eastern lowland departments (Santa Cruz and Beni)—made its voice heard in the deliberations.[79] Like social constitutions in Mexico, Cuba, and Guatemala, Bolivia's 1938 document was the product of a compromise: reformist and revolutionary forces used the convention to promote change, even as conservative elements tried to mitigate the scope of those changes.[80] For all the many points of dispute, both conservative and socialist delegates concurred on one issue: they insisted on the need for a strong and unified nation. And their concern with unity and strength centered heavily on the status of Indians. The "national problem," convention delegates agreed, was the "Indian problem."

THE NATION

From the outset, the delegates put the problem of national unity and state strength at the center of the debate. Not just defeat in war but its presumed link with the nation's ethnic diversity led the deputies to argue about the best form for the state. A group of delegates from Santa Cruz, Beni, and Potosí—composed of traditional party members as well as affiliates of new reform groups—backed a decentralization initiative. Although the initiative's sponsors sought to distribute state revenue more equitably by these means, they were not simply motivated by a defense of regional interests. These delegates insisted that decentralization was the best way to strengthen the nation. Their proposal called for the organization of regional blocks of departments with similar ethnic and geographic characteristics. Only if politicians took account of these "telluric and ethnic," "racial and geographic," elements, one advocate declared, could the nation overcome its "backwardness."[81]

The bloc opposed to this decentralization initiative above all feared that it would debilitate the nation at a time when unity was the most pressing aim.[82] This coalition, which included many future members of the MNR, listed geographic distances, lack of roads, and "racial factors" as obstacles that kept a "spirit of cohesion" from taking hold. Its supporters argued that the nation would achieve "cohesion" only under a strong central state.[83] The war made the problem of national unity an especially urgent one because it revealed, as one deputy put it, how "complex our nation is" with respect to "the racial, geographic, and spiritual, that is, [the] linguistic"— "its three fundamental features." The troops had been unable to "march en masse" and "because their composition was so diverse, they could not coordinate . . . in the hour of danger." This delegate called on the nation to "join together in language and spirit."[84]

Appeals both for and against centralization thus emphasized unity. Yet neither side explicitly invoked the concept of assimilation. "Our nation is truly . . . heterogeneous," one deputy said, implying that it was almost irrevocably so.[85] Even the most forceful proponent of a strong central state, the future MNR leader Wálter Guevara Arze, suggested that the nation was irreversibly varied. Ever since the foundation of the republic, he said, geography and demography had "conspired against . . . [Bolivia's] needs, against its constitution." And by "demography" Guevara Arze meant the preponderance of Indians. Drawing on his recent experience in the bureau of Statistics, Guevara Arze cited some numbers: for every 4,000 whites and 10,000 mestizos, 18,000 Indians were born. Then he interpreted the figures for his colleagues: they proved that the Indian "element" was going to "absorb" whites and mestizos. "Over the long term," he concluded, "Bolivia would . . . be . . . an eminently indigenous country even when the

Indian has been incorporated into western civilization."[86] Although Guevara Arze was the most passionate proponent of this view, other deputies shared his sentiments. Convention delegates repeatedly stated that at least two-thirds of the national population was indigenous. Not a single deputy denied the figure. Where late-nineteenth-century liberal ideologues had forecast the indigenous population's demise, antioligarchic legislators of the 1930s reluctantly recognized that Indians constituted the nation's permanent majority.[87]

When the assembly voted on the decentralization initiative, the majority opted against it in favor of a strong central state.[88] But the debate does not just illustrate the importance that the winners placed on the powers of centralization. It also illuminates the meanings of unity. For delegates both in favor of and opposed to decentralization, unity involved both homogeneity and diversity; the delegates desired sameness, but they did not think they could easily rid the nation of difference.[89] Control of territory and ethnic difference were the nation's challenges. To unify the nation, many believed Bolivia needed a strong, interventionist state.[90]

NATIONALITY AND CITIZENSHIP

Bolivia's 1880 Constitution stipulated that citizens be Bolivian; twenty-one years of age if single and eighteen years if married; literate; and listed in the Civic Registry. It also required ownership of property or an annual income of 200 bolivianos from work other than domestic service. Citizens had the right both to vote and be elected, but the 1880 Constitution established higher age and income qualifications for election to Congress.[91] When the 1938 delegates considered the chapter on "citizenship and nationality," they approved few changes yet attached great significance to the debate. One deputy called the discussion a chance to alter the very concept of citizenship.[92] The convention not only grappled with who should vote, but why.

In its proposal, the ad hoc constitutional commission removed the property and income requirement, and the delegates quickly approved this major initiative, more than doubling Bolivia's electorate. Still the polity remained highly exclusionary: just 3.1 percent of the population cast ballots in the 1940 elections, one of the lowest proportions in Latin America at the time.[93] And although the commission took away one rule, it proposed another: the completion of primary school. If the proposal were approved, not just literacy but schooling would determine who received political rights.

The future MNR leader Víctor Paz Estenssoro kicked off the discussion with a strong objection to the primary school clause. The proposal ignored

Bolivian reality, he said, for large numbers of people without schooling knew how to read and write. And since isolated areas of the country had no schools, the proposal clearly discriminated. Finally, it prejudiced working-class children: since they needed to work to help support their families, they could not attend school. As the debate progressed, deputies considered a second proposal obliging citizens to obtain work certificates.[94] A requirement for such credentials, Paz objected, would be just as unfair as the one for the completion of primary school, since work certificates automatically excluded the peasantry. Other deputies opposed the certificates because they were easy to forge and would not guarantee an "honest exercise of citizenship."[95] Eventually, the delegates rejected the proposal, as well as a substitute initiative to make union membership a prerequisite for citizenship.[96] In doing so, the convention voted down a central tenet of military socialism. Obligatory unionization or work certificates would have favored formal sector workers while enhancing state control.

As the convention delegates contemplated the meanings of political rights, they delved more deeply into the connections between morality, education, and citizenship. Both qualities were essential to a third proposal: to make women citizens on the same basis as men. Some of the delegates who intervened in this discussion supported women's suffrage but endorsed higher standards for men and women both. In essence this sector hoped to exclude "ignorant," "depraved," or "morally defective" men by tightening the rules for male suffrage and allowing only select women to vote.[97] A second group of delegates instead insisted that the criteria for men and women should differ. They even argued that different groups of women deserved political rights for different reasons. For some delegates, the crux of the matter was professional experience or economic power. For others the question was connection to the fraternal community of patriots through loss of a loved one in war. One delegate suggested that women should be declared citizens if they were widowed mothers or mothers of fallen soldiers.

And then there was the question of work. Augusto Céspedes, a future leader of the MNR, presented the most passionate speech on the working woman's (*mujer del pueblo*'s) capacity for citizenship. He started with a critique: rather than technical, pedagogical, or physiological qualities, citizenship for both men and women should be based on their "productive capacity" and economic contributions. Most women of the "dominant class" did not truly contribute, he declared, but the "mestiza and female indigenous classes of our country" exemplified this "virtue for hard work and productive activity."[98] Another delegate agreed, adding that working women's productive activities had already brought them into the political arena. In Bolivia, he said, the mujer del pueblo sustained small-scale commerce, and in the course of such work those enterprising women constantly lobbied against abuse. If they already exercised the right to associate and petition, how could the convention deprive them of citizenship? One more deputy called attention to women's services for the state: since women paid taxes, worked, and had children who would eventually perform military service, they fulfilled obligations just like men did and deserved to participate in elections.[99] Even as some delegates praised the merits of the working woman, others nevertheless displayed unease about the war's perceived gender displacements. The conflict with Paraguay, some argued, had "accentuate[d] the disorientation of feminine sensibility" by pushing more women into the workforce, corrupting others who cheated on husbands or became prostitutes, and freeing still others for the "frivolous" pursuits of the "modern woman."[100] Only work with "virtue," these delegates implied, could make women eligible for citizenship.

Over the course of the spirited debate, a few delegates briefly alluded to Indian citizenship. Augusto Céspedes declared that the convention should grant citizenship to the "two and a half million productive men who were not citizens: Indians."[101] In part, he used the plea as a rhetorical strategy to oppose elite women's suffrage: unless all men were included, Céspedes concluded, no women at all should vote.[102] Two other delegates endorsed political rights for Indians once they had graduated from, or taught in, indigenista schools.[103] One lone delegate argued that military service should serve to "incorporate the indigenous population into the citizenry." But he too stressed an educational bottom line. In an amendment to the original proposal, this delegate endorsed citizenship for Indians who graduated from indigenous, public, or private schools; could read and write; or were teachers.[104]

Given the considerable involvement in the war by colonos and comunarios, the scarcity of comments on Indian political rights is striking. Yet the remarks that a few of the delegates did make are revealing. When these deputies endorsed Indian citizenship, no one reminded them that the new Constitution they were ratifying—which removed the property/income requirement—already allowed Indians (and non-Indians) to vote as long as they were literate. This silence confirms a hidden status quo: most of the delegates took Indianness as a given condition of political exclusion.

In the end, the delegates rejected the ad hoc commission's proposal to give the vote to those women who held the same educational qualifications as men. The tally of 55 opposed versus 31 in favor pitted socialists and conservatives against each other on both sides. Indeed the 1938 convention did little to expand formal political rights for anyone. This is not particularly surprising: the military socialists' primary concern, after all, was social rights.[105] And the socialist delegates, who might have supported a wider suffrage, were not yet vying for votes. The mass parties of the post–Chaco War era—the PIR and the MNR—emerged only in the early 1940s. Elite women's movements did demand the vote, but only for women with schooling.[106] Neither working women nor the caciques apoderados openly lobbied for suffrage rights.

Above all, the citizenship debate sheds light on its contradictory meanings. The deputies' heated arguments harbored inconsistencies, and revealed citizenship's unstable significance. They not only disagreed about who should and should not vote. They thought that citizenship meant—and should mean—different things for different groups of people.[107] For some people (men) it meant being literate. For others (elite women) it meant advanced degrees, professional experience, and a lofty, moral state. For still others (mestizas) it meant hard work, independence, vital contributions to the economy, or civic engagement. For Indians it might also mean work, but most often it would be the product of a kind of education that encompassed not simply literacy but a civilizing process termed "rehabilitation." Citizenship did not expand evenly in Bolivia, and the 1938 delegates did not conceptualize it in linear terms. By eliminating the property/income requirement, the new Constitution expanded Bolivia's electorate, but it also retained restrictions that barred women and most Indians and peasants from voting. Just as the legislators considered new kinds of inclusion, they entertained novel forms of exclusion. Still, despite their hesitancy, the deputies had opened up a debate about a more inclusive polity. On the heels of World War II, as competition between anti-oligarchic parties intensified and a discourse of democracy began to take hold, another constitutional convention would revive their debate.

THE ECONOMIC, THE SOCIAL, AND THE DOMESTIC

After discussing "citizenship and nationality," the delegates turned to proposals for two entirely new chapters on economic and social issues. One of the first changes they approved was a section on the "Economic and Financial System" that limited the rights of foreign companies. The amendment built on Toro's March 1937 confiscation of the U.S.-owned Standard Oil— the first such expropriation in the hemisphere (preceding Mexico's more renowned oil nationalization by a full year).[108] Another forceful article allowed only the state to export oil, even if the oil was privately produced. With a pitch to include minerals in this restrictive provision, Paz Estenssoro and delegates on the Left came close to recommending the nationalization of the all-important tin industry.[109] Although this proposal and many other radical initiatives were defeated, the new chapter's final version did embrace far-reaching aims: it called for an "economic system" to ensure a "dignified human existence for all inhabitants," via state regulation of commerce and industry if public need required it.[110] A second new chapter on the "Social System" made the state the guardian of both capital and labor, and called for extensive social welfare and labor legislation. The new provision encompassed everything from maternity leave to minimum work hours to health insurance. It also made workers' right to unionize a constitutional guarantee.[111]

Armed with the new social welfare provisions, delegates next addressed an entirely new chapter on "The Family." The first article of this section states that "marriage, the family, and motherhood benefit from the protection of the law." The next article declares that the "law does not recognize inequalities among children; all [children] have the same rights." A subsequent paragraph deems the "defense of the physical, mental and moral health of childhood a primordial responsibility of the State."[112]

Of all the articles in the family chapter, that which granted equal rights to all children stirred the most debate. The delegates' contentious discussion hinged on the distinction between "natural" children—those conceived when the parents could marry—and "illegitimate" ones born from adulterous or incestuous unions or relationships with priests. Those who backed the law argued that it would alleviate heightened rates of adultery, illegitimacy, infanticide, and abortion by requiring fathers to provide for their "natural" and "illegitimate" children. They claimed, further, that the reform would "put a break on men's sexual passions" since it would force them to weigh their economic means against their sexual adventures. Those who opposed the reform instead maintained that it would drive a wedge within families: natural and illegitimate children would vie for the legitimate ones' inheritance, while wives would suffer the scandals of their husbands' transgressions.[113]

Much like the discussion of female suffrage, the debate over illegitimacy thus posited a close relationship between morality, rights, and social hierarchy. Some representatives insisted that the "morality" or "immorality" of birth marked individuals with a built-in social difference; others embraced a more gendered form of morality that required discipline from irresponsible men. One lone deputy connected the debate with an issue of enormous concern to workers and peasants. He mentioned the rights of the parents of "natural" children who had perished in the Chaco War: whether or not they were entitled to the benefits their sons' patriotic deaths accrued had not been legally established.[114] To be sure, many delegates hailed the law as a means to eliminate the "odious distinctions" of status between legitimate and illegitimate children.[115] Rather than endorsing social benefits or inheritance rights, however, the delegates who favored children's equality above all backed the law in the name of morality, male discipline, and family strength. In large part they endorsed the reform because the state could not maintain abandoned children.[116]

In the end, children's equality barely passed: the president of the convention cast the deciding vote in a 39-to-39 tie. What the approved reform concretely offered, moreover, remained profoundly ambiguous. Unlike similar reforms in Cuba (1940) and Guatemala (1945), Bolivia's law did not ban notations of legitimate or illegitimate birth status. And while the legislators seemed to assume that equality before the law implied identical rights to inherit, the new Constitution did not mention the question of inheritance. Nor was Bolivia's Civil Code altered on this count. If legal equality implied equivalent inheritance rights, the inference lacked force.[117] The delegates used the issue to reflect broadly on the meanings of equality, but they left fundamental questions unresolved. What criteria would determine who received extensive social guarantees, and how far would those rights stretch? Just how much equality would the new Constitution promise?

THE PEASANTRY

Of all the initiatives to modify the Constitution, none generated more controversy than those concerning rural property rights. Deputies first broached the issue when they discussed the chapter on "Rights and Guarantees." They rejected the ideal of "absolute" property that was enshrined in the 1880 liberal charter, and approved a new article guaranteeing the inviolability of property "as long as it served a social function."[118] The assembly sought to deny the right, as one deputy put it, to "abuse or even destroy property." This measure passed fairly smoothly. But the delegates revisited the issue during the final days of the assembly, and this time they engaged in heated debate.[119] In its proposal for the new Constitution, the ad hoc commission had designed an entirely new chapter—absent from the 1880 Constitution—concerning the "Agrarian and Peasant Regime." The proposal contained two contentious points: the lands of Indian communities were inalienable and could not be seized, and fifty peasants grouped together in a community could request expropriation of land they cultivated for the owner, so long as the owner received compensation.[120] The reform's proponents echoed the military socialists' emphasis on social over individual rights but allowed deeper change: the expropriation of haciendas.

This was not the first time Bolivian politicians contemplated agrarian reform. Tristán Marof had been promoting a radical redistribution for more than a decade. In 1932, Senator Jaime Mendoza—an influential writer, doctor, socialist, and pacifist with ties to student and labor movements— implored the legislature to consider an agrarian reform.[121] Although Presidents Toro and Busch opposed the idea of land reform, momentum was strong in 1938: delegates on the Left fully expected the socialist bloc to ensure passage. In the end, the convention did not approve the proposals. But the dispute established an enduring framework for ongoing debate about the status of individual and collective property, the social function of agriculture, and the modernization of the Indian community.

Over the course of the discussion, two future leaders of the MNR, Víctor Paz Estenssoro and Wálter Guevara Arze, elaborated distinct plans for change. Paz endorsed the subdivision of large, unproductive estates that served no "social function"; he said they should be expropriated for exploitation by peasants, especially ex-combatants. Cooperatives might be formed to make those plots more productive, but Paz insisted that subdivision was necessary to stem the emigration of landless peasants from Tarija (his home region), Santa Cruz, and the Beni.[122] Guevara Arze rejected the division of the land; instead he endorsed the delivery of unproductive latifundios to Indian communities in their entirety. He said the land in Cochabamba was already so divided up that agricultural production had stagnated; he also warned about the risks of further partition. The "indigenous community regime," Guevara Arze maintained, was the source for large-scale agricultural organization and Bolivia's only solution to "semi-colonial" nationhood.[123] Indeed he believed that the Indian community was Bolivia's great advantage over Mexico and other countries. Destruction of the large estates did not have to lead to subdivision: in Bolivia it was possible to hand them over whole to Indian communities.

Like many of the deputies who opposed land reform, Guevara Arze linked the agrarian question with "race." Bolivia was one of the "rarest" countries in the world, he declared, as it possessed a vast territory comprising distinct regional zones and "almost antagonistic races." Still, Guevara Arze insisted that the weak constitution of the nation—and the possibility that it would cease to exist—was not caused by "race." He condemned the deputies who called Indians an "inferior race" and believed—"as they did in Germany"—in "superior races"; he also reminded his colleagues that such charges could not be scientifically proven.[124] While discarding race, Guevara Arze nevertheless maintained openly discriminatory positions: he considered Indians the cause of Bolivia's "backwardness." Bolivia had an "Indian problem," Guevara Arze claimed, but it was an economic and cultural predicament that would be resolved by giving Indians "pants and shoes." Distribute land, he argued, so Indians can "dress like we do," "improve their condition as men," and become an "integral element of the nation."[125] Ten years earlier, Tristán Marof sardonically called Bolivian sociology the tailor's job: "With his scissors he makes social classes, cutting the fabric of their suits."[126] But where Marof viewed dress as a mirror image of class hierarchy and oppression, Guevara Arze saw it as a sign of deficiency: not just land but social and cultural improvement would make Indians "men." In short, Guevara Arze associated "new clothes" with a gendered vision of modernization that linked consumption to manhood.[127] If Marof saw the Indian community as the basis for a different kind of modernity, Guevara Arze instead insisted that the community—its agriculture and its men—needed to be modernized.

Where, then, did the intellectual origins of Guevara Arze's plan lie? In the shadow of his comments on semicolonialism, "new clothes," and "race" hovered allusions to the Mexican Revolution and its agrarian reform. Indeed the constitutional commission's proposed chapter on the "Agrarian and Peasant Regime" relied heavily on article 27 of Mexico's 1917 Constitution. That law gave the state the right to expropriate and distribute land, either in the form of *ejidos* (a type of corporate landholding unit) or as small plots; although the law sustained the rights of private property, it allowed the state to limit its size. Armed peasant revolutionaries compelled Mexico's convention to approve this radical framework, but the intellectual logic behind the reform derived from the social theorist Andrés Molina Enríquez's vision of property regimes as phases congruent with stages of social evolution.[128] Molina Enríquez admired Hispanic corporatism and viewed the 1910 revolution as an opportunity to recuperate the corporate society of Spanish colonialism. In turn he depicted Mexico's reform laws of 1855–61 as a "disastrous" attempt to deprive Indian communities of the juridical standing necessary for their development and evolution.[129]

Guevara Arze and other delegates may have been familiar with Molina's views via exposure to Frank Tannenbaum's works on the Mexican Revolution, which replicated Molina's own vision of the Indian community. In the years just preceding the 1938 constitutional convention, the Columbia University professor traveled to Bolivia to visit the famed indigenista school in Warisata. Tannenbaum was interviewed by Bolivian journalists in August 1938 and apparently knew some of the convention delegates.[130] When Guevara Arze made his pitch for agrarian reform, he pointed to a conversation or speech that Tannenbaum had delivered in Bolivia. Guevara Arze reminded his fellow delegates that the U.S. scholar "told us": "The Indians [indios] are approaching the standard of living of the whites and the mestizos; the day they become aware of their true situation they will initiate a bloody rebellion demanding restoration of their land."[131]

For Guevara Arze, Tannenbaum's observation conjured up Bolivia's still feudal and colonial society, which he considered a mirror image of Mexico's social structure before its agrarian reform. "Independence," Guevara Arze declared, could only be achieved via agrarian revolution. In contrast to Mexico, however, the Bolivian Revolution could proceed without bloodshed. Why? Guevara Arze believed it was because Bolivia possessed a unique agrarian structure naturally suited to large-scale production: the "Indian community system."[132] Predating the Incas, and designed to cope with poor, infertile land, the "indigenous communitarian ethos" (sentido comunitario indígena) was "biological in our country," Guevara Arze said. It was the natural product of a challenging topography, and it could be the pulse of an independent economy. By these twists and turns, Guevara Arze managed to make "demography"—meaning the predominance of Indians —both the "cause of Bolivia's backwardness" and the solution to its "semicolonial" predicament.[133] "We must do this by law or it will come by force"; and if no revolution came at all, Guevara Arze stated ominously, the nation would disappear.[134] Like Andrés Molina Enríquez, Frank Tannenbaum identified the abolition of the Indian community as the reason behind Mexico's 1910 agrarian revolt. It followed—and this is precisely what Guevara Arze argued—that peacefully relegalizing the Indian community would stave off revolution in Bolivia.

For all the delegates who backed change, the debate by and large lacked references to the people who struggled to recuperate their land. A few telling exceptions nevertheless reveal that the position of those opposed to agrarian reform had been hardened by the demands of Indian communities. If the initiative for land reform were approved, one such delegate warned, not just 50 but 50,000 peasants would come together to claim all the hacienda land surrounding their communities.[135] Pro-reform delegates were also aware of indigenous pressures, but their motivations differed from those of their potential constituency. Just as the convention was in session, the congressional Commission for the Protection of Indians (Comisión de Protección de Indígenas) received a wealth of petitions from community leaders of diverse regions, including Santos Marka T'ula. The socialist delegates Fernando Siñani and Félix Eguino Zaballa sat on that committee, and they signed off in favor of requests for deslindes as well as the longstanding demand for a new "Revisita General de las Tierras de Origen" (i.e., a general inspection of communal land boundaries). The committee also endorsed specific claims much like the ones the caciques apoderados had lodged in the 1920s: it approved petitions concerning unjust imprisonment; authorization for schools; and abusive treatment by tax collectors, corregidores, and subprefects.[136] Guevara Arze's arguments for agrarian reform did not, however, build on these longstanding grievances. His defense instead centered on a contrast between the insecurity and abuse suffered by indebted resident workers, versus the independence achieved by the former colonos who created unions in Cliza and Vacas.[137] He augured a nation of enterprising communities immersed in the market but managed, modernized, and sheltered from uncertainties by the state. The legislative proposal to protect community land rights, in short, did not directly validate indigenous demands. It was a means to modernize Indian communities and the economy while strengthening the state.

After a lengthy debate, the delegates rejected the initiative for agrarian reform on a vote of 49 to 36.[138] The final version of the chapter—entitled "The Peasantry"—included just three short articles. Article 165 declared that "the State recognizes and guarantees the legal existence of indigenous communities."[139] Article 166 stated that indigenous and agrarian legislation would be sanctioned with attention to the nation's diverse regional characteristics. And article 167 indicated that the state would foment peasant education via "indigenous nuclear schools." In line with the new emphasis on social rights, the chapter made a fundamental change: it reversed the 1874 Disentailment Law, which had abolished the Indian community. The 1938 Constitution provided only a mild juridical guarantee, however, without redress for prior usurpations or protection against future encroachments, and with no recognition of indigenous political authority. The proposed clause concerning the inalienability of communal land no longer figured. If the 1938 Constitution recognized corporate rights, it did not truly challenge landlord power.

✳ Conclusion

As the 1938 convention reveals, Bolivia's populists and military socialists—the "generation of the Chaco"—espoused both new and old ideas. On the one hand, the Chaco War led reformist politicians to reconceive the relationship between society and the state. For although the short-lived Toro and Busch regimes failed to establish new institutions or regulatory mechanisms, the military governments offered hopeful decrees and novel constitutional guarantees rooted in the state's role as an active arbiter of rights and responsibilities, not only individual ones but those that were social. Convention delegates debated forward-looking initiatives for agrarian reform, citizenship, and children's equality. The Constitution they finally ratified excluded the most radical initiatives and wound up being a fairly good reflection of the military socialists' moderate, urban-centered program. But one crucial article would have critical significance for rural communities. Bolivia's 1880 liberal Constitution had commenced its chapter on "Rights and Guarantees" with an article declaring that "slavery does not exist in Bolivia. . . . Any slave who sets foot in Bolivian territory is free." The 1938 charter reiterated this declaration of freedom, with one difference: the new Constitution not only declared the nonexistence of slavery but prohibited "personal services." "No form of servitude is allowed and no one can be forced to render personal services without consent and fair compensation."[140] The article did not explicitly mention *pongueaje* (domestic service for a landlord), but it did not have to: local communities would make that leap themselves. As we will see in chapter 5, the Constitution and other military socialist laws gave hacienda colonos a powerful language with which to talk about their rights as workers.

Like their oligarchic predecessors, however, the military socialists held fast to an "Indian problem"—to the idea that Indians were an obstacle to the nation's progress and unity and therefore that they needed to be "rehabilitated." Although a few delegates championed the role that Indian communities would play in the nation's agrarian future and dismissed hierarchies of biologized "race," the 1938 convention did not significantly reconceptualize the place of Indians in the nation. Some delegates spoke against the social prejudice associated with "illegitimate" birth, but the convention did not explicitly address class, gender, or racial prejudice; nor did it articulate expansive guarantees of equality. National unity and state strength instead drove the event.

If the post–Chaco War governments replicated oligarchic discourse in their angle on the Indian question, they clearly parted company in their approach to gender and the family. Convention delegates denounced the war's ill effects on gender norms and family life, and linked the regulation of the family with state power. The family, like Indians, became a target of state intervention. Still, if gender became an arena of political preoccupation, it did not occupy the same place as ethnicity in the legislators' reflections. The delegates viewed ethnic diversity as a cause of the defeat to Paraguay, and they considered it an obstacle to national unity. In the case of women and the family, it was instead the war that debilitated, and created risks or threats. When the convention expanded women's social rights, it also aimed to restore a gendered moral order many deputies believed the war had disrupted and put at risk.

For all its limits, Bolivia's 1938 constitutional convention disclosed things that social movements had compelled politicians to publicly say.[141] And it offered important guarantees to women, children, workers, and peasants. Although the Constitution retained the idea of citizenship as an exclusionary moral value, it offered new social rights and at least placed on the table ideas about social equality.[142] Still, the new rights privileged particular groups over others. Even though union membership or work cards did not become prerequisites for social security benefits (as they did, for example, in Vargas's Brazil), social protections ultimately hinged on employment in the formal sector.[143] Peasants, domestic workers, and the multitudes of people employed in informal arenas—many of them women —would not benefit from the new provisions. Of course everywhere that "social constitutions" were approved in early-twentieth-century Latin America, there were trade-offs between concerns with state strength and

6 President Germán Busch, circa 1938.
   Courtesy of the Archive of La Paz.

social reform.[144] But the timing of Bolivia's constitutional convention differed significantly from other such conventions, and that difference tipped the scale. On the heels of a terrible national crisis, worries about state and family strength outweighed concerns with equality and social change.

Some of the most progressive elements of the 1938 Constitution remained dead letters until after the 1952 revolution, when procedural legislation was finally approved. Moreover, the Constitution itself initially faced a varied fate. In the climate of increasing radicalism that followed the 1938 assembly, President Busch temporarily suspended the Constitution, outlawed communist and anarchist organizations, and followed up with a series of laws on morality in government. Yet despite this conservative turn, he passed a progressive labor code in May 1939 and announced the following month a radical decree that required mine owners to deposit all foreign exchange earnings in the Central Bank. Before being persuaded against it, he even threatened owners who dared to dodge the rules with the complete confiscation of their assets and the death penalty. As a result of these blows against the tin oligarchy, strong support for workers, and valorous conduct in the Chaco—which won him an almost superhuman standing—Busch became a martyr of the Left after his August 1939 suicide.[145] The president left no note explaining this tragic action. Perhaps he killed himself at the age of thirty-five out of political exasperation and a sense of dishonor: unable to truly tackle the mining oligarchy, Busch left unfulfilled the nationalist ideals of the thousands of young men whose terrible sacrifice he had witnessed in the Chaco.[146] The uncertain circumstances of his death only enhanced the president's fame. Indigenous leaders who later appealed to provisions of the 1938 Constitution invoked Busch's name. And impoverished homes throughout the countryside displayed the president's portrait (see figure 6 above).[147]

In the end, the 1938 convention's conclusions were not directly determined by the rural mobilizations of the pre–Chaco War era. But those movements clearly influenced the military socialist regimes and the constitutional convention debates. And they cast a shadow that could grow. The first major outcome of the military socialists' laws was an unintended one: the wave of rural strikes to which we now turn.

CHAPTER FIVE

THE UNRULY COUNTRYSIDE

Defending Land, Labor Rights, and Autonomy

In September 1942, landowners affiliated with Oruro's Sociedad Rural sent a harried memo to President Enrique Peñaranda (1940–43). The members of this regional landlord association were alarmed by a cycle of rural work stoppages and purported shortages of food. "Unless the Government arrest[ed] the 'agitators' among the Indians," they charged, "the situation [would] get out of hand." They also "fear[ed] the spread of the communal control of land by Indian communities which . . . [would] result in the loss of taxes for the government and a reduction of agricultural production at a time when the country [was] seeking to become more self-sufficient as regards food."[1] To curb the unrest, President Peñaranda prohibited urban labor unions from organizing among hacienda colonos.[2] But the rural strikes would persist through Peñaranda's overthrow and the years that his successor, Colonel Gualberto Villarroel, held power (1943–46).

The unrest that galvanized the countryside in the late 1930s and early 1940s took root in a deepening crisis of the hacienda system. It was also the product of military socialist policies and the rural activism of resurgent urban labor organizations. Shortly after Congress approved the 1938

Constitution and the Bolivian Confederation of Labor Unions (CSTB) convened its second national congress, in 1939, a wave of rural strikes engulfed
the departments of Cochabamba and Oruro.[3] Not coincidentally, these
were the two areas of hacienda expansion where rural unionization was
significantly advanced, and where contact between colonos and urban
labor leaders had already taken hold.[4] Government authorities blamed
"outside agitators" for a spate of rumors about the end of hacienda servitude and the restoration of land or "community." But such tales gained
meaning, and became believable, only in the context of spiraling local
struggles over labor rules, access to land, economic autonomy, and the
military socialists' unenforced laws.

The emergence of hacienda colono demands for land and community in
the years after the Chaco War complicates prevailing views of the rural
unrest. Scholarly works on this period generally emphasize an overall shift
from Indian community-based resistance to hacienda-centered movements
that accompanied the rise of peasant leagues, mineworker unions, and
populist political projects.[5] Disputes over labor and service obligations certainly gained prominence in the post–Chaco War era, and haciendas were a
central theater of the disturbances. But claims regarding land and community did not diminish in the years leading up to the 1952 revolution. They
remained vital to rural mobilization. And they were articulated not only by
members of Indian communities but by hacienda workers. Rather than a
straightforward shift from one distinct project or persona to another—from
land to labor, or from indio to campesino or rural worker—post–Chaco
War rural movements often merged the category "worker" with the term
Indian. Class became prominent, but it did not efface ethnicity.

Even in Cochabamba, where peasant unions played a key role in the
rural mobilizations of the 1930s and 1940s, ethnicity remained a significant
political force. The hacienda colonos of Cochabamba's central valleys occupy a leading place in the literature on the post–Chaco War countryside,
for they created Bolivia's first peasant union (in the village of Ucureña), in
1936.[6] But peasant mobilization stretched beyond Cochabamba's central
valleys in these years, and it was spearheaded by both colonos and comunarios from diverse areas of the department (see map 3). A close focus on
a wider geography of conflict casts a new picture of the unrest: confrontations with landlords, tax collectors, and state officials were influenced not
only by the labor-oriented discourse of the military socialists and the
burgeoning federation of workers, but by the community-based demands
of the 1920s cacique apoderado networks.

Map 3 Map of rural unrest in Cochabamba, 1939–47, including sites of the earlier cacique apoderado networks

Much like leaders of the earlier movements, the new generation of rural activists avidly petitioned government authorities. But where the caciques apoderados combined appeals to colonial titles with attention to republican "protection and guarantees," post–Chaco War activists often expressed their demands for change in a language of "freedom" and "rights." Colonos and comunarios requested permission to rent the land, or demanded release from taxes and service duties that landlords and local authorities inflicted on the "indigenous race." At times they cited the 1938 Constitution and other laws that had been decreed "in favor of the peasantry" to advance their varied pleas. Although the grievances were validated by recent laws, they were not easily rectified, for the Toro and Busch regimes affirmed rural workers' right to organize without curtailing the power and property of large landowners. In the end, the military socialists did little to improve rural working conditions. Instead their reforms unleashed a morass of conflict over the status of private property, the rights of rural workers, and the powers of the law.[7]

✳ Labor and Servitude on Haciendas of Cochabamba

The rural unrest of the 1930s and 1940s exposed what Bolivia's reformist and revolutionary intellectuals deemed the "feudal" nature of the hacienda. Indeed, Bolivian landlords relied on an especially severe system of service tenantry known as *colonaje*. As haciendas became more market-oriented in the post–Chaco War era, the burdens of an already arduous system multiplied.[8] Landlords in certain parts of the country violated long-standing customary arrangements by heightening labor and service duties and transferring taxes to resident workers. In many places, local authorities further burdened colonos and comunarios with an endless repertoire of levies on everything ranging from the celebration of religious festivals to the production of chicha. Landlord power was not without limits, however, and colonos were not merely victims of heightened hacienda oppression. As conditions deteriorated, hacienda colonos struggled to recuperate diminishing forms of livelihood. The many complaints that Cochabamba colonos lodged with government authorities reveal that landlords had to negotiate with resident workers even as they imposed more onerous conditions. Since landowners' disregard for labor agreements helped catalyze the unrest, the following pages briefly describe the hacienda labor regime in Cochabamba, one of the two main areas of conflict.

Cochabamba's landlord class consisted of men and women whose estates ranged from as little as 400 hectares (about 990 acres) to as many as 30,000 (about 74,130 acres).[9] The number of colonos residing on the properties also varied significantly, from just a dozen to more than 2,000.[10] In Cochabamba, the largest haciendas were owned by elites who lived in the departmental capital and sometimes doubled as prefects, mayors, members of municipal councils, senators, or congressional deputies. This elite class could wield significant influence over the designation of corregidores and other cantonal and provincial authorities. And only this most privileged cluster of landowners belonged to the regional Sociedades Rurales that sprang up in Cochabamba and other departments in the 1930s to promote productive strategies and guard landlords' property rights. In 1936, the regional organizations joined together to establish a national association, the Sociedad Rural Boliviana.[11]

In Cochabamba and other regions, large landowners maintained control of resident workers via a hierarchy of Indian and non-Indian hacienda administrators, sometimes harsh punishments, and their own gestures of paternalism (see figure 7).[12] Because most landlords lived in provincial towns or the departmental capital, they assigned the management of their properties to non-Indian administrators who were often relatives; sometimes the administrator was the owner's wife.[13] To assist with the organization of work and the administration of justice, hacendados also appointed alcaldes, kurakas, and hilacatas from among the colonos they considered loyal to them. These Indian authorities supervised agricultural labor, notified colonos for work, and enforced the fulfillment of service obligations. In exchange, the Indian supervisors received larger usufruct plots and exemption from pongueaje and other duties. Non-Indian majordomos fulfilled duties similar to those of the hilacata, but they were paid or rewarded with a specific percentage of the crop.[14] Although landlords delegated many responsibilities, some owners visited their properties frequently and at times personally adjudicated conflicts among colonos or between colonos and administrators. In Cochabamba this intimate involvement was facilitated by many landlords' knowledge of Quechua. An air of reciprocity and fatherly care could legitimize arduous labor conditions. On workdays, haciendas often provided a share of food and coca for the colonos (*sama y asanta*). At special moments in the agricultural cycle, the owner also offered chicha.[15]

Although specific rules varied from one property to another, labor

7 Hacienda colonos with the landlord and administrator, early-twentieth-century La Paz. The landlord is the figure on the far right. The administrator is probably the man seated in the center. *Credit: Julio Cordero. Courtesy of the Cordero Family Archive.*

obligations followed customary arrangements that were fairly common throughout Bolivia. Typically, colonos who resided on large estates received usufruct rights to a small subsistence plot (*pegujal*) in exchange for labor on the hacienda demesne and sometimes also rent, either in cash or in kind (see figure 8).[16] Colonos were also obliged to fulfill service duties. These diverged from one estate to another but usually entailed transporting crops to markets or mills, repairing irrigation ditches, caring for the owners' livestock, spinning (*hilado*), making muko (*mukeo*), running errands or delivering messages (*cacha*), and completing turns of domestic service (*pongueaje* for men, *mitanaje* for women).[17] The rotating turns of domestic work obliged resident workers to move temporarily to the landlord's home for periods of about a week. When colonos needed to fulfill the pongueaje duties in an owner's urban residence, they often had to travel long distances by foot, carrying with them all of the food they would consume during the week of service. Technically, mitanaje duty applied to *huarmisapas*: this is a Quechua term for single women and widows who paid rent for a hut and a small plot by providing domestic service or shepherding the landlord's farm animals. Many owners—particularly in Cochabamba—also obliged the colono's wife, daughters, or sisters to fulfill mitanaje services.[18] Where the total number of colonos was low, pongueaje

8 A colono family dwelling (*choza*), La Paz highlands, 1943. Colono houses were generally
one-room adobe structures with thatched roofs. *Credit: Julien Bryan. Courtesy of the Julien
Bryan Film Archive.*

came around so frequently that the costs to the workers' own agricultural
production were enormous.[19]

The burdens of pongueaje occupied a special place in post–Chaco War
debates about the hacienda. In the nineteenth century, Bolivian politicians
and intellectuals rarely used the terms *pongo* and *pongueaje*. The words
gained currency in the early twentieth century as reformist and revolutionary critiques of the great estate began to circulate. "Pongo" stems from the
Quechua term *punkurina* or *punku puerta* (doorman); it was used to designate the person performing this service because the pongo slept in the
doorway, the spot reserved for a dog.[20] Not surprisingly, reformist politicians of the post–Chaco War era took the pongo to exemplify the misery of
hacienda servitude as well as the nation's backwardness and its enduring
colonialism.[21]

In reality, pongueaje was just one of many labor and service obligations
that weighed on peasant households. For hacienda colonos not only had to
do the agricultural work but were also required to use their own tools,
manure, oxen, plows, and donkeys to complete it. And since usufruct
rights did not include access to pasture land, colonos had to pay a fee
in kind (*herbaje*) to graze their own livestock. Finally, to show "thanks"

for the usufruct rights, resident workers customarily offered the landlord "gifts" of eggs, wool, hens, firewood, fertilizer, or sacks for transporting goods. When colonos did not complete the required labor, owners or administrators punished them by confiscating clothing or tools, which were only returned once the work was doubly fulfilled. Landlords with multiple properties further penalized wayward workers by making them toil on estates far from the property where they lived.[22]

Hacienda colonos generally distributed these extensive burdens among members of the household. For assistance, they also turned to *arrimantes*, landless men and women—often extended family members—who owed their obligations directly to the colono. Although the division of labor was not rigid, men typically engaged more directly in agricultural tasks, especially plowing (see figure 9). Women shared the work in the fields, but their most important chores were household labor, spinning wool, and caring for sheep and other small animals. They could also be obliged to weave the sacks their husbands and fathers used to transport the owner's goods to market.[23] Women moreover played a key role in the making of muko (*mukeo*), chicha's principal ingredient; this was a fundamental task on Cochabamba haciendas.[24] *Colonas* frequently gathered with children and the elderly to make muko into the late hours of the night.[25]

The making of muko figured centrally in Cochabamba's hacienda labor regime precisely because chicha was the region's principal agricultural product. The industry had been important to the regional economy since colonial times, but it became Cochabamba's chief trade in the early twentieth century. And to one degree or another, the popular beverage touched just about every place and person in the region. The central valley districts of Cercado, Cliza, Punata, and Quillacollo, which specialized in corn cultivation, formed the center of Cochabamba's chicha industry; together these areas accounted for two-thirds of the production of muko and chicha (see map 3). Chicha was produced and consumed throughout the entire department, however.[26] In highland provinces, where the potato reigned supreme, hacendados sought to benefit from the lucrative business in chicha even though they did not themselves grow corn. Landowners in these districts purchased maize, sent it to local mills for grinding, distributed the flour to colonos for mukeo, and then sold the muko to chicheras (chicha producers). Some of the muko was even exported to other departments.[27] With an eye on tax revenues, departmental authorities schemed during the early decades of the century to boost chicha pro-

9 Corn harvest, Cochabamba, 1943. *Credit: Julien Bryan.*
Courtesy of the Julien Bryan Film Archive.

duction and promote related industries. One such official commented on chicha's profitable linkages with both the wood trade and pig breeding, since many chicheras were known to fatten hogs with the scraps from chicha manufacture. In "more civilized countries," this authority lamented, capitalists would have "attended with care" such a great "source of wealth," but the Bolivian pig was destined to "remain forever in the hands of our chicha manufacturers."[28]

The chicheras who put would-be capitalists to shame were female entrepreneurs who controlled nearly every aspect of the industry. They also owned land, buildings, and livestock, and wielded significant power as moneylenders.[29] A chichera's success was based on her ability to manage an extraordinarily labor-intensive process that required costly utensils, precision, and care (see figure 10).[30]

At particular junctures, hacienda colonas also participated profitably in the multifaceted process of chicha production as *mukeras* who produced small surpluses of muko directly for chicheras.[31] There is no evidence that hacienda colonas manufactured and sold their own chicha, however.[32] Alongside persistent relations of servitude, the chicha economy created

10 Corn grinding, Cochabamba, 1943. The tall white hat is emblematic of this region.
Credit: Julien Bryan. Courtesy of the Julien Bryan Film Archive.

pockets of opportunity, but these opportunities were entwined with obligation. On many estates, colonos' overall duties surely increased as landlords sought to benefit from the market in muko.³³ Still, hacendados sometimes removed another obligation when requiring mukeo, or even paid colonos for a portion of the muko allocation.³⁴ Cochabamba's expanding chicha economy was one key cause behind colonos' intensified burdens in the 1930s and 1940s, but that same economy laid bare their autonomy and the limits of landlord power.

Although hacienda servitude persisted in Cochabamba until the 1952 revolution, its evolution followed distinct subregional paths. In the department's central valleys, the large estate gave way to smallholding in the late nineteenth century and the early twentieth, but it did so without fully extinguishing the hacienda. In highland provinces, haciendas instead remained the dominant form of land tenure until the 1953 agrarian reform. In 1916, for example, the provinces where large estates prevailed—Ayopaya, Tapacarí, Arque, and Mizque—together registered 19,174 colonos, while the valley provinces of Cercado and Cliza, where smallholding was most advanced, recorded less than half that number.[35] Still, the great estates of the highland provinces also began to show signs of weakness in the early twentieth century. Landlords weighed down by mortgages sold off significant portions of land, rented out entire properties to third parties, or saw their holdings reduced by customs of partible inheritance. Extensive haciendas survived throughout the department, but even in highland provinces the estates began to be intermingled with medium-sized properties.[36]

At the same time, even as estate owners continued to rely on colonaje, they increasingly engaged other types of workers. During the early twentieth century, hacendados began to combine colonaje with sharecropping (*compañía* or *aparcería*); this was especially the case in the department's central valleys. For landowners, sharecropping shifted production costs and risks to the peasantry. For peasants, it allowed the production of larger surpluses for the market, yet it did so without exempting them from the servitude typical of colonaje.[37] A third group known as *arrenderos* also labored on haciendas: these were colonos who rented from townspeople land that they used to supplement plots held in usufruct. At times of the most intensive labor or for tasks requiring a large group of workers, hacendados also hired day laborers (*labradores* or *jornaleros*). Some such workers were colonos paid for additional duties at the same or half the rate received by wage workers. The paid work thus constituted another obligation to the landlord: it could be imposed unilaterally.[38] Finally, although hacendados generally leased and sold colonos with their property, and sometimes even rented colonos to third parties, the colonos were not strictly tied to the hacienda; particularly in the department of Cochabamba, their lives were defined by movement. Among the many "wanderers" who populated the countryside in the early twentieth century, some were locally respected leaders who had been evicted by landlords; others were arrimantes who had been expelled by colonos. Many more were people fleeing abusive landlords: they moved from one hacienda to another, or migrated to mines or cities in search of work.[39] On the Finca de Totorani, for example, a group of colonos had already abandoned the estate when another contingent reminded the owners that "no one [could] force another [to work] against his/her will." They reported their "firm resolve to leave the property for a place where" they would be "treated like human beings."[40]

From the perspective of Cochabamba as a whole, it is impossible to say that one tendency—heightened peasant autonomy or heightened labor oppression—took the upper hand after the Chaco War. For while the system of colonaje was especially severe in the highlands, some landlords in these areas entered into rental and sharecropping arrangements with colonos and recently dispossessed comunarios, just like hacendados of the valleys. The reverse was also true: even where the hacienda most clearly entered into crisis—in the central valleys—the latifundio and labor servitude remained a significant force. In fact, colonos who purchased their own parcels of land often retained other plots in usufruct and thus continued to owe service duties to a landlord.[41]

Ultimately, it was the tension between autonomy and servitude that typified land and labor systems in the Cochabamba region. And rather than a straightforward divide between the valleys and the highlands, the tension marked labor relations within subregions and sometimes even inside a single property. As the many disputes discussed below reveal, landlords throughout the region were compelled to negotiate with resident workers. Indeed the evidence suggests that hacendados in some cases imposed more onerous duties precisely in order to offset their own diminishing fortunes and control.

In response to worsening conditions, hacienda colonos throughout much of the region protested pongueaje, "forced services," and being treated like slaves.[42] But their claims also reveal the political and economic space that colonos had carved out within the hacienda—and beyond its boundaries. The very requirement to transport landlord goods to markets or mills could connect colonos to a wider world.[43] Resident workers were not confined within a closed or all-encompassing estate, as often thought. Even where the hacienda was most entrenched, colonos had begun to doubt the legitimacy of rigid labor rules—and sometimes even the owners' right to possess the land.[44]

✳ Hacienda Injustice

It is no accident that hacienda unrest escalated in the years following the Depression, which dealt a great blow to Bolivia's tin-based economy. At the onset of the twentieth century, tin replaced silver as Bolivia's primary export product. By the 1920s, earnings from tin represented greater than 72 percent of the country's total export revenues. Diminishing world prices and declining production levels following the 1929 crash threw the tin economy into crisis. The thousands of mineworkers who joined the ranks of the unemployed endured the greatest hardships, but small business owners, merchants, and public employees also suffered. In Cochabamba, the crisis took a toll on the landowning class: when the mining centers entered into crisis, Cochabamba landlords saw one of their primary agricultural markets wither.[45] And since a disproportionate number of the mineworkers originated from Cochabamba, the layoffs added extra friction to life in this region. Men who were drawn from Cochabamba to northern Chile during the late-nineteenth-century nitrate boom could also find themselves abruptly pushed back to their native countryside.[46]

In Cochabamba's central valleys, which were already densely populated, the returning migrants increased pressure on land and other resources at a time of heightened insecurity. Dynamics differed in the department's highland areas, where landlords historically faced labor scarcity. These shortages probably worsened after the Chaco War. Since the bulk of the Bolivian fatalities were peasants, the supply of workers automatically diminished in some parts of the countryside. Furthermore, many veterans did not return to their rural homes but migrated to the cities. The government's pursuit and punishment of draft evaders may have also added to the shortages, as the director of a rural school observed.[47] The peculiar characteristics of this regional economic crisis clearly shaped the rising wave of hacienda conflict, in both highland and valley provinces.

Another cause for the burdens colonos endured—and the protests they waged—was the attempt by postwar governments to alleviate a crisis of food supply. The situation was particularly devastating in urban centers, which were inundated with new migrants. Already in the 1920s, Bolivia relied heavily on imported food, and the first post–Chaco War governments did not initially seek to reduce this dependence.[48] Instead, the military socialist leaders continued to promote imports while laboring to control the cost of basic goods. They created state stores to sell food at controlled prices, and subsidized the cost of imported primary goods by effectively burdening mine owners with a hidden tax.[49] The conservative military regimes that followed Toro and Busch shifted away from state regulation of consumption and distribution toward an emphasis on increasing food production. In line with the 1938 Constitution, these governments pressured landlords to give their properties a "social function" and raise agricultural output. A September 1939 decree issued by General Carlos Quintanilla's interim regime outlined measures to boost productivity. The decree encouraged agriculturalists to use fertilizer and thus eliminate the need to leave land fallow; required growers in appropriate zones to increase the cultivation of specific crops; and obliged all landowners to register and submit detailed production data to the Ministry of Agriculture three times a year. In return, the ministry promised fertilizer, machinery, and seed at cost. Prizes in money and in kind were offered as incentives, while fines would be levied on property owners who did not produce.[50] After taking power in 1940, General Peñaranda similarly promoted economic modernization via agricultural self-sufficiency as part of his plan for "Resurgimiento Nacional" (National Revival).[51]

There is no evidence that the promised inputs ever reached the haciendas. Instead, landlords sought to heighten production by increasing labor demands and reducing the size of colonos' usufruct plots. And they did not just bring more territory under cultivation: they monopolized the best land for hacienda production, leaving resident workers with less fertile terrain.[52] These practices cut into peasants' subsistence and security; in some cases, they also reduced the time and space available to produce small surpluses for the market.[53]

The wealth of documentation from Cochabamba in fact shows that colonos, comunarios, and ex-comunarios not only protested labor obligations but also disputed their declining access to land and diminishing economic autonomy. One such set of demands centered on the time colonos needed to work their own usufruct plots. For example, peons on the Finca de Totorani (Ayopaya) complained in 1941 about the inability to "work on [their] pegujales [plots]" since they were required to "toil on the hacienda lands the entire week, day and night."[54] They objected to being forced to work from six in the morning until after six in the afternoon. They also complained that the hilacatas and majordomos made women and children work as much as the men, leaving no time for anyone to tend the colonos' pegujales or herd their sheep. In Tacorama (near Ramadas, Tapacarí), where resident workers enjoyed access to woodland, a dispute in turn centered on landlords' attempt to keep some colonos from hiring other colonos to fulfill their own hacienda duties. Without this form of subcontracting, the first group protested, they could no longer conduct a business in charcoal.[55]

Landlords not only burdened colonos with labor duties but also with a multitude of taxes. Over the course of the early twentieth century, government authorities had begun to implement the catastro, the land tax billed semiannually to all owners in line with a property's yearly income. Rather than paying the tax themselves, many landlords transferred its cost to resident workers. As if this were not enough, municipalities—which were often controlled by hacendados—levied duties on the consumption of locally produced goods. Such municipal taxes required approval from the Senate, but this was rarely denied. The plethora of local duties took a disproportionate toll on small-scale producers and consumers; unlike landlords, these groups rarely wheedled exemptions.[56] In Cochabamba, the exactions centered on chicha and muko, thus burdening the chicheras who controlled production and distribution of the beverage. But they also affected colonos and comunarios who manufactured chicha for their own consumption, especially at the time of fiestas.[57] Whether or not such forms of production were taxable was a central source of contention in the Cochabamba region. In Tapacarí as early as 1938, two "indígenas" aided by a lawyer advised indigenous comunarios that, being comunarios, they owed no tax at all for any aspect of chicha production. A flier the men circulated referenced a 1926 administrative resolution that protected the "indigenous class" from mistreatment by muko tax collectors. The presiding judge eventually ruled that all chicha was taxable, whatever its alcoholic grade and whether produced for commercial purposes or private consumption.[58] Surely the decision was a serious blow to colonos and other small-time producers.

Beyond the weight of the tax itself, colonos also suffered from the arbitrary acts of the collectors, who worked without the government's oversight. Typically, rural tax collection was assigned to local authorities (corregidores or subprefects) or farmed out to private collectors who bid for collection contracts (licitadores).[59] An excessive range of taxes—sometimes charged several times for the same thing—combined with ambiguities in the law left small-scale producers and workers subject to abuse.[60] The varied assessments generated conflicts in the locales where they were charged. And while laws were passed in the 1920s to put checks on municipal power, military socialist governments did little to curb the town's authority to require taxes at will.[61]

Finally, the question of the land figured centrally in the disputes that colonos waged with landlords and local officials. One recurring point of conflict had to do with the definition of the usufruct plot. Comunarios newly incorporated into haciendas, as well as colonos on long-established estates, liberally interpreted the boundaries of these arriendos, pegujales, or jappis. Landlords in turn insisted that colonos obtain permission to cultivate land beyond the usufruct plot, and then demanded a proportionate increase in service duties.[62] Owners' attempts to move colonos from high-quality parcels to less-productive terrain also sparked conflicts. In the end, landlords often expelled the recalcitrant workers from the property altogether. From the perspective of many colonos, the usufruct plot was land worked by successive generations of a family: it belonged to them.[63] As elsewhere in Latin America, then, hacendados' use of land to secure labor "caused relatively autonomous small holder units to become embedded in the great estates, placing those enterprises at risk."[64] That very risk was at the heart of hacienda unrest in Bolivia in the 1940s.

✳ Military Socialism, the Language of Rights, and the Limits of State Protection

Almost as quickly as Toro and Busch announced measures favoring the peasantry, colonos and comunarios invoked the new language and laws. They protested excessive duties, and called on authorities to enforce the "new constitution," the "laws passed in favor of the peasantry," or "our rights."[65] Rich with historical referents and usually prepared with the aid of sympathetic lawyers, colonos' recurrent appeals marked a new phase of rural mobilization that was closely tied to unions and leftist parties. In particular places—especially in the Cochabamba districts of Cliza and Vacas—colonos capitalized on Toro's obligatory unionization decree and even waged successful battles to rent the land. Although the overall growth of the rural unions remained limited, the Chaco War and military socialism undeniably sparked a powerful process of organization.[66]

Colonos from Cliza, Anzaldo, Sipesipe, Tapacarí, and Ayopaya lodged petitions in the 1930s and 1940s; so did comunarios, indígenas, and Indian alcaldes of Arque and Tapacarí. Their earliest claims centered precisely on unionization and servitude. One such plea from a "sindicato agrario" in Ghochi (near Punata) requested the sublease of an upper valley hacienda. "With the advent of the socialist era proclaimed by the current Military Government Junta," the union members said, "we have opened our eyes believing our unhappy fate has changed and that the moment has arrived for us to think about our economic and intellectual renewal."[67] In another appeal from Challa (Tapacarí), the petitioners reminded the prefect that they were not "pariahs": their "personhood . . . its rights and prerogatives, was recognized by constitutional law."[68]

In their claims to government authorities, colonos and comunarios often referred generically to the "laws decreed in favor of the peasantry."[69] Once the National Convention ratified the 1938 Constitution, they referenced it, too, especially the article that prohibited personal services (article 5). "No one can force anyone against his/her will," the colonos of the Finca de Totorani (Ayopaya) said.[70] Some petitioners also cited the clause stipulating that private property fulfill a social function, or noted that the "economic regime" must ensure a dignified existence for all inhabitants, including the most "humble" ones, who contribute to the economy.[71]

As they demanded the abolition of uncompensated work, colonos and comunarios posited a fundamental opposition between abuse and progress, and between slavery and freedom. Up to a point, their petitions replicated the language of the military socialists. In his 1936 presidential address, Toro, for example, linked the creation of rural unions with the recognition of "the indígena" as a legal entity (*persona jurídica*). Indígenas, he suggested, were capable of "achieving moral and spiritual improvement and economic well-being on [their] own." He also called this experiment in autonomy a "decisive step toward the [colono's] definitive liberation from pongueaje."[72] He did not, however, outlaw the obligatory domestic service. For Toro, pongueaje was not just a degrading duty but the highly symbolic opposite of independence; in turn he considered independence a superior moral status that colonos could achieve only gradually. Rural petitioners appealed astutely to this military socialist rhetoric, but they did not simply espouse the same abstract propositions. Their petitions commenced with thick descriptions of the harsh conditions of colonos' daily lives, and concluded with pleas to work the land on their own terms.[73]

Along with support for rural unions and schools, the military socialists gave colonos' claims greater institutional weight via the recently established Ministry of Labor. State authorities no longer simply validated petitions with (unenforceable) orders, as they had done in the 1920s. Now they also dispatched investigative commissions that were supervised by the new ministry. And at times these commissions allowed Indians and peasants to circumvent biased local officials. Still, if labor inspectors and judges offered recourse to justice, these authorities also carried out eviction proceedings. The Ministry of Labor provided novel forms of redress, but it did not necessarily back rural workers' interests.

The contradictory role of state authorities is well illustrated in a 1942 petition from the alcalde of Hacienda Yayani (Ayopaya), Hilarión Grájeda, who spoke on behalf of the "indígenas of Yayani." As shown in chapters 7 and 8, Grájeda would figure prominently in the 1945 Indigenous Congress and in Ayopaya's 1947 revolt.[74] His 1942 appeal underscores colonos' determination to enforce the law. It also shows how some resident workers used knowledge of legal matters to recuperate communal forms of authority within great estates.

The Yayani hacienda was one of many in Ayopaya province that encumbered colonos with an especially severe system of labor obligations. Although the terrain in this northeastern zone is ecologically diverse, spanning the semitropical to the arid highlands, the bulk of the land lies at altitudes higher than 3,200 meters (10,500 feet) above sea level. A small number of Indian communities (*comunidades originarias*) populated the area, but it was dominated by great estates.[75] Yayani, like other Ayopaya haciendas, specialized in potatoes, which could be grown year-round and sold easily in Cochabamba's central valley markets. Estates in the province also produced and sold large amounts of muko.[76] From Morochata, the closest town, Yayani was only accessible by mule or on foot. The isolation and intensive agricultural production here and on other Ayopaya haciendas militated toward the particularly harsh system of labor and service obligations.[77] Grájeda's appeal for rights thus illustrates how colonos had begun to capture economic and political autonomy, even in a province where haciendas prevailed and servitude was severe.

Grájeda and other leaders submitted their 1942 petition to the minister of labor and social welfare on behalf of 160 colono families. The petition protested the renters' violation of an agreement that had been approved by the Ministry of Labor in 1940. It also denounced the labor judge for refusing to enforce the accord. Among its many provisions, the 1940 contract specified that the owner or renter could not arbitrarily change colonos' usufruct plots; that colonos could not be evicted without a sentence; and that no new obligation "of an onerous nature" could be imposed without colonos' consent and fair payment.[78] The clause concerning usufruct plots is especially noteworthy since the substitution of plots—a strategy landlords used to increase production—fundamentally violated colonos' autonomy and livelihood. In addition, the 1940 accord specified that colonos who transported the landlord's goods to market and saw to his personal errands (cacha) receive food and three bolivianos per day. It even set down specific rations for pongos, restricted their duties, and abolished mitanaje.

For post–Chaco War reformist politicians, pongueaje and mitanaje symbolized the most egregious aspects of the hacienda system. An agreement to standardize them thus stands out. Yet the 1940 Yayani accord was not exceptional on this point. In many parts of the country, pongueaje had already been eliminated, primarily because colonos refused to comply but sometimes also as a concession by the owners. On some properties, colonos could pay for an exemption or the landlord hired third parties.[79] Reportedly pongueaje was completely eradicated in Oruro before 1945.[80] The gradual demise of the obligatory domestic service thus sprang not only from the campaigns waged by reformist politicians but from the transformation of land and labor markets and from colonos' ongoing protests and negotiations.

Still there were limits to colonos' gains. Two grievances lodged in Grájeda's complaint were not addressed by the 1940 accord: whipping (*flagelamientos*) and the act of rape (*estupro* or *violación*) against "single and married women."[81] The absence echoed a deeper silence. In its expanded consideration of civil and social rights, Bolivia's 1938 Constitutional Convention—and Busch's 1939 labor code—failed to address corporal punishment and the sexual abuse perpetrated by owners of rural properties. Furthermore, if pongueaje had been cut back or completely phased out on some estates, it persisted in diverse forms on many other properties. Some colonos protested forced labor and obligations "at odds . . . with natural laws."[82] Others denounced particularly brutal conditions. On another property in Ayopaya, for example, colonos declared that the owner's lover beat a pongo for letting a baby chicken die and then deprived all of the pongos of food.[83] Finally, if pongueaje had loosened in some places, conservative politicians stubbornly defended the institution. When a delegation of Indians submitted a petition to the Bolivian Senate in 1943 demanding pongueaje's abolition, a group of legislators upheld the onerous service as a civilizing force—because it brought Indians into contact with cities.[84]

Agreements like the one from Ayopaya potentially alleviated the harsh conditions of hacienda work, but the accords could also protect landlord interests. For example, the 1940 Ayopaya agreement prohibited colonos from planting in hacienda lands beyond their own pegujal without prior consent, and required colonos who missed work to compensate the owners during rest days. The concluding item in the accord underscored the limits of colonos' persistent struggle for justice: it stated that disagreements between owners and colonos would be resolved by the "nearest" authorities. As colonos wished, this rule removed such arbitration from landlord control. But it could also block them from seeking out higher authorities who were more removed from the owner's influence.

Even if landlords signed labor agreements to guard their own interests, the existence of such accords signaled an important change. Colonaje, by definition, was based on a verbal contract that landowners renewed generation after generation or when a property was rented out or sold. Bolivia's Civil Code contained no provisions regarding such accords, and hacendados were not subject to laws regarding payment, hours of work, or living conditions.[85] The appearance of written agreements in the post–Chaco War era shows that colonos, even in isolated areas, maintained contact with lawyers who could oblige landlords to consent to certain legal norms.[86] But the absence of effective regulatory mechanisms in turn meant that owners often violated those contracts just as quickly as they might assent. The problem for the *ayopayeños* as for colonos in many other places was not just the burden of work. Added to their trouble was the unenforceable status of contracts and laws.

Still the colonos persisted in their efforts to make the powers of the labor agreements real. Sometimes they extracted rulings against the owners or exposed corrupt officials. Grájeda, for example, did not just object to the renters' actions; he requested the dismissal of the labor judge. The judge, Grájeda reported, hit a colono who had demanded enforcement of the 1940 accord. And he told the colonos that their contract lacked force because the national authorities who crafted it "had nothing to do with things here" and had taken advantage of the Indians' good faith. "All this helps us see," Grájeda declared, "that the official responsible for protecting us . . . is instead an instrument of the landlord, who does not just rule against the colonos but actually mistreats them and commits unspeakable abuses."[87] On the basis of Grájeda's plea, the Ministry of Labor instructed the Cochabamba prefect to hold an administrative hearing against the labor judge. The prefect in turn blamed the landlords. An article in the La Paz daily *El Diario* reported that he instructed subprefects to have peasants pay catastros, herbajes, and other taxes directly to state authorities, who would then deliver the payments to landowners. Apparently the prefect did this because "the latifundistas demand exorbitant sums from the peasantry."[88]

For Grájeda and other colonos, such measures probably meant no real redress. The evidence instead demonstrates that local officials repeatedly ignored the law. In 1941, colonos on Lobo Rancho (Cliza) denounced a government commission charged to investigate labor violations because it took testimony from the owner's witnesses without hearing from any witnesses for the workers. What's more, the authorities tried to force the colonos to sign compromising documents they could not read; one colono who refused to sign his name was arrested.[89] In another plea, two Indian alcaldes from Arque, speaking on behalf of 300 colono families, protested the actions of the chicha tax collector. They said he charged them exorbitant duties for "a mere refreshment that we routinely make for our own use . . . [from] quinoa and barley, without using any muko." They even accused the man of creating an independent tax bureau for his own benefit, without any institutional authority.[90] Appeals such as these evoked images of unjust, immoral, unproductive authorities and landlords. They depicted male landowners as people who lived off of others' work, or as drunkards, omisos (deserters of war), thieves, and rapists. And they portrayed female latifundistas as adulteresses or "evil women."[91] These "corrupt" arrangements left colonos with no protection: we don't even have the "right to say a single word," a 1941 petition from the Finca de Totorani reads.[92]

As they denounced broken agreements, unjust taxes, and immoral authorities, colonos such as Grájeda acquired prestige as legitimate leaders who were conversant in the law. For the constant adjudication of fellow colonos' claims, which often entailed great risk and hardship, could enhance an individual's authority. Traditionally, colonos in positions of influence were men beholden to the landlord. During the military socialist era, however, colonos on some haciendas began to substitute their own appointees for the alcaldes de campo, kurakas, or hilacatas who had been selected by landlords. It is not clear that landlords always recognized these indigenous delegates, but some owners clearly had to accept them.[93]

Hacienda colonos' attempts to replace illegitimate authorities did not take place in a vacuum. Up to a point, those activities replicated the caciques apoderados' ongoing efforts to elect and secure the official recognition of local and supralocal community authorities. In the 1940s, members of the earlier networks struggled, in particular, for the recognition of alcaldes.[94] Take, for example, a 1940 petition from Andrés Marka T'ula (son of Santos Marka T'ula) and other caciques from all nine departments of Bolivia. This lengthy communication requested the election, recognition, and protection of alcaldes mayores, regidores, alguaciles, escribanos, and other indigenous authorities. The claimants rooted their request in a diversity of colonial and republican documents, much like the caciques apoderados had done in the 1920s. They even suggested that their plea could draw support from the 1938 Constitution and the 1939 Eucharistic Congress.[95] The varied orders, circulars, decrees, and church resolutions they cited did not have the status of laws. Nor did the 1938 Constitution actually call for the election of alcaldes: it simply relegalized the Indian community. The petition from Andrés Marka T'ula and others never-theless underscores the importance that indigenous leaders continued to place on the election of their own authorities, and it shows how they creatively merged scattered utterances from ambiguous rulings to advance those pleas.

Two additional political tendencies specific to the post–Chaco War era shaped the rise of locally legitimate hacienda alcaldes such as Grájeda. First, there was the labor federation of Oruro (Federación Obrera Local, FOL). This regional organization maintained close contact with hacienda and Indian community leaders in the 1940s and apparently promoted the election of hilacatas and indigenous *alcaldes escolares* (alcaldes in charge of education) on haciendas.[96] Second, there was the network of Alcaldes Mayores Particulares, which emerged in 1936 and concentrated its activities in Quechua-speaking areas of Chuquisaca, northern Potosí, and Cocha-bamba. This post–Chaco War movement gained a following among comu-narios as well as colonos, but it took deepest root among colonos in places where haciendas were long entrenched and where it was difficult, if not impossible, to locate colonial land titles. Affiliated members maintained (sometimes tense) connections with the earlier networks of caciques apo-derados, and like those leaders they labored to establish schools and re-cuperate usurped land.[97] Indigenous activists associated with the Alcaldes Mayores Particulares movement would play important roles as hacienda unrest deepened in the mid-1940s (see chapters 7 and 8).

It is uncertain how many hacienda communities in Ayopaya and be-yond managed to impose their own locally legitimate alcaldes or hilacatas. But it is clear that colonos throughout the country did not simply protest labor abuse in the 1940s. Their grievances were intertwined with struggles over power, both within the hacienda and outside of it. In La Paz, the early-twentieth-century process of hacienda expansion involved the incorpora-tion of communities into haciendas; although they became colonos, the dispossessed comunarios often maintained communal authority systems within the estate.[98] As the petitions reviewed here reveal, a similar process took place in Arque and in parts of Tapacarí. It might even be said that something comparable occurred within Ayopaya's most deeply entrenched haciendas, where colonos apparently created internal systems of representation that mirrored those typical of communities and "ex-communities." Although Ayopaya's colonos were not the only ones on long-established haciendas to create such systems of representation, the extent of the process in this region was unusual, and it helps explain the intensity of the insurgent movement that erupted there in 1947 (see chapter 8). In short, the line between "hacienda" and "community" was not everywhere so stark. Like community-based struggles, hacienda unrest of the late 1930s and early 1940s revolved around questions of economic and political autonomy and representation.

✳ Sit-Down Strikes

Surprising elements of continuity characterized rural social movements from the 1920s to the 1940s. But the resurgence of organized labor, the rise of antioligarchic political parties, and the internal transformation of hacienda life also produced new kinds of leaders and new forms of protest. Hand in hand with juridical procedures, evicted colonos and hacienda-based leaders on select properties began to wage work stoppages and other disruptive actions. Their protests often revolved around peculiarly local grievances much like the ones expressed in the above-discussed petitions. Many striking colonos sought to enforce existing contracts or customs. Others also summoned a "law"—recently passed or soon to be announced —that would suppress pongueaje and all other duties to the hacienda. When they alluded to the military socialist decrees, striking colonos sometimes even combined calls for an end to pongueaje with prophecies about a law to distribute land.

The press and government authorities referred loosely to rural protests of the post–Chaco War era as sit-down strikes (*huelgas de brazos caídos*).[99] This illusively straightforward term masks an enormously varied practice. Either staying in their homes or retreating to the hills, colonos sometimes simply refused to appear when administrators called them to work the landlord's fields. Or they might collect the hacienda harvest but keep it for themselves. Still others dedicated themselves to their own plots exclusively. In some cases, landlords accused colonos of taking land for themselves that was previously cultivated for the estate.[100] Other such strikes involved withholding payment for grazing rights or rental plots, refusing to fulfill personal service in the hacienda home, or failing to transport landlord goods to market.[101] Hacienda colonos of course waged strikes before the Chaco War, especially in parts of Chuquisaca, Cochabamba, and La Paz.[102] Indeed some such strikes were perceived as direct assaults against the owners' property and power.[103] That said, hacienda unrest intensified and spread in the period after the Chaco War. The upsurge had as much to do with increased labor burdens and the loss of prior autonomy as it did with the rise of military socialism, which boosted resident workers' organizational capacity.

In the late 1930s and early 1940s, the bulk of the hacienda agitation was confined to Cochabamba and Oruro. Cochabamba figured centrally due in part to the peculiar effects of heightened chicha and muko taxes in an overarching context of hacienda decline. Increasingly vigilant collection of the taxes not only augmented burdens and abuse but also infringed on colonos' and comunarios' independent economic activities. Less is known about the genesis of the strikes in Oruro, but the groundswell of work stoppages, especially in the department's eastern corner, stemmed in part from the organizing drives of members of Oruro's urban anarchist labor federation. Some of these early strikes were confined to a single hacienda; others united colonos from several different properties. Often they revealed, or exacerbated, conflicts among colonos with different privileges, status, or rights.[104] Although the multivariegated actions rarely unified all resident workers in any given place, they could garner support from significant majorities.

A 1939 court case concerning unrest on Hacienda Tacorama (near Ramadas, Tapacarí) vividly reveals how colonos could connect grievances over work rules with predictions about favorable laws.[105] The case also sheds light on a process of rural organization that extended beyond the well-known peasant unions established in Cliza and Vacas. And it shows, like the above-mentioned dispute from Ayopaya, the contentious place of written labor agreements. Lodged before Cochabamba's Superior Court, the lengthy suit from Tacorama commenced in November 1938, when a landlord initiated eviction proceedings against two colonos he and neighboring hacendados had accused of instigating an uprising involving more than 300 men, women, and children from ten properties. After the judge ruled in the owner's favor, a police commission arrived to enforce the eviction. In the course of that expulsion, at least eight people were killed, and the evicted colonos' homes were destroyed. Several colonos then filed complaints against the police commission for using excessive force. They also denied any involvement in an uprising.[106] The colonos claimed that the dispute instead concerned landlords' violation of established labor customs and rules.

The crux of the matter, according to the landlords, was the colonos' utter disregard for their authority and property. The defendants had not just exceeded the boundaries of their plots (pegujales) and invaded the hacendados' terrain. The owners claimed that the accused colonos actually "thought of themselves as landlords," "refused to share the production," and went about the work "in their own exclusive interest." They acted, in short, on the "erroneous and dangerous belief that the land belonged to them." The landlords suggested further that the defendants had grounded their illegal action in the law. Two ringleaders had been "harvesting anarchy and corrupting the indigenous class on these properties," one landlord declared, and they had "convinced the colonos to ignore the rights of the owners, [because the landlords] were going to be expelled by the Government or by revolutionary authorities who would distribute the land among the colonos." Ultimately, the landlords blamed the colonos' lawyers; they said the attorneys offered to defend the colonos so they could "continue to be like true property owners."[107]

To counter these accusations, the defendants testified that the dispute arose from complaints they had submitted to the newly established Ministry of Labor. Their grievances concerned abrupt shifts in grazing fees, reductions in the size of usufruct plots, increased turns of pongueaje, and the landlords' refusal to honor accords regarding many other duties.[108] The defendants also denied that they had ever tried to take the land. They blamed the landlords for concocting the story in order to evict them. Some colonos nevertheless testified for the landlords. One such witness declared that the two "ringleaders" "went around this estate and neighboring properties . . . spreading the word that a lawsuit was going to be declared in their favor . . . that the land . . . was theirs and that the landlords would soon be evicted with their hands tied behind their backs." The partner of a murdered colono gave additional weight to this account: "Just when the haciendas were going to be ours," she lamented, "our president [Busch] died." Another witness declared that their lawyer told them not to fulfill pongueaje and other duties, "because the Supreme Government had abolished them." One more said the leaders told him "we would be owners of our sayañas [plots] . . . with just a small uprising and another visit to the Prefect."[109]

The varied claims and counterclaims make it difficult to say exactly who promised what to whom, or to know whether the lawyers actually said what the colonos and landlords said they said. What matters is the link that the defendants, plaintiffs, and witnesses set up between the law, the government, and the promise of land. Just about all sides in the dispute presented evidence of such connections. Witnesses' statements further confirm that local actors merged legal maneuvers with illegal ones; rather than opposing poles, they viewed petitions and uprisings as interconnected modes of political practice. And violence, from their perspective, was a given element of both.[110]

In the course of the Tacorama trial, the landlords expressed alarm about a wave of similar strikes on other Cochabamba properties. They insisted on harsh punishment for the ringleaders and urged the government to resolve the standoff between owners and colonos with "extreme measures" that would ensure a rational and efficient agricultural industry.[111] The owners of Tacorama viewed the 1938 Constitution as an attempt to deny their own property rights, and noted their opposition to it. But they also invoked the charter strategically at face value by reminding state authorities that they could never fulfill the "social function of property" condition if the government did not enforce colonos' obligation to work.[112] As the landlords pursued their case, they expressed anxiety about their own declining authority. Like the colonos, they appealed to the state for mediation and force.

Colonos waged dozens of other such strikes in Cochabamba from 1939 onward. Like the Tacorama conflict, these protests exposed landlords' diminishing power. A 1941 case from Ayopaya, for example, reveals how colonos could become embroiled in hacendados' inheritance battles and divorce trials. Their complaints also unveil the sexual abuse that some landlords perpetrated against colonas.[113] Indeed, delegates to the 1945 Indigenous Congress would list *abusos deshonestos* (indecent assault) as one of the most common forms of violence that landowners perpetrated.[114]

If the hacienda enclosed—and disclosed—intimate conflicts, lies, and violence, then it was also beginning to show the very misfortune of the old elite. Throughout Cochabamba, established landowners were compelled to rent, divide, or sell their holdings. In the process, new men and women of property emerged among upwardly mobile townspeople, small-scale merchants, hacienda administrators, and even among individuals of modest origins. Some such men became caudillos, local power brokers with popular followings. Consider the case of Remberto Camacho, a Cochabamba-based lawyer who called himself the "Redentor de los Indios" (Redeemer of the Indians). In the early 1940s, Camacho persuaded alcaldes and other Indian officials on haciendas of Ayopaya to boycott the muko tax, one of the most important sources of revenue in the department.[115] According to witnesses, Camacho's exploits had recently commenced when, by "miracle of marriage," the lawyer had become the owner of a vast property called Moyapampa in Cantón Calchani.[116] By claiming powers superior to the subprefect and working through the hacienda alcaldes, Camacho had persuaded small-scale producers of muko or chicha to circumvent the "corrupt" licitadores and deliver a lower rate directly to the prefect, the Departmental Treasury, or himself. The boycott created much turmoil for tax collectors, as well as for large landowners in the region whose control over their own colonos was surely defied by Camacho's subversive message.

Leaders of rural strikes not only protested exorbitant taxes but reportedly spread rumors about laws to eliminate pongueaje and distribute land. In Anzaldo in 1941, a majordomo was accused of provoking unrest among colonos eager for the end of pongueaje. Landlords in the area claimed that the foreman, his wife, and an ex-colono had been inciting sedition. Apparently the foreman assured the colonos that the land was theirs, that the government would support them, and that the authorities had already passed resolutions to end pongueaje and all other services to the hacienda. He pressured the colonos to abandon all agricultural tasks and, according to one witness, told them that the government had passed laws reducing fees for herbaje. The foreman denied the charges, but he did confirm the rumors of favorable laws: the colonos rebelled of their own accord, he declared, precisely because they had heard about propitious decrees.[117]

The Anzaldo conflict was hardly an isolated incident. Around the same time, colonos on Lobo Rancho (Cliza) reportedly urged the owners to comply with the government's directive against pongueaje.[118] In Sacabamba (Anzaldo), where landlords had increased resident workers' obligations and violated longstanding customs, three colonos were accused of instigating a sit-down strike or "indigenous rebellion" to end pongueaje and take back the land. A witness declared that one of the leaders possessed papers documenting the peasants' property rights all the way back to the Inca empire. The accused instead claimed that the owners pursued the case to retaliate against them because they had initiated a lawsuit demanding the return of goods and land seized by an administrator.[119]

Where did the news about favorable laws, pongueaje, and land restoration originate? Ironically, the government was one source of the reports. General Peñaranda's minister of government sent a memo to prefects in May 1941 ordering them to announce publicly that "the service of postillonaje or pongueaje . . . is hereby prohibited and all such services or assistance must be paid for . . . at the market price."[120] This ambiguous circular provoked a flurry of objections from landlords. National authorities eventually revoked the measure and explained that it only applied to the services that comunarios owed local authorities, which had already been abolished by a series of nineteenth-century laws; the ban did not cover colonos' obligations to hacendados. Despite the retraction, duplicates of the "law" had already begun to circulate and some of those copies surely reached the hands of local leaders. A spate of rural strikes immediately followed the circular's release.[121] A fundamental air of uncertainty about pongueaje thus reigned, for the ongoing debates, decrees, petitions, and publications about this degrading duty obscured its legal status and fostered an expectation that it was about to end or had already been abolished.[122]

Another starting place for the rumors may have been the successful example of colonos in Cliza, who obtained the abolition of pongueaje on their hacienda in 1937. Surely the leaders from Cliza fed information to other colonos after consulting with sympathetic lawyers in Cochabamba.[123] Likewise, colonos who established unions in other provinces carried promising news to more isolated areas of the department.[124] Many of the men who spread rumors about favorable decrees were probably former colonos who had been expelled from properties for "disobedience" or constant "complaints."[125] A large number of displaced colonos, who worked as rural day laborers or went looking for work in the city, populated the Cochabamba region. Whether from a new urban base or from an old one in the countryside, members of this mobile group played a leading role in the 1940s agitation.[126] Testimony from some rural activists suggests, moreover, that "ringleaders" on one property were aware of unrest on others. A number of colonos made trips to La Paz and other cities, where they established contact with other rural leaders and acquired knowledge about favorable "laws" and "decrees."[127] Finally, men affiliated with the La Paz–based cacique apoderado networks probably helped spread the word.[128] Whatever the source, the rumors about laws were not simply imposed by outside "agitators." They appeared hand in hand with colonos' denunciations of lawlessness and with their demands for adherence to contracts and rules. The rumors were bound up with attempts to negotiate the boundaries of the landlord's domain. And they were intertwined with contests over possession, ownership, and the conduct of local officials.

The rural protests of the early 1940s had no single source. They were shaped by a dense, multidirectional network of colonos, comunarios, lawyers, labor leaders, sympathetic politicians, and even some disaffected hacienda administrators or majordomos. Some of the lawyers who supported peasants' claims had been delegates to the 1938 constitutional convention. Others were well-known leftist intellectuals or labor leaders. For example, Alipio Valencia Vega—cofounder of the Partido Obrero Revolucionario (POR) and a close comrade of Tristán Marof—advised comunarios of Ventilla (Arque) in a 1942 dispute over taxes.[129] In Sacabamba, colonos were assisted by Faustino Castellón, leader of the anarchist Federación Central Obrera. At one point, this group even planned to hook up with Marof himself. A 1937 petition from Ayopaya underscores another vital association: it linked rural petitioners with the Federación Obrera de Trabajo (FOT). Likewise, colonos in Larimarca received backing from members of the Cochabamba FOS.[130]

Ultimately the conflicts described in the preceding pages illustrate a crisis of the hacienda from within. Labor and service burdens clearly increased on many properties from the late 1930s onward. But rather than showing that landlords had achieved a tighter grip, the documents evince their inability to control resident workers—who organized fellow colonos, consulted with lawyers, or simply abandoned the property. To recover power and increase production, some landlords, renters, or administrators not only added obligations but inflicted harsh punishments; others exercised their right to expel resident workers. For all its severity, landlords' attempt to strengthen labor and service requirements was part and parcel of their slowly eroding hegemony.

* Indigenous Congresses and the Ties between City and Countryside

The outbreak of hacienda-based conflicts so perturbed the Peñaranda government that it ordered a series of investigations into rural labor conditions in Cochabamba and Oruro. The commission's reports amply confirmed colonos' grievances against excessive obligations. The team of government officials also agreed that colonos exchanged those arduous duties for a plot of land barely sufficient to maintain a family's basic needs.[131] Despite the incriminating evidence, Peñaranda's government did not seek changes in rural labor systems. Instead, the regime decided that the root of the problem was urban workers' political agitation. In February 1943, the president cancelled all articles in statutes of workers' organizations that alluded to "agricultural labor or peasant activities."[132] Although the government refused to address the underlying causes of the unrest, it was not entirely mistaken about the role that workers from the city played in rural strikes.

Urban labor organizers renewed their ties with peasant leaders immediately following the Chaco War. And after the CSTB's second national congress, in 1939, the labor movement began to establish direct connections with rural communities and espoused pro-Indian initiatives. A document entitled "La CSTB y el problema del indio" affirmed the principal demands that colonos and comunarios had lodged during the preceding decades: it called for a new revisita and the abolition of pongueaje. In the form of a general petition against communal land usurpation, ill-treatment, and servile labor, the CSTB also revived a number of complaints that had been presented to the 1938 constitutional convention.[133]

The labor movement's rural political agenda gained added weight with the creation of the Partido de la Izquierda Revolucionaria (Party of the Revolutionary Left, PIR) in 1941. The PIR's founding program displayed indigenista tendencies and stressed the party's resolve to "actively incorporate peasants into the ranks of our movement." While the PIR endorsed the technical "improvement" of Indian communities, it also called for an agrarian reform that would eliminate the "unproductive, feudal latifundio," end Indian servitude, and convert Indian communities into agricultural cooperatives.[134] Of the three most influential reform parties of the post–Chaco War era (POR, PIR, MNR), the PIR was the first to develop a network of activists engaged in organizational work in the countryside.

More important, the alliances that PIR activists and labor leaders forged with hacienda colonos resonated beyond isolated hacienda protests in the form of well-publicized urban indigenous congresses. The first such congress was not directly controlled by Bolivia's labor movement but was an intercontinental affair: the Primer Congreso Interamericano de Indianistas (First Inter-American Congress of Indianists). Originally slated for August 1939 in Bolivia, the conference instead took place in 1940 in Patzcuaro, Mexico, but not before Bolivia's organizing committee printed a preliminary agenda and published expectant announcements in the press.[135] Fourteen thematic sessions planned by an assortment of Bolivia's political and intellectual elite—conservative and radical—included a striking number of 1938 constitutional convention delegates and prominent leftists. Not surprisingly, the Bolivian organizers revived the very questions the 1938 convention delegates had left unresolved: land reform, the juridical status of Indian communities, Patronatos Indígenas, and the Revisita de Tierras. As such, the suggestive agenda broached the fundamental demands of the 1920s caciques apoderados. That an unequal dialogue would take place was also clear: interpreters would render into Spanish presentations made in Quechua and Aymara by select indigenous delegates, but the organizers did not promise to translate the Spanish talks into native languages.

Although the Inter-American Congress was ultimately convened in Mexico, its preliminary program continued to resonate in Bolivia. And the most controversial points were sustained not only by the PIR and the CSTB but by indigenous alcaldes such as Hilarión Grájeda. Two meetings of Quechua-speaking "indígenas" were held in Sucre in 1942 and 1943 under the auspices of the CSTB and the PIR-affiliated student federation. Although sponsored by urban activists, the gatherings revealed traces of the demands expressed in colono strikes and cacique apoderado petitions. Both meetings endorsed a worker-peasant alliance, hacienda takeovers, and the abolition of uncompensated services. The 1942 event also called for a review of communal land boundaries and the nullification of all indigenous land transfers effected without state intervention.[136] The meeting brought together Quechua-speaking delegates from Cochabamba, Oruro, Potosí, and Chuquisaca.

A third indigenous congress, convened in Sucre in August 1944, reiterated the platform of the first two meetings. Its organizational base further confirmed the ties between rural activists and urban labor leaders. The congress was jointly sponsored by a committee of caciques and alcaldes mayores from Sucre, Oruro, Potosí, La Paz, and Cochabamba; the Sucre Prefecture; and the board of Sucre's labor federation. The organizers advocated new judicial institutions, such as a Patronato Nacional de Indígenas. They also called on the government to extend urban workers' rights to rural laborers. Compensation for evicted colonos in line with the 1939 labor code and full support for peasants' "obligatory unionization" fell under this heading. The program even endorsed maternity leave for mitanis (until pongueaje was abolished). Other fundamental demands in-

cluded a general review of land titles (revisita), the investigation of fraudulent land sales, and an agrarian labor code.[137] To dramatize the persistence
of colonial oppression during more than 100 years of republican rule and
"liberal, egalitarian constitutions," all three regional congresses (1942, 1943,
and 1944) were held on or close to Bolivian Independence Day (6 August).

The labor movement's role in the genesis of the indigenous congresses,
and its emphasis on urban and rural "workers," did not lead to the suppression of Indianness as a political identity. Instead, the burgeoning labor
organizations gave new impetus to the longstanding struggles of the cacique
apoderado networks. Those earlier movements had changed significantly
during the Chaco War years, but they were not fully suppressed. Although
the national network no longer maintained the same level of coordination,
the "caciques indígenas" continued to submit petitions to national politicians.[138] And while the demands that hacienda colonos expressed during
the late 1930s and early 1940s figured centrally in Bolivia's first indigenous
congresses, community-based leaders also influenced those events. Both
comunarios and colonos helped make indigenous rights and guarantees a
central focus of the regional assemblies—and of post–Chaco War political
culture more broadly.

✳ Conclusion

The rural conflicts traced in this chapter reveal that military socialism was a
double-edged sword for hacienda colonos. While the military's laws and
state agencies potentially empowered peasants and Indians, the new government officials could be just as corrupt or beholden to landlords as the
local agents the colonos sought to circumvent. Rather than suppressing
unrest or enhancing state control, the tensions between empowerment and
oppression that marked the era of military socialism helped foster new
waves of mobilization. The law figured centrally in those struggles, partly
because the military socialists' favorable rulings created expectations without augmenting government control of laws and decrees. Had pongueaje
been eliminated, or was it still allowed? When the authors of the 1938
Constitution declared that "no one can be forced to render personal services without consent and fair compensation," did they abolish this degrading duty? The answer was unclear. This ambiguity helped fuel the unprecedented wave of sit-down strikes that vexed the Bolivian countryside in the
post–Chaco War era.

Following the 1939 death of Busch and the interim period of conservative governments led by Generals Carlos Quintanilla and Enrique Peñaranda, a third bearer of the military socialist torch would take power: Colonel Gualberto Villarroel. Junior officers grouped in Razón de Patria (Cause of the Nation, RADEPA), a secret military lodge forged in Paraguayan prisoner of war camps, backed Villarroel's coup, which he undertook on 20 December 1943 together with the newly established MNR. Pressured by escalating conflict in the countryside, the Villarroel-MNR regime would convene the continent's first *national* Indigenous Congress and announce a series of historic decrees. These actions inspired strikes, uprisings, and a spate of stories about revolutionary laws, all on a much greater scale than before Villarroel took power. The unrest of the late 1930s and early 1940s nevertheless shows that news of favorable rulings began to circulate well before Villarroel summoned the Indigenous Congress. To be sure, such rumors would acquire greater force after the 1945 assembly. But the demands grew out of the local conflicts and congresses that sprang up in the decades before the rise of Villarroel-MNR populism. In the beginning, MNR leaders looked on those things with uncertainty or disdain.

CHAPTER SIX

THE UNWILLING CITY

Villarroel Populism
and the Politics
of Mestizaje

About a month after the new government took power, Colonel Gualberto Villarroel held an improvised victory rally. The president, the MNR leader Víctor Paz Estenssoro, and several other officials addressed a cheering crowd from the balcony of the Government Palace. Summing up the aims of the new regime, Villarroel uttered his most memorable refrain: "We are not enemies of the rich, but we are better friends of the poor."[1] This impossible pledge to favor the poor without estranging the rich—couched in a language of intimate ties—encapsulates the military populist's ambitious but doomed reformism. The Villarroel regime aimed to increase productivity and consumption while granting dignity and sustenance to the nation's indigenous and mestizo masses, to the "man who suffers . . . the mineworker . . . [and] the indio."[2] To achieve this vision of abundance and health, the president promoted social and economic reforms that targeted both rural and urban realms.

From the beginning, the Villarroel regime found itself isolated internationally and besieged domestically by opposition from the Left and the Right. The government thus linked its drive for social reforms with the quest for political allies. Principally it promoted the increasingly powerful mineworkers, by granting recognition to their national federation, the Federación Sindical de Trabajadores Mineros Bolivianos (Federation of Bolivian Mineworker Unions, FSTMB), in June 1944.[3] Like other Latin American populists, Villarroel and the MNR also courted urban labor. Since most labor unions had already joined the PIR-controlled CSTB, which opposed the new government, the Villarroel regime tried to create a parallel labor federation.[4] Much like Argentina's Juan Perón (1946–55), Villarroel also cultivated the support of informal-sector workers.[5] Above all, his government courted the women who sold basic goods in the nation's urban markets. The market women were not just critical providers of urban sustenance; they were also one of the most autonomous sectors of the labor movement. For while the PIR-led labor federation swept up male unions after the Chaco War, it did not gain control of the unions established by female vendors, domestic workers, florists, and other women workers.[6] As wives and mothers of male artisans and factory workers, the female vendors in addition served as potential mediators between the regime and a generally antagonistic labor movement. By showing support for the nation's mestiza market women, the regime demonstrated its affinity with workers and the poor.

As Villarroel and the MNR labored to attract urban followers, they also aimed to create a sense of national unity via symbols, rituals, and institutions. Like the Busch regime in the 1930s, the Villarroel-MNR government sought to establish schools and military barracks in frontier zones as a means to fortify the nation's borders and limit external influences.[7] But Villarroel and the MNR went beyond denouncing foreign threats to national unity: they also believed in the need for a zealous attack against the internal barriers to nationhood. And while Busch viewed regional differences as component parts of a harmonious corporate whole, Villarroel and the MNR considered them dangerous obstacles. In his first annual address to Congress, Villarroel signaled the need to create a sense of nationality, to "commence the struggle against all regionalism . . . which poisons the atmosphere and sickens the social organism."[8] History occupied a special place in this quest for national unity. Villarroel stressed the need to "restore the spiritual values of our past [and] unite men from all parts of the country in the same faith, creating a national consciousness."[9] The President's MNR allies delved more deeply into historical struggles. Their programmatic texts located the essence of a national culture and consciousness in the anticolonial heroism of mestizos.

Although the Villarroel-MNR regime heralded unity, its vision of an idealized, mestizo nation was ultimately a selective one: it relied on the gendered image of a regional and racial type, namely the mestiza market women of Cochabamba. These women came to stand for moral, healthy, hardworking mothers devoted to the family and the nation. Villarroel and the MNR promoted ideals of mestizaje, national harmony, and family health in texts as well as in public rituals and social policies. As the nationalist politicians valorized a particular vision of the mestizo/a nation, they also relegated the rural indigenous majority to a subordinate political and symbolic place.

✳ The Mestizo Nation

Colonel Gualberto Villarroel was thirty-five years old when he and a group of reformist military officers overthrew General Peñaranda's conservative government. The conspirators opposed the Peñaranda regime largely because of its pro-U.S. stance and violent opposition to the labor movement.[10] Their main pillars of support were the newly established MNR and the junior officers grouped in Razón de Patria (RADEPA). Via military schools that were established in Cochabamba during the first period of military socialism, members of this secret lodge had gained a certain prominence within the army. Their influence increased during Peñaranda's brief reign (1940–43), as a series of political crises diminished the generals' control of the armed forces. When Villarroel first took power, the United States and most Latin American countries refused to recognize his government due to the MNR's alleged ties to Nazi Germany. Since the Villarroel regime depended heavily on tin exports to the United States, it acceded to the U.S. demand that all MNR members be removed from the cabinet (see figure 11). The MNR nevertheless continued to play a critical role from the sidelines; and after Villarroel's government was officially recognized by the United States in March 1944, party members were reassigned to several cabinet posts.[11] The military's alliance with the MNR remained fraught with tension, however. The party's leaders continuously clashed with the more conservative members of RADEPA, while Villarroel got caught in an ineffective mediating role in between. When four high-profile opposition politicians were killed by the military in 1944, a rift also developed within the MNR. These crosscutting tensions troubled the political alliance and eventually contributed to its downfall. Villarroel and the MNR nevertheless

11 President Gualberto Villarroel (seated in the center) and his cabinet after the March 1944 purge of the MNR ministers. *Courtesy of the Archive of La Paz*.

collaborated closely and pursued a fairly unified program for the government's two-and-a-half-year rule.[12]

Gualberto Villarroel was utterly unknown when he took power. The president was born in 1908 in Villa Rivero, a village in Cochabamba's central valleys (a small shrine still adorns the family's humble adobe home, now a national monument). As a teenager, Villarroel attended the Colegio Militar in La Paz. This academy was one of the army's most important recruiting tools: it gave the chance of upward mobility to men of modest means. Although Villarroel served as an officer in the Chaco War, he did not distinguish himself as a hero; nor did he endure the suffering of the prisoner-of-war camps. When the war was over, he became an instructor in one of Toro's advanced military institutes in Cochabamba. Along with other teachers at these schools—almost all of whom were majors and colonels who had served in the Chaco War—Villarroel promoted RADEPA's advance. Not by chance, RADEPA itself eventually became known as the "Grupo de Cochabamba."[13]

The rapid rise of RADEPA after the war with Paraguay paralleled the MNR's ascent. The party was established in 1941 by middle-class lawyers and

journalists in their twenties and thirties; a good number of its founding members were veterans of the Chaco War (see figure 12). In many cases they were also descendents of semi-impoverished oligarchs, sons of ex-presidents, or sons of managers of failed companies.[14] Shortly after the MNR's founding, its leaders established urban branch committees (*comandos*) that recruited professionals and white-collar workers to the organization's ranks. As the MNR rose to become one of Bolivia's leading electoral forces, it competed for popular support with two other antioligarchic parties.[15] The first of these was the Trotskyite Partido Obrero Revolucionario (POR), which was founded in 1934 by exiled leftists under the direction of Tristán Marof and drew its followers mainly from the mineworkers.[16] The third party, the Partido de la Izquierda Revolucionaria (PIR), was established in 1941 under the leadership of José Antonio Arze and Ricardo Anaya. Both men were prominent lawyers who had helped organize Bolivia's first national university student congress in Cochabamba in 1928. With the support of outstanding labor leaders, the PIR easily became the party of the Bolivian labor movement.[17] In the early 1940s, it won a much greater mass following than that of either the MNR or the POR.[18] In fact, only a few thousand people joined the MNR in these early years. The MNR nevertheless increased its political profile when it took significant numbers of congressional seats in the 1942 and 1944 elections.[19]

12 Founding members of
the MNR, circa 1941,
including Alberto
Mendoza López (fifth
from the left), Víctor Paz
Estenssoro (sixth from
the left), and Hernán
Siles Zuazo (seventh
from the left). *Courtesy
of the Luis Antezana E.
Private Archive.*

In large part, the MNR gained political clout via the party's passionate defense of striking mineworkers who were murdered by the military in the 1942 Catavi Mine massacre. More than 9,000 workers had gone on strike to demand improved conditions and the complete enforcement of Busch's 1939 Labor Code. The government eventually sent troops, declared the action illegal, and arrested the leaders. After a series of clashes, soldiers killed thirty-five mineworkers and an unknown number of women who accompanied the workers in a protest march. Leaders across the political spectrum condemned the army's egregious act, but the MNR made the most vocal plea by sponsoring a congressional resolution to censure the Peñaranda regime. This was the first time a standing government was accused by Congress of killing workers or Indians. And it turned out to be an astute political move. Before the massacre, Bolivian mineworkers had affiliated most closely with the Trotskyite POR. The MNR's defiant denunciation of the bloodbath, defense of workers' right to strike, and demand for the dismissal of Peñaranda's cabinet helped the party gain the support of the mineworkers union.[20]

In a more general sense, the MNR and RADEPA also derived influence from a sense of shared sacrifice in the devastating conflict with Paraguay. Since many MNR leaders had served as officers, the party belittled men who evaded their patriotic duty. The nation's harrowing experience in turn led

Villarroel and the MNR to agree on a fundamental premise: the defeat to Paraguay compelled Bolivians to expand state institutions and strengthen the nation. Penned by the *cochabambino* José Cuadros Quiroga, a journalist affiliated with the pro-Nazi strand of the MNR, the party's 1942 manifesto pledged to "struggle for the consolidation of the state and the security of the patria," to make Bolivia an "organic, unified, and strong nation," and to "fortify the national character."[21] The manifesto promised its followers that the MNR would supersede the pulls of regionalism, gain control of the mining "superstate," and foment a prosperous agricultural economy. It mixed tirades against Jews with the glorification of the nation's mestizo origins. Only with the launching of the MNR party did embryonic praise of mestizaje become full-scale affirmation.

A mix of domestic and continental trends surely influenced the MNR leaders who championed their nation's mestizo roots and identity. With the post-1898 upsurge in U.S. imperialism, discourses of mestizaje spread widely in the early twentieth century.[22] Writers and politicians in many Latin American countries increasingly rejected racial theories that equated hybridity with degeneracy, and revalorized race mixture as an idiom of national strength. As they vindicated autochthonous traditions and championed social reforms, the nationalist politicians also labored to create a unique and "healthy" national type. Domestic political dynamics also shaped mestizaje's emergence, for populist politicians of the 1930s and 1940s drew on ideals of racial unity in their efforts to forge multiclass political pacts. In some countries, power struggles between regional elites also drove the positive appraisals of hybridity. Multiple in their meanings, manifestations, and political effects, the mestizaje projects were thrashed out in diverse realms ranging from theater and music to literature and the essay.

Although mestizaje was a prevalent metaphor for union during the heyday of U.S. imperialism (1898 to the early 1930s), not all Latin American intellectuals took mestizaje as the symbolic expression of nationhood. But whether they privileged mixture, purity, or whiteness, their ruminations on national unity asserted and reinscribed racial differences and hierarchies. The influential Mexican intellectual José Vasconcelos theorized that the mixture of races would foster a "cosmic race" through a process of "spiritual evolution," but his scheme ultimately privileged whiteness.[23] In Nicaragua and El Salvador, idealizations of mixture valorized the indigenous past, but they were predicated on the disappearance of living indigenous cultures.[24] Argentine intellectuals of this era denounced mixture altogether, and even recommended the prohibition of marriage between "widely separate races" on the grounds that such unions would breed degeneration and endanger Argentine nationality.[25] In the Andes, prominent intellectuals similarly considered race mixture a wholly dangerous prospect for much of the early twentieth century. Yet unlike Argentines, who privileged whiteness, Andean intellectuals often extolled the purity of ancient indigenous pasts. When Andean thinkers embraced mestizaje, they did so with great ambivalence or as the emblem of discrete, regionally circumscribed proposals.[26]

In Bolivia, affirmations of race mixture followed a more uneven path than they did in many other Latin American countries. As La Paz–based Liberal Party leaders abandoned promises to decentralize the state after the 1899 civil war, regional elites from Cochabamba championed mestizaje in an effort to defend local interests and culture. These devoted regionalists rejected the paceño Alcides Arguedas's denunciation of hybrid people and totalizing denigration of Bolivian culture in his widely circulated *Pueblo enfermo* (1909). Instead they reclaimed the character of the nation's "distinct races and castes or social classes" and recuperated their role in the nation's past.[27] In the 1930s, intellectuals from other regions also began to attribute positive qualities to mestizaje by suggesting that it could be a sign of national integration, cultural mediation, and evolution.[28] But these were often tentative formulations based on hyphenated mestizo subjects—the "mestizo-indio" and the "mestizo-blanco"—that went against the very idea of mestizaje as an idiom of unity.[29] Only a few delegates mentioned mestizaje at the 1938 constitutional convention, and they generally viewed it as a negative force that would augment "heterogeneous tendencies."[30]

As Villarroel and the MNR competed with other political parties for the support of urban workers and war veterans, they nationalized Cochabamba's regionalist defense of mestizaje. First the revolutionary-nationalists transformed the local attack against Arguedas into a general defense of the "national-popular." Then they dislodged mestizaje from ideas about political risk and biological decline.[31] The MNR's 1942 program condemned Arguedas's historical opus for denigrating Bolivians because they were Indians and mestizos. And it rebuked his work for blaspheming such heroes of anticolonial liberation as the mestizo leader of the 1809 revolt in La Paz, Pedro Domingo Murillo.[32]

Like proponents of mestizaje elsewhere in Latin America, MNR ideologues thus rejected the idea that race mixture was dangerous. But there was a difference. The primary ground for the party's reappraisal of mestizaje was not the fusion of culture or blood: its reassessment instead centered on historical struggle.[33] According to the MNR's founding members, three essential elements defined the Bolivian nation: its "varied geography . . . , common history, and [a] race caught up in the process of mestizaje [mestización]." Geography, history, and race: three things deemed intractable problems in 1938—by socialists and conservatives alike—had now become Bolivia's greatest advantages. The MNR's 1942 manifesto denounced foreigners who considered Bolivians "racially inferior," and acclaimed the "legacy of the sons of the Sun [that we] carry in our blood." Its authors also lauded the "mestizo consciousness" that Bolivians had forged in the struggle against colonialism. More than anything else, this foundational text heralded the "glorious tradition of the independence revolution, which put to test the talent and valor of the mestizo and the Indian."[34]

Carlos Montenegro's 1944 Nacionalismo y colonaje, a crucial tool for the formation of party leaders and militants, further illustrates how the MNR defense of mestizaje rested on a particular reinterpretation of Bolivian history.[35] Although this influential text notes that Indians participated in heroic anticolonial struggles, it always couples Indians with mestizos; Montenegro completely overlooks the events in which Indians and indigenous projects figured first. The 1780s rebellions waged by Tupac Amaru and Tupac Katari, the 1899 uprising led by Zárate Willka, the 1921 revolt in Jesús de Machaqa, and the 1927 rebellion in Chayanta—all of these episodes go unmentioned. Instead the narrative focuses on events in which mestizos and creoles took the leading role. To be sure, Nacionalismo y colonaje and other founding texts of the MNR do not entirely exclude Indians, but they do relegate indigenous people to a place apart from mestizos. Indians only stand out when the heroic struggles of the past give way to the harsh realities of the present. And it is here that marginality becomes the defining feature. "Peasants" sometimes figure as members of a unified multiclass alliance against "anglo-yanqui" imperialism. But references to "Indians" center on oppression or "redemption," not political action. Indians join mestizos and creoles as faceless components of a unified Bolivian pueblo, but indigenous political agency is erased.[36]

As the MNR identified Indians and mestizos—the "people"—as the national essence, it pointed to the oligarchy as the "antinational" core. The country's three biggest tin-mine owners were Bolivians, but the smelting factories they used were located in England and the United States; Simón Patiño, the wealthiest of all, lived abroad and took his profits out of the country. For Bolivian nationalists, the "national" tin industry thus signified foreign enterprise. The MNR manifesto also identified a second antinational power, Jews and "international Judaism," which were described as forces that permeated national boundaries to weaken national culture and consciousness. Drawing on metaphors of debility and disease, the party program viewed both Jews and tin oligarchs as conduits of the "virus that destroys the Nation."[37] When the party launched its tirades against Jews, therefore, it made them a gloss for foreign domination in general. The German-born Jewish mining magnate Mauricio Hochschild became a symbolic bridge for the two forms of antinational behavior, and Hochschild figured centrally in the party's anti-Semitic diatribes.[38] The conflation also emerged forcefully in the MNR's support for immigration restrictions.

Affirmations of mestizaje throughout Latin America coincided with the enactment of racialized limits on immigration.[39] But the peculiar trajectory of Jewish immigration to Bolivia meant that anti-immigrant sentiments were largely anti-Semitic ones, and that anti-Semitism was in turn a key component of mestizaje. As they praised mestizos, nationalist ideologues denigrated Jews. In 1939, when almost every other country in the world had closed its doors, President Busch granted refuge to approximately 10,000 European Jews; by the end of World War II, Bolivia would give asylum to an estimated 20,000 Jewish refugees.[40] Since Bolivia never attracted large numbers of immigrants, Jews also made up a disproportionate share of Bolivia's total foreigners.[41] Busch's remarkable decision —influenced by Hochschild's lobbying and financial contributions—coincided with the regime's programmatic objectives: Busch hoped that immigration would spur domestic agricultural production and mitigate dependence on costly imported foods.[42] Although destined for colonization schemes in Bolivia's underpopulated eastern lowlands, the great majority of the Jewish refugees remained in the cities of La Paz and Cochabamba, where they sought employment in sectors that did not compete with Bolivian enterprise. Nationalist and anti-Semitic groups nevertheless accused them of infiltrating Bolivia's commercial nexus to the detriment of local merchants and consumers, who were plagued by shortages and price hikes. As the number of Jewish immigrants increased, more refugees became unemployed, competed with Bolivians for jobs, or tried to eke out a living as itinerant vendors. Anti-Semitic agitation intensified in this tense context.[43] The fears of foreign domination culminated in proposed laws to curtail Jews' commercial activities and to bar their immigration.[44] Efforts to restrict immigration had commenced with the Busch and Peñaranda governments, but the MNR alone called for specific rules against Jews.

The nationalism of the MNR and Villarroel thus constituted a heterogeneous mix. Rather than calling for the transformation of "Indians" into "mestizos," the MNR program stressed their marginality. With mestizos, Indians could act heroically; on their own, they were a downtrodden group that needed to be uplifted and incorporated into the national economy as able producers and consumers. Guevara Arze's 1938 conviction that Indians constituted Bolivia's indelible majority did not inspire the 1942 manifesto, nor did the MNR's early embrace of mestizaje hinge on the assimilation of Indians. It relied, above all, on their subordination.[45] At the same time, the party's positive reassessment of mestizaje was bound up with anti-Semitism.[46] In many different ways, then, racial hierarchy was ingrained within the MNR vision of national unity. Along with the subordination of Indians, and anti-Semitism, a third essential element of 1940s mestizaje was its regionalist bent. When MNR representatives had the chance to expound their version of history in Bolivia's National Congress, they identified Cochabamba as the "accurate image of Bolivian nationality." They said the region was a privileged one given its position in the center of the national territory, and they declared that it was inhabited by an "energetic, industrious race, [by a race] capable of exploiting this advantaged situation to uplift the nation."[47] The "mestizo" of MNR nationalism was a peculiar regional type.

✳ Reforming the Family

The Villarroel-MNR quest for a unified, mestizo nation not only signified a spiritual struggle; it was also a battle to improve the population's physical condition and its social well-being. And unity did not just mean fortifying the nation's borders via immigration controls. It involved a movement to strengthen the family and motherhood. In the 1920s, nationalist intellectuals mapped visions of health and progress onto the body of the upper-class mother: the future of the nation hinged on the fulfillment of criollo women's maternal duty.[48] Villarroel and the MNR instead made the working-class, mestiza mother an icon of and vehicle for a strong nation. Populist reformers targeted working women in part because they had achieved great organizational strength. Female workers were a potential political constituency the MNR did not want opposition parties to catch. But mestiza mothers also became a symbol of unity and an object of state policy because reformers deemed their "improvement" critical to the nation's social and "racial" advance.

Villarroel considered the struggle for physical and economic progress one of the greatest goals of his December "Revolution." To achieve the spiritual and physical improvement of mothers, children, and workers, the president thus endorsed a range of social welfare programs. His 1944 congressional address called for Regional Minimum Wage Committees to design wage proposals in line with conditions in specific geographic-economic zones.[49] The government also planned to expand the Worker Social Security (Seguro Social Obrero), public housing for workers, aid for victims of the Catavi massacre, and social assistance for children and orphans of the war.[50] To develop the nation's economic potential, finally, Villarroel backed a "plan for the physical and moral rehabilitation of the Bolivian worker" that would "put to use the positive energy of our indigenous and mestizo masses."[51]

Villarroel's social reform plan never truly materialized, for his minister of finance, the MNR leader Víctor Paz Estenssoro, pursued an orthodox economic policy that undermined the regime's overall social program.[52] The president's most noted accomplishments instead resided in the legal realm. Most historians highlight a series of labor laws that built on Busch's impressive but largely unenforced 1939 code. In February 1944 Villarroel approved the Fuero Sindical (special union rights), which protected union leaders from arbitrary dismissal or transfer. His government also provided a yearly bonus (*aguinaldo*) for blue- and white-collar workers.[53] The 1945 family reforms have received less scholarly attention, but they were equally significant changes. And they sparked a much bigger public debate, one that connected anxieties about family, race, and morality with the struggle for progress and nationhood. Congressional delegates, women's groups, lawyers, scholars, and church representatives all weighed in on the disputes. They deemed the laws a moral triumph or a moral threat. In the course of the controversy, the MNR would have to defend its own moral credentials and the decency of hardworking "cholas" and "mestizas."[54]

The debate about how to strengthen families and the nation's racial health was waged in large part at a special legislative convention that

Villarroel convened between August 1944 and August 1945. A strategy to legitimize Villarroel's rule, the Convención Nacional was empowered to "normalize the institutional life of the Nation," "consolidate the ideals of the National Revolution," and "regenerate" the country.[55] The senators and deputies, who were elected expressly for this convention, launched their discussion of a series of divisive reforms with a pitch for female suffrage, which was first proposed—and rejected—at the 1938 convention. The revived debate considered two distinct schemes, one backed by the MNR delegates Hernán Siles Zuazo and Augusto Guzmán and that would give women the vote on the same terms as men, the other that would authorize the vote only for women who completed primary school and in municipal elections exclusively. With the founding of the MNR and the PIR in the early 1940s, and heightened competition for electoral support, women's suffrage took on greater political significance. The MNR nevertheless remained split on the issue; not all members of the party backed Siles's and Guzmán's broad initiative.[56] Following a heated debate—packed with opinions much like those aired by congressional delegates in 1938—the 1945 representatives approved an article that allowed literate women to vote in municipal elections. This measure necessarily brought some working women into the electorate.

Delegates to the 1945 convention also revisited the question of children's equality. Drawing on works by the country's most eminent legal scholars, one group of deputies called for a procedural law to implement the 1938 constitutional reform that had abolished inequality.[57] Some delegates insisted that all children should enjoy not just the same legal status but equal rights to inherit.[58] They endorsed an amendment to the 1938 law that would allow paternity tests to ensure such rights when the father was unknown. Delegates opposed to all of these laws objected for many different reasons, but their arguments centered on immorality (the reforms encouraged "free love") and "abuse" (poor women would trick rich men into providing for their "illegitimate" children).[59] Opponents within and outside of Congress viewed the laws as an assault against class and patriarchal privilege.

Female suffrage and children's equality generated fierce disagreements, but the proposal to legalize *concubinato* (common-law union) triggered an even bigger storm. What caused the commotion? Its proponents explicitly offered social status and material protection to unmarried women. This remarkable measure—one of the first of its kind in Latin America—recognized common-law unions as marriage "after just two years of cohabitation, as demonstrated by the birth of a child or other forms of evidence."[60] Those who endorsed the law argued that it would benefit "the immense majority of Bolivian people [who] live together in cohabitation [concubinato], not only in the mines but also in the countryside." They claimed that it would aid urban workers, artisans, and mineworkers, or the "mestizo class." Many advocates of the law associated concubinato with conditions of exploitation and abuse, and with images of urban women seduced and abandoned by deceitful men. The reform, one such delegate said, would assist these "self-sacrificing, valiant" women, who not only lost rights but also dignity when their partner (*concubino*) deserted them. One passionate supporter backed the law because it would legalize and protect Bolivia's "true" families, and do away with the "feeling of caste" that typified the "existing matrimonial regime."[61] Many advocates viewed the legalization of common-law unions as a patriotic gesture, as something rooted in and suited to national customs.[62]

If some supporters of concubinato and equality-of-children laws championed social equality and national mores, others took inspiration from ideas about heredity and "race." Like their counterparts elsewhere in Latin America, Bolivian intellectuals and politicians believed they could strengthen the nation biologically via public hygiene, pronatalist initiatives, and the reform of family law and inheritance rights. Their convictions drew force from a peculiar brand of eugenics that was shaped by Lamarckian ideals. With the help of science and social work, these reformers assumed, it would be possible to forge stronger families and a "true" nationality from heterogeneous peoples and cultures.[63] Although Bolivia never created eugenics associations like those established in Mexico, Argentina, and Brazil, Bolivian politicians drew encouragement from the science of heredity.[64] They argued that marriage and family reforms would help mold healthy families and a strong race while promoting population growth.[65] In their quest for morality and growth, the Bolivian reformers did not, however, center exclusively on women's maternal functions; nor did they pass laws for intrusive regulatory procedures. Rather than marriage certificates, pregnancy registers, or training in the skills of motherhood, the Busch and Villarroel governments above all favored social entitlements and labor protections. They wrote family subsidies into the Constitution and passed laws to protect women's workplace health.[66] If immigration could not boost the nation's population and propel Bolivia toward a prosperous future, family policy would. And it would do so not only by enhancing women's domestic capabilities but also by protecting mothers at work.

After a fiery debate, the convention approved the concubinato reform, paternity tests, and family subsidies. The vote was precariously close, with 43 in favor and 41 opposed, and it provoked a swift public protest.[67] When the convention announced its decision, representatives of women's groups and the church launched a campaign for repeal. A 16 August rally opposite the Government Palace reportedly drew a crowd of "women of all social classes." The sponsors implored the convention to modify the equality-of-children clause so only legitimate and recognized natural children—but not "illegitimate" ones—would possess equal inheritance rights; "illegitimate" children who could prove they were related to the father would have the right to food, but they would not have the right to inherit. The protesters also pressed the deputies to cancel the concubinato article.[68] Elite women's groups around the country pledged their loyalty to the cause. Ladies from Oruro, Potosí, and Tarija expressed solidarity by sending letters and telegrams to the Cochabamba daily *El País*.[69] In La Paz, opposition parties and women's organizations circulated anonymous pamphlets and fliers condemning the concubinato law.[70]

In response to these attacks, the MNR party paper, *La Calle*, enthusiastically endorsed the concubinato law as a means to achieve both morality and equality. A 16 August article called the reform the best means for encouraging marriage and eliminating concubinato over the long run. It also viewed the law as a triumph for social justice, since it conferred dignity and status on the *concubinas*.[71] Mocking the "aristocratic ladies" who demonstrated against the law, this sarcastic piece asserted that the women could not "swallow" the site of "concubines" elevated to the status of "señoras." A second *La Calle* article, published after the Catholic women's rally, clarified the party's position. Rather than promoting cohabitation, the article explained, the law imposed marriage on couples who had lived together for two years. It ended with words of counsel to the "most cherished and noble ladies": "You have not thought about the majority of defenseless Bolivian women [and] about the thousands of cholas who want to be married. . . . You are not defending the common woman [*la mujer del pueblo*]; you are acting with prejudice to maintain a privilege of caste, or better said, the privileges of the rich."[72] Just like the conservative groups that opposed the law, the MNR thus deemed itself the best defender of the virtue and status of the "mujer del pueblo." As the party critiqued elites for refusing to share the status of "decent people" with the masses, it also aimed to attract the political support of working women, who were hailed as moral, marriage-seeking "cholas."

In their attempts to uplift the family and the national "race," Villarroel and the MNR stressed women's productive labor rather than focusing exclusively on their reproductive duties. Their arguments relied on a specific image of the working woman or chola, which diverged somewhat from the well-known figure of pre-revolutionary literature. Bolivia's celebrated mestiza novels of the 1940s evince elite men's dual sensibility about the urban, working-class woman: they vacillated between eroticized fascination and fear that they would be emasculated or "cholified" (*encholado*).[73] For the nationalist ideologues who penned these works, the nation's emblematic mestiza mother was an educated and acculturated woman who rejected the coarse, overly sexualized culture of working-class "cholas" and who embodied the antithesis of all "disorderly" women.[74]

Such political debates as the concubinato dispute and the battle over women's suffrage reveal that Villarroel and the MNR embraced a distinct strand of revolutionary nationalist mestizaje. As they competed with opposition parties for the support of urban workers, MNR politicians brandished images of hardworking, decent "cholas," who would be their loyal patrons. In doing so, they made women's work compatible with morality and strong families. Yet their valorization of the chola was bound up with anxieties about the "masculinization" of elite women as expressed, for example, in the debates over female suffrage.[75] "Cholas," not wives or daughters of their own class, were the women who should work. To justify the political association with working-class women, MNR politicians had to stress those women's moral standing and show that their family reforms would enhance that sense of decency. Endowed with the status of marriage —safe as a señora—mestiza or chola concubinas would no longer pose a threat to morality or male power.

✳ Honoring the Mestizas

Villarroel stayed close to the Government Palace after taking power. Besieged by domestic and international opposition, the still-provisional president desperately sought to consolidate his precarious rule. Only after five months had passed did Villarroel venture away from the capital. Not by accident, his first trip out took him to the 1944 Mother's Day procession in Cochabamba. This apparently innocuous event had immense political significance, for Mother's Day not only honored the mother. It commemorated the mestiza market women—*heroínas*—who had fought and died in Bolivia's most remembered battle of the wars for independence, the 1812 confrontation between Cochabamba market women and royalist forces on a hill called the Coronilla. Thanks to Villarroel's support, a small regional tribute to the heroínas became Mother's Day, one of Bolivia's most important and broadly publicized national festivals.[76]

Just as Villarroel and the MNR tried to cultivate urban support via social and economic reforms, so did the regime look to popular culture and civic ritual as arenas where it could broaden its social base while espousing a vision of national harmony. With the nationalization of the local Heroínas Day celebration, Villarroel staged a myth of cultural, political, and economic integration. His patriotic performance took inspiration from a familiar account: Nataniel Aguirre's 1885 novel, *Juan de la Rosa*, which located the nation's historical origins in Cochabamba's mestiza heroism. Virtually ignored in the nineteenth century, the market women of independence war lore became a formative figure of Bolivian political culture in the 1940s. But Villarroel's civic holiday did more than simply honor mestiza patriots or the Cochabamba region: it made mestiza market women—who were vilified in the media and discriminated against on the street—emblems of the nation, thus redeeming them.

The Heroínas Day festival exemplifies the attempt by Villarroel and the MNR to cultivate unity by heightening peoples' affinity with national icons and rituals. For just as the regime promoted this and other national celebrations, it placed limits on the multitudinous rites practiced by communities, cities, and regions. Reviving an unenforced 1903 edict, the 1945 Congress approved a law that eliminated state support for all local festivals and made Independence Day (6 August) Bolivia's sole national holiday.[77] Ironically, Heroínas Day escaped the prohibition, perhaps because the regime already viewed Cochabamba's independence war lore as a story of national glory. A pro-government paper commenting on the event certainly conflated region and nation: it called the Cochabamba women's battle the sign of a united Bolivia. Since the women had been "free from all regionalist prejudice," their heroism was "the purest and most sincere nationalist ideal."[78] As a tribute to the mother, this commemorative occasion hid its local roots in images of patriotic female sacrifice. Heroínas Day was the only regional celebration that Villarroel designated a national holiday. Authorities obliged all market women, teachers, and schoolchildren in Cochabamba to attend the extravagant ritual. Residents of other cities were exhorted to tune in to the festivities on the airwaves.

Only under the auspices of Villarroel and the MNR did Bolivians forge a deep and fundamental connection between Cochabamba market women, Mother's Day, and the nation. Local rituals to commemorate the heroínas may have commenced as early as the first decades of the nineteenth century. And they certainly expanded following the 1912 centennial celebration. These later commemorations subtly linked the 27 May heroines of San Sebastián with the mother. One year after a bronze monument of the heroínas was inaugurated on the Coronilla, the Bolivian government decreed an explicit commemoration of Mother's Day. Yet the 1927 law that made 27 May a day to honor mothers in all schools did not mention the heroínas. Only in 1944 did Villarroel's populist regime declare a national holiday to venerate the mother "on a par with" the heroínas.[79] The class dynamics of the event also changed considerably during the era of military socialism. In the 1920s, elite patriotic associations convened the ceremony: images, articles, and rituals of the era portrayed the heroínas as writers, as agents of an illustrious culture without connections to urban workers or artisans.[80] In the 1940s, a mutual aid society of market vendors dubbed the Hijas del Pueblo (a local synonym for *cholitas*) instead took charge.[81] One highlight of the 1944 celebration was the "coronation" of the queen of the Hijas del Pueblo at a *verbena popular* (popular soirée) in the working-class neighborhood Cara-Cota (near the Alejo Calatayud Plaza and market).[82] In the 1920s, the president crowned the feminist poet Adela Zamudio at a ceremony in the Cochabamba social club; two decades later workers and artisans made a market vendor the queen.

The 1940s coronation of the mestiza vendor neatly symbolized the recent rise to prominence of the Hijas del Pueblo. Established in 1923 by sellers in Cochabamba's 25 de Mayo Market, the Hijas del Pueblo was formed in response to a proposed municipal ordinance to raise the price of stalls in the Central Market or evict sellers altogether. The women's initial effort to organize produced a great uproar that resulted in the arrest of several vendors.[83] With Toro's 1936 obligatory unionization decree, Cochabamba market women formed the Sindicato de Comerciantes Minoristas (vendors union), but the Hijas del Pueblo did not join. Instead the group forged close ties to Catholic Action, which played a prominent role among

Cochabamba vendors and domestic workers and made important inroads into the Hijas' leadership.[84] During General Peñaranda's government, the Hijas del Pueblo continued to hold close ties with the church and the military, eschewing any formal links with organized labor. Not just the market chief but also the head of Cochabamba's Military Regiment No. 7 attended the Hijas' inaugural meeting when the group was reestablished in 1941.[85] By the time Villarroel took power, the Hijas del Pueblo had already gained widespread support: the association boasted 600 members among the city's "popular classes."[86]

Although the Hijas called on vendors in all markets to join the association, the organization took deepest roots in the city's most modern venues, the 27 de Mayo and 25 de Mayo markets, where high-status vendors and consumers congregated.[87] Reputedly styled by French designers, the 25 de Mayo Market boasted decorative ironwork, marble tables for meat sales, and vendors in well-pressed uniforms.[88] Merchants there were prohibited from selling with their children, a customary practice in the less prestigious "sectional" markets (see figure 13).[89] *Arroceras* (grain sellers), who occupied the second-highest position in the market (just behind the meat sellers, *carniceras*), prevailed in the Hijas' leadership. Intermediary groups, such as sellers of fruit or vegetables, also joined. Ambulant vendors and women who "sold from the ground" possessed the lowest rank in the market, and it is doubtful that they belonged to or were offered protection by the Hijas del Pueblo. Not just products but patrons determined a vendor's status: after a process of reciprocal scrutiny and negotiation, *caseros* (regulars) exchanged loyalty for preferred prices and goods. The market, in short, was a privileged site of social interchange; not just money reigned but commercial exchange based on affective bonds between consumers and sellers.[90] In the 1930s and 1940s, struggles over prices and shortages of basic goods made the market a focal point of state regulation.

Of the many organizations forged by working women after the Chaco War, the Hijas del Pueblo offered a particularly suitable image for the Villarroel regime. Members of the Hijas most likely engaged in contests with the market police, especially once municipal authorities began to exert greater control in the marketplace. But the organization did not publicly confront the authorities via petitions or rallies. Instead it seemed to support the market chief's efforts to impose order, hygiene, and price controls. Nor did the Hijas participate in national labor conventions, as La Paz women's unions did. The Hijas del Pueblo openly claimed a civic, apolitical

13 A market in the city of Cochabamba, 1943. *Courtesy of the Julien Bryan Film Archive.*

status, while providing mutual aid to its members and charitable service to the community. Members of the organization participated actively in civic rituals, wearing a special uniform—blue *polleras* (layered skirts)—that was adopted solely for such appearances. Since the Hijas del Pueblo maintained close relations with the army, Villarroel's well-publicized support for the organization not only underscored the regime's defense of urban workers but also the political importance of the military. And because the Hijas del Pueblo publicly identified with a church that guarded conservative social views, the celebration allowed Villarroel to exhibit allegiance to religion, morality, and family, just as his opponents were decrying the regime's "immoral" defense of concubinato.

Beyond these tactical considerations, the Hijas' Heroínas Day parade had deep ideological significance. While appealing to female vendors for political support, the Villarroel regime also sought to realize a particular vision of national unity that celebrated the mestizas' independence-war glory. Villarroel took the mestiza market women's 1812 defense of the patria as the inspiration for a "new Bolivia." As an ideal image, the mestizas bridged private and public spheres, for they stood simultaneously as mothers of a healthy "race," custodians of an abundant market, and brave patriots who died defending national independence and honor. For Villarroel, the marketplace was itself ripe symbolic terrain, signifying all that the government sought to offer: abundance, welfare, integration. This message had utmost importance as waves of rural strikes threatened to interrupt harvests, block the transport of agricultural goods, and destabilize prices—problems that were often blamed on female merchants and that could potentially topple the precarious regime.[91]

The principal moments of the Villarroel-era Heroínas Day celebration indeed focused special attention on the market women grouped in the Hijas del Pueblo. The centerpiece of the celebration was the *romería* (pilgrimage) to the Coronilla, the historic hill where the heroínas confronted Spanish forces in 1812. Sandwiched between a flag-swearing ceremony for military cadets at Bolívar's monument and a lunch for the officers based at Cochabamba's post-graduate military school, the romería filled a two-and-a-half-hour slot on the morning of 27 May that culminated in a ten o'clock mass for the Virgen de las Mercedes.[92] The Hijas del Pueblo carried the image of the Virgin from the cathedral to the top of the Coronilla, which was bedecked by Villarroel and his wife; several top-ranking government officials, including the minister of defense and the minister of education; and two local authorities, the prefect and mayor.[93] By order of the mayor's office, all public markets were closed.[94]

In addition to the mayor of Cochabamba and the commander of Military Regiment No. 7, the founding president of the Hijas del Pueblo, Teodosia Sanzetenea de Terrazas, delivered a speech on the Coronilla that 27 May.[95] Directing herself to "His Excellency, the President of the Republic," Sanzetenea declared that the light of the Virgen de las Mercedes had guided Cochabamba's "humble Women of the Market" in "ardent love" and defense of the "Patria and its liberty."[96] With this speech—probably crafted by a lawyer—the Hijas del Pueblo projected a palatable image of national loyalty. Sanzetenea's words were not just stock, patriotic refrains, however; instead they point to the market women's own investment in this historic moment. In its 1941 founding statement, the Hijas vowed to "solemnize every year the heroic deed of 27 May 1812, as they [were] direct heirs."[97] For Cochabamba's 14 September celebration, the women not only marched but also organized a float that authenticated the 1812 battle.[98] Pride in the heroínas was hardly limited to the Hijas del Pueblo. When a shoemaker mocked the heroínas battle at a 1944 party in a Cochabamba *chichería* (chicha tavern), the women gathered there "started hitting and scratching him."[99]

If the Hijas del Pueblo occupied a prominent place in the Villarroel-era program, the military almost overshadowed the women. Military cadets and members of the "women's auxiliary service" lined up to greet the president's arriving plane and led several processions together with the police and the army over the course of the three-day affair.[100] The army also sponsored its own cultural events, including a literary contest for the mother and a performance of the musical "La Coronilla." Certainly these activities not only bolstered the image of the heroínas, but also the military's own role in society. Indeed, Villarroel paid tribute with this holiday to one of his most important allies within the army, Cochabamba's Regiment No. 7, whose patron saint was the same one the market women had carried into battle that fateful day: the Virgen de las Mercedes, "Imagen Sagrada Guerra y Patrona de las Armas de Bolivia" (sacred war image and patron saint of the Bolivian armed forces).[101]

Heroínas Day, finally, was very much the president's performance. The prefect, the mayor, and "outstanding elements of . . . society" paid tribute to Villarroel with a banquet at Cochabamba's Social Club. The president in turn honored all of the Cochabamba valley provinces with a visit, "to understand the needs of each one." On the way, he broke ground for several public works projects: a workers' housing development, a stadium, a slaughterhouse, an equestrian club, and the much-touted Cochabamba–Santa Cruz highway, which was viewed as a crucial step toward progress and unity since it would join two major agricultural regions for the first time ever. No less important, Villarroel showed that he too was a man of respect and sentiment by making a visit to his own mother.[102]

As the president, the market women, schoolchildren, teachers, and the military participated in these many commemorative acts, Cochabamba's leading newspapers made their own nationalistic tribute to the heroínas. Some articles focused narrowly on the intimate link between motherhood and the patria.[103] Other articles, which were published in the MNR's *La Calle*, directly connected the heroínas with nationalist ideals, mestizaje, and the strength of the Bolivian "race." One such piece deemed the heroic women the ancestors of "our mothers," said that their "exemplary legacy lived on in the spirit of the nation," and called Bolivian women "ideal mothers," the "bulwark on which the progress of our race is based." Reaffirming these glorious traditions would help "the people" resist the influence of "strange and antinational ideologies."[104] Although *La Calle*'s tribute to motherly sacrifice lauded both the "madre india" and the "madre chola," it placed special emphasis on the chola, who it exalted as the mother of the "mestizo people" because she was "aggressive, egalitarian and passionate." These laudatory remarks were a far cry from the anti-india and anti-chola tirades that accompanied the inauguration of the 1926 monument for the heroínas.[105] Although distinct interpretations continued to circulate, the MNR now clearly linked the heroínas with positive appraisals of mestizaje.[106]

That Bolivia's commemoration of Mother's Day linked maternal sentiments with nationalism and racial "improvement" was not at all unusual. Mother's Day celebrations around the world were shaped by local and national political interests, ranging from disputes over female suffrage to the agendas of the flower industry. They also took root in the cult of the mother that emerged in the early twentieth century hand in hand with child welfare schemes, plans to improve domestic hygiene, and pronatalist agendas that stressed women's "duty and destiny . . . to be the 'mothers of the race.'"[107] In line with these international trends, Peñaranda's Ministry of Health and Social Welfare used Mother's Day to award prizes to impoverished but "moral" mothers with four or more children.[108] Loosely, Villarroel and the MNR also linked Mother's Day with the birthrate: it was to resolve a perceived crisis of depopulation and "illegitimacy" that the president endorsed the 1945 family laws.

As we have seen, however, Villarroel-MNR support for Mother's Day did not focus solely on population or maternal duty. For the revolutionary nationalists, Mother's Day as Heroínas Day above all signified anticolonial struggle, a struggle the nation must begin anew. In a message "to the Mothers of Bolivia" that appeared in several national newspapers, the president stated, "bowing with devotion before [all the mothers of Bolivia], I ask them to make the example of the Coronilla the reality of the new Bolivia."[109] In another speech he referred to the heroínas as women who fought "with sacrifice, abnegation, and valor for political and economic independence . . . [and] a new era of progress."[110]

For all the government's attempts to fix the meaning, the Mother's Day procession also spoke for itself. And at the level of the spectacle, the market women not only played anticolonial mothers who championed the nation's mestizo origins and its political and economic advance: they occupied center stage. In the 1920s, elite patriotic associations took the leading role in the heroínas festivities.[111] During the Villarroel era, market women reclaimed the celebration from the ladies of high society. And as they took up the historical narrative first publicized by Cochabamba's regional oligarchy, the market women grouped in the Hijas del Pueblo substituted protagonists. They claimed to be the true descendents of the heroínas; in turn their performance affirmed Cochabamba's and the nation's mestizo origins. Moreover, the Hijas' version, which gave the name heroínas to the "humble Women of the Market," succeeded in being that most broadly publicized by the regime.[112] During the Villarroel presidency, the Cochabamba celebration was broadcast by radio to reach homes throughout the republic.[113] The parade might also be viewed as an official reading of Aguirre's novel, since its promulgation coincided with the incorporation of *Juan de la Rosa* into the secondary-school curriculum. In a 1943 congressional session commemorating the centennial of Aguirre's birth, one MNR deputy applauded the statesman for rejecting foreign influences and defending Bolivian independence, for putting faith in the masses and extolling "the virtues of the mestizo."[114]

In the end, the populist regime took the Hijas' rendition of the 1812 battle for its own legitimizing myth, as evidence of its alliance with the people. Yet even if the populist state swallowed up popular culture, the holiday was also a chance for Cochabamba market women to reconstitute their own traditions—and the networks of power on which they were based.[115] As recent studies have shown, public rituals like the heroínas march are terrains of negotiation. If they are a means by which the state constitutes subjectivities, they are also a place where local groups gain access to and appropriate government institutions.[116] With social policies and family reforms, Villarroel and the MNR cast a wide net, but the regime's cultural politics ultimately privileged women from one region. Every mother might receive benefits, but the Cochabamba market women stood above them as symbols of the nation's traditions and its mestizo essence.

✳ Controlling the Market Women

Along with healthy families, robust mothers, and a collective "mestizo" spirit, Villarroel and the MNR deemed well-provisioned markets critical for national strength, security, and sovereignty. The MNR's 1942 manifesto decried a railroad system designed for foreign trade, bemoaned the decline of agricultural production, and denounced the escalating cost of living. When Villarroel and the MNR took power, they vowed to develop the internal market and control the prices of basic goods in order to ensure sustenance for the nation's "middle classes." But social peace and progress not only depended on the development of the market. They required control of the very vendors Villarroel and the MNR tried to incorporate into a populist political pact via progressive social reforms. Some vendors—such as those grouped in the Hijas del Pueblo—adroitly managed the state's intrusions and even benefited from them via negotiations with municipal authorities. However, most vendors suffered mistreatment by more vigilant officials, and they resisted the new controls. Rather than achieving harmony, Villarroel's populist policies ultimately deepened divisions within the urban body politic.

The Villarroel regime was not the first to intrude in the marketplace. Efforts to regulate markets had already commenced in the 1920s, when elites sought to modernize urban space and improve public hygiene with laws that prohibited ambulant vending and required merchants to register with the city.[117] After the Chaco War, marketplace conflicts intensified as inflation mounted and prices of basic goods skyrocketed. Unlike Toro and Busch, Villarroel and the MNR managed to bring into check the dramatic cost of living via price control and monetary stabilization policies that helped secure middle-class support.[118] But these policies did not always curb costs. Instead the campaign to ease consumption engendered everyday conflicts over prices and marketplace order. And these conflicts besieged a specific agent: merchants and vendors.

To end speculation and instill order in the nation's markets, the Villarroel regime created new rules and policing mechanisms with powerful implications for local trade. In June 1945 the Cochabamba mayor established a special municipal police force to regulate commerce and industry.[119] A string of news articles attests to the new officials' watchfulness: dozens of vendors were fined, arrested, or evicted by the police for charging inflated prices.[120] Newspapers published their names to enhance the shame. Cochabamba's *jefe de mercados* (director of markets), Guillermo Aldunate, ordered his personnel to impose sanctions with the "greatest energy," but the market chief himself became the fiercest enforcer of rules.[121] Aldunate personally confiscated exorbitantly priced goods, and then gained the public's sympathy by distributing liberated products to charities or selling them at reduced prices. Furtive peaches, hens, eggs, and other choice goods reached exasperated consumers by these means.[122] Even the mayor intervened directly in the war on prices. In June 1945 he toured the 25 de Mayo and Calatayud Markets accompanied by the entire corps of the newly created Market Police, personally seeing that vendors—despite continuing protests—complied with orders to reduce prices by a full 40 percent.[123] To prevent conflicts between vendors and facilitate police intervention, market stalls were clearly delimited with lines and numbers.[124] The city also banned ambulant sales, with "severe sanctions" for the violators.[125]

For all the intensity of the crackdown, the struggle to end hoarding, speculation, and unregulated sales was an uphill battle for municipal authorities, who faced complaints from recalcitrant vendors and consumers alike. To evade controls, sellers engaged in everyday forms of resistance. One news report noted that obligatory price signs had "disappeared" from the fruit stands.[126] When the signs vanished, municipal authorities turned to loudspeakers, with officials blaring prices to the public.[127] And when it was clear that these would not deter price hikes, either, the director of markets instituted an elaborate system of punishment. Following a period of complete suspension from vending, market women caught speculating would be allowed to sell in outlying markets. Only after "purg[ing] their sins" in these less desirable sites could they gain reentry to the Central Market. As for recidivists, permanent relegation to the sectional markets would be their fate.[128] In July 1946, Aldunate expelled vendors selling in an underground market filled with garbage and infectious flies near the Plaza Calatayud.[129] Just a few months later the press once again denounced unhygienic conditions, deficient sewers, exorbitant prices, missing scales, and the resurgence of covert markets.[130] Municipal authorities could not succeed. The protracted war on prices was hardly confined to Cochabamba. Market women in La Paz faced the same onslaught, and they responded to the attacks with a renewed process of organization nurtured by the anarchist FOL.[131]

As journalists and other analysts groped for explanations, they generally blamed the unruly market vendors for the deepening crisis. In doing so, these wary observers drew on and perpetuated negative stereotypes of female sellers. Many news articles depicted market women not only as treacherous negotiators who evaded municipal regulations, but as "dirty, thieving, grouchy mujeres del pueblo [plebeian women]" who did whatever they pleased. One piece stressed the "terror" they instilled in housewives with their "insolence," "arbitrary behavior," and shameless speculation.[132] Another depicted sellers scolding customers who complained about irregularities.[133] Apparently the vendors even intimidated the police.[134] Local police stations and courts, finally, heard a glut of disputes over marketplace turf that erupted in verbal slurs between market women and sometimes even in physical violence.[135]

Just as they blamed the market women, the journalists also held wealthy buyers responsible for the shortages and marketplace strife. They claimed that these well-to-do patrons voluntarily paid prices above fixed rates to monopolize goods for their own businesses. The damaging descriptions of merchants and consumers often paired female vendors—mujeres del pueblo—with "Jewish" merchants, who robbed the people and thought nothing of municipal fines.[136] The images of Jews depicted them as "money-grubbers" who controlled the press, the banks, and politics.[137] The stereotypes of female vendors instead highlighted grime, vulgarity, grouchiness, and erratic behavior. But the derogatory labels overlapped significantly, as they equated "cholas" with rich and power-hungry "Jews" bent on ruling the marketplace.

By making price controls and monetary stabilization a high priority, Villarroel and the MNR managed to control inflation.[138] Yet their campaign had clear costs: the reduction of prices was only achieved via continuous combat between authorities, consumers, and vendors. Conflict, vigilance, evasion, and violence enveloped the marketplace during the tumultuous Villarroel years. And the violence was both physical and symbolic, involving fines, arrests, evictions, and insults. Wealthy consumers were sometimes attacked, but female vendors bore the brunt of the aggression. In La Paz, municipal campaigns against sellers were coupled with widespread discrimination against plebeian women, at work and in everyday life.[139] The regime's quest for support exacerbated these quotidian dynamics by making vendors the target of authorities' and the people's scrutiny. If market women potentially benefited from the regime's social policies, they were also its victims.

✳ Conclusion

Even as mestizaje became a compelling idiom of national unity for reformist and revolutionary intellectuals of the post–Chaco War era, so did it remain for them a volatile, contested site of racial, cultural, and national meanings. The MNR's programmatic declarations located the essence of a national culture and consciousness in the independence-war heroism of Creoles and mestizos. The party's public rituals associated that national essence with mestizas even more directly. But Villarroel and the MNR commemorated a very specific image of the mestiza, the patriotic ones from Cochabamba, whose descendents—the Hijas del Pueblo—publicly sided with the church, the state, and the military. Interventions by MNR politicians in debates over social policy in turn imbued *mestizas* and *cholas* with ideals of productivity and decency.

Villarroel populism used social reforms and civic ritual not only to forge national symbols and loyalties, but to cultivate political support. For all its efforts to gain the backing of market women and other urban workers and middle sectors, the regime nevertheless failed to establish a solid political base. In La Paz, workers, students, and women would join oligarchic men in a multiclass front to oust the Villarroel regime (see chapter 8). Even in Cochabamba, where the heroínas festival was rooted, the labor movement remained largely opposed to Villarroel. Workers, artisans, and market women in both Cochabamba and La Paz figured centrally in the July 1946 uprising against the government.[140]

By the early 1940s, Bolivian populists had embraced mestizaje, and their ideals were clearly centered on mestizos/as. But the populist discourses that valorized mestizos or mestizas did not erase Indians; instead the rhetoric inscribed Indians with a subordinate status. Just what did the revolutionary nationalists then mean by *mestizo*? Their self-perceptions are telling. When it came to situating themselves within an imagined mestizo unity, some vacillated and settled on a fissured national subject: if they were "mestizo-whites," the Indians they sought to incorporate were—or would be—"mestizo-Indians." Although the populist regime valorized urban mestizo sectors, it was also forced to seek other allies. As we will see, Villarroel and the MNR reluctantly turned their attention to the nation's rural hinterland. Faced with forceful currents of indigenous mobilization and the pressing need to control the countryside, MNR revolutionaries would also put more stake in bifurcated visions of the nation.

CHAPTER SEVEN

"THE DISGRACE OF THE PONGO AND THE MITANI"

The 1945 Indigenous Congress and a Law against Servitude

"When you return to your land, *principales* and *caciques* . . . I entrust you to watch over everyone's work and ensure the peace, and I make you my representatives in this task."[1] Thus declared President Gualberto Villarroel on 10 May 1945, as he welcomed the delegates to Bolivia's first national Indigenous Congress. Approximately 1,500 representatives gathered in a makeshift auditorium near the Government Palace for the five-day meeting. They hailed from large estates and communities of virtually every region of Bolivia. With this unprecedented encounter, the Villarroel-MNR regime sought to harmonize rural labor relations and develop the nation's agricultural potential. The government also aimed to institutionalize power in the hands of the state and create a legal order in the countryside. In the end, Villarroel instead bestowed the law directly to the hands of local indigenous leaders: the president not only called caciques and principales of haciendas, communities, and ayllus his representatives; he entrusted them to keep order and peace. Rather than resolving a perceived crisis of the law, the Indigenous Congress exacerbated the turmoil by empowering the delegates to be agents of the law.

There is much irony in Villarroel's act. Given the populist regime's fundamental interest in forging national unity, why would its leader so wholeheartedly back an indigenous congress and even affirm indigenous authorities' local power? The 1945 Indigenous Congress draws attention to the ambivalent but integral connections between the 1940s revolutionary-populist project and a deep history of indigenous mobilization. Dominant images of the MNR associate the party with an assimilationist program rooted in Hispanicization, private not communal property, and mestizo (or campesino), not Indian, identity. As we have just seen, Villarroel and the MNR certainly privileged "mestizos" as symbols of national unity and strength. The government also viewed assimilation or "incorporation" as a central strategy for establishing a "culture of legality" that would integrate indigenous peoples into state institutions and the national economy.[2] But the MNR program was more flexible than commonly perceived. In these early years, some nationalist leaders considered differentiating the rights of Indians and non-Indians a viable means to create a modern legal order.

Tensions between assimilationist and anti-assimilationist conceptions of the nation ultimately typified the populist project articulated under the short-lived Villarroel-MNR regime. And as social mobilization intensified in the early 1940s, prominent populist politicians concluded that the incorporation of Indians was an impossible or even dangerous goal. The disputes over indigenous rights and guarantees that marked legislative debates of the 1920s thus continued to be a central locus of Bolivian political culture in the decade after the Chaco War. Such contests over rights and guarantees were not restricted to elite interlocutors but had to contend with interventions by Indian and peasant leaders, in word and action. The following discussion of the 1945 Indigenous Congress traces struggles to define the meanings of Villarroel's decrees against pongueaje and other forms of servitude. Dialogues about the law were the terrain where tentative alliances could be forged between indigenous leaders and populist politicians. They were also the place where those alliances would unravel.

✳ Villarroel, the MNR, and Indigenista Congresses

Bolivia's national Indigenous Congress was an extraordinary undertaking in the broader Latin American context. Reform governments in Guatemala and Ecuador convened constitutional assemblies in 1945 that adopted legal changes much like those approved at Bolivia's 1938 convention. Mexico and

Peru in turn convened indigenista congresses in the early 1940s. But no specifically indigenous congress took place on a national scale anywhere else in Latin America during this period. How did rural activists manage to organize a national assembly across Bolivia's vast geographic and linguistic divides? And why did they mobilize, specifically, for a congress?

The 1945 event undoubtedly drew inspiration from the Inter-American Indigenista Congresses. With the first such interregional congress in Patzcuaro in 1940, Mexico's Instituto Indigenista Interamericano (Inter-American Indigenista Institute) launched a continental quest to incorporate "the Indian."[3] Although some of Bolivia's official representatives to Patzcuaro raised subtle questions about this goal, and about the proper—or even possible—balance between unity and diversity, the delegation wholeheartedly endorsed the enterprise for inter-American cooperation, knowledge, and solutions to the so-called Indian question. Bolivian scholars and politicians also identified with a central aim of the institute's research program: the search for a common definition of "the Indian."[4] Indeed the committee on international relations of Villarroel's 1944 legislature declared that Bolivia would receive the most benefits from the institute's initiatives, because "the true laboratory for understanding the social experiences of [the Indian] is our nation." Indigenismo in Bolivia, the committee stressed, was inspired by a "generous impulse," but it had not produced any data. "We don't even know how many [Indian] communities still exist in the Republic."[5] With the convocation of its own indigenous congress in May 1945, Bolivia finally determined to create an affiliate of the Inter-American Indigenista Institute.[6] In a most general sense, then, the inter-American meeting motivated the Villarroel-MNR concern to create a nationally unified and internationally coordinated policy on the "Indian question."

The 1945 Indigenous Congress nevertheless differed sharply from the inter-American events in one fundamental respect: the main impetus behind the Bolivian assembly was not the state but forceful indigenous movements. Opposition parties even accused the Villarroel regime of convening the congress "out of fear."[7] In part, the remarkable organizational process that culminated in the 1945 congress was facilitated by the contacts hacienda colonos had forged with urban labor leaders and lawyers in the years just after the Chaco War. The movements of the 1940s also drew some impetus from the social and organizational networks that had been established by the caciques apoderados in the decades before the war, for although the apoderados were weakened after the conflict with Paraguay, the connections formed among far-flung leaders did not dissolve so easily. The caciques remained active in the 1940s, and they offered lodging, and probably also counsel, to Indigenous Congress delegates.[8] Efforts to arrange the 1945 event benefited from these preexisting organizational ties.

Bolivia's first *national* Indigenous Congress also took impetus from the regional assemblies that preceded it. As previous chapters have shown, regional indigenous congresses were already an established feature of Bolivia's political landscape before Villarroel took power. The idea for a national indigenous congress surfaced during one of these earlier encounters.[9] We should also consider the possible links between the Indigenous Congress, the 1938 constitutional convention, and the Inter-American Indigenista Congress originally scheduled for 1939 in La Paz. Not a few of the delegates to the 1938 convention contributed to the preliminary program for the (cancelled) 1939 event, and that program revived controversial questions left unresolved by the 1938 assembly, such as land reform and the revisita. One such delegate, the young socialist Félix Eguino Zaballa, would serve on the official organizing committee for the 1945 congress. Villarroel and many future MNR party members appeared in the preliminary program for the 1939 event. If the 1945 Indigenous Congress built on earlier indigenous congresses, it also evolved in dialogue with these official legislative forums.

Finally, the Villarroel-MNR regime itself played an important role in the 1945 congress. For although the government's participation was compelled by the pressures of rural mobilization, once committed, the regime used the event to promote its own reform program, attract new political allies, and counter inroads in the countryside made by the leftist opposition. Indeed the Indigenous Congress is forceful evidence of political ties that Villarroel and the MNR sought to forge with rural communities in the 1940s. Of the three antioligarchic parties that were established after the Chaco War, the MNR was the least indigenista. The party's most closely targeted supporters were mineworkers, urban labor, and the middle class; its manifesto made no explicit call to mobilize Indians. "Peasants" were sometimes mentioned as members of a unified multiclass alliance against imperialism. But declarations about "Indians" centered on oppression or "redemption," not political action. The party's views on the early 1940s indigenous congresses discussed in chapter 5 are equally revealing. The MNR did not back the Quechua assemblies of 1942 and 1943, but its paper, *La Calle,* expressed sympathy for a proposed congress of the Quechua, the

Aymara, and the Guaraní.[10] These three groups, the newspaper argued, should be seen as one entity, because their common interests outweighed cultural and linguistic difference. At the same time, the paper questioned "up to what point it was advisable . . . for the *indios* . . . to go to the extreme of holding congresses, and whether such assemblies were beneficial to the country and the indios."[11] *La Calle*'s stress on the shared experience of linguistic groups dovetailed with the continental quest to define and fix the meaning of "Indian." Its articles also unveil the MNR's fundamental ambivalence about indigenous political participation.

In large part, the Villarroel-MNR regime backed the 1945 Indigenous Congress because it deemed the event vital to its effort to forge a more prosperous and unified nation. As for indigenistas in Mexico and Peru, Villarroel considered education and the modernization of agriculture crucial state projects. Social well-being and the creation of a legal order were equally central goals. One fundamental objective of the 1945 congress was to promote a broader program for rural development.[12] If any objective was paramount, it was to extend the state to a rural hinterland that was viewed as stateless. And in many respects, the countryside was just that. A legal structure—a primary "effect" of the state—did not exist as an abstract formal arrangement in Bolivia's pre-revolutionary countryside; in the hinterland, there was not the slightest illusion that the law existed above social practice, that it stood separately from society as part of the state.[13]

Of Villarroel's many projects, one of the most important was to impose the law on presumably a lawless countryside. An oft-repeated symptom of unrule in early-twentieth-century Bolivia was the fact that landlords controlled the courts. As one congressional deputy put it: "In Bolivia, the *gamonales* [landlords] are stronger than the law."[14] Yet Villarroel's remedy of choice was not so much institutions (courts) or even agents (judges), but the law itself. Rather than violently transforming institutions, the president announced in a 1944 speech, the key goal of his revolution was to give "juridical form to a constant and gradual transformation of the state, to grant the state more vigor, efficiency, and technical capacity for its many activities."[15] Villarroel evidently considered the law the most powerful force in society; he put great stake in his own decrees and insisted they would last even if he himself were killed.[16]

In agreeing to convene the 1945 Indigenous Congress, Villarroel and the MNR clearly worried about regulation and control. Yet the mix of alliance and ambivalence that characterized MNR-Indian relations in the pre-revolutionary era militated toward the opposite. The president not only encouraged rural leaders' longstanding requests to authorize their own schools, but endorsed the expansion of the Oficina Jurídica de Defensa Gratuita de Indígenas (Office of Free Legal Assistance for Indígenas) that was first established in 1943. Designed to bring independent action under state management, the juridical office actually enhanced contact among rural and urban activists, and heightened opportunities for organizing across regions. Lawyers affiliated with the institution even endorsed some of the key demands advanced by rural leaders. A preliminary program for the Indigenous Congress prepared by two such attorneys argued that the overarching goal should be to incorporate Indians into the national economy and polity. To achieve this end, however, the lawyers called for special legislation that would officially recognize Indian communities, land rights, and authorities (caciques, hilacatas, alcaldes, and kurakas).[17] While Villarroel himself privileged the ultimate authority of the state, he too viewed indigenous leaders as indispensable envoys of justice.[18]

In the end, the Villarroel regime successfully controlled the official agenda of the Indigenous Congress. Still, it could not manage the *unofficial* agenda the new organizational contacts facilitated. In part this was because some of the indigenista politicians who backed indigenous demands in the 1940s were not just distant orators but men who maintained close contact with rural communities and at times served those communities as legal advisors. Likewise, Bolivia's local indigenous leaders gained impressive access to the national media, legislators, and laws. This unusual articulation between the local and the national, between highly mobilized rural communities and urban political spheres, helps explain why Bolivia convened an Indigenous Congress just as other Latin American countries were convening indigenista ones.[19] It also points to the unique significance of the Bolivian event. Mexico held its Inter-American Indigenista Congress after the revolutionary state had demobilized peasant movements, largely via a major agrarian reform. Bolivia's Indigenous Congress instead took impetus from rising rural unrest, competition over reformist and revolutionary agendas, grave political instability, and an unfinished process of constitutional change.

✳ The Comité Indigenal's Congress

The primary motor behind the 1945 Indigenous Congress was a nongovernmental entity known as the Comité Indigenal Boliviano (Bolivian Indigenous Committee). Comprised of at least fifteen representatives from

14 President Villarroel and members of the Bolivian Indigenous Committee at the Government
Palace, 29 September 1944. The president is in the center of the back row; on his right is
Luis Ramos Quevedo; on his left is Victoriano Condori Mamani. The man third from the left
in the front row is holding the alcalde's *bastón de mando* (staff of office). From the cover
of the bulletin *Congreso Indigenal Boliviano en la Ciudad de La Paz, 2 de Febrero de 1945*
(1944). *Courtesy of the U.S. National Archives.*

all over the country, the committee was first established in 1938 or 1939. A
complete list is not available, but we know that the group included Victoriano Condori Mamani, a hacienda cacique or alcalde from Oruro; Hilarión Grájeda, Ayopaya's well-known alcalde; Dionisio Miranda, a hacienda colono and longtime leader from Sipesipe; the lawyer Juan B. Arce;
and a labor organizer by the name of Luis Ramos Quevedo. In September
1944, the committee initiated a meeting with Villarroel that launched the
organizing drive for the congress (see figure 14).[20]

During the organizational phase, Ramos Quevedo served as the committee's principal spokesperson. Despite his prominent place, Ramos was a
profoundly enigmatic figure. Journalists stressed the labor organizer's urban roots. They claimed he was a "fearsome boxer" from Oruro who also
worked for the La Paz police department; after spending some time ar-
ranging presentations by a foreign anarchist theater troupe, Ramos reportedly surfaced in La Paz as the "Conductor of the Indigenous Race" and
organizer of the Indigenous Congress.[21] The peasants of Ayopaya remember Ramos very differently: as the selfless son of a smallholder (*piquero*)

from Cochabamba's Valle Bajo.[22] For a time, Ramos belonged to Oruro's labor federation (Federación Obrera Sindical, FOS) and probably served as its "secretary of indigenous issues."[23] This position was first instituted by the Sucre FOS to defend peasants in their encounters with state authorities; other regional labor federations adopted it following the second congress of the Bolivian Confederation of Labor Unions (CSTB) in 1939.[24] As a member of Oruro's labor federation, Ramos maintained close contact with members of the 1920s cacique apoderado networks. He backed the land claims of the caciques and defended them when they were detained.[25] Ramos also waged battles against the hacienda regime, especially in Cochabamba and Oruro, and he probably helped organize the 1941–42 strikes on Oruro haciendas. Victoriano Condori (a member of the Indigenous Committee) and eight other "Caciques and Alcaldes" charged with inciting unrest on Oruro estates in March 1945 reportedly received instructions and funds from the labor leader.[26] As the divergent characteristics and competing hopes invested in Luis Ramos Quevedo suggest, the "true" identity of this remarkable individual is difficult to disentangle. Rather than straightforward answers, the controversy raised a larger query: who was an Indian and who would speak legitimately for indigenous causes?[27] The rising wave of indigenous mobilization, with its extensive rural and urban roots, put these questions at the center of the disputes that began to converge around the 1945 Indigenous Congress.

As Ramos worked to bring about the Congress, he deftly obtained audience with government officials and, for a time, their confidence. In December 1944, the minister of government, Major Alfonso Quinteros, advised prefects and mayors throughout the nation to guarantee "committees, agrarian unions, representatives, delegates, Apoderados and Alcaldes Escolares" full freedom to organize the Indigenous Congress. At Ramos's request, the Ministry of Communication waived all postal and telegraph fees for the Indigenous Committee.[28] Ramos and the other members even received government credentials, complete with the president's signature.[29]

Ramos and the Indigenous Committee effectively used this official assistance to steal the initiative from the government: before state authorities could prepare an agenda for the congress, the committee publicized its own. In December 1944, it designated 100 special delegates to circulate an eight-page "independent newspaper" among "indigenous districts throughout the Republic," advising Indians to send delegates to the congress.[30] Messengers reportedly distributed almost 25,000 copies of the bulletin.[31]

Congreso Indigenal Boliviano en la Ciudad de La Paz

2 de Febre ro de 1945

EL ESCUDO NACIONAL

EL LIBERTADOR SIMON
BOLIVAR.

EL DIVINO NIÑO JESUS, NA-
CIDO PARA SALVAR A
LA HUMANIDAD

EL FUNDADOR DE LA REPU-
BLICA, MARISCAL ANTONIO
JOSE DE SUCRE

El Excelentisimo Señor Presidente de la República, Teniente Coronel Don Gualberto Villarroel, con
una parte del Comité Indigenal Boliviano.— A su dere-
cha, el Compañero Luis Ramos Quevedo, Secretario
General y a su izquierda, el compañero Victoriano Condori Mamani, Secretario de Relaciones.— (Foto saca-
da en el Palacio de Gobierno el 29 de septiembre de
1944).

15 The cover of the bulletin *Congreso Indigenal Boliviano en la Ciudad de La Paz, 2 de Febrero
de 1945* (1944). The cover juxtaposes national emblems with an image of President Villarroel and members of the Bolivian Indigenous Committee inside the Government Palace.
It simultaneously conveys the Committee's loyalty to the nation and its political clout.
Courtesy of the U.S. National Archives.

With this artfully designed publication, Ramos and the Indigenous Committee illustrated the president's support for colonos and comunarios, all the while affirming the committee's allegiance to the government. The title of the bulletin reads: "Congreso Indigenal Boliviano in the City of La Paz, 2 February, 1945." Its cover is cloaked in patriotic imagery: it bears the portraits of "the Liberator," Simón Bolívar; the "founder of the republic," Mariscal Antonio José de Sucre; and an image of the Bolivian national emblem. A picture of Jesus, centered beneath the national emblem, expresses the committee's hopes for a new age: he is identified as "the divine child Jesus, born to save humanity." Below this set of figures is a photograph of Ramos and other members of the Indigenous Committee posed next to Villarroel; it shows them gathered at the Government Palace for the September meeting with the president (see figure 15 above). The words on the banner just above Villarroel's head are hard to make out, but they seem to say: "Sindicato Agrario de Caracollo. La Tierra Para El Que Cultiva. Fundado El Año 1939" (Agrarian Union of Caracollo. The Land for He Who Works It. Founded in the Year 1939). This striking placard underscores the committee's concern with the land, and confirms its close ties to union activists in Oruro's northeastern corner (see map 1 for Caracollo's location). But perhaps the most notable feature of the image is Villarroel's willingness to pose at the Government Palace next to a banner that affirms colonos' land rights. To accentuate the nation's indigenous origins, the final page of the paper is decorated with an image of the archaeological ruins in Tiwanaku. Scattered throughout the body of the text appear pictures of government officials, members of the MNR, sympathetic congressional deputies and journalists, members of Villarroel's cabinet, and the former president Germán Busch. All of these public figures are described generously as defenders or protectors of Indians and workers.

The committee had especially laudatory remarks for the president of Bolivia's National Convention, Alberto Mendoza López: it deemed him an "authentic protector and deputy of the Indians in the National Convention" who was "elected by Indians" (see figure 16). Mendoza had already been a congressional deputy from 1926 to 1930; later he served as a delegate to the 1938 constitutional convention and as minister of treasury and statistics for Germán Busch. Before he helped found the MNR and represented the party in the 1942 legislature, Mendoza belonged to Tristán Marof's Partido Socialista Obrero Boliviano (Bolivian Socialist Workers' Party, PSOB). In an October 1944 legislative session, Mendoza backed Ramos Quevedo's call to repeal the Saavedra-era decree barring Indians from the principal streets and squares of La Paz.[32] And as a congressional deputy for the heavily indigenous district of Omasuyos (La Paz)—his place of origin— Mendoza had dealt personally with indigenous constituencies. In 1944, the lawyer helped elaborate a petition to the minister of education and indigenous affairs from the alcalde mayor of an ex-community in Omasuyos. As the petitioners wrapped up a grievance about land usurpation and abuse, they concluded: "The law should be the same, and it is; and . . . indígenas and minors benefit from special protection." In its hybrid conceptualization of rights, the claim is reminiscent of the cacique apoderado petitions of the 1920s. But Mendoza and the alcalde mayor took the link between equality and protection a step further: in view of Indians' right to "special protection," the petition states, the office of Education and Indigenous Affairs "had the responsibility to be more demanding with the white adversary than with the Indian." "Protection," in this context, had nothing to do with tutelage. Instead, it signified a legal system that would be more rigorous with "whites."[33] Indeed, the committee itself linked Mendoza's role as "authentic protector" with Indians' decisive participation in national politics. According to the Indigenous Committee, Mendoza had been "elected by Indians." He was *their* deputy.

But what did the Indigenous Committee really mean when it said that Indians—who were essentially barred from voting as a result of the literacy requirement—"elected" Mendoza as their deputy? For the nineteenth century and much of the early twentieth, electoral politics centered largely in urban areas. By the 1940s, however, political parties were drumming up support for congressional candidates in the mining camps and in some cases even among the peasantry.[34] Even if Indians did not actually cast ballots for Mendoza, communities from Omasuyos may have formed a collective base of support for the deputy that could be mobilized at a time of electoral contention. And if the communities of Omasuyos exhibited such support during the July 1944 campaign, surely they expected Mendoza to honor their contribution to his victory. Perhaps the phrase "elected by Indians" was a challenge: to hold the elected official to a pledge.

Hand in hand with its expressions of allegiance to Mendoza and other MNR leaders, the Indigenous Committee bulletin offered up tributes to Villarroel and RADEPA (see figure 17). And in those accolades, it similarly underscored Indians' political sway. The bulletin first summarizes the committee's September meeting with the president; it then lauds Villarroel for his revolutionary spirit and dedication to Indian freedom and equality:

Doctor Alberto Mendoza López, auténtico protector y diputado de los indios en la Convención Nacional.— Su sacrificio y defensa desinteresada de muchos años, nunca puede ser bien pagada.

16 Alberto Mendoza López, "authentic protector and deputy of Indians in the National Convention." From the bulletin *Congreso Indigenal Boliviano en la Ciudad de La Paz, 2 de Febrero de 1945* (1944). *Courtesy of the U.S. National Archives.*

"Don't abandon the struggle; work the land with enthusiasm, fulfill your obligations, but don't let yourselves be humiliated. We are all equal, there should not be any pongos or mitanis in Bolivia," it says the president told them. But the bulletin does not just emphasize the president's part. The next section of the paper contains legalized copies of government guarantees that certify the committee's right to organize the Indigenous Congress. One additional missive assures Ramos that the Ministry of Government sent circulars to prefects and mayors of the republic advising them to protect Indians from abuse by hacendados and the police; to lift the decree prohibiting Indians from entering the principal streets and squares of cities, "because [the Indian] has the right to walk wherever he wants, just like anyone else"; and to enforce article 5 of the Constitution, which outlawed slavery and servitude. After laboring clandestinely for five years to end "the disgrace of the pongo and the mitani," the committee had been "recognized by the Government."[35] The upcoming Indigenous Congress, the committee thus emphasized, was not the government's initiative but the product of its own action.

Like the caciques apoderados of the 1920s, the Indigenous Committee professed allegiance to the Bolivian state. But there was a difference: rather than submitting a humble entreaty to generic executive authorities, the committee expressed loyalty to a particular government—that of Villarroel and his MNR allies, who were in turn depicted as defenders of indigenous

-: Homenaje del Indio al Gobierno Nacional :-

Fotografía de Cadete. del que fué ilustre Teniente General Germán Busch. Gran Presidente de Bolivia, que pusiera en práctica los ideales de emancipación económica y que promulgara la Nueva Constitución Política del Estado de 1938, cuyo artículo 5o. eliminó la vergüenza nacional del pongueaje y mittanaje. Los indios, muy particularmente, dedican su respetuoso recuerdo al prócer desaparecido.

Excelentísimo Señor Presidente Constitucional de la República de Bolivia. Teniente Coronel don Gualberto Villarroel, nacido —en Cochabamba— para la felicidad de nuestra Patria, el 15 de diciembre de 1908.— Cuenta en su vida 36 años a los cuales ha vencido en la Carrera Patriótica de las Armas con incomparable honor y eficiencia las pruebas más ennoblecedoras de la Historia Nacional.— Nuestro joven y apreciado Mandatario es un altísimo exponente del Gran Ejército Joven y un representante destacado de la intelectualidad de la raza.— Su personalidad completa en las condiciones que requiere un gobernante, aseguran un porvenir grandioso a la Nacionalidad.— Dotado de excepcionales sentimientos de generoso humanitarismo con los que asumió la Jefatura del Gobierno en 20 de diciembre de 1943, se preocupa por la organización del país bajo un régimen científico que verdaderamente defiende y protege al trabajador, ya sea empleado u obrero, por igual a los que trabajan en todas las industrias, y muy preferentemente al minero y al agricultor.— Las garantías y consideraciones otorgadas al indio y el sincero deseo de elevar su condición social, económica y educacional, son objeto de real agradecimiento de la masa de millones de indios que ven en el Presidente un amigo y un Salvador.

Sr. Mayor don Edmundo Nogales, Ministro de Agricultura. Ganadería y Colonización. Nació en La Paz, el 1o. de enero de 1911.— Muchos son los merecimientos que tiene dentro del Gobierno Libertario de las clases oprimidas, como principal dirigente y actor. Ultimamente, con relevante habilidad ha enfocado la contrarevolución dirigida a encumbrar hombres ambiciosos, personalistas que trataban de envolver nuevamente al trabajador y al indio en bárbara y caprichosa tiranía.— Se espera mucho de su invariable probidad, sugerencias de un régimen agrario justo y productivo a la economía nacional y a la posición del indio.

Sr. Mayor don Jorge Calero. Ministro de Educación. Bellas Artes y Asuntos Indígenas. Nació en La Paz, el 14 de noviembre de 1907. Como militar y gobernante ha demostrado sus altas condiciones. Su incesante trabajo por la educación, le distinguen como a un hombre progresista y patriota que se desvela por la más noble finalidad de mejorar la cultura nacional, en la que estudia con el mayor interés la forma de sacar al indio de su ignorancia y analfabetismo.

Doctor Germán Monrroy Block, figura política joven que en la Convención Nacional demuestra su afecto a las clases trabajadoras y al indio.

Señor Teniente Coronel don José Celestino Pinto, Ministro de Defensa Nacional.— Nació en Cochabamba, el 19 de mayo de 1906.— Desde 1928 en que se graduó de Subteniente sirve a la Patria en la Digna Profesión Militar.— Sus méritos de guerra en la Campaña del Chaco, su talento militar y su experiencia en el ramo, le han llevado a la Cartera que ocupa actualmente. Su colaboración al Gobierno y sus aceptadas disposiciones de reorganización del Ejército son muy reconocidas.— Su cariño al trabajador y al indio le recomiendan muy gratamente.

Sr. Mayor don Antonio Ponce, Ministro de Obras Públicas y Comunicaciones. Nació en Cockabamba, el 31 de marzo de 1909.— Digno y Calificado miembro del Noble y Redentor Ejército Joven, se ha posesionado en el sitial honroso y justiciero de liberación de las clases asalariadas y sufridas como el obrero y el indio, dentro del más amplio sentido nacionalista.

NOTA DE REDACCION.— Escrito de acuerdo a la mentalidad y reducido lenguaje del indio.

17 "Homage of the Indian" to President Villarroel and members of his cabinet. From the bulletin *Congreso Indigenal Boliviano en la Ciudad de La Paz, 2 de Febrero de 1945* (1944). This striking page illustrates the Bolivian Indigenous Committee's affinity with young military officers of the post–Chaco War era and highlights its own concern with the rights of workers and Indians. The committee commends Germán Busch (upper-left-hand corner) for promulgating the 1938 Constitution, because its article 5 "eliminated the national shame of pongueaje and mitanaje." It also extols Villarroel (top center) for defending and protecting workers, especially those who labor in the mines and in agriculture. Similar praise goes to the other officials for siding with workers and Indians. The page in addition reveals the paternalistic ethos of some members of the committee: the caption states that it was "written in accordance with the mentality and limited language of the Indian." *Courtesy of the U.S. National Archives*.

rights. The bulletin addressed the government and the army as political partners. And it identified Indians as members of the national political community, who "elect" congressional deputies. Rather than protection and guarantees, it demanded *rights* and guarantees. For the Indigenous Committee, loyalty was a two-way street: the Villarroel-MNR government deserved the committee's praise only because it backed their own struggle for equality and freedom.

The next segments of the bulletin detail the group's objectives. Referring to itself as the "true and only social authority of the Indians," the committee first quoted a February 1944 petition that Ramos had submitted to the National Congress demanding clarification of article 5 of the 1938 Constitution.[36] In that appeal, Ramos not only maintained that the law explicitly outlawed pongueaje; he suggested it was "established to liberate the *compañero indio*." The bulletin itself then takes pongueaje more broadly as a sign of degradation, inequality, and enslavement. Its conflation of pongueaje and slavery was not just dramatic strategy; it was the means to advance a specific interpretation of a much-disputed guarantee (article 5). Landlords insisted that colonos' unpaid duties were fair payment for the land they held in usufruct. Since Indians were not in any sense bound to the property of the owner, they argued, the labor and service requirements could not be considered slavery or servitude.[37] For Ramos and the Indigenous Committee, compensation was not the only point. The fundamental problem was discrimination: "A man can NEVER serve as a PONGO and a woman NEVER AS A MITANI, even if the patrón wants to pay in silver or gold; . . . THE LANDLORDS SHOULD WAIT ON THEMSELVES." Finally, the bulletin established an intimate connection between Indian freedom and

Bolivian freedom: servitude and "slavery" not only infringed on Indians' constitutional rights, but epitomized the nation's feudal and dependent status. Bolivia's future, it thus followed, hinged on the liberty of its Indians. "This Congress," the committee stressed, "is to save the INDIAN and BOLIVIA."[38]

After delineating these basic principles, the Indigenous Committee turned to the details of the Indigenous Congress. Up to a point its instructions echoed government directives: the committee called on each community and hacienda to send two delegates to the meeting. It also asked them to select the "best" from among the alcaldes, hilacatas, caciques or kurakas, alcaldes escolares, or apoderados, and advised that they should all be "comrades of much confidence in the struggle for *los indios* . . . who appreciate our concerns and issues."[39] To exclude labor activists and "outside agitators," the government would insist on delegates who were involved exclusively in agricultural labor. The Indigenous Committee embraced the same rule, but to ensure that "those responsible for the oppression of the Indian—landlords or merchants" did not "interfere."[40] The committee concluded its message with a call to *all* Indians: "Come to La Paz . . . make any sacrifice . . . compañeros and compañeras: We must be many so the government will listen to us and grant laws that recognize our rights and guarantees."[41] Even as it pledged loyalty, the committee openly challenged the government's rules.

Neither the Villarroel regime nor the Indigenous Committee had full control of the delegate selection process, however. As discussed in chapter 5, not all alcaldes or kurakas were locally legitimate leaders. Where they were not, hacienda colonos tried to elect their own recognized leaders to represent them at the congress.[42] In some areas, landlords deceived these delegates or blocked their travel. Elsewhere, well-respected leaders managed to circumvent landlords' interference. In the end, the 1,659 delegates who assembled for the May 1945 congress represented a mix of legitimate local leaders and individuals who had been hand selected by landlords or state authorities.[43] As per the Indigenous Committee's instructions, these delegates held local assemblies, sometimes clandestinely, to prepare demands and petitions that stemmed from their own experience of exploitation and abuse.[44] By rail or by foot—at least an eight-day journey in many cases—the delegates would bring those concerns to the assembly. Two thousand Indians reportedly took part in the event as spectators.[45] Many more made the trek to La Paz, but the police refused to let them attend the congress or even enter the city's center. Approximately 150 women participated in the congress, primarily from Oruro and Cochabamba.[46]

Although the Indigenous Committee bulletin solicited local input, it also instructed the "compañeros and compañeras" to "support and defend" the committee's own twenty-seven-point agenda, which was included in the bulletin and reprinted in the national press.[47] Of the many demands in this richly detailed program, the most notable include: "That the Indian [indio] be free, secure in his life and work, and respected the same as everyone; that there be special laws and authorities for the Indian; and that there be Committees of lawyers paid by the government to defend the Indian." Not coincidentally, the list begins and ends with the long-standing claim that the land "belong to the Indians;" that it be "returned to the Community;" that it belong to "those who work it . . . the Indian."[48]

If controversial demands for land and justice were paramount to the Indigenous Committee program, there is also a second set of very different claims in the long list: appeals to civility, order, progress, and modernization. The authors offered to "civilize" themselves in exchange for land, respect, and fair wages. Their program thus interspersed demands for land and labor rights with promises to "serve Bolivia better" through education, sports, military service, and the modernization of agriculture. It urged respect for indigenous cultures while professing love for the patria. It not only demanded justice and land but also requested that "male and female Indians" be taught the "good customs of the city . . . that the Indian be taught Spanish without neglecting to perfect his use of the native languages quechua and aymara . . . that [the Indians] be provided with machines and instructed in their use . . . that the state assist with women's and men's change of dress and clothing."

Were such appeals to modernization and national unity instrumental and strategic? Were they designed to appease state authorities? Or were they more than strategic? Did they express genuine convictions? Quite likely, the Indigenous Committee's very incursion into the national arena masked substantive local differences between leaders who favored multiethnic or multiclass alliances, on the one hand, and those who favored autonomy, on the other. Such differences notwithstanding, this particular document reveals points of agreement and points of disagreement between local projects and state projects. Thus it cannot simply be considered an instrumentalist ploy, something designed to appease government ears. The authors do not suppress Indianness or communal land claims. Nor do they reject "modernization" or bilingualism in favor of "pure" indigenous cultures. The Bolivian Indigenous Committee requested changes in dress and clothing, but it did not specify for which contexts or encounters. Was the point to transcend the negativity projected on Indian clothing—and on Indians—by city people?[49] The document is ambiguous, but no irreversible conversion is announced. If any message was paramount, it was the coming of a new age when Indian rights and respect would prevail: "After such a long wait, the HOUR OF THE INDIAN has finally arrived."[50]

The Indigenous Committee prepared this remarkable program without the government's involvement. The program did not bear the government's seal, and the Ministry of Education—the agency first responsible for the congress—had not even reviewed it. Yet the program circulated among rural communities as though it possessed an official status: the national press referred to the program as the "basis for discussions that would take place at the Indigenous Congress."[51] And the commissions sent to rural communities—with government sanction—most likely presented it as a certified agenda. The twenty-seven-point program, in short, was and was not an "official" document. This liminal status gave the program its power. Neither a disingenuous ploy nor a simple capitulation, the agenda expressed sincere loyalty to a Bolivian government that recognized indigenous authority and rights.

With some reluctance, the government agreed to convene the Indigenous Congress on 25 December 1944. But officials soon rescheduled the event for February 1945.[52] Delegates were advised to arrive in La Paz five days before the meeting, on 28 January. When January rolled around, the government once again pushed back the assembly.[53] Either because they thought the meeting was still scheduled—or because they knew it was not—more than 1,000 "indígenas" from provinces of La Paz, Cochabamba, Oruro, and Potosí arrived in the capital in late January and made their way to the Government Palace for a meeting with Villarroel. "Alcaldes, caciques, and leaders of communities" filed through the city's main thoroughfares holding "the classic staffs, richly adorned with silver," and a Bolivian flag.[54]

The massive, unplanned showing surprised Villarroel, but he agreed to meet informally with the delegates before they returned to their communities (see figure 18). In these relatively casual encounters, the delegates asked the president for tools and irrigation; an end to pongueaje and other abuses "against their persons and property;" a commitment to investigate

18 President Villarroel listening attentively to "representatives of indígenas" who arrived in La Paz, late January 1945, for the (cancelled) Indigenous Congress (published in *La Razón*). *Courtesy of the U.S. National Archives*.

land and title grievances that stemmed from eviction by hacendados; a new revisita; and the return of all usurped territory.[55] As these demands suggest, the impetus for the Indigenous Congress came from both communities and haciendas, and the first participants made land a high priority. Like rural petitioners of the early 1940s, these delegates also intertwined demands for land and labor rights with concerns about the abuse of power. And their pleas included the caciques apoderados' principal claim for a general inspection of land boundaries. The unexpected convergence of the delegates in January illustrates the extensive phase of consultation that preceded the May congress, and confirms that rural leaders—not just outside "agitators"—publicly articulated demands both approved and frowned upon by the government. It also shows how Villarroel courted political backing via horizontal gestures of support and exchange. The president not only heard the delegates' concerns; he invited the "main" leaders to meet with him at the Government Palace and later visited them in their temporary quarters at the La Paz Police Academy for about four hours. At the end of the meeting, he "commenced a slow and patient tour," and "listened carefully to the requests that each one formulated, on behalf of their constituents and themselves."[56] This personal investment and willingness to admit delegates to the halls of government surely enhanced the president's legitimacy vis-à-vis rural communities. As the Aymara scribe Leandro Condori Chura put it, Villarroel did not just "favor the poor"; like Busch, he showed that he favored "the Indian."[57]

During the months leading up to the congress, government officials continued to consult with local communities, sometimes under more formal circumstances (see figure 19). With assistance from the Villarroel government, the Miners' Federation, and departmental union federations, regional meetings were held in the La Paz districts of Laja, Kollana, and Cañaviri. These congresses not only showed labor's continuing involvement in rural activism; they revealed the ongoing competition for peasant backing between the MNR and the PIR, which enjoyed the support of the labor movement. The events were also visible evidence of the regime's pro-Indian designs. Villarroel attended two of these gatherings with members of his cabinet and a few diplomats.[58] The president predictably called for an end to hacienda servitude. More surprising, he endorsed a system of salaried rural labor, an idea that exceeded the official recommendations ultimately approved by the Indigenous Congress. Although the president did not mention land conflicts, surely his presence at these local meetings buttressed the legitimacy of peasant demands. Villarroel made personal overtures to rural leaders right up until the congress was convened, assuring them that the government was on their side. Certainly Busch made similar gestures, but Villarroel held court with a wider constituency of comunarios and colonos. These were still relations of patronage, but they were less narrow ones.

As the date of the Indigenous Congress neared, landlords used the newspapers they controlled to publicly denounce true and untrue incidents of subversive activity. They blamed an apparent upsurge in work stoppages on outside "agitators."[59] In Oruro, colonos staged a sit-down strike of such "serious proportions" that "they [the Indians] now believed that . . . all the land would be returned to them."[60] One such report connected the incident with a newspaper signed by Luis Ramos Quevedo.[61] The denunciations of subversion were especially pronounced in Cochabamba and Oruro, where rural strikes were centered in the early 1940s. Refusals to work or fulfill related obligations outweighed acts of violence.

In this increasingly tense context, government officials grew to distrust Ramos Quevedo. The new minister of government, Major Edmundo

19 Government ministers Major Nogales (center) and Lt. Col. Pinto (to Nogales's right) amidst Indians and peasants, prior to the May 1945 Indigenous Congress. On Nogales's left may be Luis Ramos Quevedo. The photo gives a vivid sense of the waves of mobilization that led up to the congress. *Courtesy of the Luis Antezana E. Private Archive; from* DATA, Revista del Instituto de Estudios Andinos y Amazónicos *3 (1992) (Universidad Andina Simón Bolívar)*.

Nogales, reported that Ramos "had been agitating among the Indians for six or seven years and swindling them."[62] The *oficial mayor* of government, Carlos Morales Guillén, charged further that Ramos had printed and sold false property titles to Indians, and then used the funds to purchase several properties for himself.[63] Not everyone condemned the man's moral fiber, however. According to another source, Ramos had attracted thousands of followers and accumulated hefty sums, but not for his own enrichment: the money was earmarked for the "República Indigenal" (Indigenous Republic), of which Ramos would be the first president.[64]

As the charges against Ramos Quevedo mounted, government authorities began to withdraw their support. Eventually, they identified him as the principal agent of an elaborate antigovernment program. By the end of April 1945, Ramos and five other "agitators" were in jail.[65] Ramos was first sent to Beni but then reportedly escaped to Brazil or La Paz, where he may have worked as a rural teacher. Although he never resurfaced, this "Conductor of the Indigenous Race" left a powerful trace. In La Paz, colonos had gathered in the night to read confidential memos Ramos dispatched to them from Oruro.[66] The elusive leader also assembled an extraordinary network in the countryside, complete with *chasquis* (Quechua for messengers) who carried political leaflets and newspapers from one district to the next.[67] When Ramos was first arrested, telegrams demanding his release poured in from Cochabamba, Potosí, and Tarija.[68] And the delegates who attended the May congress arrived expecting a discussion of the demands circulated by him and the other jailed leaders. News articles published after the Indigenous congress confirm that many of the items Ramos publicized were discussed at the assembly, even though they no longer figured in the official agenda.

The final organizing phases for the May event can be read as the government's unrelenting effort to rein in the meeting. As reports of political agitation poured in, authorities intensified their crackdown. The oficial mayor of government claimed that Indians had circulated handbills "urging all Indians of the Altiplano to attend" the Indigenous Congress. He warned that the city—with a population of approximately 250,000—would be inundated with 50,000 Indians, "creating serious police, food, housing, and sanitation problems." By the end of April, the government had placed between 150 and 300 people in "preventive detention." Authorities also exerted control over the movements of the rural populace. From 26 April onward, patrols were established in La Paz and other departments to inspect the military service certificates of men in transit. Individuals without the documentation and all "agitators" would be sent to an agricultural colony following a "very brief" trial. Since few men possessed the certificates, the government found this an effective means to limit the numbers of colonos and comunarios who would reach the capital for the congress.[69]

✳ The Government's Congress

To manage the May meeting, the government created an official organizing committee comprised of representatives from various ministries. This official body drafted a formal agenda for the congress and continued to act as an advisory board once it commenced.[70] The committee selected four overarching topics for discussion: hacienda labor and unremunerated services; education; rural cooperatives; and a rural police force (to maintain order, protect Indians from abuse, and ensure that Indians complied with work rules).[71] Education remained a central concern, but the Ministry of Education no longer held responsibility for the event: now the Ministry of Government was in charge. This shift not only made issues of order and control primary; it put MNR party members at the head of things.

Although government officials prevailed on the committee, those officials did not all take the same stance. Along with three representatives from the Ministry of Government and two from the Ministry of Agriculture, the committee included the lawyer José Flores Moncayo, head of the La Paz Oficina Jurídica de Defensa Gratuita de Indígenas; Félix Eguino Zaballa, a member of Congress and prominent socialist deputy to the 1938 constitutional convention; and Toribio Claure, a representative of the Ministry of Education. Originally an ally of Elizardo Pérez's ayllu-based pedagogy, Claure joined the opposition to this project in the late 1930s and was one of the few original ministry employees who remained on the conservative Concejo Nacional de Educación (National Council on Education).[72] The final member of the official organizing committee was Carlos Montes, director of the Sociedad Rural Boliviana—the organization of large landowners that so vociferously opposed the assembly. Four other representatives from the Sociedad Rural were also allowed to join, with "voice but no vote." The Minister of Government gave them seats to assuage their fears about strikes and disorder.[73] The national labor federation (CSTB) asked to participate on the same conditions as landlords, noting that it had already sponsored two indigenous congresses, but the government evidently refused.[74] These decisions were prophetic ones. Villarroel would not directly confront landed interests, but he would not give landlords unchecked influence, either. Nor would the government allow the CSTB—which was controlled by the PIR—to participate in rural policy making. Both landlords and workers would later join the coalition that overthrew the Villarroel regime.

Less known and equally unexpected, a U.S. citizen also attended the official organizing committee's planning sessions.[75] Ernest Maes, a University of Michigan–trained sociologist, was invited to participate because he was director of the Servicio Cooperativo Interamericano de Educación (Inter-American Cooperative Education Service, SCIDE), which was implementing educational projects in a number of highland communities.[76] Maes's work was part of an incipient U.S. development agenda that emerged out of the geopolitical maneuverings of the World War II era. In the early 1940s, the U.S. government promised Bolivia significant economic assistance in exchange for joining the Allied cause, resolving conflicts that stemmed from the 1937 nationalization of Standard Oil, and ensuring access to Bolivian tin. As long as the war lasted, the United States provided limited aid in order to obtain tin at favorable prices. With the end of the war, the United States enjoyed the leverage of an extensive tin stockpile, and its

promises of far-reaching assistance evaporated.[77] This context of unfulfilled promises explains Villarroel's frustrated remark to U.S. Embassy staff
in April 1945: "If the United States helps us, we will do it [modernize the
countryside] in five years, but if not we will do it in 10, 15, or 20; but in any
case, it will be done."[78]

The combination of expectation and irritation that marked United
States–Bolivian relations with the close of the war helps explain Ernest
Maes's inclusion on the organizing committee: the government put Maes—
like the landlords—at a distance, inviting him to attend meetings without making him an official member. Certainly Maes was asked because
Bolivian officials believed—or wanted to believe—that the United States
would provide extensive aid. But his presence did not signal a simple
capitulation to U.S. pressure. Maes's participation could enhance the legitimacy of a project to modernize the countryside that was already embraced
by Bolivian officials but opposed by powerful rural sectors. Keeping his
participation informal preserved the aura of independence.[79]

If U.S. policy broadly influenced Bolivia's 1940s development agenda,
the orchestration of the Indigenous Congress made it clear that Bolivia's
modernizing push would not be dictated by the United States. The Congress was convened in a makeshift auditorium near the Government Palace
(Luna Park) from 10 May to 15 May. The inaugural session, which was aired
on the radio, showcased the government in all aspects practical and ceremonial. A host of high-ranking Bolivian officials bedecked the center stage:
the president and his cabinet, the prefect and mayor of La Paz, the arch-
bishop, representatives of government ministries, the organizing committee, and about seventy-five members of the armed forces. The only ambas-
sadors invited to the congress were those from Mexico and the United
States. But while the Mexican envoy joined Bolivian officials on the dais,
the U.S. ambassador was given a seat in the audience. If Villarroel and the
MNR valued the scientific stamp of U.S. development agencies, in this
public setting they gave more weight to the nationalist and revolutionary
credentials that Mexico's attendance could lend.

An indigenous directorate accompanied government officials on the
podium. Francisco Chipana Ramos, a young Aymara Indian from the altiplano, served as president of the congress; Dionisio Miranda, a sixty-year-
old Quechua Indian from Cochabamba, filled the vice-presidential post;
and Desiderio Chilina, from the eastern lowlands, was named secretary-
general (see figure 20).[80] At the outset, Chipana Ramos must have seemed

20 Francisco Chipana Ramos, president of the Indigenous Congress (left), and Dionisio
Miranda, vice-president, May 1945 (published in *La Razón*). Chipana Ramos has a *ch'uspa*,
the small woven bag used to carry coca leaves. Miranda is holding the alcalde's bastón de
mando. *Courtesy of the U.S. National Archives.*

an especially suitable appointee, for his biography epitomized the values of
learning, social renewal, and nationalism that the populist regime embraced. A Chaco War veteran, Chipana Ramos served as Busch's personal
messenger during the war and spent some months working on the construction of the famed indigenista school in Warisata. Indeed, one ob-
server suggested that Chipana Ramos's prestige among the "indigenous
masses" was based precisely on his connections to Busch.[81] When Villarroel came to power, Chipana Ramos collaborated closely with the MNR as it
began to establish a network of supporters in the countryside.[82] Although
Chipana Ramos maintained contact with labor leaders, at the time of the
Indigenous Congress he lived in an "agricultural community," just as the
government wished.[83] In the eyes of the authorities, he was not only socially appropriate but politically dependable. The vice-president of the
congress, Dionisio Miranda, possessed less obviously reliable credentials.
Miranda, a colono from Hacienda Chacapaya in Sipesipe, was known
throughout Cochabamba's Valle Bajo and Tapacarí as a respected peasant leader. In the early 1940s, Miranda worked together with Luis Ramos
Quevedo to organize peasants on haciendas, and he later joined Ramos

Quevedo on the Bolivian Indigenous Committee. A man with extensive political experience, Miranda diligently presented local demands to national authorities in La Paz, probably over a period of many decades, and enjoyed the support of lawyers from the Oficina Jurídica de Defensa Gratuita de Indígenas.[84] Both men's activities exemplify the close ties that local indigenous leaders had forged with indigenista politicians and legal advisors.

These three indigenous officials were not actually elected but hand-picked by the minister of government, Major Nogales.[85] Nogales could not, however, impose completely malleable appointees. All three men were prominent local leaders, and for alleged involvement in the unrest that followed the 1945 congress, two of them—Miranda and Chipana Ramos—would be pursued by the police.[86] Even as the government took control of the congress, it had to bargain with indigenous constituencies.

The opening session of the Indigenous Congress included speeches by the president; the minister of government; Chipana Ramos; the minister of labor; and the MNR representative Hernán Siles Zuazo. Their presentations were delivered in or translated into Spanish, Quechua, and Aymara. Each day, commissions of delegates from each region met to discuss one of the four official topics and then exchanged ideas with the indigenous directorate and members of the organizing committee.[87] At plenary sessions in the afternoons, the entire assembly debated points discussed by these subgroups. For the most part, the delegates simply approved the resolutions proposed by each of the four committees, but there were also many spontaneous interventions, including some harsh criticism of the clergy.[88] In addition, five government representatives gave plenary talks that outlined official positions on the four overarching themes. These presentations, which were written under the pressure of "requests, suggestions and complaints," reveal the regime's underlying concern to regulate rural labor, quell unrest, and increase agricultural production by balancing the interests of landlords and colonos.[89] The talks also evince the authorities' divergent opinions about just how much the government should protect the interests of landowners versus those of workers. Rather than forging a consensus, the government's difficult balancing act deepened political divides.

Carlos Morales Guillén, oficial mayor of government and head of the official planning committee, gave the first and most important presentation. His speech focused on the regulation of hacienda labor, which

Morales linked with the recent unrest.[90] The source of the agitation, he stressed, was the system of uncompensated services and gifts. Yet rather than focusing on services per se, Morales called attention to the connections between colonaje and legal procedures. Although Morales noted the wholesale failure of existing legal protections, he granted extensive powers to the law. Ultimately he attributed the unjust system of labor and service duties to the absence of a comprehensive legal code and special courts equipped to deal with violations. Instead of clear and uniform norms, a disorderly system prevailed that was based on the whim of individual landlords and then reinforced by incompetent subaltern officials. The fundamental problem, Morales declared, was local authorities' immoral behavior and their failure to enforce the law. Concretely he sought to replace the corregidor post—an unsalaried position subject to corruption and abuse—with officials (*intendentes*) trained in the National Police Academy. Finally, Morales identified hacienda servitude—colonaje—as the sign of a lawless society and the banner for more effective institutions and laws.

But Morales did more than just invoke the colono or the pongo as a symbol of economic backwardness. His speech affirmed in abundant detail the same grievances that drove members of the Indigenous Committee to lodge petitions, wage strikes, and organize assemblies. First, Morales noted that the people who filled the corregidor post were themselves often renters or administrators of estates. Second, he stated that police commissions committed "unjustifiable excesses." Third, he noted that tax collectors routinely exhorted unjust sums from the "indigenous class" without providing receipts. He identified the collector of the muko tax, who demanded hefty sums even from nonproducers, as the most egregious offender. More than just hindering the economy, Morales concluded, colonaje degraded the nation as a whole, for this unregulated system of labor epitomized the absence of a rule of law. Although he stressed the mutual rights and obligations of landlords and colonos, Morales did not hesitate to take sides. He reminded his audience that the new Constitution not only made property rights contingent on their social function but protected the rights of workers.

Other official presentations reiterated Morales's central points about the legal and moral deficiencies of the state. A short speech by the Ministry of Labor's José Antonio Lloza, on "Legislation Pertaining to Indians and the Community Question," blamed the "abuses committed by landlords and authorities" for the "existing state of belligerence and tension." To ward off an uprising by the "indigenous class," Lloza maintained, provincial authorities needed to know and enforce the many laws that protected Indians and colonos.[91] A presentation on law enforcement by Dr. Reynaldo Bustillos, secretary-general of the official organizing council for the congress, echoed Morales's concern with "complete regulation." The cause of the "constant agitation" among Indians, Bustillos concluded, was not simply the "cruelty and abuse inflicted by the landlord or the authorities"; the disturbances were also due to the absence of a comprehensive body of agrarian legislation "that would establish mutual obligations." For it was the dearth of such laws and the resulting "juridical chaos," he said, that gave way to "inhuman customs" and "unprecedented violations" in the first place.[92] Hand in hand with the development of a special rural police force, Bolivia needed an agrarian labor code. Those laws mattered more than the police itself, according to Bustillos. Like Morales, Bustillos gave the law transformative powers: a legal order would make up for and expunge human disorder.

Not all of the official speakers agreed that universal rules were the answer. Like many landlords, the Ministry of Agriculture's Jorge Alcázar insisted that hacienda labor systems were too diverse and complex to be regulated by a single code.[93] Trying to create general rules for all agricultural workers would not only prejudice "the nation's incipient agricultural production . . . [but] create chaos for Indians and landlords alike."[94] Indeed, Alcázar stated that commissions to study peasant labor should include representatives from the Sociedad Rural. No other speaker contemplated landlords' direct involvement in the expansion of the local state; the other presenters instead purported to transcend class interests by creating uniform norms.

The last official intervention shifted attention away from the law altogether. In a lengthy speech on "Indigenous Education," the Ministry of Education's Toribio Claure gave education the magical powers that Morales and others attributed to legal procedures. Like Morales, Claure stressed the need to stem the tide of rural strikes, to modernize agriculture, and to strengthen the nation itself.[95] But he argued that a grand educational plan, not laws, would accomplish this feat. Drawing on the resolutions of the 1940 Inter-American Indigenista Congress at Patzcuaro, Claure claimed that education for Indians must not be based on racial differences but should pursue the same aims as education for other social groups. His proposals belied this professed concern with parity and echoed the segregationist plans of the 1920s. Claure endorsed a comprehensive

21 Closing session of the Indigenous Congress, 15 May 1945 (published in *La Razón*). This
photo shows the marked attention to indigenous symbolism that characterized the final
session of the congress. The delegates in the front row are wearing the traditional dress
of an altiplano region; several of them are holding the alcalde's bastón de mando. The two
delegates in the center of the third row are dressed in the attire used for a lowland festival
dance. *Courtesy of the U.S. National Archives*.

plan of health, education, agricultural and social reforms—a "crusade to
rehabilitate the indígena"—that would make Indians modern agriculturalists and keep them on the land. Rural education, he maintained, should
instill morality, order, Christian doctrine, and patriarchal norms. As Indian men became productive agriculturalists, Indian women would be
"dignified and prepared in a superior way for their role in the home."[96]

Deliberations over these official presentations resulted in four decrees
that were publicly recited on the final day of the congress (see figure 21).[97]
The first one called for the suppression or remuneration of any and all
nonagricultural labor or service that colonos were required to provide to
landowners (mail delivery, weaving, mukeo, etc.). The second abolished
pongueaje and mitanaje. The third called for schools on rural properties
(but with no reference to schools for Indian communities). And the fourth
mandated the preparation of an agrarian labor code as well as some immediate regulations such as a ceiling of four days on the rural work week.

An underlying concern of all four decrees was the need to bring the law to what was considered a lawless countryside. An article in the first decree prohibited peasants from collecting ramas in money or in kind. Henceforth, anyone caught taking up such collections could be charged with fraud. With this clause, the government aimed to stifle the independent organizing process that had produced the Indigenous Congress in the first place. Another article in the same decree criminalized the fraudulent sale of "copies of legislative initiatives, [and] other dispositions or material containing counterfeit property titles or other propaganda." The consideration here was twofold. Rural leaders were frequently accused of exchanging false property titles for the ramas they collected from rural followers. But the measure also criminalized the sale of proposed laws, presumably because they were passed off as real ones. This clause was similarly directed at rural "agitators," but they may not have been the only target. Bolivia's National Congress was itself accused of selling Indians legalized copies of parliamentary documents that registered decisions of benefit to them. The chief of the congressional editorial staff indignantly denied the allegation.[98] Even if untrue, the charge reveals the depth of anxieties about the law and what was perceived to be a widespread trafficking in legislative initiatives and property titles.

The majority of the items listed in the Indigenous Committee's twenty-seven-point agenda did not figure in the official program or government decrees. Most notably, the items about land had been eliminated. Indeed an official circular sent to prefects of all departments explicitly stated that there would be no return of communal land.[99] A close look at the proceedings of the congress reveals, however, that the question of the land was not entirely suppressed. By the time the Indigenous Congress was convened, some MNR leaders who allied with Villarroel had already made statements favoring some kind of land reform.[100] Villarroel himself on many occasions stressed the importance of the land, and in certain contexts focused special attention on the usurpation of communal property.[101] In a meeting with U.S. Embassy officials, the president described how "many times . . . Indians had been forced off their lands and . . . coerced or tricked into disposing of [them]."[102] He indicated further that the government planned to inspect registrations of rural property to determine who the real owners were, and that it would resolve cases where the land had been illegally obtained. Villarroel also stated that "such measures on behalf of the Indians and other social reforms which the Government contemplated were going to cause a lot of grumbling and discontent in the country." But "it was a case of 200,000 against 2,000,000 and the Government was going to do right by the 2,000,000." Much like the caciques apoderados had insisted two decades before him, Villarroel concluded that "Indians had been oppressed for hundreds of years, first by the Spaniards and then by the citizens of the Bolivian Republic."[103] His public statements about land were more hesitant, but Villarroel probably shared the expansive views with indigenous leaders in his unrecorded encounters with them. During a May 1945 stay in Tarabuco (Chuquisaca), one opposition leader recalled, Villarroel openly offered to distribute land to Indians.[104]

If Villarroel was generally reticent in public, the prominent MNR politician Hernán Siles Zuazo broached the question of the land in a widely publicized speech to the Indigenous Congress delegates. His words were broadcast live on the radio and quoted the following day in several newspapers. Speaking in the name of the MNR party, Siles declared that "the land should belong to those who work it." This is precisely what the Bolivian Indigenous Committee led by Ramos had claimed. Siles later regretted the words, but he could not retract them.[105] Several other speakers mentioned the land at the Indigenous Congress. The talk endorsing a rural police force noted "the constant usurpation of communal lands due to the expansionist voracity of some landlords, who use either violent or juridical means."[106] A presentation on cooperatives posed a powerful contrast between the liberal attempt to "disregard and even destroy Indian communities" and the corporatist recognition of communal property.[107] Finally, shortly after the congress ended, the minister of labor himself reported that delegates had presented a demand for "the return of lands that . . . [had] belonged to [colonos] since the colonial era and had been seized from them by the landlords."[108] Although the official organizing committee emphasized labor issues, these subtexts about the land would have lasting resonance.

Given the demands and expectations of the delegates, the four formal decrees were only modest gains. Some of the outlawed labor requirements continued to be imposed on many properties: landlords simply changed the names of the duties. New and old authorities charged with implementing the provisions of the congress failed to do so. And Bolivia's National Congress could not settle on an agrarian labor code, as the Indigenous Congress stipulated. Nor did it ratify the four decrees.[109] The National Congress did not possess effective mechanisms to enforce them anyway. Thus the law remained ever more forcefully in the hands of landlords and local authorities.

There was, however, one significant shift. Delegates returned with knowledge of favorable decrees and the president's overt backing. In at least one case, and probably in others, the minister of government explicitly ordered a colono to deliver duplicates of the rulings to local authorities.[110] And while the government planned to publish the laws in native languages, the proposed pamphlets did not appear. This predicament made indigenous delegates the main messengers of Villarroel's edicts. Of course making colonos direct conduits of the law wholly contradicted the institutionalizing mission of the Indigenous Congress.

Despite their shortcomings, the laws imparted some important new rights to colonos and comunarios. The decree outlawing unpaid service duties not only placed limits on non-agricultural work requirements; it made colonos "absolute owners" of their crops and gave them explicit permission to sell those products in markets. The decree also eliminated landlords' prerogative to purchase colonos' goods for negligible sums; if landlords did purchase the items, they would have to pay the going price. The same law barred landlords from taking colonos' crops or livestock in exchange for pasture rights (*herbaje* or *pastoraje*). This change had special significance in Cochabamba, where landlords allowed colonos to graze their animals on hacienda land only if they handed over one-tenth of all the animals born in a given year. The decree in addition forbid landlords from requiring resident workers to contribute to the catastro (land tax), in money or in kind. The decree abolishing unpaid services thus addressed grievances that had been fundamental to the rural strikes and petitions of the early 1940s. Still it did not overlook landlords' concerns. One article in the law obliged colonos to transport hacienda goods to towns and cities, "following an agreement regarding payment and, if necessary, with the intercession of the closest political authority." Moreover, another decree—the one that mandated the preparation of an agrarian labor code—preserved hacendados' right to use colonos' animals for agricultural labor without compensating them. It also prohibited resident workers from providing replacements for their work unless the landlord agreed, thus further restricting colonos' economic autonomy.[111]

Without doubt, the decree outlawing pongueaje contained the most expansive guarantees. The text of the law, which bore the influence of Morales's keynote address, took this unremunerated service as the absolute absence of rights. The decree not only forbid landlords from requiring the domestic service but prohibited all local authorities (political, judicial, and ecclesiastic) from demanding uncompensated services of colonos, comunarios, or "residents of cities and towns." Any official who violated the law would be dismissed from his post. The decree also noted that "slavery [did] not exist in Bolivia" and underscored every person's "right to fair payment for the work they voluntarily undertake." Finally, it linked the abolition of pongueaje with "the indígena's . . . possession of civil rights . . . [as a] member of the [national] community." With the eradication of pongueaje, it could be said, Villarroel not only prohibited a degrading duty but conferred to Indians the civil rights that all Bolivians were owed. Indeed the Indigenous Committee itself linked the end of pongueaje with a larger sense of respect and rights: "If our hopes are realized . . . THE INDIAN WILL GO TO SCHOOL, NEVER AGAIN WILL [THE INDIAN] BE THE BEAST OF BURDEN. [THE INDIAN] WILL BE THE CITIZEN WHO WINS RESPECT FOR BOLIVIA."[112] Citizens, from this perspective, were those who were not subjected to servitude.

Not just the content of Villarroel's decrees carried weight. What made the laws historic was the locus of enunciation. Their force resided in where and to whom they were announced and in who would be authorized to convey them. In theory, the decrees would be transmitted to and through representatives of the state. If effectively established, such mechanisms of communication between local and national authorities might have ensured greater governability.[113] But that goal was not achieved. Rather than resolving a perceived crisis of the law by professionalizing, codifying, and institutionalizing legal practice as planned, the Indigenous Congress exacerbated the turmoil by empowering indigenous delegates themselves to be agents of the law.

On the final day of the congress, the government threw a large party in a field adjacent to the La Paz cemetery. Military bands played. Villarroel and other government officials shared food and drink with the delegates, and conversed with them in Quechua. This encounter of solidarity and confraternity left poignant memories with many delegates, for it evoked the bond that rural leaders had established with "their" president.[114] In large part, Villarroel presented himself to Indians as a father who would provide for his children if they behaved. The president did not rule by paternalistic means exclusively, however. Villarroel was a protective figure, one who bestowed not just gifts but also laws that would outlive him. His four most important offerings were rights conferred in a public assembly, to indigenous delegates who had already claimed those rights over decades of petitioning, strikes, and rebellions. While Saavedra in the 1920s and Busch in the 1930s met privately with indigenous leaders, Villarroel addressed them publicly in a national forum. The president did not just bestow rights: he made indigenous leaders bearers of his laws.

✳ The Aftermath of the Congress

Delegates' physical return to haciendas after the Indigenous Congress was difficult, and sometimes it could only be accomplished furtively. Their efforts to inform fellow colonos about the congress were also fraught with obstacles. Landlords sought to obstruct the decrees, intimidate colonos, and punish so-called agitators. Over the course of the year following the May meeting, sit-down strikes became common on haciendas in many regions, as colonos themselves tried to enforce compliance with Villarroel's laws.[115] During the early 1940s, such strikes had been centered in Cochabamba and Oruro, but the department of La Paz was also affected in 1945.[116] Delegations of peasants from throughout the country traveled to the capital to denounce reprisals and request "guarantees." Rather than enforcing the decrees, they complained, local officials imposed fines if they did not fulfill duties just outlawed by the president. Much like before the Indigenous Congress, government authorities accused local leaders and "outsiders" of copying and distributing proposed laws and fraudulent land titles.

In the months following the congress, the press gave extensive coverage to a series of conspiracies that involved contests over the meanings of the 1945 decrees. In Tapacarí, a family was blamed for turning its house into a "Permanent Secretariat of Indians" where typed copies of laws abolishing pongueaje were distributed and promises of imminent land distribution were announced.[117] Another, more celebrated, episode involved Mizque's Manuel Andia, a chicha producer whose parents were small landowners. Although Andia maintained ties with the Alcaldes Mayores Particulares movement (chapter 5), the principal object of his activism was not so much schools as unjust taxes and tax collectors.[118] In December 1945, Andia reportedly provoked disturbances on properties in both Mizque and Aiquile: he promised to distribute land, eliminate haciendas, and abolish taxes. As Andia's movement gained adherents, some observers even claimed that he pledged to "restore the Inca empire." Reportedly no taxes at all had been collected in the area for a full three years due to Andia's proclamations.[119] The opposition press depicted the movement as a plot manufactured by the government and MNR militants who implanted themselves in

Aiquile as judge and defender of Indians with the aid of the local police. The Villarroel-MNR government instead attributed this incident and others like it to poor understandings of the 1945 decrees.[120] In fact, Andia himself carried news of the Indigenous Congress to colonos in Aiquile.[121]

In the face of the escalating unrest, government authorities called on Dr. Humberto Calvi, legal advisor and director of indigenous affairs for the police, to correct peasants' "misinterpretations" of Villarroel's 1945 decrees.[122] In December 1945 Calvi was called to a strike in Capinota to clarify the scope of the laws and ensure that colonos fulfilled their obligations. Calvi also accompanied a police commission to Ayopaya to "explain to the peasants the true meaning of the agrarian-social laws promulgated . . . by the First Indigenous Congress." The laws were being interpreted in an "irregular manner" there, causing "grave abnormalities in agricultural production." In July 1946, Calvi journeyed to Aiquile, home of Manuel Andia, to adjudicate conflicts resulting from colonos' "faulty interpretations" of the laws.[123] As part of its effort to quell the unrest, the government even arranged a meeting between Calvi and indigenous delegates and "ringleaders" from the entire department of Cochabamba. Addressing his audience in Quechua, Calvi outlined the "true" meanings of the decrees so "the indígenas" would "correctly interpret each article."[124]

Without doubt, the expectations unleashed by the Indigenous Congress and Villarroel's decrees helped trigger the unrest of 1945–46. The Sociedad Rural itself blamed the agitation on the president's laws. Of course, observers held "demagogues," government agents, and lower-level MNR militants responsible for the disturbances.[125] But the primary cause of the agitation, one landlord stressed, was the "twisted" interpretation of the May laws, "which have driven the peasant . . . to adopt rebellious and insolent attitudes toward his bosses."[126] Writing in 1951, the future agrarian reform commission member Raimundo Grigoriú suggested more broadly that the atmosphere of intense political conflict and agitation surrounding the 1945 Indigenous Congress led Indians to "misunderstand" the decrees: they assumed that the laws would make them owners of the land and exempt them from all obligations to the hacienda.[127] The government itself anticipated such developments, for the decree outlawing pongueaje provided sanctions against peasants who invoked the law falsely to dodge their agricultural obligations. The most influential outcome of the Indigenous Congress was an unintended one: a powerful association between the government, the land, the end of hacienda duties, and a law against servitude.

✳ "Special Justice" for Indians

The months following the May 1945 Indigenous Congress were a time of intense political agitation and expectation. In this turbulent atmosphere, Bolivia's National Congress debated one of the most interesting if least-remembered legislative initiatives of the pre-revolutionary era: a resolution for "special justice."[128] The proposed law called for the creation of indigenous juries that would conduct oral trials in native languages in line with local "uses and customs." The initiative's sponsor was none other than Hernán Siles Zuazo, founding member of the MNR and future president (1956–60, 1982–85). Initially, Siles said that the special tribunals should restrict themselves to petty crimes among peasants (campesinos) or indígenas.[129] Toward the end of his congressional address, he suggested that the indigenous tribunals should also hear crimes between peasants/indígenas and rural powerbrokers. The "white mestizo," "exploiter of the Indian's labor," Siles concluded, must also submit to peasant juries and thus to the "jurisdiction of the national majority."[130]

That the leading member of a party dedicated to ideals of national unity and "incorporation" would propose a system of indigenous juries in and of itself is extremely noteworthy. That he did so at the height of indigenous demands for the return of usurped communal land, the reincorporation of evicted colonos, and an end to abuse by landlords and local authorities makes this proposal all the more compelling. In part, Siles justified the measure with appeal to an age-old fear of "race war." Continual recourse to ordinary courts by peasants/indígenas often ended in conflicts, he warned. Those conflicts could push the nation to a civil war more destructive than one in an ethnically homogeneous nation, because it would be rooted in "racial hatred." Siles also articulated a second compelling reason: he considered the measure for "special justice" a means to fortify the nation.[131] A stronger nation, Siles implied, would be achieved not only by expanding the state's Hispanicizing institutions to rural areas but also via the opposite: by recognizing indigenous language, law, and custom.

Siles's unusual measure breathed a very short life. Initially criticized, temporarily approved, and then repeatedly modified, it was finally transferred to the "Commission on Indigenous Affairs," which amounted to a relatively swift legislative death. Many practical objections were raised, about jurisdictional limits, for example, and whether court resolutions should be in writing. Whether or not customary justice violated human rights, a key criticism of similar measures proposed in the 1990s, was not an issue then. Instead the obstacle that most thoroughly buried this unprecedented measure for indigenous justice was the inability to decide whom it was for: "Indios"? "Campesinos"? "Campesinos indígenas"? The "indigenous race"? A race, or a class? The National Congress could not agree on terms.

To a certain extent, Siles's 1945 recommendation resembled the protective and paternalistic ethos of the 1920s plans for special laws and Patronatos Indígenas. The 1945 measure for special justice departed from the earlier model, however, by appealing not simply to special protections but to indigenous language, law, and custom. At least implicitly, debates over the initiative also recognized that Indianness was not confined to rural spheres but was very much an urban identity. Indeed, the blurring of ethnic and spatial boundaries made it impossible for lawmakers to come to any agreement about just whom special justice would be for.

Such blurring of boundaries was itself a tool the government capitalized on in its surveillance of indigenous movements. In the 1920s, government authorities often charged that indigenous leaders were not really "Indians" but instead "mestizos" masquerading as Indians; it was a strategy to discredit their demands. A similar pronouncement was made about the elusive figure Luis Ramos Quevedo. As officials grew to distrust Ramos's political intentions, they began to spy on him, and to raise questions about his "true" racial identity. Government authorities eventually concluded that Ramos was not an Indian. And it was this presumed unmasking of his identity that partly led to Ramos's imprisonment.[132] In his public appearances, Ramos in fact consistently presented himself as a non-Indian: in a February 1945 interview he said he had learned about the "idiosyncrasy of the Bolivian indígena by living with the keshuas [Quechuas] and the Aymaras," thus suggesting that he was neither.[133] The Indigenous Committee bulletin also implied that Ramos was a non-Indian who "lived closely with the Indian, like no one else had ever managed to do."[134] Before Ramos became a political threat, the government never questioned his ethnicity.

In part, such queries reinvoked liberal-oligarchic ideologies of race. Accusations that Ramos was not really an Indian conjured up longstanding assumptions about purity and danger; about the innocence of Indians versus the nefarious interference of mestizos, labor organizers, or "communists"; and about the sanctity of rural society versus the contaminating effects of cities. Indians were defined as beings who needed representation and protection or else they would be exploited by "outsiders" under any number of names. The questions about Ramos cut simultaneously to the realities of racial blurriness in twentieth-century Bolivia. There was much rural–urban migration in the 1920s, but those movements were even more pronounced after the Chaco War; by the mid-1940s, many of Bolivia's major cities had been significantly "Indianized." The questions about Ramos thus display authorities' distress about the lapse of presumed boundaries—rural/urban, "indian"/"mestizo" divides—by a new generation of organizers who were themselves the product of such transgressions.

In the late 1930s, some public advocates began to question and even reject "race" and the derogatory term *indio*. Bolivia's reformist and revolutionary intellectuals did not fully expunge or outlaw the words, however. The discussion of special justice vividly shows how they vacillated about what to call rural inhabitants and rural–urban migrants. Unlike Ecuadorian state authorities, Bolivian officials never eliminated the category "Indian" from the census.[135] Rather than discarding the term, they sought to stabilize the meaning of Indian and refix Indians' social place.

If law and society had changed dramatically, debates about the 1945 proposal reveal that its backers had not shed the paternalistic vision that motivated their pre–Chaco War indigenista counterparts. Like proposals of the 1920s, the 1945 measure for special justice presumed an indigenous population that lived outside the law, beyond the state's courts and decrees. It assumed that Indians were innocent, uneducated beings who needed to be protected from mestizos and other "urban dangers." The debate over Siles's tabled proposal can thus be summed up as a forward-looking recognition of indigenous rights, and a backward glance at special protection. For Siles could simultaneously affirm indigenous justice and praise colonial law; he said at one point that the laws of colonialism were superior even to those just passed by the Indigenous Congress. And one of his colleagues could declare Bolivia an indigenous nation but lament the lack of unity, the inability to "mix" Indians with whites and mestizos. And Siles could recognize indigenous authorities but slip and call their historic encounter with the president a "Peasant Congress."[136] The recognition of Indianness—in the legal realm—was fraught with tension. Indians should be bearers of the law; indigenous language, law, and custom should be elements of the nation's legal order. If such ideals were to be realized, however, Indians had to be safely ensconced in rural realms. Indigenista thinking of the forties was a thing in flux. "Unity" and "incorporation" were goals, but vague and distant ones that were often combined with a call for rural seclusion. As some legislators who debated the MNR's "special justice" proposal implicitly acknowledged, the latter was not only a new mode of colonization: it was utterly unrealizable.

✴ Conclusion

There are many reasons why vacillation between assimilationist and anti-assimilationist norms so deeply marked antioligarchic political projects of the 1940s. One crucial factor was precisely the unique strata of indigenous political and intellectual leaders who continuously intervened in the public sphere. That public sphere had changed and expanded significantly by the 1940s. Powerful public dialogues marked this decade. Greater ideological diversity characterized the debates, and many new political entities participated in them. What had been isolated, private conversations between indigenous leaders and elite politicians in the 1920s could now be public discussions convened in national arenas and broadly publicized by the press. In pursuit of competing aims, powerful and not-so-powerful allies endorsed indigenous claims for land and justice to an extent not previously witnessed. This continuous force of indigenous mobilization helps explain why indigenous protection and guarantees were such a powerful impetus, and why some populist politicians thought they could be—had to be—a means of national unity.

Twentieth-century indigenismo of the type elaborated by Villarroel and the MNR undoubtedly struck a paternalistic posture, one that usually implied the negation of Indian agency. Yet the specific alignment of political forces is what ultimately gives meaning to such doctrines. As the Indigenous Congress and the debate over "special justice" show, indigenous rights and guarantees were a strategy of rule rooted in hierarchical concepts of race. Yet it would be wrong to consider such concepts a tool of domination alone. State authorities were patently unable to control the circulation and meaning of laws and decrees, even when their own institutions were the source of the powerful papers. Villarroel-MNR populists sought to regulate rural peoples and communities in the interests of "modernization," but they did not manage to suffocate Indian agency. Nor could they simply reinforce images of Indians as illiterate or "backward" beings, as obstacles to "progress." This is not to suggest that Villarroel's populist indigenista project affirmed full equality, for it did not. Yet the government was unable to completely stifle the public interventions of rural–urban interlopers such as Luis Ramos Quevedo, Hilarión Grájeda, Dionisio Miranda, and many lesser-known Quechua and Aymara leaders who insisted that Indianness was compatible with literacy, legal expertise, technical innovation, rights, and the "renovation" of the nation.

It was just this seizing of rights and representation that irked landlords grouped in the Sociedad Rural. Once the Indigenous Congress concluded, the association expressed numerous complaints concerning the deleterious effects the decrees would have for the nation's agriculture.[137] Its harshest criticism had less to do with production than with the impact of the laws on Indians' sense of themselves: "The most serious aspect of the social question is the fact that the indígena is allowed to believe that everything in the country represents his efforts, his hardships, his sacrifices, and even his blood, and that as a result he has the full right to demand whatever he wants from the authorities and the whites. With this policy, which is likely to spark a race war, the government forgets that it is the white who works the land the most, who contributes the greatest percentage in taxes, while the Indian contributes almost nothing."[138]

The power this passage attributes to "the indígena" is striking. If the words display hacendados' fears, they also suggest the efficacy of decades of petitions, strikes, assemblies, and other interventions by indigenous leaders in the public sphere. The remark does not just register a complaint about insolence; it replicates the language and logic of longstanding indigenous demands, demands that the state recognize Indians' contributions to the economy and the nation, offerings of work, blood, and taxes. The landlord association objected, above all, to the fact that public authorities had allowed "the Indian" to think he had "full rights."

In reality, Villarroel did not endow Indians with "full rights." Although the president sometimes spoke in favor of land reform and salaried agricultural labor, his government did not legislate a land reform; nor did his laws significantly alter the labor system on haciendas. Uncompensated service ended, but agricultural work itself would still go without pay. Such inconsistencies continued to mark Villarroel's rural policy after the Indigenous Congress concluded. In October 1945, the National Convention approved a law that suspended all lawsuits to evict colonos from haciendas and prohibited the colonos' dismissal. The Villarroel government vetoed this sweeping measure for two reasons: because it put landlords in an "indefensible position in the face of [colonos'] . . . recognized impunity" and because it "constituted a grave threat to agricultural production."[139]

On the basis of such rulings, it might seem that the government ultimately sided with the landed elite. Yet Villarroel's policies were not all of one piece, and they were too little to earn the landlords' cooperation. Despite profound contradictions, the president repeatedly showed with symbolic and legal acts exactly where his "friendship" lay. When members of the Sociedad Rural submitted requests for modifications of the four Indigenous Congress decrees, the president's office returned their pleas with a note stating that their missive did not follow protocol. And although the president permitted the Sociedad Rural to hold its third national convention in 1945, he did not officially sponsor the meeting, as Toro and Busch had done in 1936 and 1939.[140] By demonstrating with such seemingly innocuous gestures that he was a "better friend of the poor," Villarroel found that he could not avoid becoming an "enemy of the rich."

For the far-flung delegates who journeyed to La Paz in May 1945 and later returned to their communities bearing the president's decrees, such displays of personal loyalty left perhaps the most lasting impression. One delegate remembered the powerful stance Villarroel took against the oppression of the hacienda:

> President Villarroel arrived with some soldiers and gentlemen and greeted us in Quechua. Later he said to us: "Compañeros campesinos, you are seated in this place . . . because it is your place. And you should rest because certainly many of you have traveled great distances on foot; but the effort you have made will not be in vain. Now you should get to know each other, as peasant brothers from all parts, because all of the peasants must unite, that is why I have called you here. . . . From now on you will have to go to school and you will no longer be the animals of the landlords; the landlords will have to work the land, and they will moor the oxen to plow the land and from now on there will be no more pongos or mitanis. You will be free. Now it is your turn to be gentlemen. If I end up dying, I will die content knowing you are free." That is what President Villarroel told us.[141]

This striking recollection highlights Villarroel's concern with education, just as it underscores his insistence on equality and freedom. The president did not simply condemn pongueaje and mitanaje; nor did he just posit a process of social improvement (for Indian men). In the delegate's remembrance, Villarroel actually inverted the social hierarchy. Landlords would work the land, while peasants would be freed; hacienda colonos would take a turn at being "gentlemen." With the allusion to his own death, finally, Villarroel revealed his utter devotion to the colonos' freedom.

Ultimately, it is the connection between the law and the president's looming death that resonates most forcefully in the rare windows we have on Villarroel's unofficial thoughts. In the face of virulent opposition, Villarroel considered his own demise imminent, and he saw the legacy of his December 1943 revolution as the law. Fermín Vallejos, a former colono from Raqaypampa (Mizque) recalls that Villarroel said: "This decree-law will not die. I may disappear, surely they will kill me like a dog. My days are numbered. But this law will last no matter who becomes president."[142] The president's words were prescient ones indeed.

CHAPTER EIGHT

"UNDER THE DOMINION OF THE INDIAN"

The 1947 Cycle of Unrest

On 21 July 1946, a popular revolt overthrew the Villarroel-MNR regime. The movement to depose the president culminated in an act of spectacular violence: he was hung from a lamppost outside the Government Palace alongside the corpses of several other high-ranking officials. Against a backdrop of urban strikes, rural unrest, and acts of state repression, an unlikely anti-Villarroel coalition was formed: the Frente Democrático Antifascista (Democratic Antifascist Front, FDA). It brought together Liberal, Republican, and PIR politicians; striking teachers; upper-class women; students; and workers.[1] This multiclass movement, which claimed to defend democracy from "Nazi-Fascist" tyranny, toppled the government without any collaboration from the police or the army. The brutal end to the revolt remains clouded in myths about the ire of an unruly plebe and the violence of vengeful women. But we can say with certainty that the desecrated bodies were paying for political assassinations, wage freezes, restricted civil liberties, "anti-marriage" reforms, and contentious pro-Indian policies. Villarroel and his associates paid twice: first with their lives, and then with the spectacle of a postmortem lynching.

The anti-Villarroel movement drew much legitimacy

from the global anti-Fascist current of the immediate postwar period. And its position was reinforced by the United States, which erroneously labeled Villarroel's government Fascist. But domestic polarization ran deep in 1946, and those local factors ultimately explain the overthrow and its extreme brutality. At center stage was the government's conflict with mine owners, who resented an April 1945 decree that once again mandated deposit of export earnings in the Central Bank. Teachers in turn joined the July movement because the government's fiscal austerity left them with miserable raises. Tensions with landowners also played a fundamental role, for the 1945 Indigenous Congress and Villarroel's decrees profoundly antagonized the landlord association, as we have just seen. Following the 1945 Congress and during the final months of his presidency, Villarroel organized massive rallies of peasants and workers in La Paz and Oruro. These visible displays of support only heightened the association between Indians and the president—and the rage against both. As opposition spread, the governing coalition itself began to unwind.[2]

A series of conservative civilian and military governments followed Villarroel's 1946 demise. Hand in hand with this conservative backlash, the president's overthrow triggered a cycle of rural rebellions. These wide-scale but largely unstudied uprisings commenced in mid-January 1947, just after the presidential elections, and came to a denouement only in about June of the same year. Encompassing haciendas and communities in the departments of Cochabamba, Chuquisaca, La Paz, Oruro, and Tarija, these were arguably Bolivia's largest rural uprisings of the twentieth century.[3] Rebels hailed from areas where private estates were deeply entrenched. They also came from places where Indian communities remained visible figures of a recently expropriated past. They agitated in areas where labor organizers had longstanding contacts, and in places where the 1920s cacique apoderado networks were based. Emboldened by the 1945 anti-pongueaje decree and other "laws decreed in favor of the peasantry," leaders of the 1947 uprisings variously claimed land, "community," schools, unions, the end of "slavery," the destruction of haciendas, and local government by Indians. Much more was at stake than the obligations of work: the rebels denounced an unlawful system of domination.

The few existing works on 1947 rightly recognize this cycle of unrest as a critical turning point that marked the apex of indigenous movements and the shift to MNR-led insurrection. For all the truth it contains, this view of the rebellions obscures significant continuity, both before and after 1947.

Despite heightened aggression against landlords, the 1947 unrest resembled the protests that preceded Villarroel's overthrow.[4] Protagonists engaged in work stoppages, demanded land and education, called for official recognition of unions, insisted on enforcement of the 1945 decrees, and denounced abuse by landlords and local authorities. To pressure the government, gather adherents, and make themselves known, they employed a wealth of tactics ranging from petitions and manifestos to the physical occupation of strategic territory and the circulation of rumors, titles, and laws. The events of 1947 certainly constituted a full-scale assault against landlord power; but armed action was not the only strategy, hacienda colonos were not the only actors, and the repression—for all its vigor—did not completely suppress rural political action.

If the uprisings resembled and belonged to a longer cycle of unrest, why did outright rebellion reach a high point in 1947? In part, the rebellions were linked with regional political trends. The period between World War II and the beginning of the cold war represented a "critical conjuncture" in Latin America.[5] Between 1944 and 1946, the region witnessed processes of democratization, radical labor movements, and the rise of the Left. This political opening closed down quickly with the shift to cold war containment. From 1946 to 1948, the Right gained ascendancy throughout Latin America: labor movements were restrained and scrutinized, communist parties were outlawed, and democratic gains were reversed. Guatemala constitutes a notable exception to this pattern, both because the democratic opening lasted until 1954 and because direct U.S. intervention helped close it down. But Bolivia also defies the rule. Political space both opened and closed after Villarroel's bloody overthrow. After taking power in 1947, President Enrique Hertzog of the Partido Unión Republicana Socialista (PURS) certainly cracked down on the MNR and the FSTMB (Federation of Bolivian Mineworker Unions), which were blamed for political agitation in the mines and the countryside. His government did not simply suppress political activism, however. An unlikely confluence of circumstances even led the president to include members of Bolivia's Communist Party (the PIR) in an otherwise conservative cabinet.

However much Hertzog contrasted his "democratic" approach with Villarroel-MNR "Nazi-Fascism," his government actually sustained key aspects of the Villarroel-era reforms. Hertzog not only kept the Indigenous Congress decrees in place but adopted a virtual replica of the 1945 Constitution (after first abrogating it). His prefects in addition sent circulars to subprefects and corregidores reminding them to enforce the May 1945 decrees.[6] To ensure that landowners complied with "the laws that favored the indígenas," Hertzog himself promised to dispatch rural inspectors under the supervision of the Ministry of Labor and Agriculture.[7] Up to a point, Hertzog also permitted a renewed process of labor organization in the cities. But he discouraged unionization in rural areas and sided with mine owners against striking workers.[8] Finally, and most importantly, even though Hertzog's government retained Villarroel's 1945 laws, landlords refused to heed them. With the death of Villarroel, hacendados sought to reimpose their hegemony in the countryside.

The unusual combination of political suppression and opportunity that marked Bolivia's postwar conjuncture helped pave the path for the 1947 rebellions. Of course, a longer history of rural mobilization, populist politics, and agrarian change shaped rural movements after Villarroel's overthrow. But a close look at the rebels' visions in the two main areas of 1947 unrest—Cochabamba and La Paz—shows that the revolts were very much the product of a state-making process over which the state itself had incomplete control. Whether through recourse to Villarroel's decrees, or via union drives for land and education, the protests sprang from and exposed a deepening crisis of state power that successive governments were utterly unable to resolve. In Bolivia, the interlude between World War II and the cold war was a highly contradictory one: its ultimate outcome would not be the suppression of popular movements but a revolution with deep—and deeply divided—rural roots.

* "The Laws . . . Were Decreed for Us and Not for the Landlords"

For Margarita Coca viuda de Coca, civilization hung in the balance on 7 February 1947. This was the day the "indiada" toiling on her Ayopaya haciendas assassinated her husband, the lawyer José María Coca. According to the widow's testimony, the colonos "destroyed, burned, and robbed" the hacienda house, killed the caretaker, and mortally wounded Dr. Coca with several close-range shots to the chest. After attacking and disfiguring Coca's cadaver, the rebels sacked and destroyed furniture, the house, and everything else they could not carry away. Taking with them a typewriter, a sewing machine, clothes, potatoes and maize, and Coca's horse, most of the insurgents abandoned the premises. Two men left to guard the dead owner then proceeded to burn "all of Dr. Coca's papers and documents, including property titles, loan papers, and books of laws."[9] With this symbolic act of violence, they destroyed the legal trappings of the landlord's domain.

Of the many sites of rebellion, the Ayopaya uprising stands out for its magnitude and resonance. Centered at the Hacienda Yayani (see map 3), the uprising encompassed numerous other properties in the area and reportedly involved anywhere from 3,000 to 10,000 individuals. Between 4 and 10 February, colonos of Ayopaya and several other properties attacked and pillaged Yayani and eight other estates. They also ransacked the offices of the corregidor in two adjoining towns. And they paid a visit to the tax collector, where they "charged [their] own tax" while retrieving garments that had been confiscated from colonos who failed to pay various duties (probably for chicha and muko).[10] In addition to killing Dr. Coca and his caretaker, the insurgents murdered Lt. Col. José Mercado, who had been called to guard the Yayani hacienda during the tense months immediately preceding the uprising. The rebels also destroyed the school in Yayani and threatened to hang the husband of the landlord-contracted teacher.[11] Pursued by the police and the military, some of the rebels took flight to Oruro, where they expected to receive reinforcements. Others retreated to the adjacent province of Tapacarí. Local inhabitants joined them there in attacks against several other highland properties. Indeed, Tapacarí became a second central theater of the unrest. Rebels in this province above all fought against grazing charges (herbaje), a persistent source of conflict on many Cochabamba properties and something that was outlawed by the Indigenous Congress decrees. Because some cantonal authorities in Tapacarí had spoken against the fees, the prefect even accused them of instigating the 1947 unrest.[12]

Why did colonos on so many Ayopaya haciendas rise up against landlords, local authorities, and tax collectors in 1947? Scholarship on the revolt emphasizes the heightened labor burdens on Ayopaya estates and suggests that the rebels, who forged a close bond with Villarroel, were motivated by landlords' failure to heed the president's decrees against exploitation and abuse.[13] Focusing on trial testimonies, the following discussion illustrates that the rebellion involved a much wider contest over the meanings of Villarroel's 1945 laws. In the course of the rebellion, the Ayopaya rebels connected an imaginary law for revolution with Villarroel's real decrees against servitude. In doing so, the insurgents not only appropriated and redefined the state's decrees against pongueaje and other service duties: they enacted their own vision of justice and the law.[14]

The 1947 Ayopaya uprising was facilitated by hacienda colonos' tightly knit organization and by the direction of several outstanding leaders who had knowledge of the law. Colonos and landlords alike knew the three men who spearheaded the revolt as *cabecillas* and *alcaldes*. An office of colonial origin, the indigenous alcalde was situated both to serve local government —primarily in a judicial capacity—and to represent the community before outside powers.[15] *Cabecilla*, in turn, means "ringleader." In the pre-revolutionary era, the term was used in a derogatory sense by landlords and local authorities to denote rural "agitators" who led strikes and rebellions. But peasants and Indians also used the label to describe their own leaders.[16] Witnesses from Llajma and Moyapampa (two haciendas near the border between Ayopaya and Tapacarí) provided a very specific definition of the word: they identified as cabecillas the men who traveled to La Paz to demand schools or attend the Indigenous Congress.[17]

If the legitimacy of the cabecillas derived from outside contacts, their prestige was also based on local service to hacienda colonos as alcaldes. Consider the case of Hilarión Grájeda, one of the principal leaders of the 1947 rebellion and a key player in the 1945 Indigenous Congress. After advancing through several other hacienda posts such as *alcalde segundo* and *alcalde de fiesta*, Grájeda had been named alcalde de campo of Yayani.[18] According to republican legal codes, the alcalde de campo was a judicial and police agent of an ayllu who was appointed by the municipal council.[19] In Ayopaya—and probably in other provinces and departments —this figure was the highest indigenous authority of one of four hacienda *suyus* (Quechua for sections). Although landlords or the state could demand judicial and supervisory duties of the alcaldes, a significant degree of colono input figured in the alcalde de campo's selection, for candidates first had to work up the ladder of less prestigious posts.[20] The lower-level alcaldes also owed the community important political duties: they took charge of collecting ramas for the cabecillas who traveled to La Paz to wage colonos' legal battles, and they played a critical role in the organization of insurgent forces. For inciting disobedience and encouraging workers to shirk their agricultural duties, Grájeda had been evicted from Yayani; at the time of the 1947 rebellion he lived in hiding somewhere in Ayopaya, where he held secret meetings with colonos from various haciendas. Before this revered—and sometimes feared—alcalde was driven out by the owners, he campaigned for many years against pongueaje and mitanaje, and lobbied authorities for schools.[21] Much like the caciques apoderados, Grájeda and other hacienda alcaldes derived their authority from both official and community sources. Neither landlords nor state officials could fully control the actions—or the image—of hacienda alcaldes such as Grájeda.[22]

A second principal leader of the Ayopaya uprising, Antonio Ramos, also exemplified the cabecilla-alcalde figure. Like Grájeda, Ramos maintained external ties, possessed knowledge of the law, and attested to an established record of service to other colonos. And he too had reached the highest level of authority on Parte Libre, another Ayopaya hacienda. But there was a difference: by calling himself an alcalde mayor, rather than an alcalde de campo, Ramos merged his own standing as an established local leader with an official colonial-era post. The alcalde mayor position, which dates to the sixteenth-century Toledan period, was originally a municipal authority in Indian towns. Like ordinary alcaldes, the alcalde mayor served principally as an enforcer of the law, yet he enjoyed a higher status than the other alcaldes.[23] In seizing this particular label, Ramos gave new meaning to the post. He noted in an interview with the Cochabamba daily *Los Tiempos* that the title put him in a "position of superiority" over the other leaders. He also said that the designation had been conferred by the government in La Paz and that it made him the "principal agent of all the demands of the natives in [his] region before the Oficina de Defensa Gratuita."[24] By making the state's recognition of his status a crucial characteristic of the position, Ramos asserted his own power over other local leaders while insisting on his own legitimacy before the state.

As cabecillas and alcaldes, Grájeda and Ramos labored painstakingly to obtain "guarantees" to enforce the Villarroel decrees, to no avail. While Villarroel was still in power, Ramos traveled to La Paz to file complaints regarding colonos' service obligations. When he returned to Parte Libre after one such trip, he said, "we fixed things . . . with the owner . . . and worked with considerable effort." But the arrangement did not last. In August 1946, a month after Villarroel's murder, a new renter reimposed all of the obligations that had been abolished by the deposed regime and told the colonos "your President has died. . . . Everything has changed."[25] In January 1947, Ramos once again journeyed to La Paz to visit the Defensa Gratuita, where lawyers reassured him—he testified—that "all" the obligations had in fact been abolished. When he asked for "guarantees," the lawyers gave Ramos some documents. Upon his return to the hacienda, the renter threatened Ramos once again and confiscated the "papers of guarantee."[26]

Like Ramos, Grájeda grew increasingly frustrated by the landlords' and hacienda administrators' refusals to observe the laws against service duties. But he emphasized specific kinds of abuse. Grájeda testified in court that the single cause of the Ayopaya uprising was the "multiple abuses" committed on the hacienda "against the married, single, and young women." He also declared that the hacienda administrators "made us work without rest, and for whatever insignificant thing . . . took our livestock." The owners, Grájeda declared in a communiqué, "never comply with the decrees" and put the colonos in a state of "terrible slavery."[27]

For the rebels of Ayopaya, the refusal of the landlords to heed the law implied much more than the imposition of outlawed duties. The denial meant that the owners had violated their rights and were holding them in a kind of bondage. The Villarroel decrees in turn conjured up freedom from a form of labor that colonos equated with slavery. The laws also meant liberty to graze their own animals, consistent legal norms, and an end to the abuse of women. For the insurgents, Villarroel's laws heralded the end of the hacienda system itself—the end of an unlawful system of racialized and gendered domination.

Another critical spark behind the Ayopaya rebellion was the rumor of a government decree that ordered colonos to rise up against the landlords. Grájeda and Ramos learned about this supposed order by way of an apparently chance meeting with Gabriel Muñoz, a "mineworker comrade" Grájeda first met at the 1945 Indigenous Congress.[28] Muñoz reportedly told Ramos and Grájeda that "the press and the authorities had declared civil war in the nation and that an order had been issued to kill all the landlords and that all the land would then be distributed among the Indians, because it was the Indians' land, and that [the Indians] should no longer work on the haciendas."[29] Grájeda and Ramos apparently achieved a broad diffusion of this striking declaration, for numerous defendants repeated it. Sometimes it was called a law; other times it was referred to as an order; occasionally witnesses said it was a rumor. One crucial detail absent in the above rendition appeared in almost every other reference to the declaration: numerous witnesses declared that all the land would be "converted into communities."[30]

Many of the accused Ayopaya rebels linked the "law" they repeatedly invoked not only with political parties, but with a government presumed to be in power. A good number referenced the MNR, its leader Víctor Paz Estenssoro, or the head of the mineworker union (FSTMB), Juan Lechín. Others instead mentioned the PIR or the "communists."[31] For some, a party's orders played no role; they had acted to avenge the murder of *their* president (Villarroel).[32] In its decision, the court fixed responsibility on Lechín and Paz. Whether or not the Ayopaya movement was linked with the MNR's post-1946 attempted insurrections remains an open question. But it is unlikely that the MNR established direct ties with the insurgents.[33] After Villarroel's overthrow, MNR leaders went into exile, above all to Argentina. While they maintained some level of organization inside Bolivia via clandestine cells, the party was ill equipped to wage armed actions. Low-level affiliates—many of them former POR and PIR members who joined the MNR—agitated in rural areas, but the MNR leadership was unable to direct or control their actions at this early date. Antonio Alvarez Mamani and Francisco Chipana Ramos (president of the 1945 Indigenous Congress) were implicated in the Ayopaya uprising. Yet while both peasant leaders later became affiliated with the party, they were not, at the time of the rebellion, associates of the MNR. Whether true or false, the ruling against the MNR and the FSTMB fit with the government's more general effort to discredit the two organizations.[34]

Over the course of the trial, some of the interrogated did present evidence that "outsiders" had forced them to participate.[35] But the association that many witnesses made between political figures and the "law" suggests that an emphasis on external forces was more than coercive cover or even simple evasiveness. The accused were not just hiding behind the MNR, Paz, or Lechín; the "mineworker comrade" (Muñoz/Barrios); or the Indian "ringleader" (Grájeda). They conjured up a "law" a local leader described to them or even read from a newspaper. That law merged the official and unofficial agendas of the 1945 Indigenous Congress. It linked decrees against pongueaje with demands to return all the land to the "Community."

Such merging of messages is most apparent through loose inference or juxtaposition. For example, witnesses frequently said that the mineworker Muñoz told them, "we would all be comunarios, because the laws favor us and were decreed for us and not for the landlords."[36] Another witness explicitly connected the two themes. Asked about the origins of the uprising, he referred to the "law passed last year" that suspended "all requirements for pongueaje, cachas [running errands], mitanis, [gifts of] cheese, eggs, etc., and that finally we would be comunarios."[37] The force of the law is further evidenced by participants' descriptions of their own actions; even after the attack on the landlords' house, some said they traveled to Oruro to learn about the laws in their favor.[38] A letter apparently sent by Grájeda and Muñoz to Juan Lechín (addressed as the country's "vice-president") substantiates Grájeda's own investment in the law. The letter first denounces landlords' repeated failures to heed the decrees against forced services. Then it reports that "luckily it has been publicly decreed that there be revolution against exploitation and misery, and because abuses are committed; we have made a revolution in defense of our rights and the truth is that we do not abuse anyone without an order; just because we are blind does not mean that we do not understand what is the order of God and the current true law."[39]

The Ayopaya trial transcript suggests that an unreal but palpable revolutionary law to make everyone comunarios and all the land a Community was one of the most important, albeit unintended, consequences of the 1945 Indigenous Congress. The similarities between the claims of the rebels and the demands of the Indigenous Committee that spearheaded the congress are too great to be ignored. Both made the same magnificent request that all the land be returned to the Community. What did that oft-repeated phrase conjure up? Did the rebels mean communal property, or a community of small property owners? Were their allusions to many communities, or just one? Who were the members?

The trial transcript gives no clarity or consensus about the meaning of such terms, but a few of the declarations provide rough clues. During the months preceding Villarroel's July 1946 overthrow, and as the MNR politician Wálter Guevara Arze campaigned for deputy in Ayopaya, the press reported on a major work stoppage. Colonos on numerous properties in the province had refused to work on the hacienda for more than two days a week and demanded abolition of all the service duties mentioned in Villarroel's decrees.[40] Statements collected for the 1947 trial reveal that much more than labor obligations was at stake in this 1946 strike. The colonos not only insisted that existing authorities enforce Villarroel's 1945 laws; they implanted their own officials. One witness to the strike said that Mariano Vera, another local leader, told the Indians of the area not to obey the landowners' orders, because they were now "under the dominion of the Indian."[41] Vera said they should heed only the alcaldes' commands, as the alcaldes were higher than any other authorities in Ayopaya. He told the Indians "not to obey any authority appointed by law," because he and the other leaders were "primordial authorities," not "ringleaders" but "alcaldes mayores." As "primordial" authorities, Vera proposed, the alcaldes were both separate from and higher than officials appointed by the state (or by the landlords). While insisting that the law favored Indians, Vera and other local leaders flatly rejected the state's legal delegates.

In their depositions to the court, landlords, foremen, and the corregidor confirmed that Ayopaya had indeed come "under the dominion of the Indian" in 1946. The colonos, they charged, appointed their own alcaldes, and even the state's local representative, the corregidor. The "real" corregidor was only so in name and title; apparently he no longer held any authority.[42] If local power resided in Indians' hands, a few of the declarations by the accused allotted a clear space for the power and property of "whites." Antonio Ramos informed participants that a kind of equality of property rights would reign. "We would all be owners of the land, all the goods would be owned in common; in the countryside for the Indians, and in the town, the stores and things for the whites, in common for everyone." This vision apparently had wide support: "It made us all so happy when he said this," one witness testified.[43]

Viewed together with this ritual of justice, the Ayopaya uprising represents much more than a struggle against labor exploitation and abuse. It also embodied a process of political empowerment and confrontation whereby the community substituted its own authorities for the state's local representatives. A second complaint voiced by landlords in the year preceding the uprising adds further weight to this interpretation. The owners not only grumbled about colonos' insistence on full enforcement of the Villarroel decrees. Their most forceful gripe concerned the colonos' constant requests that they publicly recite the decrees to the last letter. In short, colonos insisted on the full performative force of the law; they demanded that every single stipulation be read to the public in the space of power (town square) by the properly authorized individual. They did not just demand the new rights granted by Villarroel's decrees; they strove to fix the limits of local power.[44] In the end, the colonos sought to replace hacienda hegemony with their own power.

✳ Alcaldes for Corregidores, Typewriters for Teachers

Not only in Ayopaya but throughout the Cochabamba region, 1947 protests linked land and labor with disputes over state authority. Two lesser-known conflicts—from Anzaldo and Sacabamba—further reveal how the rebellions were partly spurred by local authorities' growing independence from landlords. Like the Ayopaya insurgents, hacienda colonos in other areas of Cochabamba invoked novel interpretations of the 1945 laws. Their protests thus confirm the varied meanings and marked local effects of Villarroel's decrees.

The uprising in Anzaldo—an area of haciendas and smallholdings in Tarata province—involved a promise to restore or distribute land that echoed the Ayopaya rebels' call.[45] Anzaldo also evoked another characteristic element of the Villarroel-era mobilization: those ubiquitous forged land titles the government worried about. A hacienda administrator (who doubled as teacher) accused the "instigator" of the rebellion, the merchant Virgilio Vargas, of distributing papers "with the name of titles" and telling the colonos they were sufficient to make them "absolute owners of the property." Allegedly, Vargas also promised the colonos education: he was going to bring a teacher from La Paz who would show them how to read and write on typewriters. In fact, he would get "typewriters instead of teachers, because with typewriters alone it was possible to educate every child adequately, without the need of teachers." The hacienda administrator's school was "worthless," Vargas reportedly told the colonos. Many other witnesses corroborated the administrator's testimony. Two colonos declared that Vargas "sold them papers with seals" because the land was going to be turned into a community. Several other witnesses said the papers were linked with a land redistribution the government (or revolutionary authorities) would soon carry out. They also revealed that Vargas had deep roots in the region and was known as a local benefactor who assisted colonos when they were jailed. Apparently, he also visited haciendas in the area to sell *aguardiente* (liquor) and other goods.

In his ruling against Vargas, the judge failed to note the "illegible and incomprehensible" land titles witnesses mentioned, but these curious papers were certainly the most compelling proof of the "agitator's" presumed political intentions. They bear the seal of the alcalde mayor of Lechechoto (Mizque), Toribio Miranda, who had helped establish the Alcaldes Mayores Particulares movement in the post–Chaco War era and served as an important bridge between the Alcaldes movement and the 1920s cacique apoderado networks.[46] Surely this seal gave the papers their power—not only because it offered an official aura, but because the seal served, like a mnemonic device, as an object that tied the hacienda colonos to an interpreter who could explain what the seal meant (see figure 22).[47] Although the administrator accused Vargas of selling false titles, Vargas—and the

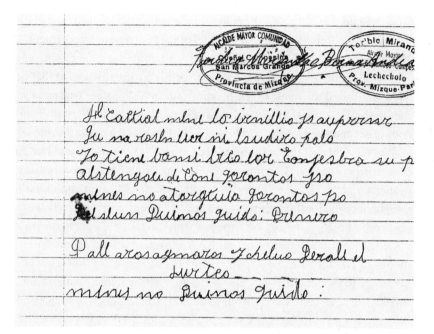

22 One of the "titles" Virgilio Vargas reportedly distributed to hacienda colonos in Anzaldo. It bears the seal of Toribio Miranda, Alcalde Mayor of Lechechoto (Mizque). *Archivo de la Corte Superior de Justicia de Cochabamba, Oficio contra Vargas y otros, 1947*.

colonos—may have viewed the papers as a forceful symbol of future hopes. Whatever the case, the papers bearing Miranda's stamp suggest a link between the agitation in Anzaldo, the Alcaldes Mayores Particulares movement, and broader disputes over power that had been unleashed by the Indigenous Congress and Villarroel's overthrow. Indeed, in Mizque-Aiquile, the alcaldes mayores had already been invested with significant local power. Striking colonos in that region not only claimed a kind of ownership of the land by marking off the boundaries of their own usufruct plots. They also named their own political authorities: alcaldes mayores. As in Ayopaya in 1946, colonos of Mizque and Aiquile in essence established their own local government. To authenticate their possession of the land, the alcaldes mayores even gave the colonos titles or "certificates."[48] Were the papers that Vargas distributed in Anzaldo the same certificates?

Oddly enough, the owner of the hacienda in Anzaldo—like the judge—overlooked Vargas's connection with Miranda and the alcaldes mayores. Instead, he suggested that the "instigator" had a different kind of ally. The landlord said that Vargas let the colonos believe that the legal advisor of the Security Police (also known as the "Chief of the Indigenous Department"), Humberto Calvi, had authorized him to "distribute land along with the relevant documents or receipts." Vargas, for his part, flatly denied that he had ever "raised the name of the Juridical Advisor." Whether true or false, the landlord's accusation is revealing, for it points to the depth of the hacienda crisis and the growing gap between landlords and local authorities.

Was the "chief of the indigenous department" of the police involved in deals with colonos and commercial middlemen? Did he defend Indians' property rights? The possibility that he might is significant in and of itself. Caught between local power networks and the rule of law, the legal advisor post embodies the limits of Villarroel's attempt to take the state to the rural hinterland. For this figure was at once a government delegate more autonomous of landlords, and one potentially beholden—or one who could be perceived to be beholden—to new local interests, whether of merchants, smallholders, or colonos.[49] Throughout rural Cochabamba, struggles for land and labor rights became connected with contests over state power.

A second case, this one from Sacabamba (an extensive hacienda in Tarata), both calls attention to local authorities' growing independence from landlords and underscores the multiple meanings of the 1945 decrees. A petition brought by two Sacabamba colonos directed its grievances against the hacienda administrator, Fructuoso Ortuño, who also served as corregidor, licitador of the chicha tax, collector of municipal taxes, and judge. Their petition accused him of offenses ranging from excessive taxation to insults, the seizure of animals, and arbitrary detention. The colonos also complained that Ortuño had violated Villarroel's decrees by making them sell chickens, lambs, and eggs for measly prices. They concluded with a demand for Ortuño's dismissal. To justify the request, the colonos invoked the 1945 decrees. Indeed, the law against pongueaje and mitanaje called for the removal from office of local authorities who required colonos, comunarios, or residents of towns to provide services or goods without payment.[50] Yet the Sacabamba colonos extended the significance of the decree to include myriad forms of abuse. Their petition thus underscores both the force of Villarroel's proclamations and their local meaning. To the petitioners, the decrees meant the right to punish or expel authorities who violated legal and moral norms in a most general sense. Although the Sacabamba colonos did not actually remove the corregidor, as the ones from Ayopaya had done, they invoked Villarroel's edicts to achieve the same end.

Taken together, these two cases show that one key source of the agitation in Cochabamba was the erosion of close ties between landlords and local authorities. In different ways, each case illustrates how new social actors— sometimes as allies of colonos and sometimes as their exploiters—contested landlords' domain. Another common element of the unrest is the role that the Indigenous Congress decrees played in the construction of a "language of contention."[51] One recurring motif of the Villarroel and post-Villarroel protests in this region was an association, direct or indirect, between the decrees, the government, and the promise of land; sometimes rebels combined that promise with allusions to the Community. Another underlying element of the unrest was the idea that Villarroel's laws had abolished *all* obligations to the hacienda. Of course, not all claims for land or labor rights were rooted in the decrees. But it is striking to note that such "misuse" was anticipated by the government, for the law itself included a clause that delineated punishments for individuals who "deceitfully invoked" the decree against servitude to avoid their agricultural duties.[52]

The 1945 Indigenous Congress was a crucial catalyst of the unrest in Ayopaya and in other Cochabamba provinces. It facilitated the transmission of laws, slogans, and prophecies between the government and rural communities; it also increased contact among rural communities themselves. These exchanges, appropriations, and misappropriations between rural and urban, state and nonstate, entities were what led the Ayopaya rebels to claim, incorrectly, that their subversive action was the law. The most threatening act, however, may not have been that violent culmination, when landlords and their homes were attacked. Before the rebels of Ayopaya ever took up arms, they insisted on the complete affirmation of the law and imposed their own authorities, alcaldes. In doing so, they not only took Villarroel's command to ensure order at its word. They exposed the state's absolute inability to control its own laws, institutions, and lawmakers.

✳ "Everyone Has the Right to Offend Us"

As in Cochabamba, Villarroel's death triggered a series of rural strikes and rebellions in La Paz by colonos who demanded enforcement of the 1945 decrees. Yet while the La Paz rebels appealed to the "laws decreed in favor of the peasantry," they did not mention the martyred president's name. And they maintained a more obvious distance from the newly agitating MNR and other political parties. In La Paz, the insurgents instead took

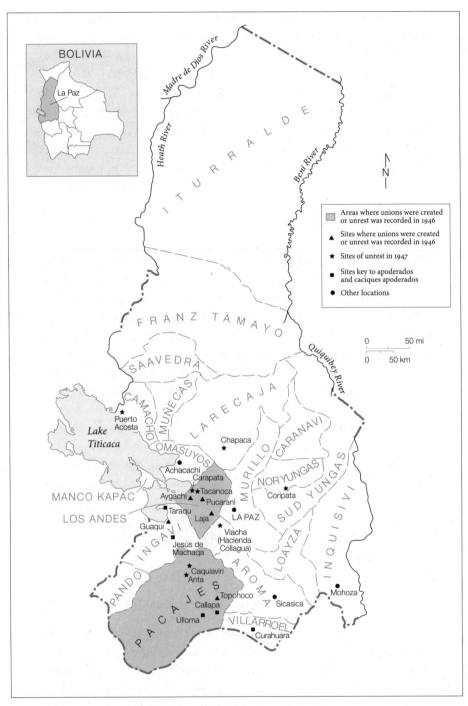

Map 4 Map of rural unrest in La Paz, 1946–47, including sites of the earlier
cacique apoderado networks

inspiration from members of the Federación Obrera Local (FOL), the anarchist association of Aymara workers and artisans. Indeed, one of the most striking characteristics of the revolts in this region was the connection between rural and urban realms. In Ayopaya, the rebels envisioned an equal but divided world: "All the goods would be owned in common; in the countryside for the Indians, and in the town, the stores and things for the whites, in common for everyone."[53] For the FOL-influenced insurgents of La Paz, by contrast, "Indian" was not an identity fixed to rural inhabitants but a supple category that crossed rural–urban divides. Nor did the cities belong to "whites." The organizers of rural unions in La Paz denounced discrimination against Indians who lived in the city, just as they demanded the end of all rural servitude.

As early as May 1946, the FOL pledged to extend its organizing drive to rural areas of La Paz (see map 4 above). But the movement to organize hacienda colonos did not truly take off until after Villarroel's overthrow, which briefly created an opening for labor activism. In August 1946, the FOL established its first rural union and began to denounce abuses perpetrated by hacendados in Guaqui (Ingavi), Topohoco (Pacajes), and Q'achuma. In November, it helped establish the Unión Sindical de Labriegos (Farmworkers Union) of Cantón Aygachi under the leadership of Estaban Quispe Yucra. Similar organizations sprung up in Caquiaviri, Laja, Guaqui, Cucuta, Araca, and Los Andes. In December, the hacienda-based unions held a plenary meeting in La Paz. They created the Federación Agraria Departamental (Departmental Agrarian Federation, FAD), and the FAD and the FOL subsequently signed a pact of solidarity. Peasants from Pacajes and Los Andes expressed strong support for the agreement. In the city, the new organization was backed by teachers, rural migrants, and members of the former networks of caciques apoderados, such as Marcelino Llanque, leader of the 1921 rebellion in Jesús de Machaqa. The FAD also forged alliances with non-Indians. Once established, its urban-based supporters fanned out to rural areas of La Paz to organize unions, schools, and strikes.[54]

The period from 1946 to 1947 was a liminal moment. The January 1947 presidential and congressional elections and tentative toleration of urban labor movements were the most patent signs of a tense political opening (see figure 23). Based on the 1945 Constitution, which allowed literate women to participate in municipal elections, the December 1947 polls included women as voters and candidates for the first time ever. And because municipal elections had not been held since 1932, these contests

23 Citizens crowded around a polling place in La Paz during the Bolivian presidential and congressional elections of January 1947 (women were allowed to participate only in December, when municipal elections were held). *Courtesy of the U.S. Library of Congress, Prints and Photographs Division,* New York World Telegram *and* Sun Newspaper *Photograph Collection.*

sparked considerable expectation.[55] In particular areas of the country—especially in Cliza and Tapacarí—the 1947 elections also involved significant mobilization in the countryside; the PIR, in particular, solicited peasant votes for its congressional candidates.[56]

In this context of political opening, the FOL's organizing drive in the La Paz countryside rapidly gained extensive support. On 8 January, an estimated 4,000 Indians bearing the Bolivian flag gathered on Hacienda Carapata (Los Andes), where they selected 200 representatives to draft a petition to the government. Signed by the "Sindicato de Labradores," the petition demanded official recognition of the union and affiliated schools.[57] Like the Ayopaya rebels, the petitioners from Carapata also asked for the "complete" abolition of pongueaje. But they did not invoke the Villarroel decrees. Instead, they appealed to the "Political Constitution of the State" and the rights of the "workers of the city." Republican guarantees figured centrally in their initial demands.

No violence was recorded at this early date, but journalists commented that some of the demonstrators carried arms. They also emphasized the sense of panic taking hold among landlords and townspeople. In early January, the Sociedad Rural denounced a widespread revolutionary movement and impending attacks against haciendas. The accusations increased over the course of the month. Landlords and townspeople condemned colonos' continued attempts to create unions; denounced actual and presumed assaults against their property; and grew ever more anxious about threatened invasions of towns.[58] A landowner in Chapaca (Larecaja) accused indigenous comunarios of attacking his hacienda in order to convert it into a Community. The assaults commenced in 1944, he declared, and were now being led by the ex-corregidor and several Indians, including both community leaders and outsiders.[59] A similar complaint was lodged in January 1947 by the owner of a finca in Pacajes. This landlord asserted that "indígenas" on neighboring properties had incited her colonos and threatened to burn the hacienda house as well as the homes of all the colonos who would not rebel. Like the owner in Larecaja, she accused the corregidor of aiding the uprising.[60] Even if false, the allegations confirm landlords' nervousness about the corregidores' loyalty. As in Cochabamba, owners not only agonized over their diminishing control of workers but fretted about an uncertain hold on local power.

The unrest in La Paz in February–April 1947 largely replicated the "strikes" of the early 1940s. On the whole, the incidents of these years were not violent uprisings, as journalists and landlords often alleged. The unrest instead involved work stoppages, insolence, the appropriation of goods, the withholding of fees, and the promise to restore land. In April, the president of the Sociedad Agrícola Industrial, an association of Yungas landowners, presented a lengthy complaint to the prefect of La Paz that called for government protection and the eviction of the indígena Faustino Ortiz. The landlord accused Ortiz of agitating on his property in Coripata and on other fincas owned by members of the society. He said that Ortiz had induced the Indians to establish a union and commit acts of disobedience and sabotage: they left work early, did no work at all, or refused to pay rental fees.[61] Individuals who testified for the landlord at an administrative hearing stated that Ortiz and his followers had convinced colonos on many properties to cease work altogether. By promising the colonos that the land would be returned to them, the instigators had persuaded them to join unions. These actions had grave consequences, the owner claimed, both for the organization of the hacienda and for agricultural production itself. Another landlord testified that Ortiz and the other leaders told the colonos there would be no more owners or administrators. Reportedly, they even pledged that the government would be "of the Indian and for the Indian." The owner and the administrator said that Ortiz came to the property drunk one day and insulted them with the following words: "You are accustomed to kicking us out like dogs. From today onward, I'll be the one who gives orders and not the *mistis* [mestizos] who I will now kick out like dogs."

Like the Ayopaya rebellion, the Yungas conflict commenced as a dispute over labor conditions but quickly drew attention to the dynamics of abuse, humiliation, and subordination to which colonos were daily subjected. It also raised questions about the configuration of power. By connecting the expulsion of the owners and administrators with the issue of who would rule, the conflict merged the end of the hacienda with the beginning of a government "of the Indian and for the Indian." The incident suggests that colonos viewed the hacienda itself as a form of rule. Eliminating it would not only pave the way for a new kind of authority, but reverse the relations of hierarchy and humiliation that characterized a state perceived to be controlled by landlords.

The La Paz–based strikes and union drives of early 1947 culminated in May and June in two highly publicized acts of violence. Of all the many protests the press might have covered, it centered its attention on these exceptional moments of outright aggression. The few scholarly references to the Altiplano unrest also focus on these dramatic incidents. Some peasants certainly had access to arms, and the 1947 rebellions did involve violence. But more than violence itself, the Altiplano's most prominent revolts exemplify elements of the largely peaceful protests just discussed: they were marked by union drives, physical appropriation of territory and goods, and anxious landlords.

The first major incident transpired in mid-May on the Finca Anta (Pacajes). Colonos here rose up and killed an administrator who was known for his abusive treatment and a teacher whom the landlord had contracted against the colonos' wishes. This well-publicized episode also included participation by comunarios on whose land the hacendado had encroached. And it sparked uprisings on several adjacent haciendas, leading landlords throughout the area to plead with the Ministry of Government for "guarantees."[62]

Another violent incident took place on Hacienda Tacanoca (Los Andes) —in one of the most important commercial agriculture zones of the La Paz highlands. This confrontation exhibits two additional recurring traits: conflicts among landlords, and colonos' attempts to unionize. The much-commented event commenced with the murders of the landowner Agustín Prieto and Prieto's niece.[63] Some sources suggest that a longstanding boundary conflict between owners of two contiguous properties, Tacanoca and Carapata, motivated the killings. According to this theory, the brother of the owner's murdered niece incited "his" colonos (of Carapata) to attack Tacanoca.[64] The documentation also connects the incident with unions and land claims, since some landlords accused colonos of organizing a union to take control of neighboring haciendas "and all those in the altiplano, in order to return the hacienda lands to the indígenas."[65] A third, lesser-known center of altiplano agitation was Puerto Acosta (Camacho), where colonos on contiguous haciendas engaged in combat with each other. The authorities accused Edmundo Nogales, Villarroel's minister of government, of involvement in this case.[66]

Beyond these hacienda-based incidents, the 1947 unrest in La Paz was characterized by more subtle protests against abuse by local authorities and the police—just as it was in Cochabamba. For example, a flurry of telegrams from the subprefect of Pucarani to the prefect of La Paz described attacks by Indians against low-level authorities and recounted colonos' complaints about mistreatment by the armed forces.[67] As the indígena Tiburcio Apaza put it when he filed a complaint against the police chief and the *carabineros* who plundered his house, "in the towns, the subaltern authorities are very abusive."[68]

Compared to the protests in Cochabamba, the ones in La Paz involved much greater participation by comunarios. In the core areas of unrest—Caquiaviri (Pacajes) and Pucarani (Los Andes)—hacienda expansion was only decades old. And where communities remained strong when the expansion commenced, many recently formed estates remained de facto communities; the bulk of the land was not in the demesne but farmed by the ex-comunarios for their own benefit. In addition, ex-comunarios often retained significant control over internal systems of authority.[69] To recuperate lost land, comunarios in some cases acted directly against landlords in alliance with hacienda colonos. Where paternalistic relations reigned on haciendas, colonos or ex-comunarios could instead become implicated in intra-landlord struggles. Making use of paternalistic bonds and the underlying threat of force, landlords took advantage of recently expropriated colonos' continued identification with the territory, daring them to defend "their" land against encroachments by neighboring landlords. It is equally possible that ex-comunarios in some cases capitalized on such disputes to wage their own battles with neighboring communities.[70] Hundreds, perhaps thousands, of such land-boundary conflicts—between adjacent landlords as well as between neighboring communities and ex-communities—were lodged with local courts from the 1920s through the 1940s.[71] Much remains to be learned about these alliances and conflicts amongst and between colonos and comunarios, but the disputes doubtlessly contributed to the growing instability in the countryside.

What political ideals drove altiplano colonos and comunarios to create unions, expel landlords, and reconstitute communities? The manifesto the FAD circulated among La Paz haciendas in February 1947 is a good starting place, for the organization played a critical role over the entire course of the unrest.[72] Although its directors presumably penned the document, that leadership included rural and urban inhabitants. When the manifesto was released, the FAD had already established unions of farmworkers (*labriegos*) in many of the altiplano cantons where the 1947 unrest would center. The manifesto cannot be dismissed as an urban call for rural union: it was the product of a rural–urban alliance already forged.

Calling hacienda colonos "worker comrades," the FAD's richly detailed program underscores the degraded position that Indians occupied as "beasts of burden doomed to work under the threat of the landlord's whip." To illustrate the claim, the authors first highlighted distinctions between workers of the countryside and the city. Although urban workers knew punishment and endless duties, they wrote, "the Indian" (a rural being in this context) enjoyed no holidays, rest, or scheduled work hours, and was not even able to eat or dress properly, let alone become educated. Yet the document does not simply mark differences. It also underscores the common experience of discrimination that all Indians were subjected to in the city, where "everyone has the right to offend us: the chola, the miste [mestizo], the gendarme, the rich and even the Indians who have been poisoned by capitalist morals." It denounces the symbolic violence by which authorities labeled all indigenous protests the subversive work of "savage" beings. And it condemns the widespread belief that Indians were the blight of the "aristocratic" nation. Countering this anti-Indian sensibility, the authors boldly declared that "peasants" were the decisive factor for "civilization"; if the nation did not recognize peasants' economic and moral worth, the manifesto warns, Bolivia would disappear.

After establishing these basic premises, the authors of the FAD manifesto listed several concrete demands that concerned the civil rights of Bolivians and colonos. First, they demanded that the "inalienability [of the home] prescribed by the Constitution . . . be a reality for all inhabitants." They insisted specifically on respect for the homes of the "agrarios" (rural workers). Surely this demand was motivated by unlawful evictions and the destruction of the homes of colonos deemed unruly by landlords. Next, the manifesto calls for freedom to organize and respect for the guarantees granted to "agrarios" by law. It also demands the abolition of pongueaje "in all its magnitude"; an end to the expulsions of colonos by landlords; the creation of indigenous schools on all fincas at the expense of landlords and the state; and the convocation of a national congress of peasants. The authors asserted that the purpose of the landlord association was to "maintain the slavery of the agrarios and to defend its egotistical interests." And they identified the FAD as an organization created to "demand respect for and compliance with the laws decreed in our favor."

Although the document repeatedly references the law, it makes no mention of Villarroel's decrees. Were the authors alluding to the limits of those laws when they demanded the abolition of pongueaje "in all its magnitude"? Or did they silently include the 1945 decrees in the broad reference to the "laws decreed in our favor"? The FAD clearly concurred with members of the 1945 Indigenous Committee (and the caciques apoderados before them), who insisted that constitutional guarantees apply equally to all Bolivians. But the absence of allusions to the 1945 decrees is just as striking. The authors wrote generically of laws "decreed in our favor," reminding their readers that those protections were not the government's gift but the triumph of a costly struggle. At the same time, the manifesto eschews all ties to political parties. The FAD was a "union organization," not a political party, the authors wrote; it maintained no connections with the "Nazi-Fascists [MNR and Villarroel], PIRistas, [or] Falangists."

The FAD's failure to mention Villarroel is not surprising, given the oppression its members suffered during his rule and the anarchist-influenced organization's fundamental rejection of political parties. But the reserve does not mean the president's decrees played no role. Without doubt, the laws figured more prominently in Cochabamba. The colonos of Ayopaya, in particular, forged a very personal bond with Villarroel and painstakingly sought to enforce his laws. According to some of the witnesses, the leaders of the Ayopaya uprising even saw their actions as a kind of reprisal for the lynching of Villarroel.[73] In many respects, the 1945 decrees had been molded to conditions in Cochabamba, for the decrees were shaped by the reports of commissions that investigated unrest in that department (see chapters 5 and 7). Documents on the 1947 unrest in La Paz lack the specific references to severely exploitative labor conditions that typified the complaints of movement leaders in Cochabamba; they do not include concrete references to manifold services, obligations, or taxes. Yet the laws and constitutional reforms passed by the military socialists clearly galvanized movements in both regions. The La Paz insurgents invoked them in general terms without risking any allusion to *villarroelismo* or the MNR, which the government blamed for the unrest. Altiplano leaders who might have mentioned the murdered president or his decrees, finally, had been wiped out. Just after Villarroel's overthrow in July 1946, 280 caciques were reportedly assassinated in La Paz for "the crime of having remained loyal to Villarroel."[74] Even if the FAD's drive for unions, schools, and the end of oligarchic discrimination was the primary external influence in the La Paz highlands, Villarroel's historic laws appeared here, too. They were a silent presence.

And so when the two major attacks transpired in Caquiaviri and Pucarani in May and June, a groundswell of agitation, both violent and nonviolent, had already taken place. As in Cochabamba, colonos and comunarios in La Paz disputed landlords' domain while calling for adherence to laws decreed in their favor. They demanded the end of servitude and "slavery" and insisted on the restoration of land and community. The crisis of the hacienda and the assault against it were national phenomena.

✳ State Repression, Civil Guards,
and the Crisis of Authority

The repression unleashed against the 1947 rebels was virulent, and it greatly outweighed the rebels' own recourse to violence. Indeed, the force of the response can be traced to Villarroel, for his decrees had augmented the coercive powers of the state. After coming to power, President Hertzog implemented the Indigenous Congress's recommendation for the creation of a new rural police force. He made it 300 men strong and equipped it with horses and cars.[75] Hertzog also used a 1945 decree that delineated punishments for unruly colonos and "agitators." Instigators of unrest and others who shirked their obligations or prejudiced agricultural production would be sent to "state colonies" organized by the Ministry of Agriculture.[76] Hundreds of individuals were detained by both governments on the basis of this and other legal provisions. If the Villarroel decrees could become a language of insurgency, they were also an instrument of control.

In addition to these Villarroel-era legal changes, the 1947 repression was rooted in a second, more local, logic. As noted above, landlords increasingly doubted subaltern authorities; at times, they even accused them of instigating strikes and uprisings. And because they no longer trusted cantonal officials to broker settlements to disputes, landlords appealed directly to prefects, who invariably dispatched troops.[77] In this context, even nonviolent protest could elicit the power of the police and the army. Yet despite the use of force, landowners' confidence was not restored. The rebellions and their aftermath only enhanced the distance between landlords and local officials. The uprisings sprang from and exacerbated a crisis of political authority in the countryside. Notwithstanding the recourse to both repression and reform, post-Villarroel governments could not create a new project of rule.

As soon as the agitation commenced in early 1947, carabineros were called out. And they were dispatched continuously on the mere suspicion of revolt. Some of the regiments were ordered to remain even after peace was restored, to "safeguard the property and lives of the population."[78] Private guards and so-called Patriotic Legions also intervened in the campaign for order, usually because landowners and townspeople considered the government's measures inadequate. The presence of repressive forces itself became a cause of renewed protest. Indians not only complained about abuse by the troops, but about the requirement to provide soldiers with food.[79]

Another critical aspect of the repression was its roots in the physical and symbolic violence against Indians that followed Villarroel's 1946 murder. The July overthrow was accompanied by anti-Indian reprisals in both the city and the countryside. And in visceral ways, the tragic unraveling of Villarroel's government drove home the force of an association between the president, pro-Indian policies, and anti-Indian violence. Take the experience of the Aymara scribe Leandro Condori Chura. Even though he did not back Villarroel, Condori was branded an agent of the president and pursued by soldiers after the assassination—all because he received Indians in his home and made documents for them.[80] Likewise, Hilarión Grájeda and other Ayopaya colonos who found themselves in the main plaza of La

Paz at the time of Villarroel's hanging were insulted as "Villarroel's Indians."[81] Simultaneous with Villarroel's murder, a number of rural indigenous leaders were killed.[82] In Mizque (Cochabamba), landlords tormented
colonos about the death of "their father" and even waged a war against his
laws; according to a former colono, once the president was dead they
tracked down his decree and "burned papers in large quantities."[83] And
when Francisco Chipana Ramos was arrested in October 1946, one of the
primary charges against him was that he had served as president of the 1945
Indigenous Congress.[84] The opposition of the Sociedad Rural to Villarroel's pro-Indian policies had been fierce, and some landlords took the
laws as a kind of betrayal. Capturing indigenous rebels was also revenge
against Villarroel.

In Ayopaya, the repression was particularly fierce, and it affected all of
the areas that joined the revolt. Various military and police units (the
Región Militar, the Escuela de Clases, and the Comandancia de la Bri-
gada de Carabineros) sent separate commissions to rural areas of Cochabamba.[85] In his office, the prefect of Cochabamba met with the regional
military chief and the police chief to synchronize actions. "Civil agents"
formed a voluntary corps to help pursue insurgents. And the owner of
Yayani rounded up a group of "young" volunteers to find the Indians who
killed Lt. Col. Mercado; he gave them arms provided by the military. By
mid-February, 160 men had been arrested for their presumed participation
in the Ayopaya uprising.[86]

Rebellions and strikes in rural La Paz met a similar fate. Following the
murders of the landlord Prieto and his niece, hundreds of people were
apprehended on the Carapata and Tacanoca haciendas. As part of a policy
to "disperse" agitators and potential agitators, 130 of the detained were sent
to Ichilo in the Santa Cruz jungle (see map 1). In theory, they were to be
provided with materials to create an agricultural colony.[87] The inhospitable
surroundings and stifling climate made this an especially brutal punishment, particularly for Altiplano detainees, who were accustomed to a cool
and arid environment. Figures vary, but at least 39 men detained in Ichilo
perished there, one by suicide.[88] Another 270 people—including dozens
arrested in the offices of the FOL—were sent to the "Justicia Ordinaria"
for processing. In Caquiaviri alone, approximately 198 indígenas were arrested. And the police raided the offices of the La Paz FOL, taking its leaders
into custody. Modesto Escobar, a leader of the FOL, and Marcelino Quispe
Yucra, secretary-general of the FAD, were among the detained.[89] The gov-

ernment accused the FOL not only of inciting unrest but also of misrepresenting its position to Indians.[90] The uprising on Hacienda Anta (Pacajes) reportedly resulted in the arrest of 1,000 colonos.[91] Finally, landowners took matters into their own hands: the owners of Carapata and Tacanoca intended to evict permanently anyone who was detained or a fugitive. They would also expel all those still working on the property who were suspected of inciting other colonos.[92]

The repression was framed by a war of words, with the opposition denouncing excessive force, landlords complaining about its deficiencies, and authorities insisting they were restoring peace without shedding blood.[93] The charged debates make it difficult to confirm overall numbers of deaths or to assess the relative weight that police and private guards played in the repression, but it is clear that many Indians and peasants were killed.[94] In Camacho (La Paz) and Tapacarí (Cochabamba), government action resulted in at least a dozen dead. In one altiplano town, a crowd unsuccessfully tried to capture and hang sixty Indians who had been detained by the police, to the cry: "If we have hung white men [Villarroel and his associates], we can also hang Indians!"[95] We do not know how frequently such acts of racialized brutality occurred. We do know that the uprisings were not followed by state policies to stamp out indigenous culture, identity, or political organization, as, for example, occurred after the 1780s Andean rebellions. Nor is there evidence that indigenous peoples actively suppressed outward expressions of culture and identity because they feared reprisals.

That said, a climate of tension, fear, and abuse prevailed in the Cochabamba and La Paz towns and communities that were affected by the 1947 unrest. Both the government and private forces created this climate of fear. And just as in 1946, the tension and abuse were racialized. Carabineros carried out punitive acts not only against Indians who participated in the rebellions but against members of their families, and even against individuals with only remote connections to the places where the attacks against haciendas took place.[96] Early on, the Ayopaya rebellion led authorities to cast a wide net of suspicion that resulted in a "wave of accusations" and "preventive" detentions in places distant from the presumed epicenter.[97]

Notwithstanding the intensity of the repression, it failed to restore the confidence of landowners or townspeople. Work in the province of Los Andes all but ceased, for landlords could not get Indians to resume their labors.[98] Owners of haciendas began to abandon their properties because they feared additional uprisings and doubted that government troops would come to their aid.[99] Landlords also questioned the loyalty of the police. In April 1947, Ignacio Zapata and María Zapata viuda de Aramayo denounced several colonos for leading a subversive movement among indígenas on the Hacienda Anta (Pacajes) and adjacent properties. This was precisely where one of the most violent uprisings would take place just weeks later. According to the petitioners, one of the accused had received "revolutionary literature" from a police officer.[100] As we have seen, hacendados sometimes also blamed corregidores for leading uprisings. Surely such mistrust was linked with changes in the configuration of local power, for these offices were beginning to be staffed by new middling sectors or by representatives of antioligarchic parties. Occasionally, Indians occupied the corregidor post.[101] Local authorities, in short, were no longer automatic defenders of landlord interests. Townspeople also worried about the corruption, partiality, or inaction of subaltern officials. One such complaint not only identified the corregidor post as a means of personal enrichment, but linked concerns about the integrity of local officials with fears of indigenous uprisings.[102] Another denounced a corregidor's failure to uphold "norms of rectitude and correct behavior" and condemned the official for responding to "any insignificant matter, particularly if it concern[ed] the indigenous race, . . . [with] the whip or the club."[103] In his 1945 annual report, the Cochabamba prefect himself complained that most of the corregidores in his department were "ignorant and incompetent and above all immoral and shameless leeches of the indigenous class."[104]

Evidence from varied sites of unrest suggests that the police and local authorities played divergent roles in the 1947 strikes and uprisings. Sometimes they sided with and shored up the interests of landlords. At other times, they collaborated with Indians and peasants who were rebelling against landlords. The documents also indicate that both Indians and non-Indians publicly questioned the authorities' ways. In Cochabamba and La Paz, the 1947 unrest exposed a growing political vacuum in the countryside. Colonos and comunarios, and eventually also landlords and townspeople, contested and sometimes even removed corregidores. At the 1945 Indigenous Congress, the government proposed to replace corregidores with intendants trained at the National Police Academy. The 1947 rebellions took place before any such change occurred. State authorities did not abandon the countryside, but their already questionable legitimacy had vanished.

✳ Rural Unrest on the Eve of the Revolution

In early 1948, the Hertzog government pardoned all Indians who had been confined to Ichilo and other remote regions for presumed participation in the 1947 rebellions.[105] It also released members of the FOL from detention.[106] The majority of the most prominent leaders—including Grájeda and Esteban Quispe Yucra—nevertheless died or remained in jail during the next five years of MNR-led revolutionary action. As a result of the repression, the FOL and the FAD were all but wiped out. Yet while state repression struck a powerful blow against rural leadership in all regions, and ruptured a movement uniquely based on rural-urban ties, it did not fully suppress indigenous mobilization. Rural unrest persisted until the 1952 revolution.

Indian and peasant grievances, conflicts, and political practices of the late 1940s and early 1950s, and their connections—and disconnections—with the MNR have yet to be studied in depth. Outright rebellion declined after 1947, but some small uprisings were carried out on or against haciendas.[107] From 1948 to 1952, the press chronicled at least forty-four actions and rumored actions throughout the countryside, ranging from rural strikes to land boundary disputes, to "subversive" meetings and leafleting.[108] In the years leading up to the revolution, rural rebels continued to invoke the laws of Villarroel. In June 1949, for example, authorities in Oruro denounced agitators who circulated leaflets that reminded colonos about the Indigenous Congress decrees and urged them "to rebel if their demands were not heeded."[109]

The complaints expressed in the protests of the late 1940s and early 1950s ranged widely, but they largely mirrored the demands and grievances of the 1947 rebels. Conflicts over boundaries between communities and ex-communities, and between communities and owners of contiguous haciendas, occurred repeatedly in Potosí and La Paz during these years. Some such collisions pitted landlords against each other, and they transformed their hacienda labor forces into small armies.[110] In Cochabamba and Chuquisaca, colonos continued to file complaints about unlawful charges for herbaje.[111] Landlords also lodged grievances with the authorities. One La Paz landowner denounced a colono from a neighboring property for harvesting and robbing the crops on a portion of his land.[112] And the owners of a property in Guaqui accused colonos who had "revolutionary ideas" of planting their own crops on hacienda land, refusing to work, and threatening to kill the landlords. According to the owners, the colonos even said that "there was no law for the patrón" and that they could do "whatever they wanted in matters concerning the estate"; they claimed that the property belonged to them.[113] In 1950, the press noted some small violent uprisings, this time in opposition to the agricultural census. Houses were burned, census takers were expelled, and the census itself was postponed. Anti-landlord violence was also recorded at this juncture. In July 1951, a group of Indians armed with sticks and knives assaulted a Cochabamba landowner. Local inhabitants suspected that the insurgents were followers of Anzaldo's Virgilio Vargas, now also known as the "son of God." Vargas reportedly told Indians of the Tarata region that pongueaje and the catastro did not exist.[114] As in 1947, Indians and non-Indians continued to denounce local authorities for perpetrating abuses against them. In some cases, recently freed leaders of the 1947 uprisings were presumed to be the instigators of renewed unrest.[115]

If violent incidents transpired, the post-1947 period also witnessed peaceful political initiatives. For example, rural activists continued to circulate "false" property titles; perhaps they even distributed the certificates that the Alcaldes Mayores Particulares had used to substantiate land claims. The press noted at least one attempt to form an agrarian union and several regional meetings of "indigenous agricultural workers." These congresses of indígenas or campesinos, which were held in the departments of La Paz (Caranguillas, Pacajes, and Incahuasi) and Potosí (Azanaques) during the four years that preceded the revolution, openly identified with Villarroel and demanded "strict compliance with the laws and decrees passed in favor of the peasantry [campesinado]." Scholars generally view these meetings as MNR-controlled events, but the leaders actually disassociated the "martyred" president's historic measures from the MNR.[116] To be sure, government authorities sometimes called the MNR the source of renewed agitation in the countryside.[117] Yet while contact between the MNR and particular peasant leaders increased during these years, the party did not manage to capture or control rural social movements.

Although the countryside remained a site of political mobilization right until 1952, tactics, demands, leadership, local communities, and the scope of the unrest changed in ways that remain to be studied. Without doubt, those changes held enormous significance for the unfolding revolutionary conflict. But it is also clear that no absolute rupture divided 1947—the height of rural indigenous mobilization—from the ensuing period of MNR-led conspiracy.

✳ Conclusion

The 1947 cycle of unrest represented a full-scale assault against landlord power, with more direct aggression against hacendados, their property, and their agents than typified the Villarroel-era agitation. This scale and scope of conflict would not be repeated until after the 1952 revolution triumphed. But 1947 was not a year of outright rebellion alone. One key feature was the same kind of sit-down strikes that colonos had carried out in the late 1930s and early 1940s. Another central element of the unrest was de facto land occupations. The year 1947 also meant verbal battles, petitions, and juridical action against landlords, local authorities, and tax collectors who were charged with a range of material and physical abuse by diverse social actors. For example, Cochabamba's Prefecture Archive contains piles of petitions from chicha producers who denounced excessive chicha and muko taxes. Occasional and full-time chicha producers assailed the licitadores who levied these lucrative assessments. Colonos in turn lodged complaints against landlords, administrators, and police they accused of labor contract violations, rape, and myriad forms of abuse.[118] Finally, 1947 was once again a time to organize unions and schools. Locating the range of rural political action that characterized this rebellious year underscores the role of Villarroel's incipient state-making plan and the importance of the laws "decreed in favor of the peasantry."[119] It also alters our perspective on the years leading to the 1952 revolution. For when 1947 is viewed in these multivariegated terms, the contrast between the before and the after is not so stark. For all its intensity, the repression is best understood as a force that altered rural movements without fully suppressing political action in the countryside. Outright rebellion diminished, but the countryside was not quiet.

A recurring motif of the 1947 protests was the association, direct or indirect, between the Indigenous Congress decrees, the government, and the promise of land; sometimes the rebels combined that promise with allusions to the Community. Especially in Cochabamba, the uprisings manifest fierce contests over the meaning of the Villarroel decrees. Through peaceful and violent means, rural leaders insisted on compliance with the laws, or they insisted on adherence to their own interpretations of them. In La Paz, Villarroel's image cast only a shadow. But the rebels in this region similarly combined struggles against servitude with the promise of land. Here, too, they demanded "respect for and compliance with the laws decreed in our favor." They also insisted on the "complete" abolition of pongueaje. Most studies conclude that the Indigenous Congress decrees were never truly implemented. The 1947 protests instead show that the "implementation" of the laws was an eminently local matter, something the Villarroel government, and subsequent regimes, could not fully manage. Yet it would also be wrong to say that the laws were only a local matter, for the communities that molded the president's words against servitude to their own conditions and visions said, and could say: the government decreed.

The point is not only that rural indigenous mobilization lasted until 1952. More important, those enduring movements for land, education, autonomy, and justice became entwined with a "government" or "revolutionary authorities" that seemed to validate their claims. At the very least, local leaders sometimes managed to make things look that way. In certain instances, indigenous leaders radicalized Villarroel's modest propositions. The populist regime's proclamations in turn granted unintended force to local leaders' actions. In specific parts of the country, colonos and comunarios maintained that Villarroel's laws—their laws—not only promised the end of pongueaje but augured land, community, and freedom. Rebels in Cochabamba and La Paz linked the decrees with the struggle for local power: time and again, they questioned the authority of corregidores. In one case, the insurgents in effect removed the corregidor from his post and installed their own appointee.

As we have seen, this seizing of local power could coexist with claims to republican laws and constitutional guarantees. Particularly in La Paz, the 1947 rebels sometimes appealed to the Constitution and insisted that the civil rights enshrined in it belonged to all inhabitants, including the "agrarios." Peasants' freedom to organize, a right the Hertzog government rescinded, figured centrally in the FAD manifesto of 1947. Surely the demand for equal rights was driven not only by violence in the countryside but also by the discrimination that Indians suffered in the city. There was one more reason for the organization's emphasis on equality: the repression its members suffered. Although the Ayopaya uprising was not directly linked with the altiplano protests, it shaped the government's response to the La Paz revolts, sparking a "wave of accusations" against Indians far from the areas of unrest.

Ayopaya sent shock waves throughout the nation precisely because the rebels seized local power there while invoking the very laws espoused by the deposed Villarroel-MNR regime, laws that subsequent governments sustained and indeed considered critical to the maintenance of rural order. In the February 1947 letter to "Vice President" Juan Lechín, Grájeda and the "mineworker comrade" linked those 1945 decrees against forced services with a "public decree" for a "revolution against exploitation and misery and . . . abuses"—with a revolution for "our rights."[120]

A decree for revolution undoubtedly strikes an incongruous chord. But the more important puzzle is the deceptively simple phrase "our rights." What did Grájeda mean when he used these words? The hacienda alcalde's struggles against cruel treatment, exploitation, and servitude stretched back to at least the early 1940s, when he labored to establish a school in Yayani and appealed to the Oficina de Defensa Gratuita in La Paz for "guarantees." Villarroel's rise to power, the 1945 Indigenous Congress, and Grájeda's own contacts with lawyers, urban labor leaders, and other rural indigenous activists radicalized the ayopayeños' objectives. Whereas Grájeda and hacienda colonos on several properties initially sought to enforce specific agreements with landlords, in 1947 they aimed to expel the owners all together. They were no longer simply lodging complaints against abuse but openly disputing the landlords' power.

In this context, land, community, and autonomy figured centrally. Some witnesses seemed to suggest that the land was going to be distributed among the colonos, perhaps in the form of private plots.[121] Many others spoke of becoming comunarios or talked about returning the land to the community.[122] Grájeda himself made several such allusions; according to one witness, he said he was "doing everything possible to make sure that all the colonos once again became comunarios."[123] In the letter to Lechín, Grájeda even referred to himself as the "compañero"—not from the hacienda, but from the "ayllu Yayani."[124] Together with the recuperation of the land, the rebels also struggled for local political power. In Ayopaya and other centers of unrest, insurgents explicitly or implicitly dislodged illegitimate state officials and replaced them with indigenous authorities. Equally important, they talked about a body of laws that belonged to them. According to some of the witnesses, Grájeda contrasted "our" rights with the rights that power holders would lose. One witness reported that he told the colonos, "the laws are for us and not for the *rosca* [oligarchy]."[125] Another declared that the miner told them the laws were "decreed for them and not for the landlords."[126]

To fully comprehend the phrase "our rights," it is worth revisiting the events of March 1946, when 2,000 colonos invaded the plaza of Cantón

Calchani (Ayopaya) and demanded that the corregidor read to them "the new decrees" their "cabecillas had brought back from the city of La Paz." Pressured by the crowd, the corregidor recited Villarroel's four decrees aloud in Quechua. When he finished, the colonos protested that the words he uttered were not the same as the ones they had already heard from their cabecillas. Apparently they believed that most of the hacienda services had been abolished, and that the number of work days had been greatly reduced. The colonos demanded an arrangement in accord with their understanding of the laws. Landlords observing the confrontation demanded that the assembled colonos resolve the matter directly with them, hacienda by hacienda. But the colonos refused to disband, insisting that they had a "common cause." When the colonos reconvened the following day, the corregidor ordered them to visit his office property by property, so agreements could be negotiated with each individual landowner. But the colonos once again refused. They also informed the authorities that they would no longer work for the hacienda nor fulfill any service duties. Finally, the colonos named their own corregidores and alcaldes for each property, and appointed the peasant leader Antonio Mamani (Alvarez) corregidor of the entire zone.[127] With these three acts, the colonos gave concrete form to their own interpretations of the law. From their perspective, the decrees their cabecillas delivered were not just rules to regulate labor obligations; they were laws that applied to public space and power. The question that arose from their confrontation with landlords and the corregidor was: Who would determine the meaning of the law? And from the colonos' perspective, it was not the corregidor or the landlords who gave the law significance, but their own leaders. Ultimately, it was the colonos themselves.

Indigenous activists had long appealed to republican laws and constitutional guarantees. But when Grájeda said in 1947 that he and the ayopayeños were waging a revolution for "our" rights, he was no longer referring exclusively to republican laws, or even to Villarroel's decrees. To be sure, the 1945 measures enhanced the rights of colonos, but they did so without significantly curbing hacendados' power. By combining the demand to satisfy "our" rights with direct attacks against the landlords, Grájeda turned the legal hierarchy on its head. And that is what made the law in his letter to Lechín a revolutionary one. Far from "misunderstandings," as government authorities and the landlord association charged, the rebels' disputed interpretations of the law revealed the true meaning of Villarroel's decrees.[128] In practice, they could be revolutionary laws.

Ayopaya's Hilarión Grájeda and Pucarani's Esteban Quispe Yucra faded from the pages of the nation's news after the 1947 rebellions and repression. Occasionally, words appeared about the course of the rebels' trials, but the demands and actions no longer captured front-page headlines. It would be wrong, however, to see the suppression of the uprisings as the complete defeat of the insurgents' radical re-readings of the Villarroel decrees and other laws "decreed in our favor." Rural contests and conflicts during the months immediately following the revolutionary triumph of 1952 showed that the visions of the 1947 rebels, and the visions of the caciques apoderados before them, remained living influences. As post-1952 rural unrest would reveal, neither state repression nor the MNR's growing power fully dislodged an impression that "all" the land would be "converted into communities," or undid the idea of a government "of the Indian and for the Indian." Although Villarroel had never promised such things, the lasting impression was in part the legacy of his brief rule—and of his spectacularly brutal end.

CONCLUSION AND EPILOGUE

Rethinking the Rural Roots
of the 1952 Revolution

Bolivia's revolution of April 1952 united competing groups and visions under the shadow of a rapidly disintegrating political order. The insurrection itself was a brief, relatively bloodless affair, but its popular intensity surprised even the revolution's leaders.[1] Three days of fighting by miners, workers, party militants, townspeople, the police, and discontented members of the army in all of Bolivia's major cities ended in the collapse of the military.[2] Both elite and plebeian women joined the revolutionary commandos responsible for the insurrection's triumph. In the course of the fighting, civilians collected weapons that had been discarded by the police or soldiers. Later, they established popular militias in factories, mines, rural communities, and provincial towns; these armies of the people eventually offset the police and the army, taking over their internal responsibilities (see figure 24).[3] As power shifted in the countryside and the cities, peasants mobilized for labor rights and land. Against this tumultuous backdrop, leftist and conservative factions of the MNR battled for control of the state.

Like Latin America's other twentieth-century revolutions, Bolivia's 1952 Revolution is striking for the competing hopes, interests, and demands that diverse actors invested in the victory. At the moment of triumph, the revolution was an extraordinarily plural moment that individuals and communities experienced with expectations of genuine change.[4] Scholars generally single out the miners as the force that radicalized what seems to have begun as a moderate affair. Led by Juan Lechín, mineworkers in Oruro and Potosí spearheaded the campaign for tin nationalization, worker control, and other sweeping social changes. Bolivia's revolutionary regime proved unable to control the militant workers, who had an independent-organizing tradition and the power to shut down the country's most important industry.[5] The demands of no other group in Bolivia were recognized to the extent that the revolution acknowledged those put forward by workers.[6] Rightfully, historians thus emphasize mineworkers' profound place in the origins of the revolution. In doing so, they tend to downplay the revolution's extensive rural roots.

A striking disjuncture marks the literature on the revolution. The commonly held view of the insurrection is three days of fighting led by miners, workers, and townspeople, with the countryside playing almost no part. The immediate revolutionary period instead evokes the antithetical image of a rural world turned upside down. Indeed, as soon as the revolution triumphed, peasants and Indians began to lodge petitions in which they demanded land, tax reductions, a labor code, and schools. Rural districts soon became the site of strikes, and by the end of 1952 the countryside was enveloped in violence. The agitation commenced dramatically with the takeover of several haciendas, and it became most pronounced in Cochabamba's central valleys and the area around Lake Titicaca in La Paz. These were the two regions that together made up the heart of Bolivia's commercial agriculture.[7] But agrarian violence was also reported in many other parts of the country, where hacienda colonos began to carry out sit-down strikes much like those that were staged in the 1940s. Once again, colonos championed wide interpretations of Villarroel's decrees.[8] The unrest was not directed against landlords and the hacienda regime exclusively. Confrontations with majordomos, the police, local and regional authorities, and tax collectors reached great heights in the spring of 1953. In Cochabamba, one key object of ire was the chicha-tax collector. Here both verbal intimidation and brutal physical reprisals, including kidnapping and murder, played a role as power relations were overturned.[9]

Because the violence that plagued the countryside in 1952–53 was so fierce, this phase of the revolution has been compared to the "Great Fear"

24 Peasant militia, 1952. *Courtesy of the Archive of La Paz*.

of the French Revolution.[10] The conflicts pitted peasants against landlords, landlords against peasants, peasants against townspeople, and peasants against peasants. They entailed direct assaults against property but also more subtle strikes against ethnic hierarchies and the symbolic order, actions that sometimes involved very specific expressions of gender power and aggression.[11] In an effort to control the spiraling violence, the MNR on 12 April 1952 created the Ministerio de Asuntos Campesinos (Ministry of Peasant Affairs, MAC), which was charged to enforce the Villarroel decrees. The agitation nevertheless continued unabated, and less than a year later, in January 1953, peasant mobilization effectively forced the revolutionary government to create a commission for agrarian reform. Soon the MNR began to legalize colono land takeovers, and in August it proclaimed the agrarian reform in the Cochabamba village of Ucureña. The declaration provoked another wave of land invasions in other parts of the country. As landlords fled the countryside, more takeovers took place.[12]

Not just violence encased the countryside after April 1952. There was also a peaceful deluge of petitions. These were accompanied by the ancient land titles that the cacique networks had unearthed in the 1920s and kept alive. Peasants from the community of Chrungalla revived a petition they had been presenting to government authorities over the past seventy-two years. And the Ayllu Hilata (near Curahuara, La Paz) pressed for the return of usurped land with documents dating to the Spanish colonial era.[13] For highland Indian communities, the agrarian reform represented the long-awaited revisita that caciques apoderados had struggled for during the 1910s and 1920s.[14] In the Cochabamba valleys, the MNR's emphasis on the autonomy of small property owners struck a stronger chord.

As these phases of mobilization suggest, rural ferment after 1952 mirrored and built on pre-revolutionary mobilization in fundamental respects. Yet scholars rarely emphasize the links between the two. To be sure, works on the revolution never fail to mention the post-1952 agrarian unrest. Much recent work has also emphasized the waves of indigenous mobilization that marked the five decades preceding the revolution. Some studies specifically mark the 1945 Indigenous Congress and the 1947 uprisings as major turning points of the pre-revolutionary era. Nevertheless, they generally divorce these and other incidents of rural protest from the revolution's origins and course. If rural mobilization lasted to 1952, these works suggest, it was either dormant, minor, or ineffective. The Ucureña peasantry's leading place in the origins of the revolution resonates as a remarkable exception.[15]

The history of rural mobilization charted in the preceding chapters raises new questions about the sources and significance of the revolution's initial radicalism. In the following pages, I consider more fully how and why Indians and peasants have been excluded from—and occasionally included in—specific narratives about 1952.[16] A closer look at the profoundly varied local and regional trajectories of rural political action in the years leading to the revolution takes us beyond MNR-centered views of the revolutionary project and its origins. It also sheds new light on the meanings of 1952.

✳ The Countryside in the Historiography of the Revolution

Following the MNR's lead, the first works on 1952 minimized peasants' role in the origins of the revolution. Robert Alexander's *The Bolivian National Revolution*, which appeared in 1958, when the MNR still held power, typifies the early approach. Although he dedicated his book to Frank Tannenbaum, Alexander in no way connected the Bolivian Revolution with Tannenbaum's assessment of the Mexican Revolution as a radical peasant war, one that could be repeated in Bolivia. When he broached the revolution's origins, Alexander instead identified with a widespread sense of the mineworkers as the "backbone" of the movement.[17] Works produced about ten years after Alexander's study, primarily by political scientists or participant observers affiliated with the United Nations, similarly highlighted workers' radical force.[18] These early studies not only downplayed prerevolutionary rural movements but also relied on a limited definition of legitimate political participation. The authors implicitly assumed that rural political action could only influence national events if it was directly linked with the MNR.

Rural actors were not completely excluded from the first works on 1952, but, with a few important exceptions, they were generally considered influential participants only after the revolution triumphed.[19] In the late 1960s and early 1970s, a group of studies on the agrarian reform sponsored by the University of Wisconsin Land Tenure Center underscored the role of peasant participation and pressure.[20] Richly detailed, these regional and subregional studies provided a wealth of local perspectives that greatly illuminated on-the-ground politics of the reform process. While noting that the network of rural unions forged in conjunction with the agrarian reform was the result of complex links between partisan politics and grassroots mobilization, these works generally concluded that the reform itself took place either because the MNR willed it or because the peasants of Ucureña uniquely forced the item onto the party agenda.[21]

If postrevolutionary mobilization has been a privileged focus, some works do refer in general terms to varied modes of rural mobilization during the years leading to 1952. Yet they view these movements separately from the problem of revolutionary origins. In the 1972 article "Peasants and Revolution," Andrew Pearse pointed to a deep history of peasant political action stretching back to the 1899 indigenous rebellion—a history that other scholars rarely discuss in conjunction with the revolution and agrarian reform. By defining the peasants engaged in the earlier events as colonos and former colonos, however, Pearse overlooked Indian communities, land struggles, and projects for local and regional power. When directly addressing the question of revolutionary origins, Pearse, like others before him, privileged Ucureña.[22] Of the early studies by English-language authors, James Kohl's work most thoroughly recognized colonos' and comunarios' political engagement in the pre-revolutionary years, and their role in the revolution's origins.[23] While calling attention to pre-

and post-revolutionary mobilization on haciendas and communities, Kohl nevertheless considered the problem of revolutionary origins largely from the perspective of the MNR. He left for future researchers questions about the connections between pre- and post-1952 movements and the significance of rural communities' political motivations and visions.[24]

With the rise of Katarismo and renewed waves of indigenous mobilization in the 1970s, 1980s, and 1990s, Aymara intellectuals unearthed a profound history of indigenous mobilization that reached back to the 1860s and 1870s.[25] Pioneering works sponsored by the Taller de Historia Oral Andina (Andean Oral History Workshop, THOA; founded in 1983) uncovered and analyzed the political projects forged by Aymara peasants during the late nineteenth century and the early twentieth; a central focus of their research was the networks of caciques apoderados and preceptors. While providing a nuanced view of the 1953 agrarian reform and the relationship between Indian communities and MNR-sponsored unions, these works do not consider 1952 a crucial watershed. THOA's research initially focused on the period from 1866 to the very early phase of the revolution; it aimed to recuperate the history of autonomous indigenous political action that preceded the 1952 state's intrusion into rural areas and its efforts to "modernize" indigenous culture and community political structures.[26] In her 1984 *Oprimidos pero no vencidos*, Silvia Rivera (one of THOA's founding members) offered a compelling synthesis of Quechua and Aymara political struggles in the twentieth century. Rivera showed how those movements culminated in the rise of Katarismo and a break with the network of state-controlled unions that emerged out of the 1952 revolution.[27] She also mapped out the characteristics of distinct regional and ethnic projects. Accordingly, the La Paz altiplano was connected with a long historical memory that extended back to the unfinished anticolonial struggles of the late eighteenth century. Political action by the Cochabamba peasantry, Rivera argues, was instead driven by a short-term memory associated with the revolutionary state and the process of rural unionization. From this perspective, the 1952 revolution stood for MNR-controlled unions, Hispanicizing schools, private property, and a civilizing form of citizenship. It thus represented the antithesis and suppression of the anticolonial vision of Aymara activists.

While underscoring the revolution's profound shortcomings, some such works do point to rural participation in the insurrection itself, without discounting the MNR's great hesitancy to mobilize the peasantry. For example, Silvia Rivera noted the existence of peasant cells that included leaders of the 1947 indigenous uprisings who had been jailed together with MNR militants following the party's defeat in the 1949 civil war.[28] A crucial contribution of Rivera's work more broadly was to show that rural indigenous leaders pressed their communities' claims all the way to 1952.

Two recent works by Bolivian scholars further challenge urban-centered understandings of the insurrection and its initial radicalism by altering our perspective on the role of the MNR and the makeup of the rural protagonists. Revisiting rural conflict in the department of Cochabamba between 1952 and 1964, and critiquing top-down approaches to unionization, José Gordillo's *Campesinos revolucionarios en Bolivia* (2000) charts the course of an autonomous peasant project, its gendered ideologies and practices, and its negotiations and confrontations with the party and the state.[29] Gordillo concludes that this process of political engagement not only "transformed peasant subjectivities" but "created a new political culture in the country."[30] With its critique of state-centered approaches, Gordillo's work compels us to rethink the revolution from the bottom up, not only in Cochabamba but also in other regions where the trajectory of peasant action has not yet been fully explored.[31] A 1988 essay by Víctor Hugo Cárdenas—a Katarista leader and former vice-president of Bolivia (1993–97)—provides a suggestive starting point for reconsidering such dynamics of mobilization on the La Paz altiplano. While summing up the history of indigenous movements in modern Bolivia, and downplaying the 1952 insurrection itself, Cárdenas associates Aymara and Quechua colonos and comunarios with the left-wing sector of the MNR and its coalition of workers and nationalists. The essay highlights Ucureña's formidable role, but it also underscores the rising tide of unrest on the La Paz altiplano, which the MNR just barely managed to control after taking power in 1952.[32] With the support of workers and leftist members of the MNR, Aymara peasants created militias to challenge and confront hacienda abuse. On the first anniversary of the revolution, Cárdenas notes, more than 15 of these brigades—reportedly totaling 100,000 soldiers—marked the event with a march through the streets of La Paz.[33] Such extensive mobilization cannot be explained without considering the history of pre-revolutionary political activism. In fact, one such regiment materialized in the province of Los Andes: this was precisely one of the three main centers of 1947 unrest (see map 4).[34] Of course, the MNR and other outside organizers played a fundamental part in the formation of rural unions and militias: the party's agents were sent virtually everywhere after 1952.[35] But they were taking advantage of already-existing revolutionary conditions in the countryside.

In sum, the historiography does not omit rural political action, but it generally includes and excludes Indians and peasants in ways that cloud our understanding of the revolution's origins and its meanings. With the exception of a few recent works, the literature tends to focus on events that inscribe 1952 with a particular regional/ethnic image. When the revolution is associated with the countryside, it is above all linked with Quechua-speaking "mestizo" smallholders of the Cochabamba valleys and disassociated from Aymara- or Quechua-speaking Indian communities of highland areas. When scholars broach the revolution's rural origins, they tend to focus on the village of Ucureña and overlook the connections between the revolution and pre-revolutionary struggles by colonos and comunarios in many other locations. Considerations of the revolutionary process in turn highlight the formidable role of peasant mobilization in the genesis of the agrarian reform, yet scholars do so by stressing once again Ucureña's influence or by presenting the reform as a top-down, MNR-led process. Whichever the case, the revolution remains disconnected from a deeper history of rural mobilization that involved both colonos and comunarios—at times in pursuit of contrary agendas, but sometimes also in alliance with each other.

At a basic level, ignoring rural communities' wider role in the origins of the revolution makes it difficult to explain how and why such massive rural upheaval immediately followed the urban-based, three-day insurrection. By viewing peasant mobilization solely as a consequence of the revolution, many studies risk making peasant political action dependent on the ideas and activities of other actors, particularly the MNR. Not seeing the rural roots, finally, impedes a fuller understanding of the revolution itself, for the specific visions and expectations that rural communities invested in the revolutionary triumph remain obscure. Although those visions were largely suppressed, they were critical elements of the struggle to define the revolutionary project. Surely the visions and practices of nonrevolutionary peasants also played a role in these early contests, and those too remain to be explored. The MNR is often attributed with extraordinary power to mold culture, ideology, and community.[36] In reality, the early phase of the revolution was typified by mobilization that the party could not fully control.

The long history of peasant mobilization and the precarious pact between the Villarroel-MNR government and Indians and peasants were precisely what gave rural action such force after 1952. Bolivia is the only Latin American country where the revolutionary party held power before a revolution triumphed. Profound political upheaval—rural and urban—was sustained over a period of several decades, and that upheaval was further fanned by the MNR's brief co-government with Villarroel.[37] After taking control in 1952, the MNR was forced to contend with rural movements it had itself inadvertently bolstered during its first period in power. Eventually, the MNR managed to make the peasantry and its unions a loyal arm against the mineworkers, but this was not because the peasantry was less radical than the workers: it was a battle the MNR had to win. When the MNR's urban revolution triumphed in 1952, another revolution, a rural revolution, was already unfolding. That other revolution left a lasting mark on the meanings of 1952.

✳ Revolutionary Change

During its first two years in power, the revolutionary government ushered in three well-known reforms: universal suffrage, nationalization of the tin mines, and agrarian reform. The first and only change the revolutionary leaders definitively embraced was universal suffrage. The July 1952 decree, which was entitled "Establishing the Peasantry's Right to Vote," eliminated restrictions based on literacy and gender (see figure 25). As it awarded the vote to women, the law specifically noted their role in the fight against the oligarchy.[38] Notwithstanding its title, the decree did not list peasants' or Indians' contributions to national struggles or even name them in the body of the law: they were part of the "pueblo" in which sovereignty must reside.[39] This silence is significant. The MNR stressed its own role in the "liberation" of Indians, and it took full credit for the arrival of universal suffrage and land reform.[40] Although the party dubbed the decree "a great blow to the oligarchy," it did not connect citizenship rights with broader ideals of liberty and equality, nor did it link them with the history of participatory struggles to free the nation from colonial bonds.[41]

Universal suffrage came first partly because electoral practices were so central to revolutionary authority. With the decree for universal suffrage, the Bolivian electorate jumped from about 200,000 (approximately 6.6 percent of the population) to over 1 million people (33.8 percent).[42] Still, the revolution did not make a radical break with the political culture of the past. Few laws were changed, and the party dreamed up no new civic

25 The universal vote: a woman casts her ballot in a post-1952 election in La Paz. *Courtesy of the Archive of La Paz.*

ceremonies. With the exception of the ubiquitous "v" sign, the revolution-aries did not forge a novel repertoire of symbols, signals, gestures, or words. Rather than developing a distinctly revolutionary mode of political authority, the MNR drew on already existing forms of constitutional legiti-macy to solidify its rule.[43]

Expansion of the suffrage without agrarian reform or other structural changes signaled the regime's reformism; potentially, landlords could still control the rural vote. Yet once peasants had arms, unions, and the promise of land, universal citizenship became a potentially revolutionary act, and by the time of the first elections, in 1956, they had all three. Of course, the MNR tried to use the unions to manage the vote and peasant power more broadly. Moreover, elections engendered factionalist strife or they were controlled, effectively, by the party. Yet because peasants were armed, they held signifi-cant power at the local and regional levels during the early years of the revolution.[44] In this context, universal suffrage, for all its limits, acquired potentially radical significance. The word *citizen*, in practice, could be linked with union membership, land redistribution, and carrying a gun.

The revolution's second major reform was the nationalization of the tin mines. President Paz Estenssoro and the FSTMB head, Juan Lechín, signed the historic document on 31 October 1952 in the María Barzola mining camp in the Catavi-Siglo XX compound, which was owned by Simón Patiño and formed the bedrock of Bolivia's militant mineworker movement. The act was witnessed by a crowd of mineworkers who fired into the air the very guns the revolution had just bequeathed to them. The workers demanded nationalization without compensation. To appease its conservative factions and the United States, the MNR instead pushed through a policy that included indemnification amounting to 27 million U.S. dollars, or about 70 percent of Bolivia's existing foreign-exchange funds. Centrist members of the MNR carefully couched the nationalization as a restricted, "special case" measure that did not in principle oppose private property or even foreign ownership. The bill targeted Bolivia's three most egregiously "antinational" oligarchs (Patiño, Hochschild, and Aramayo), whose 163 mines and 29,000 workers became the basis of the state-owned Corporación Minera de Bolivia (Bolivian Mining Corporation, COMIBOL).[45] The mineworkers' federation, the FSTMB, in turn became the militant core of the Central Obera Boliviana (Bolivian Workers Central, COB), which was established on 17 April 1952 and grouped together all Bolivian unions in one of Latin America's most combative and independent labor federations.

Despite its moderate aims, the nationalization policy did validate the demands of the Left in its *control obrero* (worker control) provisions. The arrangement allowed worker representatives at all levels of mining administration and gave them decision-making power over issues that ranged from working conditions to questions of efficiency. Elected in workers' assemblies, the representatives also had the authority to veto decisions made by management. Finally, co-government gave the COB the right to appoint the national ministers of mines and petroleum; labor and social welfare; and peasant affairs. The COB also received the right to designate the vice-presidential candidate of the MNR. In short, the nationalization of the tin industry gave workers a major stake in the administration of the nation's most strategic economic sector. And it allowed the FSTMB to maintain independence from both the MNR party and COMIBOL management. Although workers did not receive significant material benefits from the nationalization—their real wages actually plummeted between 1950 and 1955—politically it made them a formidable force with which the MNR leadership was repeatedly forced to contend.[46]

The third major reform was the August 1953 agrarian reform, which abolished the latifundio and pongueaje, distributed land to estate laborers, and provided for the restoration of usurped communal territory. This was a historic measure, and since it implied a more sweeping transformation of property rights and relations, it provoked greater opposition than the tin nationalization.[47] Before the agrarian reform, Bolivia had one of the most unequal patterns of land distribution in all of Latin America. In 1950, 6 percent of the nation's landowners possessed 92 percent of all developed land in holdings of 1,000 hectares (2,471 acres) or more. In turn, 60 percent of all landowners owned 0.2 percent of the land in plots of 5 hectares (12.3 acres) or less.[48] The agrarian reform made an important dent in this skewed pattern, but it did not distribute nearly as much land as expected. Of a total of 36 million hectares (about 89 million acres) of farmland, about 8 million hectares (about 20 million acres, or 22 percent) were reallocated between 1954 and 1968.[49]

The limitations of the agrarian reform law were rooted not so much in the amount of land distributed as in the way it was apportioned. For while the revolutionary government abolished the latifundio, it did not confiscate all large properties. Along with small and medium farms, communal property, and cooperatives (ultimately few were established), the law recognized "agricultural enterprises." It defined these as productive rural ventures involving "large capital investment, modern technology, and salaried labor," and it allowed their owners to control as many as 2,023 hectares (5,000 acres). The law distinguished these productive properties from the unproductive latifundio, which was characterized as a large estate that was "minimally exploited by antiquated labor-intensive methods, and which perpetuate[d] a system of feudal oppression."[50] Vague and imprecise, the distinction allowed large private property to persist, often in the hands of MNR members whose party connections helped them evade expropriation.[51] In some cases, forms of unpaid labor tenantry lasted on these large properties.[52] The agrarian enterprise provision also deepened regional disparities, for the large "agricultural enterprises" were concentrated in the department of Santa Cruz, and they were privileged recipients of the reform's financial and technical resources as well as its infrastructural investments.[53] In the eastern lowlands, then, the agrarian reform promoted large-scale commercial agriculture. In the western highlands and valleys, it resulted in the expansion of *minifundios* (smallholdings) that lacked sufficient credit and other inputs.[54]

Hacienda colonos certainly benefited from the reform, but their gains were uneven. The law permitted individual parcels up to ten hectares (about twenty-five acres). On the whole, however, allotments followed existing patterns of usufruct, thus replicating prior inequalities among colonos and in many cases leaving the new smallholders with the same poor-quality land they had farmed under the hacienda system.[55] Women stood to gain the least from the reform, for agrarian judges generally granted land to the (male) head of household. True, former colonas who labored on haciendas received land. Yet single and divorced women and unmarried mothers who had not been estate workers could only acquire access to land via (often sexual) connections with married men or union leaders. Furthermore, while the universal suffrage decree gave women the right to vote, they were not authorized to participate equally with men in the affairs of the rural unions. Established hand in hand with the agrarian reform, the unions controlled members' access to land, markets, and arms, and they were the locus of political participation and rights in the countryside. Men, who were automatically considered heads of household, served as union delegates for each family; women could only be full members if they were widows or if they were single and owned land.[56] Although revolutionary policy did not simply relegate women to the domestic sphere, it "favored men and concentrated power in their hands."[57] The 1945 Indigenous Congress organizers' attention to gender parity, and their denunciations of sexual violence, had all but vanished.

The agrarian reform also gave preference to private over communal property. It thus failed to address Indian communities' longstanding demands for the recognition of territory, corporate rights, and autonomy. Essentially replicating article 165 of the 1938 Constitution, the 1953 reform guaranteed the "legal existence of indigenous communities [and] indigenous community property." Yet while stipulating that usurped land would be returned, the law limited such claims to land seized after 1900. It overlooked the fact that haciendas formed before then were also carved from community territory.[58] The law did allow collective tenure, but it tended to individualize that status. Communities were given the option of a "proindiviso" title—which included copies of the collective deed for each member—or individual titles like those dispensed to former colonos. In line with the idea that "the land belongs to he who works it," the law barred communities from maintaining land in different locations. By separating some highland ayllus from the valley lands they still possessed, the law further fragmented Indian communities.[59]

Although the agrarian reform privileged private over communal property, and ignored Indian communities' historic grievances, the outcome was neither inevitable nor easily imposed by the MNR. Available evidence indicates that Indian communities used the provision allowing the reinstatement of usurped communal land more frequently than previously thought. Indeed, they ignored the 1900 legal limit and revived the demands advanced by the caciques apoderados in the 1920s. In Cochabamba, such claims emerged in the highlands of Tapacarí and Arque, precisely where the caciques apoderados had been based. After 1952, Indian alcaldes in these provinces protested intrusion by MNR-sponsored agrarian unions, which aimed to replace the alcaldes as representatives of Indian communities.[60] Contests over land also erupted between these highland communities and Cochabamba valley peasants, for the communities asserted rights to the same valley lands that former colonos were claiming via the agrarian reform.[61] The caciques apoderados had discovered archival traces of their connections to that territory when they struggled against hacienda expansion in the 1910s and the 1920s, and the alcaldes of the early 1950s were reviving their demands. In December 1954, their dispute culminated in open confrontation between valley peasants and approximately 2,000 highland comunarios. Since the comunarios had not presented denunciations of landlords, but were in fact disputing the rights of other peasants, the federation of peasant unions labeled this highland *ayllocomunario* movement counterrevolutionary. Unions from various provinces sent out armed militias, which resulted in several deaths, arrests, and the suppression of a movement for a very different kind of land reform.[62]

Not just the memories and archival searches of the caciques apoderados remained powerful influences after 1952, but also the laws announced at the 1945 Indigenous Congress. As noted, after taking power, the MNR quickly labored to operationalize the 1945 laws via the newly established Ministry of Peasant Affairs (MAC).[63] The revolutionary government wished to use the measures to control and manage rural mobilization. Yet while the party made haste to promulgate the 1945 decrees, it was not the only entity with an interest: hacienda colonos had a stake in them, too. And so just as the Villarroel regime had done before the revolution, the MNR government now publicized those laws precisely in order to "correct" Indians' "misinterpretations" of them.[64] The government did this because post-1952 hacienda leaders were using the laws to demand not just the end of servitude or pay for work but also land.[65] Of course, not all rural communities had vivid memories of the 1945 Indigenous Congress. Some communities held negative recollections, or viewed Villarroel's laws with skepticism.

That said, there is no denying the profound influence of the Villarroel era on the rural mobilization that immediately followed the revolution. The radical course that the revolution took in the countryside surprised and disturbed the MNR. But the many communities that lodged petitions, staged sit-down strikes, and invaded haciendas had every reason to expect that *their* land would be returned. From the perspective of some rural leaders, "revolutionary authorities" or "the government" had already once appeared to decree it.

✳ Revolutionary Visions

Revolutions are exceptional occurrences involving extraordinary levels of political mobilization, the erosion of authority, profound change, and hopes for a new age.[66] Scholars seeking to explain the common cause of these uncommon events emphasize a variety of factors ranging from the revolutionary potential of the working class and various types of peasants, to repression, exploitation, structural socioeconomic forces, rivalries between great powers, and the crisis of the state.[67] As for the Bolivian Revolution, most works locate its origins in the political or economic crises of the 1930s. Many scholars identify the Chaco War itself as the primary cause, for the war not only caused a crisis of legitimacy but led a cadre of middle-class men—the so-called generation of the Chaco—to craft the reform project that triumphed in 1952.[68] The Chaco War and world depression undoubtedly shaped the coming of the revolution in manifold ways. Yet explanations that emphasize the ruptures of the 1930s run the risk of obscuring political continuities that bridged the period before the war with that which followed. More important, accounts that focus on the Chaco War often present a narrow view of the social and ethnic groups that shaped the ideas and events associated with the 1952 insurrection. Such works tend to emphasize the influence of workers and the middle class, and often root the revolutionary project in the views that were expressed at the 1938 Constitutional Convention; as a result, they may downplay the significance of rural activists' interventions in the political controversies and legislative disputes of both the prewar and postwar decades. Of course, I am not suggesting here that Indian and peasant movements alone caused the 1952 revolution. The causes of the revolution were varied, as were the groups that propelled it. But Indian and peasant political projects of the pre-revolutionary era remained alive on the eve of the revolution, and they played a role in the disputes that followed its triumph. Those enduring visions alert us to a realm of cultural and political ideals and practices that helped make a revolution conceivable.[69]

I conclude by considering in more depth the cultural origins or sources of the 1952 revolution. Such sources include the actions, experiences, and events from which varied people generated alternative visions of the nation. They alert us to the enduring significance of ideas and processes that were obscured once the revolution—and a particular memory of the revolution—was constructed and consolidated.[70] What ideas and practices made it possible to imagine the end of pongueaje, the latifundio, and restricted suffrage? What did universal citizenship and the abolition of pongueaje mean to the comunarios, ex-comunarios, and former hacienda colonos who participated in petition drives, strikes, and rebellions of the pre-revolutionary era?

If the literature on the revolution generally disconnects post-1952 agrarian unrest and the land reform from pre-revolutionary movements, the disconnect is equally apparent with regard to the question of citizenship. Most works seem to assume that the July 1952 law universalizing citizenship rights appeared suddenly with the triumph of the revolution. First, we should recall that proposals not only for women's suffrage but also for the voting rights of Indians and illiterate people were aired in congressional sessions of 1938 and 1945. Indeed, the MNR's 1945 proposal to make illiterates citizens came hand in hand with mounting rural strikes and the convocation of a national Indigenous Congress. The MNR was certainly seeking votes to help defeat electoral contenders, but it is notable that it risked such contention at a time of heightened unrest, and almost simultaneously with a proposal for indigenous tribunals and other laws that threatened landlord power. Siles Zuazo even linked the pitch to make illiterates citizens with revolutionary justice: He called it "the first milestone in the effort to take the revolution to the countryside" and "one of the first steps to repair an injustice of four centuries."[71] Although the proposal was not ultimately approved, it received strong support in the legislature.[72]

As we have seen, Bolivia's National Congress was not the only body to deliberate the meanings of rights and the boundaries of citizenship in the pre-revolutionary era. Cochabamba's caciques apoderados developed a critique of the hierarchical qualities of citizenship when they campaigned against communal land usurpation in the 1910s and the 1920s. Their claims centered most heavily on civil protections and guarantees, and their demands were as much critiques of citizenship's exclusive status as they were projects to redefine rights ethnically and "within the boundaries of equality." In requesting a survey of land boundaries, the caciques apoderados were not simply advancing a territorial claim. They were also demanding a fundamental reconfiguration of the nation's internal and external borders, of its administrative precincts, political structures, and exclusionary principles.

In the aftermath of the Chaco War, a new generation of Indian and peasant leaders articulated similar claims for civil rights and equality, but they couched their demands in a distinct political language that centered on the freedom from pongueaje. If the revisita was the fundamental form for indigenous demands in the 1920s, in the 1940s the primary idiom was a law—or the rumor of a law—to end this degrading duty. Like the caciques apoderados, Indian and peasant leaders of the 1940s conveyed and publicized republican laws and constitutional guarantees. But they no longer invoked colonial titles and laws. Now they took hold of the military socialist laws, the "laws decreed in our favor," to demand equality and freedom from the physical and symbolic domination embodied in pongueaje. In 1947, the call to end pongueaje became a call for revolution; it meant the end of a state perceived to be ruled by landlords, the end of an unlawful system of racialized and gendered domination.

Appeals for rights in the pre-revolutionary era thus had little to do with suffrage and much more to do with civil rights and social rights. When Indian and peasant activists occasionally employed the word *citizen*, they did not use it to claim voting rights; instead they utilized it in conjunction with wider demands for state protection, the enforcement of laws, or the end of all servitude. That said, rural activists of the 1920s and the 1940s of course did not overlook political rights and participation. First and foremost, they demanded political rights by practicing them—by forging supralocal networks, submitting petitions, meeting face-to-face with government officials, organizing congresses, publishing articles in their own and national newspapers, broadcasting laws, carrying out strikes, and in some cases by intervening in electoral campaigns. For indigenous ex-combatants, the right to be elected—especially to local authority posts—mattered as much as the right to vote.[73] So even though Indian and peasant activists of the 1920s and the 1940s did not demand citizenship per se, by contesting and confronting the racialized forms of domination that characterized the countryside in the pre-revolutionary era, they shaped the context in which universal citizenship would be practiced after 1952, and what it might mean.

The cultural and political origins of the Bolivian Revolution do not only have to do with ideas about rights, participation, sovereignty, and equality, but also with the way that those ideas could acquire specific meanings in practice.[74] In the Bolivian case, protections and guarantees, social rights, the end of pongueaje—all these things gained significance through the use of specific political practices. Just as important as pleas for revisitas and the circulation of laws were the regional and national congresses where colonos and comunarios aired grievances, proposed reforms, and planned political action. Indians and peasants occasionally convened such supralocal congresses before the Chaco War. But an important change took place with the rise of populist state projects in the 1930s, for the broad-based assemblies gained the support of sympathetic political parties, labor leaders, and state authorities, even as the local organizers maintained distance and independence from them. The assemblies, in any case, were becoming (an albeit still disputed) component of the national political arena.

Another important postwar change concerns the intensity of rural "subversion" and its connections with populist state projects and the law. Legal campaigns and protest both before and after the war were punctuated by rebellion, but the intensity and scope of "subversive" action peaked in the 1940s, when a new form of protest took hold: the sit-down strike. The significance of these strikes had to do not only with what they really were but with what they were perceived to be. In the minds of landlords, local authorities, and some national officials, the work stoppages doubled as rebellions to distribute hacienda land or to restore "community." Even if they were not those things—and sometimes they really were—rumors of conspiratorial aims became a constant in the 1940s; no longer exceptional occurrences, "strikes" and "rebellions" were becoming the norm. From the towns and cities, the countryside was perceived to be a place up in arms. Landlords themselves grew anxious about their declining authority and began to question the loyalty of local authorities. Hacienda colonos did not simply disobey, hacendados complained, but acted as though they were "owners." A fundamental issue from many sides was the idea that the law favored Indians and that their illegal action was grounded in laws. If rural unrest peaked in the 1940s, this period also saw a dramatic increase in repression. In the 1920s, indigenous petitioners acting within the law were often labeled subversives, but the scope of such physical and symbolic violence widened in the 1940s; the repression affected even Indians only remotely connected to lawyers, labor unions, or areas of revolt. A related factor was the deepening crisis of state power that characterized the countryside in the 1940s. During this tumultuous decade before the revolution triumphed, not just Indians but also landlords and townspeople voiced frequent complaints against local officials. In short, the strikes and rebellions of 1946 and 1947 exposed a growing political vacuum in the countryside, and that widening gap was in part the product of the populist regime's ambivalent support for the demands of rural leaders.

This revolution before the revolution—the rebellions of the late 1940s, which were in turn connected with the 1945 Indigenous Congress and the caciques apoderados networks of the 1920s—was a key source of 1952. I say this not only because many of the ideas and tactics associated with 1947 reemerged immediately after 1952. I say it also because of the expectation and fear associated with a moment that some actors themselves considered revolutionary. The leaders of the 1947 Ayopaya uprising talked about a revolutionary government they connected with the 1943–46 Villarroel-MNR regime. However fraught, the Villarroel era constituted a key condition for Bolivia's burgeoning revolutionary situation, for it allowed particular groups to perceive a viable alternative to the existing order.[75] Whether repression suppresses or fans opposition movements is an empirical question about which it is difficult to generalize. In this particular case, repression mitigated strikes and uprisings, but it did not stamp them out. The year 1947 was a constitutive moment that shaped the revolution to come. For some, the 1947 rebellions embodied the possibility of a new era. For others, 1947 induced fear. From both angles, the events of that year cast a visible image of what a revolution might be. For the MNR, it was an image of what the revolution should not be. The MNR most thoroughly molded its rural support base in regions such as Cliza and Achacachi where the 1947 uprisings had not been centered, but peasants in some areas central to the rebellions (Tapacarí and Los Andes) nonetheless became highly mobilized after the 1952 triumph.

The timing of the 1952 revolution and its connections to Latin America's "democratic opening" of the mid-1940s are indeed noteworthy. As discussed in chapter 8, between World War II and the beginning of the cold war, Latin America experienced a major democratic transition that implied commitments to social justice, wealth redistribution, and expanded political participation for organized labor. With the shift to cold war containment, this democratic opening closed down, and an opportunity for a wider democracy was lost. Bolivia and Guatemala represent noteworthy exceptions to the pattern, not only because the political opening lasted longer, but because governments in each country espoused a particular kind of *revolutionary* democracy that awakened expectations and, for a time, inspired hopes of radical social change. Just as conservative forces consolidated power almost everywhere else in Latin America, a major social revolution triumphed in Bolivia.

When the 1952 revolution is linked with the pre-revolutionary history of indigenous mobilization, Bolivia's political opening of the mid-1940s takes on new meanings. Not just the political participation of workers expanded but also that of the peasantry. The 1952 revolution, the delayed outcome of the 1940s opening, expanded political and social rights, but the revolutionary state also suppressed the demands for autonomy that colonos and comunarios had long been championing. Despite the triumph of a revolution, then, Bolivia's lost opportunity of the postwar era must refer in part to the defeat of specific visions of the polity that Indian and peasant movements espoused. For Bolivia's frustrated political opening presented an opportunity not only for social and political change but for antiracist agendas and projects of ethnic autonomy. Although the movements that forged those visions partly propelled the revolution, the revolutionary state also aimed to contain them. This tension between support and restraint of indigenous political participation was a defining feature of the 1952 revolution.

✳ Legacies of the Revolution?

The Bolivian Revolution's three major reforms (tin nationalization, universal citizenship, and agrarian reform) were bold measures in their time, but they had significant limits. Bolivian society today is marked—and being reshaped—by an acute battle over what it means for the nation to own, control, and reap the benefits of its natural resources. In stark form, the social conditions and struggles of the present also reveal the enduring deficits and in some cases rollback of agrarian reform gains and citizenship. The reasons for these shortfalls are numerous, but can they be traced, in part, to the 1952 revolution?

Assessments of this event convey starkly divided views. What some see as liberation, others view as the triumph of an oppressive, civilizing form of citizenship, as a means to assimilate and control (see figure 26). Rather than showing the period leading to the revolution as a march toward democracy or as a journey away from it, the caciques apoderados networks, the 1945 Indigenous Congress, and the 1947 cycle of unrest direct our attention to a different question: to the historical creation of arenas of participation, argument, and power. Some of the political practices or spheres discussed in this book—rural unions, indigenous congresses, the cultivation of lay legal expertise—survived in altered form. Others—the multiethnic, multiregional network of caciques apoderados—did not. Yet whether they are now actual or symbolic sites, tangible places or only memories, all of these things can be considered elements of the process of nation making. They are also sources of a revolution very different from the one that triumphed in 1952. And the visions their practitioners expressed in the past are one basis of the struggles taking place in Bolivia today over land, resources, political power, and rights.

The fiftieth anniversary of the revolution came and went in April 2002 with barely a whimper. But the October 2003 uprising that forced President Gonzalo Sánchez de Lozada to resign resurrected memories of 1952. Some observers commented that such levels of mobilization had not been seen since the days in April 1952 when the revolution triumphed. Or they said that the movement was even bigger this time around. Many analysts connected the September–October 2003 "gas war" with the earlier struggle to nationalize tin. Some also linked it with one source of the 1952 revolution, with Eduardo Leandro Nina Qhispi's intercultural vision, with the "renovation" of the nation.[76]

It is possible to draw these connections with 1952 more than fifty years after the event, because the revolution no longer simply represents the "1952 State" but also the popular uprising it restrained.[77] With the withering of that state in the neoliberal reforms of the 1980s and the 1990s, "1952" may more clearly evoke the radical forces that first propelled the revolution. If we connect 1952 with its rural roots in the 1920s and the 1940s, those radical forces become all the more visible. Not only in the city but also in the countryside, workers, peasants, and Indians claimed justice, equality, and sovereignty over the nation's natural resources even before the 1952 revolution triumphed. They occupied public space, asserted the right to participate in the configuration of power and the economy, and insisted on an end to the discrimination of the pongo and the mitani. Symbols of an enduring colonial order, these victimized figures stood not only for the oppression of intimate service in the landlord's home but also symbolized (and continue to symbolize) the deep structures of racism.

The emphasis this book has placed on colonos' and comunarios' strug-

26   The long line at the police station to obtain an identity card (*cédula de identidad* or *carnet*), circa 1950s–1960s. The identity card is one of several forms of identification required for voter registration. *Courtesy of the Archive of La Paz.*

gles over land, rights, and local power in the 1920s and the 1940s allows us to highlight a key tension that the 1952 revolution embodies. Up to a point, the revolution was a reaction against indigenous mobilization and thus a product of the liberal oligarchic project itself and its vision of modernity. The process of nation and state making that culminated in the revolution certainly engendered a more inclusive political culture, but one that was also based on new and old forms of exclusion. If caste relations receded with the expulsion of landlords, they reappeared in different guises along with new relations of domination.[78] Bolivia's national revolution, it could thus be said, embodied the fundamental paradoxes of liberalism in a society in which social and political struggles had re-created colonial divides in modern institutions and idioms.

If we take seriously this guarded approach, with its emphasis on continuity, it must at the same time be said that the revolution was a movement against colonial legacies, and against oligarchic, exclusionary liberalism. Just like the Villarroel regime at the 1945 Indigenous Congress, revolutionary ideologues championed the revolution as the triumph of a struggle against feudalism and colonial oppression, against four centuries

of servitude. By granting suffrage rights and officially recognizing a coun-
trywide network of unions, the revolution made comunarios, smallholders, and former colonos a national political force.[79] The MNR state did not
do this on its own: it formalized, within particular institutional rubrics,
what rural people had already made true in 1945, 1946, and 1947. Indigenous participation in the initial, most contested phases of the revolution
ruptured structures of separation and discrimination. Indians and peasants occupied mestizo towns, marched on major cities, and spontaneously
established a profusion of their own rural hamlets and markets.[80] These
interventions, although counterbalanced by later developments, had an
important democratizing impact that could not be easily reversed.[81] From
a long-term perspective, it is clear that the revolution alone did not effect
the changes associated with 1952: when landlords decried the specter of
indigenous agitation, and the end of the racialized rural–urban divide,
they were seeing what they had already seen. The history they looked upon,
a history of racism and antiracism, resonates today in the possibilities
being articulated for the future and in what is still perceived as threatening.[82]

✳ Introduction

Throughout the book, translations of Spanish-language quotations are my own unless otherwise noted. The spelling of Spanish-language terms and place names, which varied during the period of this study, have generally been updated and standardized. With a few exceptions, the spelling of personal names follows the original source. The spelling used in the archival citations also follows the Spanish-language original. Documents held in the provincial courts of Cliza and Punata have not been classified and are thus cited here without numbers. The same is true for the documents that were consulted in the Cochabamba prefecture archive. To preserve the privacy of the litigants and their descendents, in the few instances that slander cases are cited, the citations appear with first- and last-name initials only. Finally, a note on the maps: administrative borders shifted during the nineteenth and twentieth centuries, as new cantons and provinces were established. To minimize confusion, I have opted to use present-day boundaries. This means that some of the provinces included in the maps did not yet exist during the period of study; likewise, some places that were once provinces are smaller administrative districts today.

1 Archivo Histórico del Honorable Congreso Nacional de Bolivia (hereafter AHHCN), Box 93, No. 2 (hereafter 93-2), 1927, Guillermo Crus et al. to the Señor Ministro de Guerra, fol. 7v. In 1900, Vacas was a canton in the highlands of Punata province; it became a section of what is today Arani province after the creation of that province in 1914. Vacas was also the

name of one of the most extensive haciendas in Cochabamba; for Guillermo Cruz and other indigenous leaders, that same territory instead comprised the Vacas community.

2 The term "1947 cycle of rebellion" is from Silvia Rivera Cusicanqui, *Oprimidos pero no vencidos*. Indigenous congresses were convened in Chile and Peru in the 1920s (see Florencia Mallon, *Courage Tastes of Blood*, 89–90; Marisol de la Cadena, *Indigenous Mestizos*, 86–97). A broad-based peasant congress was organized in Ecuador in 1931, but the government stifled the initiative before it took place (N. Kim Clark, "Racial Ideologies and the Quest for National Development," 383). In the 1940s, state agencies convened *indigenista* congresses in Mexico and Peru, but these events were not spearheaded by local activists. The indigenista congresses are discussed in chapter 7.

3 Archivo de la Corte Superior de Justicia de Cochabamba (hereafter ACSJC), AG #1202, 2PP, fol. 101v.

4 On such national political networks in the Andes, see Xavier Albó, "Andean People in the Twentieth Century," 782. A rich and growing literature on rural social movements in the colonial and modern Andes has unearthed the wide scope of peasant political imagination. Two poles repeatedly marked these projects, one emphasizing Indian autonomy and power over local or national institutions, the other stressing multi-ethnic or multi-class alliances and political and civil equality. As these works show, and the present study confirms, rural activists rarely posed these visions as mutually exclusive opposites. See esp. Steve J. Stern, *Resistance, Rebellion, and Consciousness in the Andean Peasant World*, 3–25, 327–33; Rivera, *Oprimidos pero no vencidos*; Albó, "Andean People in the Twentieth Century," 379–419; Roberto Choque, *Historia de una lucha desigual*, 46, 136–37; Sinclair Thomson, *We Alone Will Rule*; Sergio Serulnikov, *Subverting Colonial Authority*; Brooke Larson, *Trials of Nation Making*. For an overview of Andean political cultures, and the recurring characteristics of Andean social movements, see Nils Jacobsen and Cristóbal Aljovín, "Concluding Remarks." On the scope of rural movements in the Andes compared to Mexico and other Latin American countries, especially before 1900, see John Coatsworth, "Patterns of Rural Rebellion in Latin America."

5 This literature is reviewed in the book's conclusion.

6 To emphasize the relationship between state policy and indigenous projects is not to say that indigenous visions were determined by the state, for they were not. On such dynamics, and the significance of local creativity, see Mallon, *Courage Tastes of Blood*, especially 237–42.

7 My understanding of the law and juridical practice is informed by Pierre Bourdieu's analysis of legal culture, or the "juridical field," as the "site of a competition for monopoly of the right to determine the law." See "The Force of Law," esp. 816–17, 821. I also draw on the insights of historical and anthropological approaches to the law and legal culture, which have stressed the multivocal character of the law; and explored how local uses of the law may shape state law and the meanings of particular kinds of rights. See Jane Burbank, *Russian*

Peasants Go to Court, 5-10; Margaret Somers, "Citizenship and the Place of the Public Sphere," and "Rights, Relationality, and Membership"; Rossana Barragán, *Indios, mujeres y ciudadanos*; John Comaroff, "Foreword"; Sergio Serulnikov, *Subverting Colonial Authority*.

8 Ley de Organización Política (in República de Bolivia, *Constitución política del Estado*, 100). On the history of amparo in Bolivia, see Enrique Oblitas Poblete, *Recurso de amparo*. Rather than focusing on individual rights, indigenous leaders' collective appeals for amparo emphasized the concept of state protection.

9 My analysis of the law and legal processes does not look at Quechua or Aymara forms of community justice. Instead, it focuses on the ways that indigenous activists, especially from the department of Cochabamba, viewed, deployed, and—under specific political circumstances—remade the meanings of laws and decrees that were promulgated by the colonial and republican states. On Aymara practices of justice, see Marcelo Fernández, *La ley del ayllu*.

10 This discussion of revolutionary conditions draws on Friedrich Katz, *The Life and Times of Pancho Villa*, 54–56.

11 José Flores Moncayo, *Legislación boliviana del indio*, 226. During the period of this study, indigenous leaders and state officials generally used the terms community and *ayllu* (a kinship group that traces its origins to a common ancestor) interchangeably to refer to a communal landholding entity that joined its members together in a system of collective rights and obligations. That system included usufruct rights to the land, which were based on exchanges of labor among families of a particular ayllu as well as on collective labor obligations. Until 1874, Bolivian law recognized the Indian community as a juridical unit. Following the usage of the time, I use the terms "community" and "ayllu" interchangeably. On the meanings of community in the Andes, see especially Thomson, *We Alone Will Rule*, 10, 23–24; Larson, *Cochabamba*, 20–25; Larson, *Trials of Nation Making*, 30.

12 On Mexico, see Katz, "Introduction"; Katz, "Rural Rebellions after 1810."

13 See Tristan Platt, "The Andean Experience of Bolivian Liberalism"; Ramiro Condarco Morales, *Zárate, El "Temible" Willka*; Forrest Hylton, "El federalismo insurgente"; Carlos Mamani Condori, *Taraqu*; Larson, *Trials of Nation Making*.

14 To be sure, pioneering works have mapped out the leading role that colonos and smallholding peasants from Cochabamba's central valleys played in the origins of the Bolivian Revolution (see especially Jorge Dandler, *El sindicalismo campesino en Bolivia*; Dandler, "Politics of Leadership, Brokerage and Patronage in the Campesino Movement of Cochabamba"). As discussed in the conclusion, however, the literature generally disassociates the roots of 1952 from the wider history of indigenous politics that marked many Bolivian regions during the first half of the twentieth century—notwithstanding evidence of sustained links between revolutionary nationalists, Indian and peasant activists, and the military populist state.

15 The term "mestizo" was used literally to refer to a person of mixed European

and Indian descent; but whether or not a person was considered mestizo or mestiza generally depended on a series of cultural signs that could shift according to context. The meanings of the term "Indian" are discussed in greater depth below.

16 The bulk of the communities were located in La Paz, Oruro, Potosí, and Sucre (Larson, *Cochabamba*, 10).

17 The following paragraphs are indebted to Larson, *Cochabamba*; Robert Jackson, *Regional Markets and Agrarian Transformation in Bolivia*.

18 Bolivia's 1900 census employed four "racial" categories: white, black, Indian (indígena), and mestizo. It tallied Cochabamba's population as 52 percent mestizo, 23 percent Indian, 18 percent white, 0.04 percent black, and 7 percent "unknown." The individuals responsible for the census defined white as the descendent of a foreigner, especially of the Spanish, and mestizo as the descendent of a white person and an Indian. Although the census essentially equated *cholos* with mestizos (the category mestizo was used for both), it considered cholos to be closer to Indians in "features and color" (*Censo general de la población de la República de Bolivia*, 30, 38). The specific meanings that local actors attributed to "cholo" nevertheless differed by region and social context. In Cochabamba, rural inhabitants associated the term with a higher position in the local social hierarchy, that is, with artisans, manual workers, and townspeople (see José M. Gordillo, *Campesinos revolucionarios en Bolivia*, 218, 228). The Cochabamba region is well known for its bilingualism. In 1945, an estimated 44.4 percent of the population was bilingual even in the city of Cochabamba. Approximately 33 percent of the "white" population knew Quechua at this time, while about 55 percent of the "non-white" population knew Spanish. While bilingualism was fairly common in rural areas of the valleys, especially among men, it was far less frequent in the department's highland provinces (Dandler, "Politics of Leadership, Brokerage and Patronage in the Campesino Movement of Cochabamba," 41).

19 According to census data, Bolivia's total population in 1900 was 1,633,610; in 1950, it was 2,704,165. The department of Cochabamba had a population of 326,163 in 1900 and a population of 452,145 in 1950 (Erwin Grieshaber, "Fluctuaciones en la definición del indio"). Today, Bolivia's total population is approximately 9 million. According to the 2001 census, 62 percent of the population considers itself indigenous (respondents were asked whether they identified with one of 33 indigenous groups).

20 In late-nineteenth- and early-twentieth-century Cochabamba, the only other area of significant Indian community settlement was Vacas, which is located just east of the Valle Alto and about 1,000 meters (about 3,280 feet) higher than it. The scope of communal landholding, and its transformation in the late nineteenth century, is discussed in greater depth in chapter 1.

21 The term mestizaje was often used to refer to "racial" mixture but it also signified a process of cultural and social change that could be both valorized and denigrated by local actors. For diverse perspectives on mestizaje in the

Andes, see especially Stuart B. Schwartz and Frank Salomon, "New Peoples and New Kinds of People"; Larson, *Cochabamba*; de la Cadena, *Indigenous Mestizos*; Barragán, "Entre polleras, lliqllas y ñañacas"; Gordillo, *Campesinos revolucionarios en Bolivia*. Although mestizaje is associated with de-indianization, it can mean the casting off of an inferior social status without the rejection of indigenous cultural practices (de la Cadena, *Indigenous Mestizos*).

22 Larson, *Cochabamba*, 137–39, 34–39, 78–79, 101.

23 On "race," place, and region see, for example, Nancy Appelbaum, Anne Macpherson, and Karin Rosemblatt, "Introduction."

24 My thoughts about terminology are informed by recent discussions of these issues in other Latin American contexts. See especially Ada Ferrer, *Insurgent Cuba*, 10–12.

25 This discussion draws on Olivia Harris, "Ethnic Identity and Market Relations"; Larson, *Cochabamba*.

26 Grieshaber, "Fluctuaciones en la definición del indio." The 1900 census apparently equated Indian with tribute payer. The next national census, which was taken in 1950, used dress and language as the markers. Tribute's long life in post-independent Bolivia is discussed in chapter 1.

27 Mario C. Araoz, *Nuevo digesto de legislación boliviana*, vol. 1, 335. In Cochabamba, former colonos who acquired independent plots of land sometimes came to be known locally as mestizos or *campesinos* (peasants). Hacienda colonos, who continued to owe labor and service duties to a landlord, were usually considered Indians.

28 Grieshaber, "Fluctuaciones en la definición del indio."

✳ *One* Peculiar Paths of the Liberal Project

1 William Lee Lofstrom, "The Promise and Problem of Reform," 37–43.

2 Flores Moncayo, *Legislación boliviana del indio*, 36.

3 Herbert Klein, *Bolivia*, 100–108. Sucre took power in January 1826.

4 The triumph of the free traders followed decades of conflict with protectionist sectors (Platt, *Estado boliviano y ayllu andino*, 36–37; Erick Langer, *Economic Change and Rural Resistance in Southern Bolivia*, 15–25). Although Bolivia's Liberal and Conservative parties were not established until the early 1880s (see below), members of the diverse group associated with free trade are known as liberals precisely because they backed key tenets of economic liberalism. But defining "liberal" and "liberalism" in the Bolivian context is not a straightforward task. Late-nineteenth-century Latin American liberalism was a hybrid creed. As Charles A. Hale has shown, it was defined by a weave of constitutionalism, economic individualism, "scientific politics," and authoritarianism ("Political and Social Ideas"; *The Transformation of Liberalism in Late Nineteenth-Century Mexico*). And, as Alan Knight recently put it, it was exceptionally varied and composed of many illiberal and "quasi-colonial" traits ("Is Political Culture Good to Think?" 44–47). Scholars of nineteenth- and

twentieth-century Bolivia generally associate late-nineteenth-century liberalism with free trade, export-led growth, land privatization policies, educational expansion, and legislation to secularize society. By "liberal project," I mean these very things, as well as the contradictions and "illiberal" elements that marked liberal policies in practice.

5 Bolivia's late-nineteenth- and early-twentieth-century constitutions defined citizenship as the right to vote. The practical significance of citizenship is discussed later in this chapter and in chapters 3 and 4.

6 I am thus suggesting that the concrete circumstances of power and contestation are key to understanding how concepts of civil, political, and property rights were imposed, challenged, and changed. This view draws on Laurent Dubois, "La République Métissée," 23–24; Thomas Holt, "The Essence of the Contract"; Alice Conklin, "Colonialism and Human Rights"; Ann Stoler and Frederick Cooper, "Between Metropole and Colony," 16. On the differences between the colonial corporate model and the postindependent resurrection of corporatism, see Nils Jacobsen, "Liberalism and Indian Communities in Peru." On liberalism's exclusionary principles, see Uday Mehta, "Liberal Strategies of Exclusion"; Holt, *The Problem of Freedom*, esp. 308–9; Dubois, *A Colony of Citizens*, 173.

7 Gustavo Rodríguez, "Entre reformas y contrareformas," 300.

8 Until Melgarejo, the state essentially recognized communal property. In contrast to Peru, therefore, Bolivia's 1826 reinstatement of tribute was accompanied by the affirmation of the community's legal status (Larson, *Trials of Nation Making*, 212–13). In 1831, President Andrés de Santa Cruz declared Indians owners of all the land they possessed for a period of at least ten years (Langer, "El liberalismo y la abolición de la comunidad indígena en el siglo XIX," 62). Later, an 1842 circular released by the Ballivián government deemed "land possessed by the originarios . . . property of the State . . . [and thus] simply a kind of *enfiteutas* for which they pay a certain amount . . . [in exchange] for use rights [*usufructo*]" (cited in Rodríguez, "Entre reformas y contrareformas," 290). To be sure, this measure was used to justify laws that ended the protection of communal landholding rights in the 1860s and the 1870s; initially, however, it served to confirm those rights (Langer, *Economic Change and Rural Resistance in Southern Bolivia*, 15; Larson, *Trials of Nation Making*, 212–13).

9 Klein, *Bolivia*, 135–41; Flores Moncayo, *Legislación boliviana del indio*, 199–201.

10 Klein, *Haciendas and Ayllus*, 115–16.

11 Langer, *Economic Change and Rural Resistance in Southern Bolivia*, 18.

12 Larson, *Trials of Nation Making*, 204–6.

13 Klein, *Haciendas and Ayllus*, 116.

14 Rivera Cusicanqui, "La expansión del latifundio en el altiplano boliviano," 102; Grieshaber, "Survival of Indian Communities in Nineteenth-Century Bolivia," 198.

15 Platt, "The Andean Experience of Bolivian Liberalism," 297.

16 Rodríguez, "Entre reformas y contrareformas," 304.

17 Heraclio Bonilla, "Peru and Bolivia from Independence to the War of Pacific," 274–75; Rivera, "La expansión del latifundio en el altiplano boliviano," 103.

18 Marta Irurozqui, *La armonía de las desigualdades*.

19 Condarco Morales, *Zárate, El "Temible" Willka*, 45; Luis Antezana, *Las grandes masacres y levantamientos indígenas en la historia de Bolivia*, 35.

20 Xavier Albó and Josep Barnadas, *La cara campesina de nuestra historia*, 173.

21 Josep Barnadas, *Apuntes para una historia aymara*, 59–60. On the uprisings against Melgarejo, see also Nicanor Aranzaes, *Las revoluciones de Bolivia*, 270–84.

22 Klein, *Bolivia*, 135–47.

23 Bernardino Sanjinés, *Venta de tierras de comunidad*, 73–74.

24 The Bolivian congress is and was bicameral. In the late nineteenth century and for the first half of the twentieth, about eighteen senators were elected (two per department) for six-year terms, and approximately seventy deputies were elected for four-year terms; the deputies represented provinces or districts within departmental capitals. In the time between independence and the 1952 revolution, sixteen unicameral conventions or assemblies (such as the one held in 1871) were convened to rewrite the constitution. On the history of elections and conventions, see Barragán, *Asambleas Constituyentes*.

25 In Oruro and La Paz, most usurped land was returned to communities, but this was not the case in Chuquisaca (Ximena Medinaceli, "Redefinición de las comunidades," 9).

26 Langer, "El liberalismo y la abolición de la comunidad indígena en el siglo XIX." On these debates, and on elites' early-nineteenth-century reflections on the Indian community, see also Seemin Qayum, "Creole Imaginings," chap. 4. For the pro-hacienda view, see Juan de Dios Zambrana, *Dos palabras sobre la venta de tierras realengas, a la nación, a la soberana asamblea y al supremo gobierno*.

27 See Langer, "El liberalismo"; Rodríguez, "Entre reformas y contrareformas."

28 José María Santivañez, *Revindicación de los terrenos de comunidad* (reprint), 120.

29 Ibid., 131–32; Santivañez, *Rebindicación de los terrenos de comunidad o sea refutación del folleto titulado "Lejitimidad de las compras de tierras realengas,"* 48.

30 Santivañez, *Rebindicación de los terrenos de comunidad o sea refutación del folleto titulado "Lejitimidad de las compras de tierras realengas,"* 44, 48.

31 Jackson, *Regional Markets and Agrarian Transformation in Bolivia*; and Rodríguez, "Entre reformas y contrareformas."

32 Santivañez, *Revindicación de los terrenos de comunidad* (reprint), 103–4, 132–33; Santivañez, *Rebindicación de los terrenos de comunidad o sea refutación del folleto titulado "Lejitimidad de las compras de tierras realengas,"* 32–41, 48.

33 Santivañez, *Rebindicación de los terrenos de comunidad o sea refutación del folleto titulado "Lejitimidad de las compras de tierras realengas,"* 10–11.

34 Ibid., 18–19. Santivañez was refuting the idea that Indians had no property

rights under the Inca (or the Spanish), only use rights. This distinction was key, as the *compradores* (buyers) used the concept of "use rights" to argue that communal lands belonged to the state and could be auctioned by it.

35 Larson, *Cochabamba*, 21–22; Jacobsen, "Liberalism and Indian Communities in Peru," 125–26.

36 Langer, "El liberalismo y la abolición de la comunidad indígena en el siglo XIX."

37 Sanjinés, *Venta de tierras de comunidad*, 64.

38 Ibid., 66–71.

39 Langer, "El liberalismo y la abolición de la comunidad indígena en el siglo XIX," 77; José Avelino Aramayo, *Apuntes sobre el congreso de 1870*.

40 República de Bolivia, *Redactor de la Asamblea Constituyente del año 1871*, 443.

41 Sanjinés, *Venta de tierras de comunidad*, 73–74.

42 Santiváñez, *Revindicación de los terrenos de comunidad* (reprint), 118. See also Santiváñez, *Rebindicación de los terrenos de comunidad o sea refutación del folleto titulado "Lejitimidad de las compras de tierras realengas,"* 47; Irurozqui, "El bautismo de la violencia."

43 Zambrana, *Dos palabras sobre la venta de tierras realengas, a la nación, a la soberana asamblea y al supremo gobierno*, 89–90.

44 Santiváñez, *Revindicación de los terrenos de comunidad* (reprint), 130. For similar views from other smallholding advocates, see República de Bolivia, *Redactor de la Asamblea Constituyente del año 1871*, 450–53.

45 Sanjinés, *Venta de tierras de comunidad*, 73–74.

46 Dubois, "République Métissée," 27; Holt, "The Essence of the Contract"; Conklin, "Colonialism and Human Rights." On "liberalism's cultural tests," see also Holt, *The Problem of Freedom*, 308–9.

47 Flores Moncayo, *Legislación boliviana del indio*, 226.

48 Ibid., 225–34. The boliviano was the decimal-based currency introduced by the Melgarejo regime in 1869 (Klein, *Bolivia*, 139). The prefect is the highest political officer of a department; the subprefect is the head of a province. Until 2005, when the prefect became an elected position, prefects were appointed by the president.

49 Langer, "El liberalismo y la abolición de la comunidad indígena en el siglo XIX."

50 Bolívar's 1824 decree (extended to Bolivia in 1825) prohibited state authorities, judges, church officials, hacendados, and owners of mines and factories (*obrajes*) from demanding *pongueajes* (domestic service) or any other unpaid personal service of Indians. Laws passed in 1829 and 1858 repeated the abolition, but only when the duty was required by political, military, or church officials. Amendments to those laws, moreover, often allowed exemptions (Flores Moncayo, *Legislación boliviana del indio*, 26–29, 51–52, 174–77, 231).

51 República de Bolivia, *Redactor de la Asamblea Constituyente del año 1871*, 271–74.

52 República de Bolivia, *Redactor de la Convención Nacional del año 1880*, 167.

53 On Bolivia, see Barragán, "Los elegidos"; Irurozqui, *"A bala, piedra y palo."* On

Peru, Cristóbal Aljovín de Losada, "Representative Government in Peru." On Latin America, Hilda Sábato, "On Political Citizenship in Nineteenth-Century Latin America." My discussion also draws on Frederick Cooper et al.'s discussion of citizenship ("Introduction," 16).

54 The 1880 Constitution required literacy; real estate or an annual income of 200 pesos from activities besides domestic service; and official registration (Ciro Félix Trigo, *Las constituciones de Bolivia*, 396). It specified higher age and income qualifications for election to congress; the higher income requirements were dropped in 1938.

55 Literacy was mandatory only from 1836 onward, but the system of indirect elections probably offset participation by illiterates. After 1838, official registration began to be enforced, and this, too, served to exclude. Two separate registration books differentiated non-citizens, who possessed civil rights, from citizens, who not only enjoyed voting rights but also had the right to government employment. To register, citizens were required to verify their status via police certificate or with testimony from two witnesses (Barragán, "La representación territorial y la ciudadanía en el sistema directo e indirecto," 8–9, 16–17). During the presidency of Manuel Isidoro Belzu (1848–55), men without voting rights gained the right to public employment (Barragán, *Asambleas Constituyentes*, 27). Voting throughout the nineteenth century and the early twentieth was an urban and highly public phenomenon that was restricted to a tiny minority (Laurence Whitehead, "Miners as Voters," 318; Barragán, "Los elegidos").

56 Barragán, *Asambleas Constituyentes*, 5–63; Barragán, "Los elegidos." Focusing on fraudulent participation, Irurozqui points to high levels of involvement in post-1880 elections by people who did not meet the criteria for citizenship. Her findings apply, above all, to urban popular sectors (*"A bala, piedra y palo"*).

57 See Laura Gotkowitz, " '¡No hay hombres!' " Nataniel Aguirre laid out these views in the novel *Juan de la Rosa*.

58 República de Bolivia, *Redactor de la Asamblea Constituyente del año 1871*, 272–74. For Aguirre's views on tribute, see also Nataniel Aguirre and Fidel Araníbar, *Intereses nacionales*, 11.

59 República de Bolivia, *Redactor de la Convención Nacional del año 1880*, 440–41.

60 Ibid., 266. For similar remarks by other deputies, see 215, 437.

61 Ibid., 171. See also 456–57.

62 Ibid., 435. See also 268, 282.

63 Nicolás Sánchez-Albornoz, *Indios y tributos en el Alto Perú*, 187–218. Tribute was also restored in postindependent Peru, Colombia, and Ecuador, but the second abolition came earlier (Columbia: 1832; Peru: 1854; Ecuador: 1857).

64 Klein, *Haciendas and Ayllus*, 113.

65 República de Bolivia, *Redactor de la Convención Nacional del año 1880*, 451.

66 Ibid., 441–42, 451–59. See also 433.

67 Indians without land (*forasteros*)—the most numerous within the tribute-paying category—were exempt from the new *contribución* (Sánchez-Albornoz, *Indios y tributos en el Alto Perú*, 214–15).

68 But it would be deposited in departmental treasuries rather than in the national one.

69 Langer, *Economic Change and Rural Resistance in Southern Bolivia*, 21.

70 Ibid.; Sánchez-Albornoz, *Indios y tributos en el Alto Perú*, 215. As late as 1930, tribute comprised up to a fifth of Potosí's departmental income (Platt, "The Andean Experience of Bolivian Liberalism," 318).

71 On such contradictions of liberal ideology, see Holt, "The Essence of the Contract," 41.

72 Platt, "The Andean Experience of Bolivian Liberalism," 300.

73 Grieshaber, "Survival of Indian Communities in Nineteenth-Century Bolivia," 237–38. This team was called the *mesa revisitadora*. On its work in northern Potosí, see Platt, *Estado boliviano y ayllu andino*, chap. 3; in Chuquisaca, see Langer, *Economic Change and Rural Resistance in Southern Bolivia*, 77–81.

74 Klein, *Haciendas and Ayllus*, 117.

75 Platt, "The Andean Experience of Bolivian Liberalism," 300–301.

76 Langer, *Economic Change and Rural Resistance in Southern Bolivia*, 2. Hacienda growth was most pronounced in Cochabamba, which supplied Potosí with maize, wheat, and chicha (see Larson, *Cochabamba*).

77 Klein, *Bolivia*, 152.

78 Langer, "El liberalismo y la abolición de la comunidad indígena en el siglo XIX," 88.

79 Grieshaber, "Survival of Indian Communities in Nineteenth-Century Bolivia," 238.

80 Rivera, " 'Pedimos la revisión de límites,' " 604.

81 Grieshaber, "Survival of Indian Communities in Nineteenth-Century Bolivia," 136.

82 Langer, *Economic Change and Rural Resistance in Southern Bolivia*, 65; Klein, *Haciendas and Ayllus*, 128–31; Larson, *Explotación agraria y resistencia campesina en Cochabamba*, chap. 5. On the increase of landless and land-deficient forasteros within Indian communities of nineteenth-century La Paz, see Klein, *Haciendas and Ayllus*, chaps. 4 and 5.

83 Jacobsen has examined these questions for the Peruvian altiplano, where a combination of "volition and coercion" marked most land transactions (*Mirages of Transition*, 227). On the unfolding of similar processes in Mesoamerica, see Aldo Lauria-Santiago, *An Agrarian Republic*; Emilio Kourí, *A Pueblo Divided*. See also Jennie Purnell, *Popular Movements and State Formation in Revolutionary Mexico*.

84 On the internal conflicts that resulted from the sales in this region, see Hylton, "El federalismo insurgente," 107; Pilar Mendieta Parada, "Iglesia, mundo rural y política," 144–45.

85 Klein, *Haciendas and Ayllus*, 110–11, 117–18, 134, 155–56; Grieshaber, "Resistencia indígena a la venta de tierras comunales en el departamento de La Paz," 115–16.

86 Klein, *Haciendas and Ayllus*, 154–59; Erick Langer and Robert Jackson, "Liberalism and the Land Question in Bolivia," 184. Even when they did not own

estates, elite women of La Paz often served as hacienda administrators. Such administration was viewed as an extension of their domestic duties (Qayum, "Nationalism, Internal Colonialism and the Spatial Imagination," 288).

87 Grieshaber, "Survival of Indian Communities in Nineteenth-Century Bolivia," 240–41; Klein, *Haciendas and Ayllus*, 156–57.

88 Langer, *Economic Change and Rural Resistance in Southern Bolivia*, 65–67, 71–80. Limited financial incentives also mitigated the effects of the land sales in this region (Langer and Jackson, "Liberalism and the Land Question in Bolivia," 183).

89 Of the sales in this department, 54 percent were made to repay debts, and 34 percent to settle court costs, primarily for conflicts with non-Indians over land (Langer, *Economic Change and Rural Resistance in Southern Bolivia*, 69).

90 Ibid., 65–71, 77.

91 Platt, *Estado boliviano y ayllu andino*, 35.

92 Platt, "The Andean Experience of Bolivian Liberalism," 318.

93 Larson, *Colonialism and Agrarian Transformation in Bolivia*; Jackson, *Regional Markets and Agrarian Transformation in Bolivia*; Rodríguez, "Entre reformas y contrarreformas."

94 Rodríguez, "Entre reformas y contrarreformas," 312–14; Larson, *Colonialism and Agrarian Transformation in Bolivia*, 146, 176.

95 AHHCN, 64-13, 1923. See also Rodríguez, "Entre reformas y contrarreformas," 320; República de Bolivia, *Redactor de la Convención Nacional del año 1880*, 386, 394–96.

96 Langer, "El liberalismo y la abolición de la comunidad indígena en el siglo XIX," 84–85.

97 Platt, *Estado boliviano y ayllu andino*, 114.

98 Flores Moncayo, *Legislación boliviana del indio*, 279–85, 295–96. The 1881 resolution was promulgated after the Indians of Achacana (a community in La Paz) refused to divide and partition the land. It authorized the surveyors to grant proindiviso titles to *estancias* (hamlets within a community) or *parcialidades* (moities) when the "indígenas of a community without exception agree[d] that the land should be granted to them in proindiviso." The law nevertheless emphasized the "advantages" of division and partition and urged the surveyors to convince Indians of those advantages "so that private property would be definitively established." On the complex significance of the colonial "composición de tierras," see Stern, *Peru's Indian Peoples and the Challenge of Spanish Conquest*, 134–35, 162.

99 On the 1881 measure, see Grieshaber, "Resistencia indígena a la venta de tierras comunales en el departamento de La Paz," 117.

100 Ibid.; Flores Moncayo, *Legislación boliviana del indio*, 284.

101 Platt, "The Andean Experience of Bolivian Liberalism," 301.

102 Grieshaber, "Resistencia indígena a la venta de tierras comunales en el departamento de La Paz"; Platt, "The Andean Experience of Bolivian Liberalism."

103 Mendieta, "El movimiento de los apoderados 1880–1889," 10–11.

104 Flores Moncayo, *Legislación boliviana del indio*, 226.

105 Ibid., 227.
106 Platt, "The Andean Experience of Bolivian Liberalism," 319; Esteban Ticona Alejo, "Algunos antecedentes de organización y participación india en la Revolución Federal"; Marie-Danielle Demelas, "Sobre jefes legítimos y 'vagos.' "
107 Platt, "The Andean Experience of Bolivian Liberalism," 319. The war lasted from mid-December 1898 until mid-April 1899. Its most immediate catalyst was the December 1898 Ley de Radicatoria, which made Sucre Bolivia's definitive capital (Mendieta, "El poder de las montañas y la rebelión indígena," 83).
108 Klein, *Parties and Political Change in Bolivia*, 15–23; Langer, *Economic Change and Rural Resistance in Southern Bolivia*, 20. For their programs, see Alberto Cornejo, *Programas políticos de Bolivia*. On the role of pro- and anticlericalism, see Mendieta, "Iglesia, mundo rural y política," 129–39; Langer and Jackson, "Liberalism and the Land Question in Bolivia," 171–77. Conservative ideas, and the significance of conservative thought before and after 1880, have received little scholarly attention.
109 See Platt, "The Andean Experience of Bolivian Liberalism," 314–15.
110 Hylton, "El federalismo insurgente," 106.
111 This strategic alliance should not be confused with "popular liberalism," which figures prominently in the historiography of nineteenth-century Mexico (see especially Mallon, *Peasant and Nation*; Guy Thomson, "Popular Aspects of Liberalism in Mexico"; Peter Guardino, *Peasants, Politics, and the Formation of Mexico's National State*). In Bolivia, indigenous activists at times appropriated liberal laws to advance anticolonial projects that merged equality with ethnic autonomy, but they did not constitute a lasting political base of the Liberal Party nor did they craft what might be called a local or popular form of liberalism.
112 Willka is an Aymara last name that refers broadly to a person with great power. Leaders of diverse indigenous uprisings used it to signal the civil and military authority their communities had granted them (Mendieta, "Después de Zárate Willka," 13).
113 Hylton, "El federalismo insurgente," esp. 112–13. The growing literature on the rebellion includes diverse interpretations of the project for self-rule, as well as works that argue against an autonomous project. See Condarco Morales, *Zárate, El "Temible" Willka*; Platt, "The Andean Experience of Bolivian Liberalism"; Rivera, *Oprimidos pero no vencidos*, 25–35; Demelas, "Sobre jefes legítimos y 'vagos' "; Larson, *Trials of Nation Making*, 229–45; Hylton, "El federalismo insurgente"; Mendieta, "El poder de las montañas y la rebelión indígena"; Mendieta, "Iglesia, mundo rural y política"; Gabriela Kuenzli, "La evolución de la revolución liberal"; Irurozqui, *La armonía de las desigualdades*; Coordinadora de Historia, *Historias bajo la lupa*. On the varied forms of violence perpetrated by Liberals, Conservatives, and indigenous forces, see Larson, *Trials of Nation Making*, 234–38; Mendieta, "Iglesia, mundo rural y política." Hylton provides an overview of the literature in "El federalismo insurgente."

114 Mendieta, "El movimiento de los apoderados 1880–1889," 12.
115 Hylton, "El federalismo insurgente"; Rivera, " 'Pedimos la revisión de límites,' " 605; Mamani Condori, *Taraqu*, 57.
116 Mendieta, "Iglesia, mundo rural y política," 143–46.
117 Ibid., 148; Demelas, "Darwinismo a la criolla," 71; Condarco Morales, *Zárate, El "Temible" Willka*.
118 Sucre is still the judicial seat.
119 Bautista Saavedra, "La criminalidad aymara en el proceso Mohoza"; Mendieta, "Iglesia, mundo rural y política," 161 n. 27; Demelas, "Darwinismo a la criolla," 71–76.
120 Mendieta, "La revolución federal de 1899," 4.
121 On the nexus between social science, "race," and the modern state, see Ann Stoler, *Race and the Education of Desire*, 39–40. After 1900, European social scientists flocked to Bolivia, where they combined geographic, anthropological, and pedagogical research with studies of the size and intellectual capacity of Indians' brains. Bolivian politicians (who sometimes collaborated in the research) used the "evidence" they gathered to buttress racist theories and policies (Larson, "Redeemed Indians, Barbarianized Cholos"; Demelas, "Darwinismo a la criolla"). The institutional expression of this union of politics and science was the La Paz Geographic Society, which included among its members leading Liberal politicians and landlords (Qayum, "Nationalism, Internal Colonialism and the Spatial Imagination"). On the links between political and scientific power, and on "scientific politics," in Bolivia and Latin America, see, respectively, Demelas, "Darwinismo a la criolla"; Hale, "Political and Social Ideas," 240–54.
122 On heightened racism after 1899, see Irurozqui, "¿Qué hacer con el indio?"; Mendieta, "Iglesia, mundo rural y política," 153–63; Grieshaber, "Resistencia indígena a la venta de tierras comunales en el departamento de La Paz," 133–34.
123 Kuenzli, "La evolución de la revolución liberal." See also Françoise Martínez, "El 'indio' en las representaciones de la elite," 10.
124 See Rivera Cusicanqui, *Oprimidos pero no vencidos*, 31–34.
125 Bolivia's army was weak in the nineteenth century and had little repressive capacity in the countryside. After 1900, a stronger, more professional army began to be created. See James Dunkerley, *Orígenes del poder militar en Bolivia*, 47–77.
126 Jacobsen, "Liberalism and Indian Communities in Peru," 156. In contrast to most other Latin American countries, Bolivia experienced no agricultural export boom in the late nineteenth century. Nor did state authorities or private entrepreneurs develop coercive labor drafts akin to Guatemala's *mandamiento* or Peru's *enganche*, for the newly booming silver mines did not initially require large numbers of new workers. Grieshaber, "Survival of Indian Communities in Nineteenth-Century Bolivia," 228–29, 257–58; Larson, *Cochabamba*, 318 n. 51.

127 Frank Safford, "Race, Integration, and Progress"; Joanne Rappaport, *The Politics of Memory*, 90–93, 101–4, 142–44.
128 Jacobsen, "Liberalism and Indian Communities in Peru," 123–24. The highland elites who coveted indigenous resources lacked sufficient influence to shape national policies in Lima.
129 Ibid., 156–60, 123–24, 139.
130 Derek Williams, "Popular Liberalism and Indian Servitude," 703–7. See also Clark, "Racial Ideologies and the Quest for National Development," 373–74.
131 On Indian communities in Ecuador, see Larson, *Trials of Nation Making*, 30.
132 Jeffrey Gould, *To Die in This Way*, 18, 42–43, 81.
133 Lauria-Santiago, *An Agrarian Republic*, 164–69.
134 David McCreery, "State Power, Indigenous Communities, and Land in Nineteenth Century Guatemala"; McCreery, *Rural Guatemala*, 181–86.
135 McCreery, *Rural Guatemala*, 250, 261–64; Greg Grandin, *The Blood of Guatemala*, 113.
136 Richard Sinkin, *The Mexican Reform*, 60, 124; Purnell, *Popular Movements and State Formation in Revolutionary Mexico*, 27; Katz, "The Liberal Republic and the Porfiriato," 50; Guardino, *Peasants, Politics, and the Formation of Mexico's National State*, 190; Kourí, "Interpreting the Expropriation of Indian Pueblo Lands in Porfirian Mexico," 81, 92. The peculiar history of anticlericalism in Bolivia helps explain the exclusive focus on Indian communities in the late nineteenth century. Bolivia's postindependent state waged one of the strongest anticlerical campaigns in early-nineteenth-century Latin America. Although church wealth was not fully liquidated, it suffered a significant blow early on (Langer and Jackson, "Liberalism and the Land Question in Bolivia," 171–77; Klein, *Bolivia*, 109–10; Mendieta, "Iglesia, mundo rural y política," 154–61).
137 Kourí, *A Pueblo Divided*, see esp. 1–4, 129–31, 199–205, 256–57. Literature on the Mexican reform process has emphasized the role of the law and the state. Focusing on Papantla (Veracruz), Kourí instead stresses market forces and the emergence of an indigenous middle class. The implications for other regions of Mexico are not yet clear.
138 Why the Bolivian campaigns entailed such considerable violence, and why the violence was more severe in some places than in others, requires more research. But the aggression (and the specific forms it took) was surely linked with the weakness of the central state and with the peculiar dynamics of class and ethnic power in particular locales. Mendieta's work on local power networks in Mohoza during the 1899 war provides some clues for thinking about violence, power, and the revisitas. See Mendieta, "Iglesia, mundo rural, y política."

✳ Two   The Rise of the Caciques Apoderados

1 Araoz, *Nuevo digesto de legislación boliviana*, 3:64–65, 234–56. A 1907 law made military service obligatory for all Bolivian men, whether or not they were citizens. On the history of the army, and the implementation of the 1907

law, see Dunkerley, *Orígenes del Poder Militar en Bolivia*. Unfortunately, there are no in-depth studies of the prestación vial tax, which was established by a 1904 law; available evidence suggests that it had differential effects. The original law required a cash payment from all contributors, but a 1913 amendment stipulated that the "indigenous race" fulfill the duty via work alone. A 1915 law specifically for Cochabamba instead stated that it be satisfied in cash only (Araoz, *Nuevo digesto de legislación boliviana*, 3:64–65); the obligation nevertheless entailed much abuse of Indians in this uregion, as landlords and rural power brokers often oversaw it (Alberto Rivera, *Los terratenientes de Cochabamba*, 25–26). Comunarios were also burdened with *postillonaje*—a colonial-era duty involving turns of postal service—which persisted despite a 1904 abolition (Esteban Ticona Alejo and Xavier Albó, *La lucha por el poder comunal*, 112–13).

2 Klein, *Parties and Political Change in Bolivia*, 45–113; Irurozqui, "Partidos políticos y golpe de estado en Bolivia."

3 On the idea of colonial situations as sites of legal experimentation, see Comaroff, "Colonialism, Culture, and the Law," 310–11.

4 De la Cadena, *Indigenous Mestizos*, 63–68, 84–85, 127–28; Knight, "Racism, Revolution, and *Indigenismo*"; Mallon, "Indian Communities, Political Cultures, and the State in Latin America"; Zoila Mendoza, *Shaping Society through Dance*, 49–55; Deborah Poole, *Vision, Race, and Modernity*, 182–87; Peter Wade, *Race and Ethnicity in Latin America*, 32–35; Poole, "Ciencia, peligrosidad y represión en la criminología indigenista peruana." Although indigenista politicians, intellectuals, and lawyers throughout Latin America generally considered themselves pro-Indian advocates, indigenismo was marked by diverse political tendencies, ranging from the left to the right. Some indigenistas established close connections with indigenous movements and overtly backed their demands for land and political autonomy; others took a tutelary approach designed to bring those movements under state control. While recent works have explored the intellectual and cultural dimensions of Bolivian indigenismo, its impact on state policy and the law in the early twentieth century has not been fully recognized.

5 Ann Zulawski, "Hygiene and 'the Indian Problem,'" 111.

6 Barragán, *Indios, mujeres y ciudadanos*, 48–54. For example, the 1886 law concerning the duties of the Policía de Seguridad made the police responsible for the protection of indígenas (Araoz, *Nuevo digesto de legislación boliviana*, 1:169).

7 Ideas about Indian protection were aired during the period of Liberal Party rule, but full-blown legislative initiatives were rare before 1920. An early proposal for special laws and courts is discussed in Irurozqui, "¿Qué hacer con el indio?," 563–64. Republican Party rule extended from 1920 to 1934 (including its offshoots: the Salamanquista Partido Republicano Genuino and Hernando Siles's Partido Nacionalista).

8 On such dynamics, see Comaroff, "Colonialism, Culture, and the Law."

9 Rodríguez, "Expansión del latifundio o supervivencia de las comunidades indígenas?"; Rivera, "La expansión del latifundio en el altiplano boliviano"; Jackson, *Regional Markets and Agrarian Transformation in Bolivia*; Klein, *Haciendas
and Ayllus*; Langer, *Economic Change and Rural Resistance in Southern Bolivia*;
Mamani, *Taraqu*; Grieshaber, "Survival of Indian Communities in Nineteenth-
Century Bolivia."

10 Cacique is the Spanish term for kuraka or mallku, ethnic lord; apoderado is a
legal representative with power of attorney. The specific meanings of "cacique
apoderado" are outlined in the next section of this chapter. Although my
research centered on the network's trajectory in Cochabamba, the analysis in
this chapter and the next also draws on the pioneering work of Bolivian scholars whose research on the caciques apoderados has focused primarily on the La
Paz altiplano. The following studies have been especially important for my
thinking on this topic: Mamani, *Taraqu*; Rivera, " 'Pedimos la revisión de
límites' "; Rivera, *Oprimidos pero no vencidos*; Choque, "De la defensa del ayllu
a la creación de la República del Qullasuyu"; Choque, et al, *Educación Indígena*;
Ticona and Albó, *La lucha por el poder comunal*; Leandro Condori Chura and
Esteban Ticona Alejo, *El escribano de los caciques apoderados*.

11 Rivera, " 'Pedimos la revisión de límites,' " 608.

12 Albó, "Andean People in the Twentieth Century," 782. The caciques' connections with lowland leaders have not been fully explored. Albó nevertheless
notes that several Chiriguano authorities from the Chaco made contact with
Nina Qhispi's network before the war (ibid., 795).

13 Mamani, *Taraqu*, 63–68; Rivera, *Oprimidos pero no vencidos*, 42–52.

14 Grieshaber, "Resistencia indígena a la venta de tierras comunales en el departamento de La Paz," 135.

15 Thomson, *We Alone Will Rule*, 49–50, 267, 273, 277; Forrest Hylton and Sinclair
Thomson, "Ya es otro tiempo el presente," 10.

16 Rivera, " 'Pedimos la revisión de límites,' " 606–7.

17 Grieshaber, "Resistencia indígena a la venta de tierras comunales en el departamento de La Paz," 135; Gonzalo Flores, "Una indagación sobre movimientos
campesinos en Bolivia," 39–49.

18 Rivera, " 'Pedimos la revisión de límites,' " 611.

19 His network may have even established connections with Peru's Rumi Maqui
movement. See Rivera, *Oprimidos pero no vencidos*, 45–46; Jacobsen, *Mirages of
Transition*, 337–43.

20 Flores, "Una indagación sobre movimientos campesinos en Bolivia," 44–45.

21 Rivera, " 'Pedimos la revisión de límites.' "

22 On Jesús de Machaqa, see Choque, *La masacre de Jesús de Machaca*; Choque
and Ticona, *Sublevación y masacre de 1921*. On Chayanta, see Hylton, "Tierra
común"; Langer, "Andean Rituals of Revolt"; Langer, "Land Struggles, Interethnic Alliances and New Kurakas"; René Arze Aguirre, *Guerra y conflictos
sociales*; Harris and Albó, *Monteras y guardatojos*. The political aims of these
and other rebellions, and their connections with the cacique apoderado net-

works, were unearthed by Aymara researchers affiliated with the Taller de Historia Oral Andina (THOA). THOA's research showed how the uprisings and political networks together expressed a multifaceted "communal project." See Rivera, "Taller de historia oral andina," 83–84; Marcia Stephenson, "Forging an Indigenous Counterpublic Sphere," 105.

23 For an example of such claims, see AHHCN, 64-20, 1923, fols. 1v–1r.

24 Mamani, *Taraqu*, 130.

25 Ibid., 143–44; Zulema Lehm and Silvia Rivera, *Los artesanos libertarios y la ética del trabajo*, 40–43; Ticona and Albó, *La lucha por el poder comunal*, 145.

26 Mamani, *Taraqu*, 128–34; Ticona, "Conceptualización de la educación y al-fabetización en Eduardo Leandro Nina Qhispi."

27 Mamani, *Taraqu*, 132. See also Archivo de La Paz (hereafter ALP), Expedientes de la Prefectura (hereafter PE), Caja 346; Vitaliano Soria Choque, "Los caciques-apoderados y la lucha por la escuela," 63–68, 72, 75.

28 Soria, "Los caciques-apoderados y la lucha por la escuela," 63–68.

29 On Nina Qhispi's self-education, see Mamani, *Taraqu*, 127–30. On vernacular forms of literacy in the Andes, see Mercedes Niño-Murcia, "Papelito manda."

30 Mamani, *Taraqu*, 132–34.

31 María Lagos, "Livelihood, Citizenship, and the Gender of Politics," 219.

32 ALP, PE, Caja 346 [1933], "De los títulos de composición," 5. On Nina Qhispi's intercultural vision, and its enduring significance, see Mamani, *Taraqu*, 150–53; Ticona, "Conceptualización de la educación y alfabetización en Eduardo Lean-dro Nina Qhispi."

33 Condori and Ticona, *El escribano de los caciques apoderados*, 118–21. For Marka T'ula's emphasis on colonial law, see also Rivera, "'Pedimos la revisión de límites,'" 624.

34 Ticona and Albó, *La lucha por el poder comunal*, 107–8. Although Nina Qhispi never identified as a cacique and associated most closely with preceptors, a number of caciques apoderados seconded his efforts. Likewise, some of the preceptors probably served the caciques as scribes. See Mamani, *Taraqu*, 127–32.

35 THOA, "Indigenous Women and Community Resistance," 153, 176, and 183 n. 20.

36 Some had fought with Zárate Willka, but there were also many newcomers.

37 For examples, see Mamani, *Taraqu*, 139; Grieshaber, "Resistencia indígena a la venta de tierras comunales en el departamento de La Paz," 136–37; Rivera, "'Pedimos la revisión de límites,'" 645; Langer, "Land Struggles, Interethnic Alliances and New Kurakas."

38 Caciques apoderados of La Paz also insisted on being called "caciques prin-cipales" and "caciques-gobernadores" (Rivera, "'Pedimos la revisión de lí-mites,'" 608).

39 Thomson, *We Alone Will Rule*, 30, 43, 48, 57; Serulnikov, *Subverting Colonial Authority*, 26.

40 According to Andean rules of succession, women could exercise power. Under

particular conditions, the colonial state also recognized female authorities. But principles of hereditary succession became more rigidly gendered under colonial rule, since the Spanish considered women naturally "incompetent," insisted on primogeniture, and viewed female power in restricted terms (Thomson, *We Alone Will Rule*, 34–35; Roger Rasnake, *Domination and Cultural Resistance*, 116). In the sixteenth century, Viceroy Toledo sought to make the inherited position of the kuraka a state-appointed one; although the effort failed, Toledo did formalize the state's role in controlling the succession of kurakas (Larson, *Cochabamba*, 71–72).

41 For the decree, see Flores Moncayo, *Legislación boliviana del indio*, 26–27.
42 Thomson, *We Alone Will Rule*, 64–139; see esp. 70, 136–37. Cacicazgo refers to the system of Indian community government headed by a cacique.
43 Ibid., 11–12.
44 Serulnikov, *Subverting Colonial Authority*, 21–26, 34, 62.
45 Larson, *Cochabamba*, 152–70, 282; Brooke Larson and Rosario León, "Markets, Power, and the Politics of Exchange in Tapacarí."
46 On the fate of the caciques and colonial policy toward them after the 1780s rebellions, see Thomson, *We Alone Will Rule*, 232–68; Charles Walker, *Smoldering Ashes*, 61–64, 74–75, 209–12; Arze, "El cacicazgo en las postrimerías coloniales"; María Luisa Soux, "Autoridades comunales, coloniales y republicanas."
47 Non-Indian elites who were not corregidores also took up this duty (Platt, "The Andean Experience of Bolivian Liberalism," 284–87). On corregidores in republican times, see also Thomas Abercrombie, *Pathways of Memory and Power*, 86–90.
48 Flores Moncayo, *Legislación boliviana del indio*, 75-76; Soux, "Autoridades comunales, coloniales y republicanas," 101–2.
49 Ticona and Albó, *La lucha por el poder comunal*, 96; Larson, "Andean Highland Peasants," 660–62. On the hilacatas and alcaldes in colonial times, and the transformation of their responsibilities in the eighteenth century, see Thomson, *We Alone Will Rule*, 45–53, 262–77.
50 On the duties of the hilacatas and alcaldes in the nineteenth and twentieth centuries, see Medinaceli, "Redefinición de las comunidades," 7; Abercrombie, *Pathways of Memory and Power*, 87. The hilacata was the highest ranking official within an ayllu; the alcalde followed in standing.
51 Ticona and Albó, *La lucha por el poder comunal*, 96; Langer, *Economic Change and Rural Resistance in Southern Bolivia*, 64–65; Guillermo Urquidi, *Títulos y documentos relativos a la propiedad municipal de Vacas*; Archivo del Juzgado de Instrucción de Punata, G. M. vs. R. G., 1892.
52 Larson, *Cochabamba*, 355.
53 Archivo Histórico de la Prefectura de Cochabamba (hereafter AHPC), Expedientes (hereafter Exp.), Los indígenas del Departamento de Cochabamba, y de los demás Departamentos, to the Señor Presidente de la República, 1924, fols. 7r–7v (hereafter Los indígenas).
54 Mamani, *Taraqu*, 56, 158. See also Choque, "De la defensa del ayllu a la creación

de la República del Qullasuyu," 466–69; Ticona and Albó, *La lucha por el poder comunal*, 97.

55 This transient nature was linked with the rotating system of authority as well as with problems of representation and factionalism that could emerge under conditions of extreme exploitation and repression (Ticona and Albó, *La lucha por el poder comunal*, 131).

56 One key characteristic of the colonial cacique's role was the maintenance of outside contacts and the ability to coordinate interayllu action (Thomson, *We Alone Will Rule*, 275).

57 Ticona and Albó, *La lucha por el poder comunal*, 99; Rivera, " 'Pedimos la revisión de límites' " 623, 632.

58 AHHCN, 64-57, 1925, fol. 24.

59 THOA, *El indio Santos Marka T'ula*, 23, 27.

60 For such allusions, see AHHCN, 64-57, 1925.

61 Thomson, *We Alone Will Rule*, 35, 57.

62 On female cacicas, see Soux, "Autoridades comunales, coloniales y republicanas"; Irene Silverblatt, *Moon, Sun, and Witches*; Thomson, *We Alone Will Rule*, 34–35.

63 THOA, "Indigenous Women and Community Resistance," 168–69, 178.

64 AHHCN, 64-23, 1923, to the Señor Presidente de la Cámara y H. Diputados. For the law see Flores Moncayo, *Legislación boliviana del indio*, 25–27.

65 AHPC, Exp., Los indígenas, 1924, fols. 1v–2v.

66 This notion of legitimacy parallels that in eighteenth-century Potosí (Serulnikov, *Subverting Colonial Authority*, 26–27, 34, 62). Honor also entered into the legitimacy of the colonial caciques (Thomson, *We Alone Will Rule*, 39–40).

67 THOA, "Indigenous Women and Community Resistance," 156; THOA, *El indio Santos Marka T'ula*.

68 AHHCN, 64-57, 1925, fol. 2.

69 Langer, "Land Struggles, Interethnic Alliances and New Kurakas."

70 Rodríguez, "El fuego de la revuelta," 162–64.

71 Grupo Tupac Amaru, *La victoria o la muerte*, 24; Klein, *Parties and Political Change in Bolivia*, 125–26, 143–44. The founders had been exiled to Argentina by President Siles in 1927.

72 Tristán Marof, *La tragedia del altiplano*, 53–60.

73 Hylton, "Tierra común"; Langer, "Andean Rituals of Revolt"; Arze, *Guerra y conflictos sociales*.

74 Marof, *La tragedia del altiplano*, 47.

75 Langer, "Land Struggles, Interethnic Alliances and New Kurakas"; Hylton, "Tierra común."

76 Klein, *Parties and Political Change in Bolivia*, 70.

77 Ibid., 67–68.

78 Ibid., 69–70. On the repression, see Choque and Ticona, *Sublevación y masacre de 1921*, 67-80, 93-136.

79 Rivera, " 'Pedimos la revisión de límites,' " 611; Mamani, *Taraqu*, 72.

80 Rivera, " 'Pedimos la revisión de límites,' " 612–14.

81 Grieshaber, "Resistencia indígena a la venta de tierras comunales en el departamento de La Paz," 134. Although Saavedra was a hacendado (he owned an estate in Achacachi, Omasuyos), he owned no land in the provinces where Liberals were prominent owners (Rivera, " 'Pedimos la revisión de límites' ").

82 Irurozqui, "Partidos políticos y golpe de estado en Bolivia."

83 Ticona and Albó, La lucha por el poder comunal, 104–28; Mamani, Taraqu, 73–75, 91. On the rebel government that was established in Jesús de Machaqa, see Ticona and Albó, La lucha por el poder comunal, 111–39.

84 Klein, Parties and Political Change in Bolivia, 70–71, 84.

85 AHHCN, 64-2, 1923, Solicitud de Aspete y otros.

86 Flores Moncayo, Legislación boliviana del indio, 328–29. In 1921, the Republican congressional deputy Rigoberto Paredes sought to have the decree elevated to the status of a law (Proyectos e informes de la H. Cámara de Senadores, Legislatura Ordinaria de 1923, 21).

87 Langer, Economic Change and Rural Resistance in Southern Bolivia, 66. For the 1916 law, see Flores Moncayo, Legislación boliviana del indio, 321–25.

88 Mamani, Taraqu, 148.

89 Albó, "Andean People in the Twentieth Century," 781.

90 AHPC, Exp., Anaya y Rocha, de Tallija, Yarvicoya y Rodeo, 1935, 1.

91 Rivera, Oprimidos pero no vencidos, 54. Saavedra's government was also responsible for a 1923 massacre of mineworkers in Uncía (Potosí), where local unions had formed a combative labor confederation (Klein, Parties and Political Change, 81–82).

92 For in-depth works on the contradictory political practices of authoritarian leaders, see Gould, To Lead as Equals; and Richard Turits, Foundations of Despotism.

93 See, for example, Wade, Race and Ethnicity in Latin America; Appelbaum, Macpherson, and Rosemblatt, "Introduction"; Larson, Trials of Nation Making; Nancy Stepan, "The Hour of Eugenics"; Richard Graham, The Idea of Race in Latin America.

94 De la Cadena, Indigenous Mestizos; Wade, "Afterword."

95 Larson, "Redeemed Indians, Barbarianized Cholos."

96 On Saavedra's political base, see Irurozqui, "Partidos políticos y golpe de estado en Bolivia." For his views about "race," see La democracia en nuestra historia, 1–38.

97 United States National Archives (hereafter USNA), Record Group (hereafter RG) 59, 824.4016, 3 May 1924.

98 Condori and Ticona, El escribano de los caciques apoderados, 62–63.

99 Alcides Arguedas, Pueblo enfermo, 69–70.

100 Humberto Mamani Capchiri, "La educación india en la visión de la sociedad criolla," 82–84.

101 Saavedra, "La criminalidad aymara en el proceso Mohoza," 203.

102 Fausto Reinaga, Tierra y libertad, 22.

103 On internal colonialism as a "geographic-territorial configuration," see Qayum, "Nationalism, Internal Colonialism and the Spatial Imagination."

104 Condori and Ticona, *El escribano de los caciques apoderados*, 62.

105 On the idea of "racial proper places," see de la Cadena, *Indigenous Mestizos*, 66.

106 Stepan, *"The Hour of Eugenics."*

107 These ideas draw on Gerald Sider, "When Parrots Learn to Talk, and Why they Can't," 3; Comaroff, "Colonialism, Culture, and the Law," 307.

108 AHPC, 1924, Exp., Los indígenas, fol. 6v.

109 Choque, "La escuela indigenal," 20–21; Mamani Capchiri, "La educación india en la visión de la sociedad criolla," 79–80.

110 República de Bolivia, Ministerio de Justicia e Instrucción Pública, *Memoria*, 1909, 282.

111 Mamani Capchiri, "La educación india en la visión de la sociedad criolla," 80; Choque, "De la defensa del ayllu a la creación de la República del Qullasuyu," 478; Choque, "La escuela indigenal," 20.

112 The Belgian educator and entrepreneur Georges Rouma, who served as the first director of Bolivia's normal institute and stressed the importance of language unification, heavily influenced Bolivia's initial policies. On Rouma's views, see Gotkowitz, "Education and Race in Early-Twentieth-Century Bolivia," 33–39; Rouma, *Las bases científicas*.

113 República de Bolivia, Ministerio de Instrucción Pública y Agricultura, *Memoria*, 1918, 37–38. See also Ministerio de Instrucción Pública y Agricultura, *Memoria*, 1917, 17.

114 República de Bolivia, Ministerio de Instrucción Pública y Agricultura, *Memoria*, 1919, 254. See also República de Bolivia, *Proyectos de ley presentados a la H. Cámara de Diputados, 1919*, 178–79; Larson, "Forging the Unlettered Indian: The Pedagogy of Race in the Bolivian Andes."

115 República de Bolivia, Ministerio de Instrucción Pública y Agricultura, *Memoria*, 1919, 256. In 1921, for example, Umala's Escuela Normal de Preceptores became the "Instituto Agrícola" (AHHCN, 140-155).

116 Gotkowitz, "Education and Race in Early-Twentieth-Century Bolivia," 17–19, 21. Cristóbal Suárez Arnez, *Desarrollo de la educación boliviana*, 206, 228–30.

117 República de Bolivia, *Proyectos de ley presentados a la H. Cámara de Diputados, 1919*, 71.

118 República de Bolivia, *Informes de Comisiones de la H. Cámara de Diputados, 1919*, 311–12. On the work-oriented pedagogy of the era and its racialized logic, see Larson, "Forging the Unlettered Indian."

119 Cited in Klein, *Parties and Political Change in Bolivia*, 70.

120 República de Bolivia, Ministerio de Instrucción Pública y Agricultura, *Memoria*, 1927, 48–49.

121 República de Bolivia, *Redactor de la H. Cámara de Diputados, Legislatura ordinaria de 1923*, vol. 4-A, 861.

122 Arguedas, *Pueblo enfermo*, 69.

123 AHHCN, 140-175, Convención Nacional, Proyecto No. 227, 4 March 1921.

124 On this indigenista strand, see Thomson, "La cuestión india en Bolivia a principios de siglo"; Qayum, "Creole Imaginings," chap. 6.

125 AHHCN, 140-175, Convención Nacional, Proyecto No. 227, 4 March 1921. The 1921 patronato plan was just one of many such initiatives for "protection." In 1925, the Salamanca-allied Republican David Alvéstegui proposed a nineteen-point scheme centered on the administration of justice (AHPC, Exp., Los indígenas, 1924, 21–23v). And in 1931, Abdón Saavedra (Bautista Saavedra's brother) proposed another "Patronato Nacional de Indígenas" to study and devise special laws (*leyes de excepción*) and schools for the "indigenous race" (cited in ALP, PE, Caja 346, "De los títulos," 1). He did so once again in 1940 (see República de Bolivia, *Proyectos e informes del H. Senado Nacional, Legislatura Extraordinaria de 1940–1941*). In the midst of the Chaco War, as indigenous uprisings were raging in the countryside, Saavedra's brother even advocated a "Ministry of Racial Improvement" to "protect the autochthonous races and incorporate them into the civilization" (República de Bolivia, *Proyectos e informes del H. Senado Nacional, Legislatura Ordinaria de 1934*, 197–99).

126 Circular Número doce del libro copiador de circulares de la Prefectura del Departamento, La Paz, 28 December 1923, reproduced in AHPC, Exp., Los indígenas, 1924, fols. 10–12. Corregidores confiscated garments as a form of punishment. On the "idea" of the state as a mask that conceals "unacceptable domination," see Abrams, "Notes on the Difficulty," esp. 58–64 and 75–82.

127 República de Bolivia, *Redactor de la Honorable Cámara de Diputados, Legislatura ordinaria de 1923*, vol. 4-A, 1042–43.

128 See República de Bolivia, *Redactor de la Honorable Cámara de Diputados, Legislatura ordinaria de 1923*; and *Legislatura ordinaria de 1926*, 2:267–68, 328–30.

129 República de Bolivia, *Redactor de la H. Cámara de Diputados, Legislatura extraordinaria de 1927*, 5:50–81, 134–41, 161–72, 209–11. See also Hylton, "Tierra común."

130 República de Bolivia, *Redactor de la H. Cámara de Diputados, Legislatura ordinaria de 1923*, vol. 4-A, 855–62, 911–16. For the constitutional provision, see Trigo, *Las constituciones de Bolivia*, 391 (article 9).

131 This idea draws on Comaroff's discussion of the paradoxes of modern colonialism. See his "Colonialism, Culture, and the Law."

132 In this respect, the sponsors of the Bolivian proposals undoubtedly drew some inspiration from Peru's Patronato Indígena. See Albó, "Andean People in the Twentieth Century," 779.

133 República de Bolivia, *Informes de comisiones de la H. Cámara de Diputados* (1919), No. 288, 538–43.

134 República de Bolivia, *Redactor de la H. Cámara de Diputados, Legislatura ordinaria de 1923*, vol. 4-A, 859. For another such proposal that was also voted down, see República de Bolivia, *Redactor de la H. Cámara de Diputados, Legislatura ordinaria de 1927*, 1:189–203. The Senate sympathized much less with these ideas (see chapter 3).

✳ *Three* The Crisis of the Liberal Project

1 AHPC, Exp., "Cuatro cuerpos de expedientes cosidos y archibados de los Vaque-ños . . . seguidos por los casiques Mariano Rosa, Mariano Vásquez, Feliciano Zalazar y otros muchos," fols. 1r–3, 19v (hereafter, "Cuatro cuerpos").

2 "Cuarto cuerpos," fol. 188v. The status of these districts shifted over time. In 1900, "Totora" designated a province, a canton of that province, and the capital of both the province and the canton. In 1926, it became the capital of the newly created province of Carrasco. Pocona (see below) was a canton of Totora province that later became a section of Carrasco province. Arani, in 1900, was a canton of Punata province; Arani province was established in 1914. On the status of Vacas, see note 1 of the introduction.

3 "Cuarto cuerpos," 190–96.

4 On this geography of power, see Qayum, "Nationalism, Internal Colonialism and the Spatial Imagination."

5 Francisco de Viedma, *Descripción geográfica y estadística de la provincia de Santa Cruz de la Sierra*, 92.

6 Jackson, *Regional Markets and Agrarian Transformation in Bolivia*, 67–68.

7 Wálter Sánchez, "Hacienda, campesinado y estructura agraria en el Valle Alto" (lic. thesis), 177–79; Urquidi, *Títulos y documentos relativos a la propiedad municipal de Vacas*, 3.

8 Sánchez, "Hacienda, campesinado y estructura agraria en el Valle Alto" (lic. thesis), 178. A hectare (10,000 square meters) is 2.47 acres. The term *estancia* could refer to a cluster of peasant households within an ayllu or within a highland hacienda; here it signifies each of the thirteen separate settlements that together comprised what some considered the municipal hacienda and others called the community of Vacas.

9 Robert Jackson, "Community and Hacienda in the Bolivian Highlands," 199, 205.

10 Lagos, *Autonomy and Power*, 37–38.

11 Jackson, "Community and Hacienda in the Bolivian Highlands," 194–200; Federico Blanco, *Diccionario geográfico de la República de Bolivia*, 2:38.

12 Jackson, *Regional Markets and Agrarian Transformation in Bolivia*, 81–82.

13 See Urquidi, "*Títulos y documentos relativos a la propiedad municipal de Vacas*," anexo no. 6, lxxvi; *Gaceta Municipal*, 1915, 364, 390.

14 Flores Moncayo, *Legislación boliviana del indio*, 317–18. See also *Gaceta Municipal*, 1915, 178–79.

15 Often means "Indian mob." "Cuatro cuerpos," 188–89, 197–99; *Gaceta Municipal*, 1917, 47; Flores, "Levantamientos campesinos durante el período Liberal," 129.

16 The following discussion draws inspiration from Serulnikov's analysis of such images in late-eighteenth-century juridical narratives ("Disputed Images of Colonialism").

17 "Cuatro cuerpos," 190–96.

18 Ibid.

19 Ibid., fol. 187r.

20 Ibid., fol. 3r. See also AHHCN, 131-21.

21 "Cuarto cuerpos," fol. 1v.

22 Flores Moncayo, *Legislación boliviana del indio*, 221–22.

23 Urquidi, *Títulos y documentos relativos a la propiedad municipal de Vacas*, 6–9.

24 Ibid., 9.

25 *La Reacción Social*, 15 March 1917, 4 (clipping attached to "Cuatro cuerpos").

26 AHHCN, 131-21; "Cuatro cuerpos," 37r–38v. For Rosa's more critical view of the 1874 law, see "Cuatro cuerpos," fols. 13r–18r.

27 Urquidi, *Títulos y documentos relativos a la propiedad municipal de Vacas*, 2.

28 *La Reacción Social*, 15 March 1917, 4.

29 Ibid.

30 "Cuatro cuerpos," 188–89.

31 Urquidi, *Títulos y documentos relativos a la propiedad municipal de Vacas*. Urquidi's 1917 report to the municipal council was published in pamphlet form in 1928.

32 AHHCN, 93-2, 1927–31.

33 AHHCN, 64-57, 1925; 93-2, 1927–31. See also AHHCN, Caja 171B, 1929.

34 AHHCN, 93-2, 1926.

35 AHHCN, 64-14, 1923; 64-27, 1923; 64-13, 1923; 64-23, 1923.

36 AHHCN, 64-27, 1923.

37 On the problem of internal discipline, see Grieshaber, "Resistencia indígena a la venta de tierras comunales en el departamento de La Paz," 137.

38 AHHCN, 64-23, 1923; AHHCN, 64-14, 1923.

39 Their situation contrasts sharply with the economic interests and objectives of the K'iche' elite of Quetzaltenango, Guatemala. See Grandin, *The Blood of Guatemala*, 110–29.

40 Their forms of association and identification were shaped and reshaped by social, cultural, and legal changes such as land usurpation, land redistribution, the 1874 Disentailment Law, and the 1953 agrarian reform. As mentioned above, hacienda colonos in many cases retained their own hilos, or small plots, even as they owed labor to a landlord (see also AHPC, Exp., Cavero, vecino de Punata, 1947, fol. 2, which reports that some of the Vacas colonos were "landowners"). But the documentation in addition suggests that the hilatarios often considered themselves to be comunarios. Still, when former colonos of the Vacas estancias appealed to the 1953 agrarian reform law, they opted for private titles (Archivo del Servicio Nacional de la Reforma Agraria, Packets 1, 5, 6, 8–10, 12–15).

41 In 1912, 24 properties of less than 10 hectares (about 25 acres) each occupied 25 percent of the land; and 2 properties of between 10 and 50 hectares (between about 25 and 124 acres) each occupied 6 percent of the land. The state-owned estancia, which totaled 267 hectares (about 660 acres), occupied 68 percent (Jackson, "Community and Hacienda in the Bolivian Highlands," 200).

42 "Cuatro cuerpos," fols. 185r–187r. See also AHHCN, 93-2, 1926, fol. 2v.

43 AHHCN, 93-2, fol. 6r.

44 Ibid., fol. 3r.

45 Ibid., fols. 1v–2r.

46 Only one of Rosa's petitions was submitted with leaders from La Paz.

47 A petition from Cruz and others said they were from "Urinsaya y Aransaya de puna y valle de la provincia Totora, Ayquili, Misque, Clisa, Punata, Tarata, todas provincias y Cantones del Departamento de Cochabamba." AHHCN, 93-2, 1927.

48 On ethnic groups and territory in preconquest Cochabamba, see Raimund Schramm, "Mosaicos etnohistóricos del valle de Cliza"; Mercedes del Río, "Simbolismo y poder en Tapacarí"; Larson, Cochabamba, 13–43.

49 See Mamani, Taraqu, 164 n. 3.

50 AHPC, Exp., Los indígenas del Departamento de Cochabamba, y de los demás Departamentos, to the Señor Presidente de la República, 1924, fol. 2 (hereafter AHPC, Exp., Los indígenas). Originarios, in contrast to forasteros, held full landholding rights and tribute obligations. On the complexities of forastero status, see Platt, "Andean Experience," 301–2. On landholding patterns in Tapacarí, see Sánchez Albornoz, Indios y tributos en el Alto Perú; Larson and León, "Markets, Power, and the Politics of Exchange in Tapacarí."

51 AHPC, Exp., Los indígenas, 1924, fols. 2–2v.

52 Larson, Cochabamba, 66–67, 77–78.

53 Jackson, Regional Markets and Agrarian Transformation in Bolivia, 81.

54 AHHCN, 64-20, 1923. See also 64-14, 1923; 64-27, 1923; AHPC, Exp., Los indígenas, 1924.

55 AHHCN, 64-13, 1923.

56 AHHCN, 64-19, 1923. For an offer to fund the revisita, see AHHCN, 64-27, 1923.

57 See, for example, AHHCN, 93-2, 1927–31; AHHCN, 64-27, 1923; AHPC, Exp., Los indígenas, 1924, fol. 86v.

58 AHHCN, 64-27, 1923.

59 Ibid. This was a rotating post. In Indian communities, as on haciendas, the alcalde de campo may have been selected from among those community members who enjoyed the others' respect. The Alcalde de Campo's dismissal in this case might have thus violated comunarios' perceived right to participate in the official's election.

60 Jacobsen, Mirages of Transition, 341; Hylton and Thomson, "Ya es otro tiempo el presente," 10.

61 AHHCN, 93-2, 1926 [1919]. See also AHHCN, 64-27, 1923; República de Bolivia, Informes de Comisiones de la H. Cámara de Diputados, 1919, No. 288, Informe de la Comisión de Peticiones a varias solicitudes de indígenas, 1919.

62 AHPC, Exp., Los indígenas, 1924, fols. 3v–4. See also AHHCN, 64-2, 1923; 75-73, 1929.

63 AHPC, Exp., Comunarios del aillo de Totora, del Cantón de Ventilla, 1930, fol. 6v.

64 AHPC, Exp., Los indígenas, 1924. See also AHHCN, 75-62, 1928; 75-66, [1928?]; AHHCN, 75-54, 1929.

65 In addition to the petitions cited in this chapter, see also ACSJC, AG #1202, 2PP,

viuda de Coca vs. Grájeda y otros, 1947, fols. 69–69v; AHPC, Exp., Manuel Cruz Vallejos, Sacabamba, 1937; AHPC, Exp., Araujo, vecino del pueblo de Caraza (Arque), 1877.

66 AHPC, Exp., Comunarios del aillo de Totora, del Cantón de Ventilla, 1930.

67 This analysis draws on Timothy Mitchell's definition of the state not as an entity separate from society but as the idea or "effect" of that separation. However, the point is not to distinguish an illusion from a reality. Rather than a subjective belief, the "effects" of the state, Mitchell argues, are material things such as border patrols and legal systems; they are the product of administrative processes and surveillance ("The Limits of the State," esp. 81–82, 95).

68 AHPC, Exp., Ramos et al. to the Sr. Ministro de Gobierno y Justicia, 1925, fol. 25r. See also AHHCN, 64-57, 1925, fol. 1r.

69 AHPC, Exp., Cruz et al. to the Sr. Ministro de Estado en el Despacho de Instruc-ción, 1928, fol. 1v.

70 Ibid.

71 Ibid., fol. 1r. For other such cases, see Huacani et al., Warisata "Escuela Ayllu."

72 See República de Bolivia, Ministerio de Instrucción Pública y Agricultura, Memorias y anexos, 1925, 1929, 1930. Indians continued to request schools during the 1940s; in one week alone, the Ministry of Education received "more than 400 Indian delegations pleading for the establishment of schools" (USNA, RG 59, 824.00/4-2345).

73 AHPC, Exp., Cruz et al. to the Sr. Ministro de Estado en el Despacho de Instruc-ción, 1928, fol. 3.

74 Mamani, Taraqu, 145.

75 See, for example, República de Bolivia, Ministerio de Justicia e Instrucción Pública, Memoria, 1907, lxv.

76 Soria, "Los caciques-apoderados y la lucha por la escuela," 61; Marten Brienen, "The Clamor for Schools"; Larson, "Capturing Indian Bodies, Hearths and Minds," 192–93; Albó, "Andean People in the Twentieth Century."

77 Mamani, "La educación india en la visión de la sociedad criolla," 82. See also Ramón Conde Manani, "Lucas Miranda Mamani," 112–13.

78 AHPC, Exp., Los indígenas, 1924, fols. 8v–9.

79 Trigo, Las constituciones de Bolivia, 390; AHHCN, 93-2, 1918–19, 1927–31.

80 For an example of the caciques' use of these laws, see AHPC, Exp., Los indígenas, 1924, fol. 10. Article 1 of the first law deemed the police responsible for safe-guarding personal and property rights (garantías personales y reales) and obliged its officers to actively pursue all criminals. Article 51 of the second law delineated the powers of the prefect; while establishing this officer's depen-dence on the executive branch, the cited passage also specified the prefect's supremacy over other departmental functionaries. For the laws, see Araoz, Nuevo digesto de legislación boliviana, 1:167; República de Bolivia, Constitución Política del Estado, 155.

81 AHHCN, 64-56, 1925.

82 Ibid., 64-57, 1925, 25.

83 AHPC, Exp., Los indígenas, 1924, fols. 6v–7v. This much-reproduced passage

confirms that the caciques copied petitions among themselves, but not without adapting their pleas to local circumstances.

84 AHPC, Exp., Los indígenas, 1924.

85 Ibid., fols. 8–9.

86 AHHCN, 93-2, 1927, fols. 7–8.

87 Ibid., fol. 7v.

88 Barragán, *Indios, mujeres y ciudadanos,* 25. The Bolivian concepts paralleled those in Mexico. See Claudio Lomnitz, *Deep Mexico, Silent Mexico,* 64.

89 Barragán, *Indios, mujeres y ciudadanos,* 23, 27–28. By civil rights I mean such things as the right to be a guardian, to act as a witness, to initiate a legal demand, or to participate in a trial, as well as constitutional guarantees concerning freedom of association, freedom to petition, and protection against arrest without warrant. As Barragán has shown, Bolivia's post-independent courts became a site of struggle over some such rights as non-citizens were deprived of them in subtle and unsubtle ways.

90 Ibid., 23–43.

91 For some local uses of the term, see Archivo del Juzgado de Instrucción de Cliza (hereafter AJIC), N. C. vs. A. G., 1897; AJIC, Soria vs. Rosetti, despojo, 1887.

92 AHPC, Exp., Los indígenas, 1924, fols. 1–1v, 79.

93 On such use of universal rights for particularistic claims, see Dubois, "République Métissée," 29.

94 AHPC, Exp., Los indígenas, 1924. See also AHHCN, 64-19, 1923.

95 AHHCN, 64-2, 1923.

96 AHPC, Exp., Los indígenas, 1924, fol. 6v, p. 79. See also AHHCN, 93-2, to the Señor Ministro de Guerra, 1927.

97 AHPC, Exp., Los indígenas, 1924.

98 Ibid., fol. 17 and p. 79. See also AHHCN, 64-2, 1923; 64-57; 64-3, 1923.

99 AHPC, Exp., Los indígenas, 1924, fols. 12–12v, 14v.

100 Ticona and Albó, *La lucha por el poder comunal,* 108.

101 Romualdo Bustos and Alejandro Mirones, *Cuestión Social Jurídica,* 2, 10, 13. For another conflict that centered on the delivery of laws to Indians, see República de Bolivia, *Redactor de la H. Cámara de Diputados, Legislatura ordinaria de 1927,* 1:195–96.

102 Grieshaber, "Survival of Indian Communities in Nineteenth-Century Bolivia," 228; Blanco, *Diccionario geográfico de la República de Bolivia,* 9–11.

103 Flores, "Una indagación sobre movimientos campesinos en Bolivia," 49.

104 Jackson, "Community and Hacienda in the Bolivian Highlands," 205.

105 Bustos and Mirones, *Cuestión social jurídica,* 10–11. See also AHPC, Exp., Comunarios del aillo de Totora, del Cantón de Ventilla, 1930, fol. 6v.

106 Bustos and Mirones, *Cuestión Social Jurídica.*

107 Lomnitz, *Deep Mexico, Silent Mexico,* esp. 62.

108 República de Bolivia, *Informes de Comisiones de la H. Cámara de Diputados* (1919), 538–43.

109 AHPC, Exp., Los indígenas, 1924.

110 AHHCN, 64-57, 1925.

111 AHHCN, 93-2, 1927–31.

112 AHHCN, 64-57, 1925, p. IV and fol. 24; AHPC, Exp., Los indígenas, 1924.

113 AHHCN, 64-57, 1925, fol. 24.

114 AHPC, Exp., Los indígenas, 1924, fols. 4–4v. See also AHHCN, 64-57, 1925, fol. 24.

115 Araoz, *Nuevo digesto de legislación boliviana*, 1:168 n. 4.

116 Ticona and Albó, *La lucha por el poder comunal*, 150.

117 ALP, PE, Caja 346, "De los títulos." For another example of Nina Qhispi's method, see AHHCN, 93-18, 1932.

118 This idea draws on Mitchell, "The Limits of the State," 93.

119 Rivera, " 'Pedimos la revisión de límites.' "

120 AHPC, Exp., Comunarios del aillo de Totora, del Cantón de Ventilla, 1930; AHHCN, 171B, 1929.

121 República de Bolivia, *Proyectos e Informes de la H. Cámara de Senadores, 1919*, vols. 1 and 2, 130–31.

122 AHHCN, 75-73, 1929.

123 AHHCN, 93-2, 1931, 67–71. On the distinct positions taken by the Senate and the Chamber of Deputies, see also AHHCN, 75-62, 1928.

124 AHHCN, 64-57, 1925.

125 AHHCN, 64-56, 1925; AHPC, Exp., Los indígenas, 1924, fols. 17, 18v; Rossana Barragán and Florencia Durán, "El despojo en el marco de la ley," 47–48.

126 This idea draws on Comaroff, "Colonialism, Culture, and the Law."

127 República de Bolivia, *Redactor de la H. Cámara de Diputados, Legislatura extraordinaria de 1927*, 5:166–68. Soruco was the only deputy to denounce the Jesús de Machaqa massacre. For more on this legislator, see Roberto Choque and Esteban Ticona, *Sublevación y masacre de Jesús de Machaqa de 1921*, 42–52.

128 Mamani, *Taraqu*, 136–37. See also Arze, *Guerra y conflictos sociales*, 29–31, 94–95.

129 Klein, *Bolivia*, 186.

130 Cited in ALP, PE, Caja 346, "De los títulos," 7–9.

131 República de Bolivia, *Redactor de la H. Convención Nacional, 1938*, 5:285–86. See also 220, 267, 286.

132 República de Bolivia, *Redactor de la Convención Nacional de 1945, Sesiones ordinarias*, 4:411.

* *Four* The 1938 Constitutional Convention

1 The 1938 convention has received only limited scholarly attention, but Bolivia's 2006–7 Constituent Assembly has revived interest in it. Klein's 1966 " 'Social Constitutionalism' " highlighted the significance of the 1938 convention for Bolivia's modern polity and underscored the role of workers and the left. Barragán's recent *Asambleas Constituyentes* situates it in a longer history

of constitution making and emphasizes the recurring themes of inequality and territorial representation over more than a century. On the 1938 convention, see also Ferran Gallego, *Ejército, nacionalismo y reformismo en América Latina*, 31–100. I thank Hernán Pruden for information on the number of delegates.

2 Klein, *Bolivia*, 205–6. On the broader Latin American trend, see Hale, "Political and Social Ideas," 280–99.

3 For an overview, see Michael Conniff, "Introduction"; Paul Drake, "Conclusion"; Knight, "Populism and Neo-populism in Latin America, especially Mexico."

4 Several recent works illuminate populism's rural roots. See esp. Gould, *To Lead as Equals*; Turits, *Foundations of Despotism*.

5 Cuba's was the most far-reaching, partly because proximity to the United States at the height of World War II conditioned a vigorous "democratic" ethos. The strength of Cuba's Communist Party—a weak entity in Bolivia—in turn facilitated the approval of radical reforms. But the article outlawing discrimination emerged more deeply from the unfulfilled promises of Cuba's 1898 Revolution. Universal male suffrage, an influential labor movement that championed anti-racist ideals, and strong representation by Cubans of color made racial discrimination a fundamental concern of the 1939 convention. Feminist movements also influenced the Cuban Constitution, for women who had already received the rights to vote and be elected (in 1934) helped place questions concerning women, children, and the family at the convention's center. But racism, not gender discrimination, drove the broad-based equality article (see Robert Whitney, *State and Revolution in Cuba*, 173; Alejandro de la Fuente, *A Nation for All*, 211, 220–22; Alejandra Bronfman, *Measures of Equality*, 159–81; Russell Fitzgibbon, *The Constitutions of the Americas*, 230; Lynn Stoner, *From the House to the Streets*, 162–64, 185). Mexico's 1917 Constitution did not include an expansive declaration against discrimination, nor did it give women the vote, but the chapter on personal guarantees made equality a goal of education (Fitzgibbon, *The Constitutions of the Americas*, 498).

6 This is not to overstate the provisions of the other constitutions. Although Guatemala's 1945 convention outlawed "any discrimination by reason of relationship, sex, race, color, class, religious beliefs, or political ideas," and although it rejected a proposed statute creating a separate juridical status for Indians (Estatuto Indígena), it failed to address the country's legacies of segregation. In place of proposed tutelary laws, the Constitution gave the executive branch responsibility for addressing "indigenous problems" (Arturo Taracena, *Etnicidad, estado y nación en Guatemala, 1944–1985*, 35–41). And, although the new Constitution granted illiterate men and literate women suffrage rights, it denied the vote to illiterate women and distinguished illiterate from literate men—and thus essentially Indians from non-Indians—via voting practices (optional and public versus obligatory and secret). See Deborah Yashar, *Demanding Democracy*, 121–22.

7 Klein, *Bolivia*, 185; Klein, *Parties and Political Change in Bolivia*, 145–54, 182–83.

8 Klein, *Parties and Political Change in Bolivia*, 134-35, 145-48, 151–54, 187; David Zook, *The Conduct of the Chaco War*, 240–41; Dunkerley, *Orígenes del poder militar en Bolivia*, 169–70; Whitehead, "Bolivia since 1930," 519; Arze, *Guerra y conflictos sociales*, 74-5; Miguel Angel Centeno, *Blood and Debt*, 58–59, 92, 228; Bruce Farcau, *The Chaco War*, 18–19.

9 Klein, *Bolivia*, 194.

10 Dunkerley, *Orígenes del poder militar en Bolivia*, 167, 174; Arze, *Guerra y conflictos sociales*, 76; Klein, *Parties and Political Change in Bolivia*, 197 n.1; Mamani, *Taraqu*, 101; Farcau, *The Chaco War*, 19.

11 For an example, see Choque, "Las rebeliones indígenas de la post-guerra del Chaco," 37.

12 Dunkerley, *Orígenes del poder militar en Bolivia*, 167, 174; Klein, *Parties and Political Change in Bolivia*, 155, 187–88.

13 Klein, *Parties and Political Change in Bolivia*, 155.

14 THOA, *La mujer andina en la historia*, 40.

15 Ibid.; Arze, *Guerra y conflictos sociales*, 47–50.

16 Arze, *Guerra y conflictos sociales*, 39–40, 64–65.

17 Ibid., 48; THOA, "Indigenous Women and Community Resistance," 157. Unfortunately, there are no detailed studies of the Chaco War army's composition, but the available evidence supports this conclusion. Because of mining's economic significance, mine owners obtained a release that allowed them to keep most of their workers out of the army.

18 Arze, *Guerra y conflictos sociales*, 48.

19 THOA, *La mujer andina en la historia*, 41.

20 Dunkerley, *Orígenes del poder militar en Bolivia*, 168.

21 Arze, *Guerra y conflictos sociales*, 2, 71.

22 Ibid., 2, 45–46. See also República de Bolivia, *Proyectos e Informes del H. Senado Nacional, Legislatura Ordinaria de 1934*, 188–93.

23 Klein, *Bolivia*, 186. On the end of the official land sales in the 1920s, see Langer, *Economic Change and Rural Resistance in Southern Bolivia*, 66.

24 Arze, *Guerra y conflictos sociales*, 29–36; Langer, *Economic Change and Rural Resistance in Southern Bolivia*, 87; Lagos, *Autonomy and Power*, 43–44.

25 Cited in Arze, *Guerra y conflictos sociales*, 35–36.

26 Klein, *Parties and Political Change in Bolivia*, 132–42.

27 Arze, *Guerra y conflictos sociales*, 95.

28 For an overview of the wartime rebellions, see Arze, *Guerra y conflictos sociales*, 60, 85–115. Although the unrest was centered in the department of La Paz, Potosí and Sucre were also affected.

29 See THOA, "Indigenous Women and Community Resistance," 158–59; Mamani, *Taraqu*, 120–24.

30 Mamani, *Taraqu*, 113–16; Ticona and Albó, *La lucha por el poder comunal*, 148 n. 13; Arze, *Guerra y conflictos sociales*, 109–10, 112.

31 Arze, *Guerra y conflictos sociales*, 112–14.

32 Klein, *Bolivia*, 192–93.

33 Dunkerley, *Rebellion in the Veins*, 27.

34 Klein, *Parties and Political Change in Bolivia*, 189–90.

35 Ibid., 243 n. 1.

36 Ibid., 241–43.

37 Lesley Gill, *Precarious Dependencies*, 31; Stephenson, *Gender and Modernity in Andean Bolivia*, 142–46.

38 Zulawski, *Unequal Cures*.

39 Roberto Fernández Terán, "Prensa, radio e imaginario boliviano durante la Guerra del Chaco," 20; Florencia Durán Jordán and Ana María Seoane Flores, *El complejo mundo de la mujer durante la Guerra del Chaco*, 13; Gill, *Precarious Dependencies*, 33; Lehm and Rivera, *Los artesanos libertarios y la ética del trabajo*, 69.

40 Fernández, "Prensa, radio e imaginario boliviano durante la Guerra del Chaco," 30–32.

41 Ibid.

42 República de Bolivia, *Proyectos e Informes del H. Senado Nacional, Legislatura Ordinaria de 1934*, 77–82.

43 THOA, "Indigenous Women and Community Resistance," 164–65.

44 On the FOF, see Ineke Dibbits et al., *Polleras libertarias*; Lehm and Rivera, *Los artesanos libertarios y la ética del trabajo*, 35-40, 69-101. The FOL (Federación Obrera Local) was an anarchist labor organization established in La Paz in 1926.

45 Lehm and Rivera, *Los artesanos libertarios y la ética del trabajo*, 70.

46 Stephenson, *Gender and Modernity in Andean Bolivia*, 24–27; Fernández, "Prensa, radio e imaginario boliviano durante la Guerra del Chaco," 10; Durán and Seoane, *El complejo mundo de la mujer durante la Guerra del Chaco*, 69–70.

47 Etelvina Villanueva y Saavedra, *Acción socialista de la mujer en Bolivia*; Durán and Seoane, *El complejo mundo de la mujer durante la Guerra del Chaco*, 28, 129, 133. On women's organizations in the 1920s and the 1930s, see also Gloria Ardaya, *Política sin rostro*, 21-29; Medinaceli, *Alternando la rutina*.

48 Klein, " 'Social Constitutionalism' in Latin America," 262.

49 Dandler, "Politics of Leadership, Brokerage and Patronage in the Campesino Movement of Cochabamba," 54.

50 Klein, *Parties and Political Change in Bolivia*, 214. See also Gallego, *Los orígenes del reformismo militar en América Latina*, 67–68.

51 Klein, *Parties and Political Change in Bolivia*, 214–16.

52 On the gendered essence of such projects elsewhere in Latin America, see Karin Rosemblatt, *Gendered Compromises*; Katherine Bliss, *Compromised Positions*; Alexandra Stern, "Responsible Mothers and Normal Children"; Stepan, *"The Hour of Eugenics."*

53 Klein, *Parties and Political Change in Bolivia*, 208–9. On the organizations of ex-combatants, see also Dunkerley, *Orígenes del poder militar en Bolivia*, 179.

54 Fernández, "Prensa, radio e imaginario boliviano durante la Guerra del Chaco," 32–33.

55 Ibid., 29–30, 35; Toribio Claure, *Una escuela rural en Vacas*, 90. See also República de Bolivia, *Proyectos de ley e informes de comisiones de la H. Cámara de*

Diputados, 1932, 37, 127. What to do with the omisos was a much-disputed question after the war. For the many proposals, see also República de Bolivia, *Proyectos de Ley, H. Convención Nacional de 1938*, 210–11, 308–11, 333; República de Bolivia, *Informes de Comisiones, H. Convención Nacional de 1938*, 98-99. On the limits of aid to soldiers' families during the war itself, see Durán and Seoane, *El complejo mundo de la mujer durante la Guerra del Chaco*, 114, 134.

56 Klein, *Parties and Political Change in Bolivia*, 224–27.

57 Ibid., 224–27, 232. Toro also established Ministries of Mines and Petroleum, and of Commerce and Industry. To put a hold on leftist influences, he later replaced Alvarez with a conservative lawyer (Klein, "American Oil Companies in Latin America," 60, 63 n. 51).

58 Antezana and Romero, *Historia de los sindicatos campesinos*, Anexos, 9–12.

59 Gallego, *Los orígenes del reformismo militar en América Latina*, 67–80. See also Whitehead, "Bolivia since 1930," 519–24.

60 Personal communication, Eduardo Arze Loureiro, 26 May 1993.

61 Klein, *Parties and Political Change in Bolivia*, 228–35, 271–73; Dunkerley, "Political Suicide in Latin America," 32; Gallego, *Los orígenes del reformismo militar en América Latina*, 114. The quote is from the "Sindicalización obligatoria" decree, reproduced in Antezana and Romero, *Historia de los sindicatos campesinos*, Anexos, 10.

62 Gallego, *Los orígenes del reformismo militar en América Latina*, 116–23; Klein, *Parties and Political Change in Bolivia*.

63 Rivera, *Oprimidos pero no vencidos*, 57; Lehm and Rivera, *Los artesanos libertarios y la ética del trabajo*, 61–75.

64 Gallego, *Los orígenes del reformismo militar en América Latina*, 194–95.

65 Ibid., 198–202. Bolivia's first local labor federation, the FOT, was loosely connected to the Socialist Party. Its local branches, which grouped together workers from diverse sectors in major cities, were established in the late 1910s. The anarchist FOL was established in La Paz in 1926 in opposition to the FOT. Anarchism was also influential in Oruro, and the La Paz FOL eventually gained control of the Oruro FOT. With the creation of the CSTB in 1936, workers created Federaciones Obreras Sindicales (FOS) in departmental capitals, and the FOT began to fade. (Guillermo Lora, *A History of the Bolivian Labour Movement, 1848–1871*, 128–37, 151, 157, 161–62, 175–76, 208; Lora, *Historia del movimiento obrero boliviano, 1933–1952*, 259–60.

66 Klein, *Parties and Political Change in Bolivia*, 216, 273, 355.

67 República de Bolivia, *Redactor de la H. Convención Nacional, 1938*, 1:455–56. Toro's statute built on the 1919 decree to educate Indians "in their own habitats" (see chapter 2). In 1936, the name of the "Ministerio de Instrucción Pública y Agricultura" was changed to "Ministerio de Educación y Asuntos Indígenas."

68 Larson, "Capturing Indian Bodies, Hearths and Minds," 192. Three schools had opened and nine more were in progress by the end of 1936 (Christine Whitehead, "Cochabamba Landlords and the Agrarian Reform," 49).

69 República de Bolivia, *Proyectos de Ley, H. Convención Nacional de 1938*, 629–32.

70 *La Razón*, 18 May 1939, 5.

71 Primer Congreso Interamericano de Indianistas, *Reglamento, Temario y Agendas*, 7–8; *La Razón*, 18 May 1939, 5.

72 Larson, "Capturing Indian Bodies, Hearths and Minds," 192.

73 See Dandler, *El sindicalismo campesino en Bolivia*; Antezana and Romero, *Historia de los sindicatos campesinos*, 1–37. For the law, see Flores Moncayo, *Legislación boliviana del indio*, 378–80.

74 Dunkerley, *Orígenes del poder militar en Bolivia*, 262 n. 72.

75 Klein, " 'Social Constitutionalism' in Latin America," 262–63.

76 This leftist bloc encompassed diverse political tendencies and included Alberto Mendoza López, Félix Eguino Zaballa, Fernando Siñani, Waldo Alvarez, Carlos Medinaceli, Wálter Guevara Arze, and Ricardo Anaya (Klein, *Parties and Political Change in Bolivia*, 281, 288–89, 124, 141–42).

77 Klein, *Parties and Political Change in Bolivia*, 272-73; Klein, " 'Social Constitutionalism' in Latin America," 262–64, 263 n. 19.

78 See Lora, *Historia del movimiento obrero boliviano, 1933–1952*, 211–16; Klein, " 'Social Constitutionalism' in Latin America," 263.

79 Klein, " 'Social Constitutionalism' in Latin America," 273.

80 On Cuba, see de la Fuente, *A Nation for All*, 210–11.

81 República de Bolivia, *Redactor de la H. Convención Nacional, 1938*, 2:433–34. On the history of regionalism and decentralization initiatives, see Rodríguez, *Poder central y proyecto regional*. Like their nineteenth-century counterparts (and unlike present-day advocates of regional autonomy in the eastern part of Bolivia), 1930s proponents of decentralization emphasized its significance for national strength or "salvation" (Rodríguez, *Poder central y proyecto regional*, 62). On the broader intellectual context of the decentralization debate in Santa Cruz, see also Hernán Pruden, "Separatismo e integracionismo en la post Guerra del Chaco."

82 In the late nineteenth century, politicians from Cochabamba championed decentralization, but they joined La Paz deputies in support of centralization in the 1930s (Rodríguez, *Poder central y proyecto regional*, 117–21).

83 See República de Bolivia, *Redactor de la H. Convención Nacional, 1938*, 2:437, 469, 479; 3:480, 495–96, 500.

84 Ibid., 3:519–20.

85 Ibid., 2:438.

86 Ibid., 2:437–38; 3:669–71; 5:277, 280.

87 On late-nineteenth-century views, see Demelas, "Darwinismo a la criolla"; República de Bolivia, *Censo general de la población de la República de Bolivia, 1900*, 35–36.

88 The count was 44 to 35.

89 On the tensions between unity and diversity in Latin America's racialized national mythologies, see Poole, "Mestizaje, Distinction and the Political Language of Culture in Oaxaca"; Appelbaum, Macpherson, and Rosemblatt, "Introduction"; Wade, "Afterword."

90 On the recognition of diversity as a means to stake political control where state power is weak, see Poole, "Mestizaje, Distinction and the Political Language of Culture in Oaxaca."

91 Trigo, *Las constituciones de Bolivia*, 396, 401–2. The 1938 Constitution dropped the higher income qualifications for senators and deputies (ibid., 433).

92 República de Bolivia, *Redactor de la H. Convención Nacional, 1938*, 3:109–11.

93 Enrique Ochoa, "The Rapid Expansion of Voter Participation in Latin America," 869–98.

94 República de Bolivia, *Redactor de la H. Convención Nacional, 1938*, 3:107–8, 110, 115.

95 Ibid., 115–16, 121.

96 Ibid., 107, 136–37, 156–57.

97 Ibid., 111–13.

98 Ibid., 116–20, 136, 139–40.

99 Ibid., 148–49, 122, 162–63.

100 Ibid., 117–18, 166, 174–75.

101 Ibid., 148–49.

102 Ibid. Other future MNRistas, including Guzmán and Paz Estenssoro, voted against female suffrage.

103 Ibid., 136–37.

104 Ibid., 110.

105 On the concern with social rights in Latin America in the 1930s, see Whitehead, "State Organization in Latin America since 1930," 84–90.

106 Marcela Revollo Quiroga, *Mujeres bajo prueba*, 36–37, 67. For an example, see *El Diario*, 14 February 1938, 3.

107 Linda Kerber, "The Meanings of Citizenship," 836. On the "instability" of citizenship in Latin America in particular, and the wavering "rules of inclusion/exclusion," see Whitehead, "State Organization in Latin America since 1930," 87.

108 Widespread belief that the Chaco War had been triggered by a struggle between foreign oil companies, and Standard Oil's unaccommodating stance toward Bolivia during the war, led both radicals and conservatives to favor nationalization (Klein, "American Oil Companies in Latin America," 56–58, 65).

109 Klein, " 'Social Constitutionalism' in Latin America," 270–71.

110 Trigo, *Las constituciones de Bolivia*, 440 (articles 106 and 108).

111 Ibid., 443 (articles 121, 122, 124, 125).

112 Ibid., 444.

113 Bolivia's Civil Code granted "natural" children recognized by fathers a third of the "legitimate" child's inheritance; it also guaranteed "illegitimate" children's right to food.

114 República de Bolivia, *Redactor de la H. Convención Nacional, 1938*, 4:304.

115 See ibid., 267, 297, 313.

116 The Bolivian outlook mirrors approaches in popular-front Chile, where offi-

cials deemed illegitimacy a problem of national security and armed social workers with tools to "domesticate" men (Rosemblatt, *Gendered Compromises*). Bolivia more fully expanded the rights of children and mothers, but without significantly developing social welfare institutions to deliver the entitlements. On the social welfare system before 1950, see United Nations, *Report of the United Nations Mission of Technical Assistance to Bolivia*, 106–11.

117 República de Bolivia, *Redactor de la H. Convención Nacional, 1938*, 5:405–10.
118 Trigo, *Las constituciones de Bolivia*, 424.
119 República de Bolivia, *Redactor de la H. Convención Nacional, 1938*, 2:545.
120 Ibid., 5:264, 269; 2:545.
121 República de Bolivia, *Proyectos e Informes del H. Senado Nacional, Legislatura Ordinaria de 1932*, 211–14. On Mendoza, see Zulawski, "Hygiene and 'the Indian Problem,'" 121–22; Lora, *Historia del movimiento obrero boliviano, 1933–1952*, 227.
122 República de Bolivia, *Redactor de la H. Convención Nacional, 1938*, 2:525–32, 540–41.
123 Ibid., 5:267, 281, 212–88.
124 For Guevara's views on "race," see also Wálter Guevara Arze, "Manifiesto de Ayopaya." The congressional delegate and future PIR member Abelardo Villalpando rejected the concept on similar grounds (Abelardo Villalpando, "La cuestión del indio," 99).
125 República de Bolivia, *Redactor de la H. Convención Nacional, 1938*, 3:495, 669–72; 5:277.
126 Marof, *La tragedia del altiplano*.
127 Ibid., 5:270, 277, 280. Guevara's views paralleled those of Ecuadorian industrialists (Clark, "Race, 'Culture,' and Mestizaje," 205).
128 On Molina's framework and its enduring influence, see Kourí, "Interpreting the Expropriation of Indian Pueblo Lands in Porfirian Mexico"; Hale, "Frank Tannenbaum and the Mexican Revolution."
129 Hale, "Frank Tannenbaum and the Mexican Revolution," 242; Kourí, "Interpreting the Expropriation of Indian Pueblo Lands in Porfirian Mexico," 93, 98, 100–104. The conservative Bolivian politician Enrique Finot similarly praised Spanish corporatism and protective laws. Finot considered such measures particularly important in a place such as Bolivia, where the "fusion of bloods has occurred only on a limited scale" (Finot, *Sobre el problema del indio*, 18–19).
130 Elizardo Pérez, *Warisata*, 242–43.
131 República de Bolivia, *Redactor de la H. Convención Nacional, 1938*, 5:281.
132 Ibid., 281–82.
133 Ibid., 2:533–35.
134 Ibid. 2:5–35, 534, 545; 3:285, 535–36; 5:212–88.
135 Ibid., 5:285–86.
136 República de Bolivia, *Informes de Comisiones, H. Convención Nacional de 1938*, 25–26, 61–68, 96–99, 143–46, 251, 330–43.

137 República de Bolivia, *Redactor de la H. Convención Nacional, 1938*, 5:228–29.

138 Landowners demonstrating outside of Congress influenced the outcome (Whitehead, "Cochabamba Landlords and the Agrarian Reform," 56).

139 Trigo, *Las constituciones de Bolivia*, 450.

140 Ibid., 390, 422.

141 The same was true of Cuba's convention. Louis Pérez, *Cuba*, 282; Whitney, *State and Revolution in Cuba*, 180.

142 On the socialization of rights elsewhere in Latin America, see Grandin, *The Last Colonial Massacre*, 7, 197.

143 On Brazil, see Robert Levine, *Father of the Poor?*, 124.

144 On Mexico, see Hale, "Political and Social Ideas," 294. On the authoritarian tendencies of corporatist thought, see ibid., 293-99.

145 Whitehead, "Bolivia since 1930," 524; Klein, *Bolivia*, 207–9; Dunkerley, "Political Suicide in Latin America," 33–34; Lora, *A History of the Bolivian Labour Movement*, 384 n. 6.

146 Dunkerley, "Political Suicide in Latin America," 31–34.

147 Guevara Arze, "Manifiesto de Ayopaya," 230.

✳ *Five* Land, Labor Rights, and Autonomy

1 USNA, RG 166, Box 48, "International Agreements—Labor, Bolivia 1942–45."

2 Antezana and Romero, *Historia de los sindicatos campesinos*, 89–90, 94–95.

3 On the intensification of the rural strikes, see Antezana and Romero, *Historia de los sindicatos campesinos*, 93–100. A truly national crisis began to unfold only after Villarroel and the MNR came to power in 1943 (see chapter 7).

4 The Oruro strikes have not been fully explored. The reasons for the upsurge in strikes in Cochabamba are discussed in more detail below.

5 See especially Albó, "Andean People in the Twentieth Century," 796. Although Albó emphasizes a clear shift, he notes that some community-based resistance persisted after the war (see "From MNRistas to Kataristas to Katari," 381). On the community-based resistance, see also Choque, "Las rebeliones indígenas de la post-guerra del Chaco."

6 The principal study is Dandler, *El sindicalismo campesino en Bolivia*.

7 The situation parallels that of Guatemala, where rural labor reforms destabilized the countryside and sparked disputes over land several years before the 1952 agrarian reform was announced (Cindy Forster, *The Time of Freedom*).

8 Jorge Dandler and Juan Torrico, "From the National Indigenous Congress to the Ayopaya Rebellion," 336, 374. Focusing on Cochabamba, José Gordillo and Robert Jackson have deemed this process a "refeudalization" of the hacienda ("Mestizaje y proceso de parcelación en la estructura agraria de Cochabamba"). Larson instead stresses an overall dynamic of hacienda crisis that probably made it necessary for landlords to negotiate with their colonos ("Casta y clase," 215). The tension between peasant autonomy and hacienda servitude is discussed in greater depth below.

9 Rivera, *Los terratenientes de Cochabamba*. A hectare (10,000 square meters) is 2.47 acres.

10 Qayum, Soux, and Barragán, *De terratenientes a amas de casa*, 30.

11 Rivera, *Los terratenientes de Cochabamba*, 97, 100.

12 See ibid., 106–7; Langer, "Labor Strikes and Reciprocity on Chuquisaca Haciendas," 263–65; Rivera, "La expansión del latifundio en el altiplano boliviano," 113–14.

13 Whitehead, "Cochabamba Landlords and the Agrarian Reform," 26; Qayum, Soux, and Barragán, *De terratenientes a amas de casa*.

14 Sánchez, "Hacienda, campesinado y estructura agraria en el Valle Alto" (lic. thesis), appendix 5 and 67–70.

15 Ibid., 99; Gustavo Rodríguez and Humberto Solares S., *Sociedad oligárquica, chicha y cultura popular*.

16 The hacienda's best land, the demesne, was cultivated by and for the owner. Colonos' usufruct plots varied in magnitude in relation to the size of the family, size of the estate, and total number of colonos. In Cochabamba, the plot was sometimes also called an *arriendo, jap'ina*, or *jappi*. In other regions, the terms *sayaña, huasipungo, melga*, or *arriendo* were used. Lagos, *Autonomy and Power*, 28–29; Qayum et al., *De terratenientes a amas de casa*, 29; Rivera, *Los terratenientes de Cochabamba*; Jackson, "Evolución y persistencia del colonaje en las haciendas de Cochabamba," 146.

17 Muko, the raw material of traditional chicha, is salivated ground corn. For duties on specific properties, see Gordillo and Jackson, "Mestizaje y proceso de parcelación en la estructura agraria de Cochabamba"; Jackson, "Evolución y persistencia del colonaje en las haciendas de Cochabamba"; Sánchez, "Hacienda, campesinado y estructura agraria en el Valle Alto" (lic. thesis), 58–62, 73–74.

18 "Primer Congreso, Principales Ponencias," 4, 6. In USNA, RG 59, 824.401/7-1845.

19 Jackson, *Regional Markets and Agrarian Transformation in Bolivia*, 38, 161; "Primer Congreso, Principales Ponencias," 3, 7; Lagos, *Autonomy and Power*, 28–29.

20 *Pregón*, 8 June 1945.

21 The same applies to *colono* and *colonaje*, which were used widely only in the late nineteenth century and the early twentieth. In colonial times, service tenants were usually called *arrenderos* (Larson, *Cochabamba*, 384–85 and 384 n. 75).

22 "Primer Congreso, Principales Ponencias," 5; Lagos, *Autonomy and Power*, 28–29.

23 Bruce Dorsey, "A Case Study of Ex-Hacienda Toralapa in the Tiraque Region of the Upper Cochabamba Valley," 15.

24 *Muko de boca*, the highest quality, was made by chewing crushed corn and pressing it against the roof of the mouth; once saturated with saliva, small palate-shaped molds were dried in the sun. A simpler form, called *huiñapo*, was produced with wet ground corn that was set aside to germinate (Olen Leonard, *Canton Chullpas*, 44–48).

25 Leonard, *Canton Chullpas*, 46. On the burdens of mukeo, see Fermín Vallejos, *Tata Fermín*, 19; Juan Félix Arias, "La política y sus modelos en la relación con el Estado boliviano," 66.

26 Rodríguez and Solares, *Sociedad oligárquica, chicha y cultura popular*; Jackson, *Regional Markets and Agrarian Transformation in Bolivia*, 11. In 1900, Cliza was a canton in Tarata province; in 1945, it became the capital of the newly created province of Germán Jordán.

27 Sánchez, "Hacienda, campesinado y estructura agraria en el Valle Alto" (lic. thesis), 94–95; Rivera, *Los terratenientes de Cochabamba*, 34.

28 AHPC, Correspondencia, Colonización y Agricultura, 1906–8, 88.

29 Rodríguez and Solares, *Sociedad oligárquica, chicha y cultura popular*.

30 On the production process, see Leonard, *Canton Chullpas*, 44–48. For a glimpse of the utensils involved, and their social value, see the early-twentieth-century wills in the Archivo del Juzgado de Partido de Cliza. Punata's 1918 register of chicheras gives a good sense of the scale of the industry in rural areas (Archivo Municipal de Punata).

31 On self-employed producers of muko, see Sánchez, "Hacienda, campesinado y estructura agraria en el Valle Alto de Cochabamba"; Rafael Reyeros, *El pongueaje*, 179-82; Gordillo and Jackson, "Mestizaje y proceso de parcelación en la estructura agraria de Cochabamba."

32 On relations between chicheras and mukeras, see AJIC, Juicio Verbal Civil presented to the Alcalde Parroquial, P. V. vs. L. Z., 1887; AJIC, To the Alcalde Parroquial, 1885.

33 Larson, "Casta y clase," 214–15; Rivera, *Los terratenientes de Cochabamba*, 34 n. 3.

34 Sánchez, "Hacienda, campesinado y estructura agraria en el Valle Alto" (lic. thesis), 55–56, 72, 100, 114, 229–30.

35 Gordillo and Jackson, "Mestizaje y proceso de parcelación en la estructura agraria de Cochabamba," 34. On the expansion of smallholding in Cochabamba's central valleys, see Larson, *Cochabamba*; Jackson, *Regional Markets and Agrarian Transformation in Bolivia*; Rodríguez, "Entre reformas y contrareformas."

36 Lagos, *Autonomy and Power*, 29–30; Jackson, *Regional Markets and Agrarian Transformation in Bolivia*, 181–82, 194, 149 (table 4.6).

37 Jackson, *Regional Markets and Agrarian Transformation in Bolivia*, 163–64; Reyeros, *El pongueaje*, 224–26. Owners typically supplied some of the seed and received at least half the yield. Although peasants working in compañia owed some of the same services to the landlord, they were not as heavily burdened as colonos (Sánchez, "Hacienda, campesinado y estructura agraria en el Valle Alto," lic. thesis, 219).

38 Sánchez, "Hacienda, campesinado y estructura agraria en el Valle Alto" (lic. thesis), 71–72, 75, 104–5; Dandler, *El sindicalismo campesino en Bolivia*, 48; Richard Patch, "Social Implications of the Bolivian Agrarian Reform," 90–93; Whitehead, "Cochabamba Landlords and the Agrarian Reform," 20–21.

39 Lagos, *Autonomy and Power*, 28–31; Klein, *Parties and Political Change in Bolivia*, 160–66; Dandler, "Politics of Leadership, Brokerage and Patronage in the Campesino Movement of Cochabamba," 34–35.

40 AHPC, Exp., Pacci, Finca de Totorani, representando a los colonos, 1941. The evidence suggests that rural workers' mobility increased after the Chaco War. The reasons are not entirely clear, but labor scarcity was probably a cause, as discussed below.

41 Dandler, *El sindicalismo campesino en Bolivia*, esp. 165–66; Lagos, *Autonomy and Power*, 28–32. For a description of the transactions between landlords and the colonos who purchased plots from them, see Sánchez, "Hacienda, campesinado y estructura agraria en el Valle Alto" (lic. thesis), 118.

42 AJIC, Nogales vs. Angulo et al., Toco-Molino, 1939; AJIC, Ugarte, Ad Perpetuam, Lobo Rancho, 1941.

43 Sánchez, "Hacienda, campesinado y estructura agraria en el Valle Alto" (lic. thesis), 121.

44 This parallels western El Salvador in the years before the 1932 uprising (see Jeffrey Gould and Aldo Lauria-Santiago, " 'They Call Us Thieves and Steal Our Wage,' " 234).

45 Whitehead, "Bolivia since 1930," 514–15.

46 Larson, *Cochabamba*, 317-18; Albó, "Andean People in the Twentieth Century," 774; Rodríguez and Solares, *Sociedad oligárquica, chicha y cultura popular*, 46–48.

47 Claure, *Una escuela rural en Vacas*, 89–90.

48 Klein, *Parties and Political Change in Bolivia*, 164, 396; United Nations, *Report of the United Nations Mission of Technical Assistance to Bolivia*, 54.

49 Klein, *Parties and Political Change in Bolivia*, 241; Richard Thorn, "The Economic Transformation," 182.

50 República de Bolivia, *Anuario Administrativo, 1939*, 2:444–46; Carmenza Gallo, *Taxes and State Power*, 97–118.

51 Klein, *Parties and Political Change in Bolivia*, 335.

52 According to the U.S. Vice Consul, this was a common complaint on haciendas. USNA, RG 84, Cochabamba Consulate, General Records, 1945, Vol. V, Box 9.

53 ACSJC, AG #774, 2PP, Tapacarí, 1939, 3rd set, fols. 121v–122.

54 AHPC, Exp., Pacci, representando a los colonos, Finca de Totorani, 1941; AHPC, Exp., Colonos de la Finca de Totorani (Ayopaya), 1941. See also AHPC, Exp., Mamani, Ayopaya y Quillacollo, 1941.

55 ACSJC, AG #774, 2PP, 1939, Tapacarí, 3rd set, fols. 121v–122.

56 On the municipal tax system, see Gallo, *Taxes and State Power*, 79–82. For colonos' and comunarios' complaints about taxes, see AHPC, Exp., Luizaga, Sipesipe, 1943; AHPC, Exp., Mollo y Falso vs. Zegarra y Alavis, Cantón Ventilla, 1942; AHPC, Exp., Alavi, alcalde del Ayllo Yarviri et al., Cantón Tacopaya, Arque, 1943; AHPC, Exp., Apaza, indígena originario de la estancia Kcochi et al., Challa, Tapacarí, 1937.

57 See AHPC, Exp., Mollo y Falso vs. Zegarra and Alavis, 1942, Cantón Ventilla; AHPC, Exp., Testimonio, Sr. don Félix Bolívar, Independencia (Ayopaya), 1944. See also Vallejos, *Tata Fermín*, 9 n. 3.

58 The Tapacarí records are attached to AHPC, Exp., Testimonio, Sr. don Félix Bolívar, Independencia (Ayopaya), 1944. Reams of documentation in the Cochabamba Prefecture Archive illustrate the conflicts that were waged over this tax in the 1930s and 1940s.

59 Andrew Cleven, *The Political Organization of Bolivia*; Gallo, *Taxes and State Power*, 99.

60 United Nations, *Report of the United Nations Mission of Technical Assistance to Bolivia*, 31.

61 That authority was not curbed until after 1952 (Gallo, *Taxes and State Power*, 79–82, 105).

62 See, for example, AHPC, Exp., Flores, casique de la comunidad Totora (Arque), 1937.

63 See AJIC, Soria vs. Rosetti, 1887.

64 Michael Jiménez, "Class, Gender, and Peasant Resistance in Central Colombia," 126.

65 AHPC, Exp., Pacci, representando a los colonos, Finca de Totorani, 1941; AHPC, Exp., Colonos de la Finca de Totorani, 1941. As discussed in chapter 4, Toro signed a decree giving colonos organized in unions the preferential right to rent land owned by municipalities or religious orders. He also approved a decree that protected resident workers from arbitrary eviction by landlords. These were very significant measures. But for the Indians and peasants who lodged petitions, the most important military socialist law was the 1938 constitution itself, which outlawed servitude. For the laws promulgated by Toro and Busch, see Flores Moncayo, *Legislación boliviana del indio*, 354–99.

66 Twenty-four peasant unions were established in Cochabamba's upper valley (Albó, "Andean People in the Twentieth Century," 797); others were created in the provinces of Arque, Punata, Ayopaya, and Tapacarí, and in the department of Tarija. Support from the FOL and the FOT contributed to their success (Antezana and Romero, *Historia de los sindicatos campesinos*, 73–78).

67 AHPC, Exp., Ugarte et al., Sindicato Agrario del Ghochi, 1937.

68 AHPC, Exp., Hermógenes y otros, Challa, Tapacarí, 1937.

69 See, for example, AHPC, Exp., Colonos de la Finca de Totorani, 1941, fol. 2.

70 AHPC, Exp., Pacci, representando a los colonos, Finca de Totorani, 1941, fol. 1v.

71 AHPC, Exp., Luizaga, pide amparo, Sipesipe, 1943.

72 Cited in Dandler, *El sindicalismo campesino en Bolivia*, 71.

73 For similar dynamics, see Grandin, *The Last Colonial Massacre*, 29.

74 AHPC, Exp., Grájeda et al., indígenas de Yayani, Ayopaya, 1942.

75 Rivera, *Los terratenientes de Cochabamba*, 70–72; Larson, *Cochabamba*, 186–88.

76 Rivera, *Los terratenientes de Cochabamba*, 34.

77 Dandler, "Politics of Leadership, Brokerage and Patronage in the Campesino Movement of Cochabamba," 45–46.

78 AHPC, Exp., Grájeda et al., indígenas de Yayani, Ayopaya, 1942. Initially, written contracts like this one applied to particular properties or provinces. As the tempo of unrest accelerated, landlords themselves tried to establish legal stan-

dards for all haciendas (Rivera, *Los terratenientes de Cochabamba*, 107-12). At the 1939 conference of the Sociedad Rural, landlords even called for a commission to draft an agricultural relations code (Whitehead, "Cochabamba Landlords and the Agrarian Reform," 54).

79 "Primer Congreso, Principales Ponencias," 6; Jackson, "Evolución y persistencia del colonaje en las haciendas de Cochabamba," 156; Sánchez, "Hacienda, campesinado y estructura agraria en el Valle Alto" (lic. thesis), 101.

80 *El Imparcial*, 4 February 1945, 5.

81 See also AHPC, Exp., Mamani, Ayopaya y Quillacollo, 1941. Estupro is the rape of a minor.

82 AHPC, Exp., Colonos de la Finca de Totorani (Ayopaya), 1941.

83 AHPC, Exp., Mamani, Ayopaya y Quillacollo, 1941.

84 *La Calle*, 14, 15 August 1943. The Senate had already debated a proposal to end pongueaje in 1942. See *Pregón*, 23 August 1942.

85 Remberto Capriles y Gastón Arduz Eguía, *El problema social en Bolivia*, 42–43; Klein, *Parties and Political Change in Bolivia*, 162 n. 1.

86 Grájeda met with lawyers and manufacturing and printing unionists during a 1940 trip to Cochabamba (Dandler and Torrico, "From the National Indigenous Congress to the Ayopaya Rebellion," 340).

87 AHPC, Exp., Grájeda et al., indígenas de Yayani, Ayopaya, 1942.

88 *El Diario*, 13 May 1942, 5.

89 AJIC, Ugarte, Ad Perpetuam, Lobo Rancho, 1941.

90 See AHPC, Exp., Mollo y Falso vs. Zegarra y Alavis, Cantón Ventilla, 1942; AHPC, Exp., Alavi, alcalde del Ayllo Yarviri et al., Cantón Tacopaya, Arque, 1943.

91 AJIC, Ugarte, Ad Perpetuam, Lobo Rancho, 1941; AHPC, Exp., Colque, indígena de la estancia de Yarviri, Cantón Tacopaya, Arque; AHPC, Exp., Cruz, indígena originario, Tapacarí, 1936. On such images, see also Gordillo, *Campesinos revolucionarios en Bolivia*, 207–9.

92 AHPC, Exp., Pacci, representando a los colonos, Finca de Totorani, 1941; AHPC, Exp., Colonos de la Finca de Totorani (Ayopaya), 1941.

93 Following a 1945 "uprising" in Capinota (Cochabamba), landlords recognized its leaders as the new majordomos (Antezana and Romero, *Historia de los sindicatos campesinos*, 124).

94 Conde Mamani, "Lucas Miranda Mamani."

95 AHPC, Exp., Testimonio de unos obrados presentados por [Andrés] Marca Tola y Rufino Villca, 1940. Alcaldes, regidores, and alguaciles were colonial-era Indian officials who served the government of official Indian towns (*pueblos de reducción*) and acted as representatives of Indian communities before outside powers. The colonial state played a significant role in the election of these officials, who acted, above all, as enforcers of the law. The alcaldes were of two types: alcaldes mayores and alcaldes ordinarios. Although they fulfilled the same duties, the alcalde mayor had a higher status. The alguaciles and regidores were lower-status officials who assisted the alcaldes and other authorities. See

Thomson, *We Alone Will Rule*, 28–48; Abercrombie, *Pathways of Memory and Power*, 87. Escribano means scribe.

96 Antezana and Romero, *Historia de los sindicatos campesinos*, 99–100.

97 Juan Félix Arias, *Historia de una esperanza*, 33–37, 68; Vallejos, *Tata Fermín*, 8; Waskar Ari, "Race and Subaltern Nationalism," esp. 22, 116, 122. Ari traces the origins, trajectory, tactics, and political project of the Alcaldes Mayores Particulares, as well as the movement's connections and tensions with the pre–Chaco War networks of caciques apoderados. In Cochabamba, the Alcaldes Mayores Particulares took deep roots in Mizque and Aiquile. *Alcalde Mayor*, as noted above, was the colonial term for an alcalde of higher status; by adding the word *particular* (private), the members of this movement signaled the independence of the alcaldes mayores, who served Indians, not the state, and promoted non-state schools (Ari, "Race and Subaltern Nationalism," 4).

98 Klein, *Haciendas and Ayllus*, 148.

99 Some 1920s incidents were known by this term, but it is usually associated with protests from 1939–46, when labor leaders agitated on haciendas.

100 See, for example, *Los Tiempos*, 18 March 1945, 4.

101 *El País*, 18 March 1945, 4.

102 On La Paz, see Mamani, *Taraqu*; on Chuquisaca, Langer, "Labor Strikes and Reciprocity on Chuquisaca Haciendas." On Cochabamba, see AJIC, Hilario Salasar vs. Facundo Claros, 1864–66; and AHPC, Exp., Comunarios de Altamachi, 1926.

103 See AJIC, Hilario Salasar contra Facundo Claros, 1864–66, fols. 9v–10.

104 See, for example, AJIC, Claure, Amenazas i otros delitos, Santa Clara, 1940. It seems likely that the peasant federation established in Oruro in 1941 played a role in the strikes in that department. On the creation of the federation, see Whitehead, "Cochabamba Landlords and the Agrarian Reform," 2.

105 ACSJC, AG #774, 2PP, Tapacarí, 1939.

106 Ibid., 2nd set, fols. 7, 43.

107 Ibid., 3rd set, fols. 114–16.

108 Ibid., fols. 52, 152–52v. See also 2nd set, pp. 108–108v.

109 Ibid., 1st set, fols. 62–65; 2nd set, fols. 25, 99v, 112–112v; 3rd set, fols. 108, 110–110v, 119–20v.

110 As Serulnikov put it for the Bourbon period: "To define peasant mobilization as illegal or extralegal draws an artificial distinction that belies both the actors' perception and the rules of political struggle" ("Disputed Images of Colonialism," 206–7).

111 ACSJC, AG #774, 2PP, Tapacarí, 1939, 1st set, fol. 52.

112 Ibid., 2nd set, fols. 109–109v.

113 AHPC, Exp., Mamani, Ayopaya y Quillacollo, 1941.

114 Servicio Nacional de Reforma Agraria (SNRA), *Evaluación de la reforma agraria boliviana: El fermento pre-revolucionario (1932–1952)*, 2:45–46.

115 AHPC, Exp., Testimonio, Sr. don Félix Bolívar, Independencia (Ayopaya), 1944.

116 Ibid., fols. 1v, 4.

117 ACSJC, AG #789, 2PP, Antezana vs. Rodríguez y otros, 1941, fols. 8–8v, 59.

118 AJIC, Ugarte, Ad Perpetuam, Lobo Rancho, 1941. For other examples, see Marianne De Jong, "En la sombra de Totora," 75, and 75 n. 90; AJIC, Calle Claure, Amenazas i otros delitos, 1940; AHPC, Exp., Flores, casique de la comunidad Totora, 1937.

119 Gordillo, *Campesinos revolucionarios en Bolivia*, 199. For more land redistribution rumors, see AHPC, Exp., Ledezma viuda de Saucedo Sevilla, Finca de Chucchihuañusca, 1937.

120 De Jong, "En la sombra de Totora," 76 n. 96.

121 Ibid., 77. See also Dandler, *El sindicalismo campesino en Bolivia*, 104–5.

122 For proposals and petitions to end pongueaje, see, *Pregón*, 23 August 1942, 3, 6; Antezana and Romero, *Historia de los sindicatos campesinos*, 88; *La Calle*, 14, 15 August 1943. As early as 1937, a decree concerning the eviction of colonos potentially undercut landlords' ability to demand pongueaje duties. According to the decree, the failure to fulfill agricultural tasks was legitimate grounds for expulsion, but the refusal to complete "personal obligations" was not (Flores Moncayo, *Legislación boliviana del indio*, 380–83).

123 Gordillo, *Campesinos revolucionarios en Bolivia*, 198 n. 4.

124 De Jong's interviews in the Pocona area allude to such journeys ("En la sombra de Totora," 72–73).

125 In addition to the Tacorama case, see AHPC, Exp., Ledezma viuda de Saucedo Sevilla, Finca de Chucchihuañusca, 1937. While Villarroel was in power, a full thirty families were expelled from just one hacienda in Tiraque (Roger Simmons, *Palca and Pucara*, 19–21, 125–26).

126 See, for example, ACSJC, AG #774, 2PP, Tapacarí, 1939, fol. 99; Gordillo, *Campesinos revolucionarios en Bolivia*.

127 See, for example, Gordillo, *Campesinos revolucionarios en Bolivia*, 198–99, 199 nn. 6–7.

128 On Santos Marka T'ula's activities, see J. Blanco, *Antonio Alvarez Mamani*. See also Claudia Ranaboldo, *El camino perdido*, 131–32.

129 AHPC, Exp., Mollo y Falso vs. Zegarra y Alavis, por cobro indebido, Cantón Ventilla, 1942.

130 De Jong, "En la sombra de Totora," 81 n. 110.

131 USNA, RG 166, Box 48, Folder "International Agreements—Labor, Bolivia, 1942–45, 10 December 1945"; "Primer Congreso, Principales Ponencias," 2–7. The investigations were carried out in 1941–42.

132 Antezana and Romero, *Historia de los sindicatos campesinos*, 89.

133 Lora, *Historia del movimiento obrero boliviano, 1933–1952*, 223–25.

134 Cornejo, *Programas políticos de Bolivia*, 194, 251–53, 262. See also Villalpando, "La cuestión del indio"; Arturo Urquidi Morales, *La comunidad indígena*.

135 For the agenda, see Primer Congreso Interamericano de Indianistas, *Reglamento, Temario y Agendas*.

136 Antezana and Romero, *Historia de los sindicatos campesinos*, 86–88, 91–92; *El Nacional*, 1 February 1945; Lehm and Rivera, *Los artesanos libertarios y la ética del trabajo*, 81; Choque, "Las rebeliones indígenas de la post-guerra del Chaco," 39–40; Rivera, *Oprimidos pero no vencidos*, 61-63; USNA, RG 166, Box 48, 7 September 1942.

137 The resolutions approved by this congress were transcribed in *Los Tiempos*, 5 April 1945.

138 See República de Bolivia, *Informes de Comisiones, H. Convención Nacional de 1938*; *El Diario*, 14 May 1942, 6.

✳ *Six* The Politics of Mestizaje

1 Luis Peñaloza Cordero, *Historia secreta del Movimiento Nacionalista Revolucionario*, 64.

2 Gualberto Villarroel, *Mensaje a la H. Convención Nacional de 1945*, 7.

3 Whitehead, "Bolivia," 530.

4 Jael Bueno et al., "Los trabajadores cochabambinos," 6.

5 Mariano Plotkin, *Mañana es San Perón*. Perón courted informal workers and women to offset male trade unions; Villarroel targeted them most likely because he lacked an urban base.

6 Lehm and Rivera, *Los artesanos libertarios y la ética del trabajo*, 61–80.

7 Villarroel, *Mensaje a la H. Convención Nacional de 1945*, 45.

8 Villarroel, *Mensaje a la H. Convención Nacional de 1944*, 70.

9 Villarroel, *Mensaje a la H. Convención Nacional de 1945*, 4.

10 Klein, *Parties and Political Change in Bolivia*, 351–68.

11 Paz Estenssoro rejoined the cabinet as minister of finance; Julio Zuazo Cueca and Germán Monroy Block became ministers of agriculture and labor. Carlos Montenegro, Villarroel's first minister of agriculture, returned to the government as ambassador to Mexico. Most other cabinet posts went to RADEPA members or its civilian allies (Peñaloza, *Historia secreta del Movimiento Nacionalista Revolucionario*, 59–61).

12 Klein, *Parties and Political Change in Bolivia*, 217–18, 336–68, 372–77; Christopher Mitchell, *The Legacy of Populism in Bolivia*, 21–22, 373; René Zavaleta Mercado, *50 años de historia*, 44–56; USNA, RG 59, 824.00/1-2146; USNA, RG 59, 824.00/6-2145.

13 Klein, *Parties and Political Change in Bolivia*, 368–70; Fernández, "Prensa, radio e imaginario boliviano durante la Guerra del Chaco." On the paternalistic relationships that junior officers established with indigenous soldiers under their command, see Fernández, "Transformaciones y prácticas de poder en el ejército boliviano."

14 Zavaleta, *50 años de historia*, 46.

15 On the MNR's growth, see Mitchell, *The Legacy of Populism in Bolivia*, 17–25. The program did not appear until 1942.

16 Klein, *Parties and Political Change in Bolivia*, 195–96; 295–96; Mitchell, *The Legacy of Populism in Bolivia*, 16.

17 Mitchell, *The Legacy of Populism in Bolivia*, 16; Klein, *Parties and Political Change in Bolivia*, 341–42.

18 Klein, *Parties and Political Change in Bolivia*, 331, 341–42; Mitchell, *The Legacy of Populism in Bolivia*, 16.

19 Mitchell, *The Legacy of Populism in Bolivia*, 19–20; Peñaloza, *Historia secreta del Movimiento Nacionalista Revolucionario*, 67–68.

20 Zavaleta, *50 años de historia*, 47; Klein, *Parties and Political Change in Bolivia*, 355–58, 363–65, 373–76; Mitchell, *The Legacy of Populism in Bolivia*, 20–21; Fernando Mayorga, *El discurso del nacionalismo revolucionario*, 85.

21 MNR, *Sus bases y principios de acción inmediata*, 37, 43; Klein, *Parties and Political Change in Bolivia*, 336–37; Mitchell, *The Legacy of Populism in Bolivia*, 18–19.

22 This paragraph draws on Stepan, "*The Hour of Eugenics*," 106, 138–39; Lomnitz, *Exits from the Labyrinth*; Lowell Gudmundson and Francisco Scarano, "Conclusion," esp. 338; de la Cadena, "Are *Mestizos* Hybrids?"; de la Cadena, *Indigenous Mestizos*; Gould, *To Die in This Way*; Appelbaum, Macpherson, and Rosemblatt, "Introduction."

23 For diverse perspectives on mestizaje in Mexico, see Knight, "Racism, Revolution, and *Indigenismo*"; Alexander Dawson, *Indian and Nation in Revolutionary Mexico*; Stern, "From Mestizophilia to Biotypology"; Poole, "Mestizaje, Distinction and the Political Language of Culture in Oaxaca."

24 Gould, *To Die in This Way*; Gould, "Revolutionary Nationalism and Local Memories in El Salvador," 141. On mestizaje in Central America, see also Charles R. Hale, "Does Multiculturalism Menace?," 500–501.

25 Stepan, "*The Hour of Eugenics*," 118.

26 De la Cadena, *Indigenous Mestizos*; de la Cadena, "Mestizos Are Not Hybrids"; Larson, "Redeemed Indians, Barbarianized Cholos"; Mendoza, *Shaping Society through Dance*; Sarah Chambers, "Little Middle Ground."

27 José Macedonio Urquidi, *La obra histórica de Arguedas*, 52; Octavio Salamanca, *En defensa de Bolivia*; Teodomiro Estrada, *Pequeña monografía del departamento de Cochabamba*.

28 Barragán, "Identidades indias y mestizas."

29 For the use of these hyphenated terms, see, for example, Federico Avila, *El problema de la unidad nacional*. For a similar claim regarding the use of the term Afro-Mestizo in Mexico, see Poole, "Mestizaje, Distinction and the Political Language of Culture in Oaxaca."

30 República de Bolivia, *Redactor de la H. Convención Nacional, 1938*, 2:672; see also 396–97.

31 On the general dynamic, see Holt, "The First New Nations," xi; Stepan, "*The Hour of Eugenics*," 137–38.

32 MNR, *Sus bases y principios de acción inmediata*, 34.

33 Bolivia was not unique in this respect. See Ferrer, *Insurgent Cuba*.

34 MNR, *Sus bases y principios de acción inmediata*, 10, 31, 38–39.

35 Mayorga, *El discurso del nacionalismo revolucionario*, 13–14, 21, 97–98.

36 MNR, *Sus bases y principios de acción inmediata*, 31, 36. On these exclusions, and

the occasional, ambivalent inclusions, see Thomson, "Revolutionary Memory in Bolivia."

37 MNR, *Sus bases y principios de acción inmediata*, 20, 28, 33–37, 41, 42.

38 These political tirades should not be confused with many people's local practices; Jews who lived in Bolivia remember tolerance and the support they received (Leo Spitzer, *Hotel Bolivia*, 134, 178–79).

39 Holt, "The First New Nations," x; Stepan, *"The Hour of Eugenics."*

40 Spitzer, *Hotel Bolivia*, ix and 203 n. 2.

41 The bulk of Bolivia's immigrants were from neighboring Latin American countries (Valerie Fifer, *Land, Location, and Politics since 1825*, 254 n. 1).

42 Spitzer, *Hotel Bolivia*, 110–22. With the specter of the Chaco War just behind him, Busch was probably also motivated by Paraguay's bid to colonize the Chaco with 15,000 Austrian Jewish refugees (Klein, *Parties and Political Change in Bolivia*, 308).

43 Spitzer, *Hotel Bolivia*, 172–73, 222 n. 23; Klein, *Parties and Political Change in Bolivia*, 337.

44 *La Calle*, 4 August 1942; MNR, *Sus bases y principios de acción inmediata*, 41–42; Spitzer, *Hotel Bolivia*, 167–68; Jerry Knudson, "The Bolivian Immigration Bill of 1942."

45 This is not to suggest that MNR rhetoric was without calls for cultural transformation, but the pleas were not full-scale assimilationist ones at this time.

46 Elsewhere in Latin America, pro-mestizo sentiments were similarly premised on the construction of other "others." On anti-Chinese racism in Mexico, see Knight, "Racism, Revolution, and *Indigenismo*"; Gerardo Rénique, "Race, Region, and Nation."

47 República de Bolivia, *Redactor de la H. Convención Nacional, 1944*, 2:1373–74. See also 1375–83; and República de Bolivia, *Redactor de la Convención Nacional de 1945, Sesiones ordinarias*, 2:431–36.

48 Medinaceli, *Alternando la rutina*; Stephenson, *Gender and Modernity in Andean Bolivia*, 20.

49 Villarroel, *Mensaje a la H. Convención Nacional de 1944*, 50.

50 Ibid., 51–53.

51 Ibid., 69. See also *Mensaje a la H. Convención Nacional de 1945*, 5.

52 The plan did provide a blueprint for social policy after the 1952 revolution triumphed. See James Wilkie, *The Bolivian Revolution and U.S. Aid since 1952*; Gallo, *Taxes and State Power*; Dunkerley, *Rebellion in the Veins*; Klein, *Parties and Political Change in Bolivia*, 380.

53 Klein, *Parties and Political Change in Bolivia*, 378.

54 During the period of study, the term chola was often used as a synonym for the "mujer del pueblo," or plebeian woman, especially those who worked as vendors, chicheras, and cooks. Though the term chola was sometimes used interchangeably with "mestiza," "chola" generally implied greater proximity to indianness. The word was often used as an insult, but it did not always carry a derogatory connotation, as the debates discussed in this chapter indicate. "Cholas" are identified by their emblematic clothing: the *pollera* (a full layered

skirt), elegant shawl, and distinctive hat (which varies by region). The diverse meanings associated with the term in the 1940s are discussed more fully below. On the history of the pollera, and its transformation into a self-conscious mark of identity, see Barragán, "Entre polleras, lliqllas y ñañacas."

55 Klein, *Parties and Political Change in Bolivia*, 374; República de Bolivia, Ministerio de Gobierno, Justicia e Inmigración, *Ley Electoral*, 88–90.

56 Lourdes Zabala, "Las Madres de la Política," 4.

57 See José Valdivieso, "La igualdad de los hijos ante la ley"; *El País*, 30 December 1944, 1 January 1945; José Antonio Zegada, "Declaración judicial de la paternidad"; Zegada, "La organización de la familia ante nuestra legislación."

58 See República de Bolivia, *Redactor de la Convención Nacional de 1945, Sesiones extraordinarias*, 2:504–6, 700.

59 Ibid., 516–17.

60 Trigo, *Las constituciones de Bolivia*, 482.

61 *La Calle*, 2 August 1945. See also *La Calle*, 4 August 1945; República de Bolivia, *Redactor de la Convención Nacional de 1945, Sesiones extraordinarias*, 2:806–7, 823, 826, 648–49, 537–40.

62 República de Bolivia, *Redactor de la Convención Nacional de 1945, Sesiones extraordinarias*, 2:556–57, 564, 639, 648–49, 807.

63 On the broader Latin American context, see Stepan, *"The Hour of Eugenics,"* esp. 106, 120; Stern, "Responsible Mothers and Normal Children," esp. 372–73.

64 On the influence of eugenics in Bolivia, see Zulawski, *Unequal Cures*, esp. chap. 5.

65 República de Bolivia, *Redactor de la Convención Nacional de 1945, Sesiones extraordinarias*, 2:697–99. The arguments replicate Cuban views (Stoner, *From the House to the Street*).

66 On such trends elsewhere in Latin America, see Stepan, *"The Hour of Eugenics,"* esp. 110. Like advocates of similar measures in Vargas's Brazil, Bolivian politicians may have viewed such protection as a means to build national vigor. On Brazil, see Stepan, *"The Hour of Eugenics,"* 168.

67 República de Bolivia, *Redactor de la Convención Nacional de 1945, Sesiones extraordinarias*, 2:837.

68 *La Calle*, 2 September 1945.

69 *El País*, 17, 25 August 1945. See also *Los Tiempos*, 18 August 1945.

70 República de Bolivia, *Redactor de la Convención Nacional de 1945, Sesiones ordinarias*, 1:181–84; *El País*, 5 September 1945.

71 *La Calle*, 16 August 1945, 8.

72 Ibid., 17 August 1945. On working women's support for the concubinato law, see also Dibbits et al., *Polleras libertarias*, 55; *La Calle*, 16 August 1945, 8.

73 Stephenson, *Gender and Modernity in Andean Bolivia*, 70–72, 175; Antonio Díaz Villamil, *La niña de sus ojos*; Carlos Medinaceli, *La Chaskañawi*.

74 Stephenson, *Gender and Modernity in Andean Bolivia*, 38–50.

75 For additional evidence, see Stephenson, *Gender and Modernity in Andean Bolivia*, 22.

76 In 1937 Busch established another major holiday: Indian Day. This event con-

tinued to be celebrated each August, but it was a less consequential occurrence than Heroínas/Mothers Day.

77 República de Bolivia, *Proyectos de Ley de la Convención Nacional de 1945*, 1:560–61; Araoz, *Nuevo digesto de legislación boliviana*, 1:243–44. For the debate, see República de Bolivia, *Redactor de la Convención Nacional de 1945, Sesiones extraordinarias*, 2:436–58.

78 *El Imparcial*, 26 May 1944.

79 República de Bolivia, *Anuario Administrativo de 1944*, 302–3; República de Bolivia, *Anuario Administrativo de 1927*.

80 Gotkowitz, "Commemorating the *Heroínas*," 217–25.

81 *Cholita* is a softened, acceptable form of address; the term *chola* is often used as an insult.

82 *El País*, 26 May 1944.

83 See Jael Bueno, "La Sociedad 'Hijas del pueblo,' orígenes y desarrollo"; Bueno, "La mujer cochabambina"; Gotkowitz, "Commemorating the *Heroínas*." On market women in La Paz, see Dibbits et al., *Polleras libertarias*; Lehm and Rivera, *Los artesanos libertarios y la ética del trabajo*; Medinaceli, *Alternando la rutina*.

84 Raimundo Grigoriú Sánchez de Lozada, "Bolivia," 93; Bueno, "La Sociedad 'Hijas del pueblo,' orígenes y desarrollo," 4–5. Catholic Action had its takeoff during an ironic revival of church power under Toro and Busch. A series of Eucharistic Congresses convened in various towns culminated in the Segundo Congreso Eucarístico Nacional of 1939. The Hijas del Pueblo marched at one such event, carrying the Bolivian flag.

85 *Actas de la Sociedad "Hijas del Pueblo 27 de Mayo,"* Primer Tomo, "Acta de Fundación" (I am grateful to Doña Alcira Patiño, honorary president of the Hijas del Pueblo, for sharing the *Actas* with me); *El Imparcial*, 15 September 1947, 5. See also Bueno, "La Sociedad 'Hijas del pueblo,' orígenes y desarrollo," 5. Some date the founding to 1939 (*El Imparcial*, 27 May 1947, 4). On the military's role, see *El Diario*, 13 May 1942. See also *El Imparcial*, 15 September 1947.

86 *El Imparcial*, 26 May 1944, 4.

87 *El Comercio*, 19 May 1926, 3.

88 Ruth Marina Mendoza, "El Mercado 25 de Mayo como espacio comunicacional," 28–29.

89 Ibid., 109–10; *El País*, 25 August 1944, 8; 1 October 1944, 8; 24 December 1944, 4.

90 On the history of the market, its internal structure, and its contemporary social dynamics, see Mendoza, "El Mercado 25 de Mayo como espacio comunicacional," 98–111. For a vivid description, see Díaz Villamil, *La niña de sus ojos*. On Cochabamba markets, see also Larson, *Cochabamba*, chap. 10.

91 On urban discontent, see Klein, *Parties and Political Change in Bolivia*; Lehm and Rivera, *Los artesanos libertarios y la ética del trabajo*, 75–80.

92 *El Imparcial*, 25 May 1944, 8; 26 May 1944, 4.

93 *El País*, 28 May 1944, 8.

94 *El Imparcial*, 26 May 1944, 1.

95 Ibid., 23 May 1944, 2; 27 May 1947, 4.

96 *El País*, 28 May 1944, 8.

97 *Actas de la Sociedad "Hijas del Pueblo 27 de Mayo,"* Primer Tomo, "Acta de Fundación," 25 May 1941.

98 Ibid., "Asamblea general del 25 de mayo de 1943."

99 *El Imparcial*, 1 June 1944, 8.

100 Ibid., 26 May 1944, 1.

101 *El País*, 26 May 1944, 4.

102 Ibid., 28 May 1944, 8; 24 May 1944, 5; *El Imparcial*, 23, 24 May 1944. The road was not completed until 1954.

103 *El Imparcial*, 27 May 1944, 1; *El País*, 27 May 1944, 3–4.

104 *La Calle*, 27 May 1944, 2.

105 Gotkowitz, "Commemorating the *Heroínas*," 220–21.

106 See *La Calle*, 27 May 1945, 4.

107 Anna Davin, "Imperialism and Motherhood," 87–91. See also Karin Hausen, "Mothers, Sons and the Sale of Symbols and Goods," and "Mother's Day in the Weimar Republic."

108 *El Diario*, 22, 23 May 1942. On post–Chaco War concerns about motherhood and the birthrate, see Zulawski, *Unequal Cures*, chap. 4.

109 *El País*, 28 May 1944, 1.

110 *La Calle*, 28 May 1944, 5.

111 Gotkowitz, "Commemorating the *Heroínas*," 220–21.

112 *El País*, 28 May 1944, 8.

113 Ibid., 26 May 1945, 4.

114 República de Bolivia, *Redactor de la Convención Nacional de 1943, Sesiones extraordinarias*, 2:487–99.

115 On such dynamics, see Gilbert Joseph and Daniel Nugent, "Popular Culture and State Formation in Revolutionary Mexico."

116 William Beezley, Cheryl English Martin, and William French, "Introduction"; Eric Van Young, "Conclusion"; Lomnitz, *Deep Mexico, Silent Mexico*, 162–63.

117 Humberto Solares, *Historia, espacio y sociedad*.

118 Klein, *Parties and Political Change in Bolivia*, 270, 273, 377–78. Although Villarroel promoted domestic agricultural production, he also increased food imports in an effort to address the longstanding crisis. Price trends continued upward, but the cost of living, which rose dramatically under Toro and Busch, leveled off during the 1940s. Villarroel was nevertheless compelled to address tensions that had built up over the preceding fourteen years (Gallo, *Taxes and State Power*, 47–53; Klein, *Parties and Political Change in Bolivia*, 347 n. 1, citing CEPAL 1958 report, 62–63; Wilkie, *The Bolivian Revolution and U.S. Aid since 1952*, 3).

119 *Los Tiempos*, 16 June 1945, 4.

120 *El País*, 26 September 1945, 4.

121 Ibid., 15 January 1944, 8.
122 *Los Tiempos*, 17 March 1945, 5; 20 March 1945, 5; 25 March 1945, 5; *El País*, 11 October 1946, 5. See also *El País*, 19 July 1944, 4.
123 *Los Tiempos*, 7 June 1945, 8.
124 *El País*, 19 July 1944, 5.
125 *Los Tiempos*, 6 April 1945, 5. For more on the campaign to regulate markets, see *Los Tiempos*, 3 July 1946, 3; *Los Tiempos*, 4 July 1946, 5. See also *El País*, 25 August 1944, 8; 1 October 1944, 8; 24 December 1944, 4.
126 *Los Tiempos*, 18 January 1945, 2; 1 October 1946, 3.
127 *El País*, 28 June 1946, 4.
128 Ibid., 31 August 1946. See also *Los Tiempos*, 22 February 1945, 5; 28 February 1945, 5; 1 March 1945, 5.
129 *Los Tiempos*, 3 July 1946, 3.
130 *El País*, 12 October 1946, 4. For more on the conflicts, see *Los Tiempos*, 8 March 1945, 5; 1 October 1946, 3; *El Imparcial*, 27 March 1945, 4; 10 April 1945, 4; *El País*, 18 June 1946, 4
131 Lehm and Rivera, *Los artesanos libertarios y la ética del trabajo*, 36–38, 75.
132 *El Imparcial*, 27 March 1945, 4.
133 *Los Tiempos*, 1 October 1946, 3.
134 Ibid., 7 April 1945, 6; *El País*, 24 December 1944, 4.
135 Gotkowitz, "Trading Insults."
136 *Los Tiempos*, 1 October 1946, 3.
137 Spitzer, *Hotel Bolivia*, 166, 168–73.
138 Klein, *Parties and Political Change in Bolivia*, 377–78.
139 See Dibbits et al., *Polleras libertarias*.
140 See Lehm and Rivera, *Los artesanos libertarios y la ética del trabajo*, 82–83.

✳ *Seven* The 1945 Indigenous Congress

1 *La Razón*, 11 May 1945.
2 On the centrality of a culture of legality to the making of nation states, see Comaroff, "Foreword," ix–xi.
3 Lázaro Cárdenas, *Primer Congreso Indigenista Interamericano*. For the presentations by Bolivian delegates, see *Educación*, IV, 1940, esp. 103–8; Finot, *Sobre el problema del indio*. On the interamerican congress, and the contradictions of Mexico's varied indigenista projects, see Dawson, *Indian and Nation*.
4 On the continental quest for definitions, see Manuel Gamio, "La identificación del indio"; Oscar Lewis and Ernest Maes, "Base para una nueva definición práctica del indio."
5 *El País*, 11 November 1944.
6 "Primer Congreso, Recomendaciones," 10. In USNA, RG 59, 824.401/5-3045.
7 *El País*, 23 May 1945.
8 Condori and Ticona, *El escribano de los caciques apoderados*, 126.
9 *La Calle*, 13 August 1942 (cited in Antezana and Romero, *Historia de los sindicatos campesinos*, 86–88).

10 *La Calle*, 12 August 1942, 5.

11 Ibid., 21 August 1943, 4.

12 Ibid., 21 October 1945.

13 Mitchell, "The Limits of the State," 94.

14 República de Bolivia, *Redactor de la Convención Nacional de 1945, Sesiones ordinarias*, 4:110. In other contexts, gamonal may also refer to a rural boss.

15 Villarroel, *Mensaje a la H. Convención Nacional de 1944*, 61.

16 Dandler and Torrico, "From the National Indigenous Congress to the Ayopaya Rebellion," 354; Vallejos, *Tata Fermín*, 10.

17 *El Nacional*, 8 February 1945.

18 See the speech quoted in René González Torres and Luis Iriarte Ontiveros, *Villarroel*, 153–54.

19 On indigenista intellectuals and "local arenas of struggle," see Gould, *To Die in This Way*, 192–99.

20 On the composition of the committee, see Dandler and Torrico, "From the National Indigenous Congress to the Ayopaya Rebellion," 341–44.

21 *Los Tiempos*, 5 April 1945, 5.

22 Dandler and Torrico, "From the National Indigenous Congress to the Ayopaya Rebellion," 341.

23 Rivera, *Oprimidos pero no vencidos*, 63; Ranaboldo, *El camino perdido*, 83. According to the Oficial Mayor of the Ministry of Education, it was the Oruro FOL that called on the government to convene the Indigenous Congress. See USNA, RG 59, 824.402/2-1545, p. 3.

24 Lora, *Historia del movimiento obrero boliviano, 1933–1952*, 208.

25 Ranaboldo, *El camino perdido*, 83–86; Rivera, *Oprimidos pero no vencidos*, 63.

26 *La Razón*, 8 March 1945, 7.

27 On such politics of authenticity, see María Elena García and José Antonio Lucero, "Un País Sin Indígenas?"

28 *El Diario*, 30 December 1944; *Boletín Indigenista* 5:2 (June 1945): 116–17.

29 Dandler and Torrico, "From the National Indigenous Congress to the Ayopaya Rebellion," 341.

30 *Congreso Indigenal Boliviano en la Ciudad de La Paz, 2 de febrero de 1945* (hereafter *Congreso Indigenal*). In USNA, RG 59, 824.00/4-2345.

31 *El Diario*, 30 December 1944. See also *El Imparcial*, 4 February 1945, p. 5.

32 *El Diario*, 30 October 1944, p. 4. For Ramos' petition, see *El Diario*, 19 October 1944, p. 9. The "elected by Indians" quote is from *Congreso Indigenal*, 3.

33 ALP, PE, Caja 313, 1930–44. Decrees of 1941 gave the Ministry of Education and Indigenous Affairs responsibility for adjudicating complaints from Indians (Flores Moncayo, *Legislación boliviana del indio*, 402-06).

34 Although Bolivia's voting population remained small until 1952, its size doubled between 1940 and 1951; mineworkers clearly played a significant role in the elections of these years (see Whitehead, "Miners as Voters"). Whether or not peasant electoral participation increased, and, if so, how such participation took place, is not entirely clear. But the evidence suggests that Indians and peasants took part in the public demonstrations that accompanied electoral

contests of the 1940s, and that candidates sometimes made campaign promises to them (for an example, see *El País*, 4 April 1946, 5; *Los Tiempos*, 24 May 1946, 5). Indeed, the MNR was accused of undertaking an intensive effort to teach Indians to write so they could register to vote; and notaries were supposedly instructed to accept the mere ability to sign one's name as fulfillment of the literacy requirement (see *Los Tiempos*, 11 April 1946, p. 4). On peasant participation in the 1947 elections, see chapter 8. As discussed in the conclusion, the MNR backed a legislative proposal in 1945 to grant voting rights to illiterate people.

35 *Congreso Indigenal*, 2–3.

36 Ibid., 3. The statement suggests that Ramos's movement competed for support and authority with other indigenous movements. Another prominent 1940s activist, who defended Ramos Quevedo after his arrest (see below) but was not in full agreement with him, was Antonio Alvarez Mamani (Mamani Alvarez). An underlying point of disagreement between the two leaders apparently had to do with the very definition of "Indian." Like the government, the Comité Indigenal led by Ramos focused its attention on people involved in agricultural labor. From Alvarez Mamani's perspective, the Indigenous Congress should take into account the entire indigenous population ("todos los aborígenes de la República"), including the fishermen who lived on the shores of Lake Titicaca, the *calleguayas* (Andean herbalists), the men who herded cattle on eastern ranches, the mineworkers, and the rubber tappers (*La Calle*, 20 March 1945, 3; see also *La Noche*, 7 February 1945). For Alvarez Mamani's views of Ramos Quevedo (and of the caciques apoderados), see Ranaboldo, *El camino perdido*, 83–88, 91–101. On Alvarez and the Indigenous Congress, see also Blanco, *Antonio Alvarez Mamani*.

37 "Primer Congreso, Principales Ponencias," 8. In USNA, RG 59, 824.401/7-1845.

38 *Congreso Indigenal*, 3, 4, 6. For more on Ramos's views, see *La Noche*, 10 February 1945; *Los Tiempos*, 4 February 1945. Use of all-uppercase words in the quotations throughout this chapter follows the Spanish-language original.

39 *Congreso Indigenal*, 4.

40 *Congreso Indigenal*, 4; *Ultima Hora*, 30 January 1945; *El Diario*, 18 December 1944.

41 *Congreso Indigenal*, 4, 6. See also *El Diario*, 18 December 1944; *El País*, 15 December 1944.

42 Dandler and Torrico, "From the National Indigenous Congress to the Ayopaya Rebellion," 344.

43 USNA, RG 59, 824.401/5-2945, 2; Dandler and Torrico, "From the National Indigenous Congress to the Ayopaya Rebellion," 344; De Jong, "En la sombra de Totora."

44 Dandler and Torrico, "From the National Indigenous Congress to the Ayopaya Rebellion," 344; *Congreso Indigenal*, 4. For sample petitions, see "Primer Congreso, Recomendaciones."

45 *Pregón*, 8 June 1945.

46 Ranaboldo, *El camino perdido*, 106.

47 *El País*, 16 February 1945, 5; *Los Tiempos*, 4 February 1945.

48 The quotes in this and the following paragraph are from *El País*, 16 February 1945, 5.

49 Abercrombie, "La fiesta del carnaval postcolonial en Oruro," 289–91, 313–14.

50 *Congreso Indigenal*, 5.

51 *El Diario*, 18, 21, 30 December 1944; *El País*, 16 February 1945.

52 *El Diario*, 21 December 1944.

53 USNA, RG 59, 824.401/2-1545, 1; *El Diario*, 30 December 1944.

54 *La Razón*, 21 January 1945.

55 Antezana and Romero, *Historia de los sindicatos campesinos*, 101; *Claridad*, 4 February 1945; *Ultima Hora*, 3 February 1945; *La Razón* 4, [1?], February 1945.

56 *La Razón*, 31 January 1945.

57 Condori and Ticona, *El escribano de los caciques apoderados*, 125.

58 Dandler and Torrico, "From the National Indigenous Congress to the Ayopaya Rebellion," 345–48; *Los Tiempos*, 5 April 1945.

59 *La Noche*, 1 February 1945; *Ultima Hora*, 3 February 1945.

60 USNA, RG 59, 824.401/3-145.

61 Choque, "Las rebeliones indígenas de la post-guerra del Chaco," 42–43. On the unrest in Cochabamba, and Ramos Quevedo's role in it, see USNA, RG 84, Cochabamba Consulate, General Records, 1945, Vol. V, Box 9.

62 USNA, RG 59, 824.401/5-2945, 11. From April to December 1944, Nogales was minister of agriculture; in December 1944 he replaced Quinteros as minister of government.

63 USNA, RG 59, 824.401/5-345. The oficial mayor is the subsecretary of a government ministry and responsible for its internal operations.

64 *Los Tiempos*, 29 March, 5 April 1945.

65 USNA, RG 59, 824.00/4-2345.

66 Choque, *Historia de una lucha desigual*, 110; Dandler and Torrico, "From the National Indigenous Congress to the Ayopaya Rebellion," 350; *Los Tiempos*, 25 March 1945.

67 Ranaboldo, *El camino perdido*, 83.

68 USNA, RG 59, 824.401/5-345.

69 USNA, RG 59, 824.00/4-2745; *La Razón*, 26 April 1945; USNA, RG 59, 824.00/5-145; *El País*, 15 May 1945, 3.

70 "Primer Congreso, Recomendaciones," 17.

71 USNA, RG 59, 824.00/4-2345.

72 Pérez, *Warisata*, 279–81.

73 USNA, RG 59, 824.401/5-2945; Federación Rural de Cochabamba, *Memoria de la tercera conferencia nacional de agricultura, ganadería e industrias derivadas realizada en Cochabamba*, 29; "Primer Congreso, Recomendaciones."

74 Antezana and Romero, *Historia de los sindicatos campesinos*.

75 USNA, RG 59, 824.401/5-2945.

76 USNA, RG 59, 824.42/9-1845. In addition to promoting educational projects, U.S.

344 ★ NOTES TO PAGES 214-20

advisers such as Maes sponsored research on rural labor systems. The work was part of an agreement between the ministries of agriculture of both countries that aimed to increase agricultural production and solve the "food problem." See USNA, RG 166, Box 517, Labor-Land Policies, 1949-46; Box 513, Folder Agr. 1947-46; *La Noche*, 31 May 1946.

77 Kenneth Lehman, *Bolivia and the United States*, 77–87; Kevin Healy, *Llamas, Weavings, and Organic Chocolate*, 19–29.

78 USNA, RG 59, 824.00/4-1145 (translation by the U.S. Embassy).

79 This analysis draws on Drake, "Introduction," xi–xxxiii.

80 USNA, RG 59, 824.401/5-2945, p. 2. Participation by Chilina and other lowland delegates has not been studied. But we know that Santos Aireyu, one of the most important Chiriguano (Ava-Guaraní) chiefs of the era, participated as a delegate for Caipipendi (near Camiri, Santa Cruz). Personal communication, Erick Langer, March 2000; USNA, RG 59, 824.401/5-3045, p. 20.

81 *Pregón*, 8 June 1945; Ranaboldo, *El camino perdido*, 64.

82 Dandler and Torrico, "From the National Indigenous Congress to the Ayopaya Rebellion," 343.

83 *La Razón*, 12 May 1945; USNA, RG 59, 824.401/5-2945, p. 2.

84 AHPC, Exp., Ramos . . . con los colonos de la Finca de Choroco, 1944, 8; Dandler and Torrico, "From the National Indigenous Congress to the Ayopaya Rebellion," 341–42.

85 USNA, 824.401/5-2945, 2.

86 Choque, "Las rebeliones indígenas de la post-guerra del Chaco," 45.

87 USNA, RG 59, 824.00/4-2345.

88 USNA, RG 59, 824.401/5-2945; Choque, "Las rebeliones indígenas de la post-guerra del Chaco," 45-46.

89 "Primer Congreso, Principales Ponencias," Advertencias.

90 This paragraph and the next draw on "Primer Congreso, Principales Ponencias," 1–12.

91 Ibid., 13–14.

92 Ibid., 33.

93 USNA, RG 59, 824.401/7-1845; USNA, RG 59, 824.401/5-2945. The MNR itself initially took this position (MNR, *Sus bases y principios de acción inmediata*, 44).

94 "Primer Congreso, Principales Ponencias," 36.

95 Ibid., 15–19.

96 Ibid., 16–18. On conflicts over educational policy and its gendered characteristics during the post-1940 conservative turn of the Consejo Nacional de Educación, see Larson, "Capturing Indian Bodies, Hearths and Minds"; Stephenson, *Gender and Modernity in Andean Bolivia*, 120–28.

97 "Primer Congreso, Recomendaciones," Apéndice.

98 AHHCN, 300, letter from the Jefe de Redacción to the Oficial Mayor de la H. Convención Nacional, 27 April 1945.

99 Choque, "Las rebeliones indígenas de la post-guerra del Chaco," 44.

100 As discussed in chapter 4, Paz Estenssoro and Guevara Arze spoke in favor of land reform proposals at the 1938 constitutional convention (i.e., before the MNR party was established in 1941). For the proposal they backed after the party's creation, see República de Bolivia, *Proyectos de ley de la H. Convención Nacional, 1944*, 52–56; *El País*, 28 October 1944, 5.

101 USNA, RG 59, 824.00/4-1145.

102 Ibid.; USNA, RG 59, 824.00/4-2345.

103 USNA, RG 59, 824.00/4-1145 (translation by the U.S. Embassy).

104 Miguel Bonifaz, "El problema agrario-indígena en Bolivia," 277.

105 USNA, RG 59, 824.401/5-2545, 4 (translation by the U.S. Embassy).

106 "Primer Congreso, Principales Ponencias," 32.

107 Ibid., 14.

108 *El País*, 15 May 1945.

109 Dandler and Torrico, "From the National Indigenous Congress to the Ayopaya Rebellion," 356-61.

110 *Pregón*, 29 June 1945. Chipana Ramos himself helped spread news of the decrees to many rural areas (Hugo Romero Bedregal, "Integración y politicización en una sociedad compuesta," 83).

111 "Primer Congreso, Recomendaciones," Apéndice; USNA, RG59, 824.401/5-2945, 8-11.

112 *Congreso Indigenal*, 5. For the emphasis on the respect that education could bring, see also 6.

113 On local authorities' state linkages, and performative powers of the law, see Andrés Guerrero, "The Construction of a Ventriloquist's Image," 586–90.

114 Dandler and Torrico, "From the National Indigenous Congress to the Ayopaya Rebellion," 356.

115 Ibid., 356–61. On the sit-down strikes, see also Antezana and Romero, *Historia de los sindicatos campesinos*, 123–27; Romero Bedregal, "Integración y politización en una sociedad compuesta."

116 On the La Paz strikes, see Choque, *Historia de una lucha desigual*, 105–20; *Los Tiempos*, 19 December 1945, 4.

117 *El Diario*, 10 September 1946.

118 Vallejos, *Tata Fermín*, 8, 29–31.

119 *Los Tiempos*, 13, 22 December 1945; Vallejos, *Tata Fermín*, 12–13, 19–20; Arias, "La política y sus modelos en la relación con el Estado boliviano," 70–71. See also *Informe del Prefecto, Superintendente de Hacienda y Minas del Departamento, Cnl. Alberto Arauz*, 135.

120 *Los Tiempos*, 11 June 1946, 5. See also *El Diario*, 3 July 1946.

121 Vallejos, *Tata Fermín*, 20.

122 This official was charged to mediate rural conflicts. Indeed, Calvi was sometimes called the "Mediator for the Indigenous Class." He was hardly a neutral figure, however. Calvi's duties included enforcing Juzgado de Trabajo decisions such as orders of eviction. Colonos in some cases attacked or denounced him for his arbitrary acts.

346 * NOTES TO PAGES 225-34

123 *El País*, 29 December 1945, 26 May 1946; *El Diario*, 3 July 1946. See also *Informe del Prefecto, Superintendente de Hacienda y Minas del Departamento, Cnl. Alberto Arauz*, 152.

124 *Los Tiempos*, 22 December 1945, 5.

125 Ibid., 24 May 1946, 5.

126 Ibid., 23 May 1946, 4.

127 Grigoriú Sánchez de Lozada, "Bolivia," 96.

128 República de Bolivia, *Redactor de la Convención Nacional de 1945, Sesiones extraordinarias*, 2:727–43.

129 Siles used these words interchangeably and maintained that the term *indígena* necessarily referred to "the man who works . . . and lives in the countryside." República de Bolivia, *Redactor de la Convención Nacional de 1945, Sesiones extraordinarias*, 2:737.

130 Ibid., 743.

131 Ibid., 757–58.

132 As officials began to view Antonio Alvarez Mamani as a political threat, they concluded similarly that he was a "mestizo" who did not belong to the "authentic indigenous class" and could not be allowed to deceive "true Indians" (*indígenas verdaderos*) (*La Calle*, 12 April 1945, p. 5).

133 *Los Tiempos*, 4 February 1945.

134 *Congreso Indigenal*, 3. According to the U.S. Embassy, Ramos Quevedo was "white" (USNA, RG59, 824.401/5-345).

135 On Ecuador, see Clark, "Race, 'Cuture,' and Mestizaje," 198; Albó, "Andean People in the Twentieth Century," 784.

136 República de Bolivia, *Redactor de la Convención Nacional de 1945, Sesiones extraordinarias*, 2:750–51, 756.

137 *El País*, 25 May 1946.

138 Federación Rural de Cochabamba, *Memoria de la tercera conferencia nacional de agricultura, ganadería e industrias derivadas realizada en Cochabamba*, 31

139 *El Imparcial*, 31 October 1945. For the debate, see República de Bolivia, *Redactor de la Convención Nacional de 1945, Sesiones ordinarias*, 4:107–59.

140 Rivera, *Los terratenientes de Cochabamba*, 120; *El País*, 25 May 1946.

141 SNRA, *Evaluación de la reforma agraria boliviana*, 2:44.

142 Vallejos, *Tata Fermín*, 10.

✳ *Eight* The 1947 Cycle of Unrest

1 Klein, *Parties and Political Change in Bolivia*, 381.

2 Whitehead, "Bolivia since 1930," 530–39; "Bolivia," 120–38. On the rallies and the threat they posed, see Simmons, *Palca and Pucara*, 197; Reinaga, *Tierra y libertad*, 29–33; SNRA, *Evaluación de la reforma agraria boliviana*, 2:60–62.

3 See Rivera, *Oprimidos pero no vencidos*, 66–75; Antezana and Romero, *Historia de los sindicatos campesinos*, 123–68; Harris and Albó, *Monteras y guardatojos*,

NOTES TO PAGES 235-38 * 347

71–72; Gabriel Ponce Arauco, "Los alzamientos campesinos de 1947"; Dandler, "Politics of Leadership, Brokerage and Patronage in the Campesino Movement of Cochabamba," 103–27; Dandler, and Torrico, "From the National Indigenous Congress to the Ayopaya Rebellion"; Choque, "Las rebeliones indígenas de la post-guerra del Chaco." The most important studies of the Ayopaya uprising are those by Dandler, and Dandler and Torrico. The authors demonstrate the close connections between the rebellion, the 1945 Indigenous Congress, and Villarroel's personal investment in indigenous rights and justice. They disassociate the rebellion from the question of the land. There are no full-length studies of other loci of unrest.

4 On these similarities, see Gordillo, *Campesinos revolucionarios en Bolivia*, 194–209.

5 Leslie Bethell and Ian Roxborough, "Introduction."

6 *El Diario*, 30 May 1948.

7 Ibid., 15 April 1947. See also Enrique Hertzog, *Mensaje al H. Congreso Ordinario de 1948*, 84-85.

8 Hertzog, *Mensaje al H. Congreso Ordinario de 1947*, 64; Whitehead, "Bolivia," 139–44.

9 ACSJC, AG #1202, 2PP, viuda de Coca vs. Grájeda y otros, 1947, Tercer Cuerpo (incomplete trial record), fol. 142v.

10 *Los Tiempos*, 3 April 1947, 5. In fact, Juan Lechín, head of the mineworkers federation, linked the Ayopaya rebellion with an increase in the chicha tax. See Lupe Cajías, *Juan Lechín*, 101.

11 ACSJC, AG #1202, fols. 69v–71.

12 Ponce, "Los alzamientos campesinos de 1947," 112, 122 n. 11, 127. See also *El Imparcial*, 15 February 1947, 1; *El País*, 14 March 1947.

13 See, above all, Dandler and Torrico, "From the National Indigenous Congress to the Ayopaya Rebellion."

14 My analysis draws much inspiration from Serulnikov's work on collective violence in Northern Potosí ("Disputed Images of Colonialism"; "Andean Political Imagination in the Late Eighteenth Century").

15 Thomson, *We Alone Will Rule*, 44–54; Rasnake, *Domination and Cultural Resistance*, 76–80. Several of the defendants were hilacatas; when questioned, they denied that they had participated in the uprising. Although some of the accused alcaldes refused to obey the cabecillas, most of them, in contrast, admitted to carrying out Grájeda's orders (ACSJC, AG#1202, fols. 68v, 81–82, 186v–187, 101v–102v).

16 Dandler, "Politics of Leadership, Brokerage and Patronage in the Campesino Movement of Cochabamba," 104 n. 21.

17 ACSJC, AG #1202, fol. 15v; see also fols. 23v, 26v, 151v–152.

18 Dandler, "Politics of Leadership, Brokerage and Patronage in the Campesino Movement of Cochabamba," 104.

19 Néstor Luis Bolaños, *Prontuario para Jueces parroquiales, corregidores, alcaldes de barrio y alcaldes de campo*.

20 For a glimpse of the various posts on Hacienda Yayani, see fol. 94. The role of the alcalde de campo on haciendas was both to assist the hacienda administrators and to represent the colonos. Although landlords designated this official, they generally selected individuals who enjoyed the colonos respect. It might thus be said that the alcalde de campo in some cases was even elected by the colonos. The position had great ceremonial significance. See Dandler, "Politics of Leadership, Brokerage and Patronage in the Campesino Movement of Cochabamba," 249.

21 ACSJC, AG #1202, fols. 9v, 196v–197; AHPC, Correspondencia, Telegram to the Prefect of Cochabamba, 27 November 1942. See also Dandler and Torrico, "From the National Indigenous Congress to the Ayopaya Rebellion."

22 Women did not occupy the alcalde post or earn the label "cabecilla," but they intervened in Ayopaya and other twentieth-century strikes and rebellions as guards, spies, and rabble-rousers who used gendered taunts to stir the men to action. See, for example, ACSJC, AG#1202, fols. 67v–68.

23 Thomson, *We Alone Will Rule*, 46–47.

24 *Los Tiempos*, 3 April 1947, 5.

25 ACSJC, AG #1202, fols. 6–6v.

26 Ibid.

27 Ibid., fols. 91–91v, 101v–102v, 107, 6–9v. See also *Los Tiempos* 3 April 1947, 5.

28 ACSJC, AG #1202, fols. 89–89v. Muñoz was also known as Barrios.

29 Ibid., fol. 7.

30 Ibid., fols. 15–15v, 72–72v, 85v, 103v, 107.

31 Ibid., fols. 7v, 10, 73, 84, 91, 103v–104.

32 Ibid., fols. 106v–107, 108. On such identification, see also fols. 108v, 179v.

33 Gordillo, *Campesinos revolucionarios en Bolivia*, 204–5. Grájeda and other local leaders did confer with PIR- and MNR-connected lawyers in the 1940s (Dandler and Torrico, "From the National Indigenous Congress to the Ayopaya Rebellion," 345).

34 Whitehead, "Bolivia," 139–43. On mineworker-MNR relations, see also Dunkerley, *Rebellion in the Veins*, 6–18; Klein, *Parties and Political Change in Bolivia*, 373–76.

35 See, for example, ACSJC, AG #1202, fol. 10v.

36 Ibid., fol. 85v.

37 Ibid., fols. 109–109v.

38 Ibid., fols. 152–152v.

39 Ibid., fol. 101v.

40 Ibid., fols. 191–191v; *El País*, 4 April 1946, 5; *Los Tiempos*, 23 May 1946, 5. Guevara Arze, who like many elites had learned Quechua from a family servant, reportedly drummed up Indian support with inflammatory anti-landlord language; with or without his knowledge, two MNR-affiliated police officials in the area allegedly promised colonos that all the land in the province would be distributed among them if Guevara won. On Guevara Arze's knowledge of Quechua, see Carter Goodrich, "Bolivia in Time of Revolution," 21.

41 ACSJC, AG#1202, fols. 189v–190; Guerrero, "The Construction," 586–87.
42 Ibid., fol. 192v.
43 Ibid., fol. 179v. According to the witness, Ramos tied this outcome to the PIR's triumph.
44 Ibid., fols. 191–192v.
45 This paragraph and the next three are based on ACSJC, AG #791, 2PP, Oficio contra Vargas y otros, 1947.
46 Arias, *Historia de una esperanza*, 30–37, 68.
47 This analysis draws on Rappaport, "Object and Alphabet."
48 Arias, "La política y sus modelos en la relación con el Estado boliviano," 70–72. For another example, see Choque, *Historia de una lucha desigual*, 119: in May 1946 landlords in Muñecas province (La Paz) accused Francisco Chipana Ramos of taking over a hacienda and appointing new hilacatas.
49 For another example of such dynamics, see AHPC, Exp., Cavero, vecino de Punata, 1947.
50 Article 2. Flores Moncayo, *Legislación boliviana del indio*, 424–25.
51 This term is from William Roseberry, "Hegemony and the Language of Contention," 355–66.
52 Article 9. Flores Moncayo, *Legislación boliviana del indio*, 421.
53 ACSJC, AG#1202, fol. 179v.
54 Lehm and Rivera, *Los artesanos libertarios y la ética del trabajo*, 80–89.
55 Revollo, *Mujeres bajo prueba*, 90.
56 Dandler, *El sindicalismo campesino en Bolivia*, 33–34, 110–11. Literacy tests and registration requirements were tightened in 1949 to keep peasants away from that year's election (Dandler, "Politics of Leadership," 42).
57 *Los Tiempos*, 19 January 1947. See also USNA, RG 59, 824.00/1-1447.
58 *El Diario*, 2 February 1947.
59 ALP, PE, 1947, Caja 481, Expediente de Amparo, Huet.
60 ALP, PE, 1947, Caja 481, Expediente de Amparo, Quisbert. See also ALP, PE, 1947, Caja 483, Lobo Aguilar to the Señor Prefecto.
61 All quotes in this paragraph are from ALP, PE, 1947, Caja 483, Gamarra to the Señor Prefecto del Departamento. For a related conflict, see ALP, PE, Hacienda Collagua (Viacha), 1947, Caja 481, Denuncia, Cardozo.
62 Lehm and Rivera, *Los artesanos libertarios y la ética del trabajo*, 90.
63 *El Diario*, 4 June 1947, 5; *Los Tiempos*, 5 June 1947, 1.
64 Lehm and Rivera, *Los artesanos libertarios y la ética del trabajo*, 92–93; Rivera, *Oprimidos pero no vencidos*, 71–72.
65 ALP, PE, 1947, Caja 481, to the Señor Prefecto del Departamento, from Campos.
66 ALP, PE, Caja 479, Expediente de secuestro de armamentos, 1947. For more examples of altiplano unrest, see *El Diario*, 2 February, 5 June 1947.
67 ALP, Caja 285 (Telegrams, 1947). For a similar case from Murillo Province, see ALP, PE, Caja 482, Ministerio de Gobierno, Justicia e Inmigración, Sección Indígenas, Carapata, 1947.
68 ALP, PE, Caja 481, 1947, Expediente de Amparo, Tiburcio Apaza. The cara-

bineros, a police force organized along military lines, were established by Toro in 1937; the institution was influenced by a police mission from fascist Italy. Juan Ramón Quintana, *Policía y democracia en Bolivia*, 44–48, 368.

69 Albó, *Achacachi*; Ticona and Albó, *La lucha por el poder comunal*.

70 For examples, see ALP, PE, 1947, Caja 481, Informe que eleva el Sr. Subteniente Aracena Sequeiros al Sr. Subprefecto; ALP, PE, 1947, Caja 481, Iturralde de Téllez Reyes to the Subsecretario de Gobierno, Justicia e Inmigración.

71 Albó, *Achacachi*.

72 The manifesto is included in ALP, PE, 1947, Caja 481, Expediente de Denuncia, Nicasio Cardozo. The quotes in this paragraph and the next three are from this manifesto.

73 ACSJC, AG#1202, fols. 106v–108, 179v.

74 Agustín Barcelli, *Medio siglo de luchas sindicales revolucionarias en Bolivia*, 196. See also SNRA, *Evaluación de la reforma agraria boliviana*, 2:62; Reinaga, *Tierra y libertad*, 34. Additional research is needed to substantiate and explicate this staggering crime.

75 Antezana and Romero, *Historia de los sindicatos campesinos*, 155; Hertzog, *Mensaje al H. Congreso Ordinario de 1947*, 27.

76 Articles 9, 10, 11. Flores Moncayo, *Legislación boliviana del indio*, 421–22.

77 Ponce, "Los alzamientos campesinos de 1947," 114.

78 *El Diario*, 4 June 1947.

79 Ponce, "Los alzamientos campesinos de 1947," 122 n. 16, 123 n. 21.

80 Condori and Ticona, *El escribano de los caciques apoderados*, 128–29.

81 Dandler, "Politics of Leadership, Brokerage and Patronage in the Campesino Movement of Cochabamba," 116.

82 See Vallejos, *Tata Fermín*, 13, 23; Arias, "La política y sus modelos en la relación con el Estado boliviano," 70–72.

83 Vallejos, *Tata Fermín*, 10.

84 Choque, *Historia de una lucha desigual*, 120.

85 *Los Tiempos*, 9 February 1947, 5; *El País*, 14 March 1947, 5.

86 *El Diario*, 15 February 1947.

87 USNA, RG 59, 824.00/6-1147. By November the number was 204 (ALP, PE, Caja 482, 1947, Ministerio de Gobierno, Justicia e Inmigración, Sección Asuntos Indígenas, Carapata). On confinement in Ichilo, see also *El Diario*, 17 June 1947.

88 *El Diario*, 4, 13 January, and 6 February, 1948.

89 Ibid., 18, 26, 29 May, and 7 June 1947. See also ALP, PE, Caja 482, 1947, Ministerio de Gobierno, Justicia e Inmigración, Sección Asuntos Indígenas, Carapata.

90 USNA, RG 59, 824.00/6-1147.

91 *El Diario*, 8 January 1950.

92 ALP, PE, Caja 482, 1947, Ministerio de Gobierno, Justicia e Inmigración, Sección Indígenas, Carapata. On repression in the Altiplano, see also *El Diario*, 31 January 1947.

93 Hertzog, *Mensaje al H. Congreso Ordinario de 1947*, 24–25; *El Diario*, 4 June 1947, 5.

94 SNRA, *Evaluación de la reforma agraria boliviana*, 2:72–74.

95 USNA, RG 59, 824.00/6-1147.

96 ALP, PE, 1947, Caja 481, Telegram to the Asesor Jurídico de la Prefectura de La Paz; and From Vallejo et al. to the Señor Prefecto del Departamento; *El Diario*, 24 February 1948.

97 ALP, PE, 1947, Caja 483, Huynoca, Alcalde Ordinario et al. to the Señor Corregidor Territorial; and Expediente de reclamación . . . de Pairumani; ALP, PE, 1947, Caja 481, to the Señor Jefe de la Policía de Seguridad, de Porce.

98 *El Diario*, 21 June 1947. On such problems in Ayopaya, see Ponce, "Los alzamientos campesinos de 1947," 112.

99 Rivera, *Los terratenientes de Cochabamba*, 124. See also ALP, PE, 1947, Caja 482, Ministerio de Gobierno, Justicia e Inmigración, Sección Asuntos Indígenas, Contrato de Sesión Temporal.

100 ALP, PE, 1947, Caja 483, Zapata and Zapata viuda de Aramayo to the Señor Ministro de Gobierno.

101 For Cochabamba, see the above-cited cases. For La Paz, see ALP, PE, 1947, Caja 481, Carrillo et al. to the Señor Ministro de Gobierno; Choque, "Las rebeliones indígenas de la post-guerra del Chaco," 37. In 1946, Ucureña's peasant union lobbied successfully to replace the corregidor with a peasant (Dandler, *El sindicalismo campesino en Bolivia*, 109–10).

102 ALP, PE, 1947, Caja 483, to the Señor Subprefecto de la Provincia Inquisivi. See also ALP, PE, 1947, Caja 483, Expediente de Amparo, Meave, which involved a complaint against the corregidor for failing to carry out an arrest order.

103 ALP, PE, 1947, Caja 481, Guillén to the Señor Prefecto.

104 *Informe del Prefecto, Superintendente de Hacienda y Minas del Departamento, Cnl. Alberto Arauz.*

105 *El Diario*, 6 January 1948.

106 Rivera, *Los terratenientes de Cochabamba*, 124.

107 *El Diario*, 15, 21 December 1948.

108 Antezana and Romero, *Historia de los sindicatos campesinos*; *El Diario*, 1948–52. See also Vallejos, *Tata Fermín*.

109 *El Diario*, 17 June 1949. See also *El Diario*, 29 December 1948.

110 Ibid., 23 September 1946. For an example of a conflict between two neighboring communities, see Expediente de Garantías, Tiburcio Benito, ALP, PE, 1948, Caja 486.

111 *El Diario*, 30 May 1948; Hertzog, *Mensaje al H. Congreso Ordinario de 1948*.

112 Expediente de Amparo, Roberto Saavedra, ALP, PE, 1948, Caja 485.

113 Pablo Cammack, Hacienda Copajira, Guaqui, ALP, PE, 1948, Caja 487. To alleviate the conflict, the owners offered to cede two hectares (about five acres) of land to every colono who wished to leave the property. The owners were U.S. evangelicals who had established several schools in the area.

114 *El Diario*, 7 January 1948. On the assault, and Virgilio Vargas's possible involvement, see ACSJC, AG #3633, 21P, Iriarte Paz vs. Aquino, Agitador Indigenal, 1951.

115 *El Diario*, 22 June 1949.

116 Ibid., 9 September 1948; 6 January 1952. See also *El Diario*, 28 April, 26 September 1950; 20 January, 16 December 1951; 6 and 10 January, 11, 19, 21 February 1952; 9 September, 12 and 31 October, 1, 5, and 7 December 1948. The FSTMB apparently backed the Incahuasi Congress (*El Diario*, 18 October 1949).

117 Antezana and Romero, *Historia de los sindicatos campesinos*, 169–202; *El Diario*, 29 September, 4 October 1949; 29 January 1950. See also Albó, *Achacachi*, 18, 24–29; *El Diario*, 30 May, 20 October 1948; Hertzog, *Mensaje al H. Congreso Ordinario de 1948*, 24–25, 82–85.

118 See, for example, Gordillo, *Campesinos revolucionarios en Bolivia*, 207–9; Ponce, "Los alzamientos campesinos de 1947," 113, 122.

119 On such scope in eighteenth-century Bolivia, see Thomson, *We Alone Will Rule*. On the "diversity of peasant consciousness and political horizons," see also Stern, "New Approaches to the Study of Peasant Rebellion and Consciousness," 9, 13–15.

120 ACSJC, AG #1202, 2PP, fol. 101v.

121 Ibid., fols. 16, 73, 81v, 189v.

122 Ibid., fols. 81v, 83v–84, 85v–86, 87v–88, 102v, 103v, 104v–105, 108v.

123 Ibid., 110.

124 Ibid., fol. 102.

125 Ibid., fols. 84–84v.

126 Ibid., fols. 85–85v.

127 Ibid., fols. 191v–192v.

128 My analysis of the "real significance" of the law and its "practical content" draws on Serulnikov, *Subverting Colonial Authority*, 147.

✳ Conclusion and Epilogue

1 Klein, *Bolivia*, 231. Ninety people died in Oruro, and four hundred in La Paz; elsewhere the revolution triumphed without bloodshed (Dunkerley, *Rebellion in the Veins*, 39; Zavaleta, "Consideraciones generales sobre la historia de Bolivia," 98–99).

2 James Kohl, "Peasant and Revolution in Bolivia"; Klein, *Bolivia*, 231.

3 Klein, *Bolivia*, 231–32; Dunkerley, *Rebellion in the Veins*, 49, 99; James Malloy, "Revolutionary Politics," 122. At the outset it appeared that the militias might fully replace state security forces, but Paz Estenssoro instead slowly rebuilt the army with U.S. aid (Whitehead, "The Bolivian National Revolution," 30). Estimates range widely, but one source suggests that as many as 110,000 peasants gained possession of arms after 1952 (cited in Dunkerley, *Rebellion in the Veins*, 99). For a more modest approximation, see Knight, "The Domestic Dynamics of the Mexican and Bolivian Revolutions," 86 n. 88.

4 Luis Tapia, "Ciclos políticos del siglo XX boliviano," 284. For a recent discussion of the diversity of projects and visions invested in the 1952 revolution, see Magdalena Cajías de la Vega, "Introducción."

5 Dunkerley, *Rebellion in the Veins*, 85.

6 Susan Eckstein, *The Impact of Revolution*, 32–33.

7 Kohl, "Peasant and Revolution in Bolivia," 252. Most works emphasize the takeovers in Cochabamba. Just five months after the revolution triumphed, landlords in some cases were also being driven off land in La Paz (Dwight Heath, "Bolivia's Law of Agrarian Reform," 47).

8 Antezana and Romero, *Historia de los sindicatos campesinos*. On the scope of the unrest, which also encompassed Oruro, northern Potosí, and parts of Sucre, see also Dunkerley, *Rebellion in the Veins*, 65–74.

9 Kohl, "Peasant and Revolution in Bolivia," 252, 254.

10 Klein, *Bolivia*, 234.

11 Kohl, "The Role of the Peasant in the Bolivian Revolutionary Cycle"; Gordillo, *Campesinos revolucionarios en Bolivia*, 213–15; Albó, "Andean People in the Twentieth Century"; Whitehead, "The Bolivian National Revolution," 45.

12 Albó, "Andean People in the Twentieth Century," 798–99.

13 Kohl, "Peasant and Revolution in Bolivia," 251; *El Diario*, 13 May, 10 December 1952. These petitions have not been studied systematically, and we do not know how extensive they were. Chrungalla is probably in the department of La Paz. The conflict there, as reported in *El Diario*, involved the comunarios' complaint against an indigenous apoderado, but the article suggests that the plaintiffs were reviving a longstanding petition against landlords.

14 Rivera, " 'Pedimos la revisión de límites,' " 642.

15 On Ucureña's consequential role, see Dandler, *El sindicalismo campesino en Bolivia*.

16 The approach is inspired by Roseberry, "Beyond the Agrarian Question in Latin America," 320.

17 Robert Alexander, *The Bolivian National Revolution*, xviii–xiv, 278–79.

18 Goodrich, "Bolivia in Time of Revolution," 5. See also Cole Blasier, "Studies of Social Revolution," 32, 50; Malloy, "Revolutionary Politics," 117; Malloy, *Bolivia*, 188.

19 The major exceptions are the works by Dandler and by Antezana and Romero.

20 See, for example, Dwight Heath, Charles Erasmus, and Hans Buechler, *Land Reform and Social Revolution in Bolivia*.

21 Heath, "Conclusions and Implications for Action," 371–72; Andrew Pearse, "Peasants and Revolution, Part II," 403, 405; Heath, "Bolivia's Law of Agrarian Reform," 42–43; Malloy, "Revolutionary Politics," 126; Alexander, *The Bolivian National Revolution*, 60. See also Kohl's critique of this conclusion in "Peasant and Revolution in Bolivia," 243–44, 258–59.

22 Pearse, "Peasants and Revolution, Part II," 402.

23 Kohl, "Peasant and Revolution in Bolivia."

24 Ibid. See also Kohl, "The Role of the Peasant in the Bolivian Revolutionary Cycle."

25 Katarismo is a political movement that emerged in La Paz and the Aymara altiplano in the early 1970s. Driven by the vision of a plurinational state and the

recuperation of native culture and identity, Katarismo led to the formation of an independent peasant federation that ended the Military-Peasant Pact established by General Barrientos in the 1960s. It also resulted in several political parties that gained national representation in the early 1990s. Urban migrants—who experienced daily the discrimination of the city—played a particularly important role in the movement (Albó, "Andean People in the Twentieth Century," 824–26, 839–49).

26 Stephenson, "Forging an Indigenous Counterpublic Sphere," 105; Rivera, "Taller de historia oral andina," 84–86.

27 Rivera's history courses at the Universidad Mayor de San Andrés (UMSA) in La Paz were an important forum for Aymara researchers who later affiliated with the workshop (Stephenson, "Forging an Indigenous Counterpublic Sphere," 105).

28 Rivera Cusicanqui, *Oprimidos pero no vencidos*, 73–74. Kohl notes additionally that peasant mobilization was part of the MNR's contingency plan if the first urban uprising failed; he also recorded the strategic inclusion of some rural activists in the 1949 civil war and 1952 revolution ("Peasant and Revolution in Bolivia").

29 Gordillo, *Campesinos revolucionarios en Bolivia*. See esp. 25–28.

30 Ibid., 31–32.

31 In her analysis of the roots of agrarian radicalism in the Cochabamba valleys, Larson also rethinks the revolution from the bottom up. Her emphasis on rural–urban networks and sites of popular culture has methodological implications for understanding revolutionary movements in other locations (*Cochabamba*, chap. 10).

32 Víctor Hugo Cárdenas, "La lucha de un pueblo," 520.

33 Ibid., 521.

34 Heath, "Bolivia's Law of Agrarian Reform," 47.

35 William Carter, "Revolution and the Agrarian Sector," 242.

36 For a critique of such approaches, see Whitehead, "The Bolivian National Revolution," 45.

37 Blasier, "Studies of Social Revolution," 35; Eckstein, *The Impact of Revolution*.

38 Flores Moncayo, *Legislación boliviana del indio*, 464–67. The law also mentioned the military, the clergy, and the police, who had been denied suffrage rights under oligarchic rule.

39 Ibid., 464. The law granted voting rights to all single men and women over twenty-one years of age and all married men and women over eighteen years of age, "no matter their level of education, occupation, or income" (466).

40 See Heath, "Bolivia's Law of Agrarian Reform," 37, 42–43.

41 República de Bolivia, Dirección Nacional de Informaciones, *Bolivia*, 76.

42 Dunkerley, *Rebellion in the Veins*, 50.

43 Ibid., 50–51; Marco Peñaloza, "Entrevista a James Dunkerley"; Malloy, "Revolutionary Politics," 118–19; Whitehead, "The Bolivian National Revolution," 40, 47.

44 Malloy, "Revolutionary Politics," 119; Whitehead, "The Bolivian National Revolution," 32–33.

45 Malloy, "Revolutionary Politics," 120–22; Dunkerley, *Rebellion in the Veins*, 58; Thorn, "The Economic Transformation," 172.

46 Eckstein, *The Impact of Revolution*, 32; Antonio García, "La reforma agraria y el desarrollo social," 413; Malloy, "Revolutionary Politics," 121–23; Thorn, "The Economic Transformation," 163; Dunkerley, *Rebellion in the Veins*, 43–44, 57–58, 60, 63.

47 Dunkerley, *Rebellion in the Veins*, 65.

48 Klein, *Bolivia*, 228.

49 For a more recent assessment that emphasizes the reform's achievements, see Whitehead, "The Bolivian National Revolution," 49 n. 13.

50 Lagos, *Autonomy and Power*, 52.

51 William Thiesenhusen, *Broken Promises*.

52 Heath, "Land Reform, Revolution, and Development," 55; Lagos, *Autonomy and Power*, 52; Thorn, "The Economic Transformation," 161; Carter, "Revolution and the Agrarian Sector," 244; Dunkerley, *Rebellion in the Veins*, 73. Although the agricultural enterprise was defined by a system of salaried labor, the law permitted some labor tenants "as long as capital investment be doubled and modern techniques be used" (Heath, "Land Reform, Revolution, and Development," 55). The agrarian reform law banned sharecropping, but the practice was briefly relegalized before the government of General René Barrientos once again abolished it in the 1960s. Along with agricultural enterprises, the law permitted ranches as large as 140,000 acres.

53 See Healy, *Llamas, Weavings, and Organic Chocolate*, 13; Lagos, *Autonomy and Power*, 65.

54 Dunkerley, *Rebellion in the Veins*, 74; Merilee Grindle, *State and Countryside*, 138.

55 Carter, "Revolution and the Agrarian Sector," 247–48; Barbara Léons and William Léons, "Land Reform and Economic Change in the Yungas," 281; Garcia, "La reforma agraria y el desarrollo social," 443; Lagos, *Autonomy and Power*, 49, 57. On Cochabamba haciendas, the peasants who received the most benefits were those who were both smallholders and colonos in the pre-reform era; this particular group not only retained plots already owned but received parcels of former hacienda land (Lagos, *Autonomy and Power*, 54–55, 57).

56 Lagos, "Livelihood, Citizenship, and the Gender of Politics," 211, 217. See also Léons and Léons, "Land Reform and Economic Change in the Yungas," 283–84.

57 Gordillo, *Campesinos revolucionarios en Bolivia*, 254–56.

58 Ticona and Albó, *La lucha por el poder comunal*, 170; García, "La reforma agraria y el desarrollo social," 421–22.

59 Ticona and Albó, *La lucha por el poder comunal*, 171, 180; Albó, "Andean People in the Twentieth Century"; Langer, *Economic Change and Rural Resistance in Southern Bolivia*.

60 This paragraph is based on Gordillo, *Campesinos revolucionarios en Bolivia*, 86–91.

61 The agrarian reform did not anticipate and failed to address the conflicts that emerged when comunarios and ex-comunarios pursued restoration of the very

land that was being claimed by former colonos. Such disputes became acute in areas where hacienda expansion had taken place in the first decades of the twentieth century, that is to say, precisely where the caciques apoderados had been based (see García, "La reforma agraria y el desarrollo social," 413, 421–22). On intrapeasant conflict in the months leading up to and following the reform, see Kohl, "Role of the Peasant," chaps. 4 and 6.

62 On a similar campaign against alcaldes mayores in Mizque and Aiquile, see Vallejos, *Tata Fermín*, 15.

63 Gordillo, *Campesinos revolucionarios en Bolivia*, 44–45.

64 *El País*, 7, 17, 19, 26 June 1952.

65 See, for example, Antezana and Romero, *Historia de los sindicatos campesinos*, 229. Such incidents led landlords to abandon their opposition to the decrees. Gordillo, *Campesinos revolucionarios en Bolivia*, 50. On the importance of the decrees after 1952, see also Gordillo, *Campesinos revolucionarios en Bolivia*, 40, 45; Dunkerley, *Rebellion in the Veins*, 67; Kohl, "Peasant and Revolution in Bolivia," 249–51.

66 Knight, "Social Revolution," 179-80; Roger Chartier, *Cultural Origins*, 192.

67 See, for example, Knight, "The Domestic Dynamics of the Mexican and Bolivian Revolutions"; Theda Skocpol, *Social Revolutions in the Modern World*; Jeff Goodwin, *No Other Way Out*, 3–34. For discussion and critique of literatures on revolutionary origins, see Gould, *To Lead as Equals*, 292–305; Knight, "Social Revolution."

68 In explaining the revolution's origins, scholars give different weight to the role of the Depression versus the role of the Chaco War. For a range of views, see Klein, *Parties and Political Change in Bolivia*; Whitehead, "Bolivia since 1930"; Dunkerley, "The Origins of the Bolivian Revolution in the Twentieth Century"; Albó, "Andean People in the Twentieth Century."

69 On ideals, practices, and conceivability, see Chartier, *The Cultural Origins of the French Revolution*.

70 Dunkerley, "The Origins of the Bolivian Revolution in the Twentieth Century."

71 República de Bolivia, *Redactor de la Convención Nacional de 1945, Sesiones ordinarias*, 5:618–19. See also USNA, RG 59, 824.0131/11-2745.

72 *Los Tiempos*, 11 April 1946; Roberto Jordán Pando, "Participación y movilización campesinas en el proceso revolucionario boliviano," 926-27. The debate apparently ended before a vote was taken, but both sources suggest that the proposal was close to being approved.

73 Choque, *Historia de una lucha desigual*, 136. See also Ticona's discussion of Manuel Chachawayna's extraordinary campaign for congressional deputy in 1927. Chachawayna was Bolivia's first Aymara candidate for Congress.

74 This idea draws on Chartier, *On the Edge of the Cliff*, 74–75.

75 On the role that such alternatives play, see Katz, *The Life and Times of Pancho Villa*, 54–56.

76 Rivera, "Reclaiming the Nation."

77 Ibid.

78 See Lagos, *Autonomy and Power*; Rivera, *Oprimidos pero no vencidos*.

79 This made the unions a vehicle of clientelism and state aid, but it also made them a potential means of independent political representation (Albó, "Andean People in the Twentieth Century," 799).

80 Rivera, *Oprimidos pero no vencidos*, 110–11; Malloy, *Bolivia*, 208; Katherine Barnes de von Marschall and Juan Torrico Angulo, "Cambios socio-económicos en el Valle Alto de Cochabamba desde 1952."

81 Rivera, *Oprimidos pero no vencidos*, 111.

82 On the ways that history "shapes our approach to the present and to what we perceive as threatening," see Patricia Williams, "Extrajudicial Activism," 11.

BIBLIOGRAPHY

✳ Archival Sources

COCHABAMBA, BOLIVIA
Archivo de la Corte Superior de Justicia de Cochabamba
  (ACSJC)
Archivo del Arzobispado de Cochabamba
Archivo del Juzgado de Instrucción de Cliza (AJIC)
Archivo del Juzgado de Instrucción de Punata
Archivo del Juzgado de Partido de Cliza
Archivo del Notario de Cliza
Archivo de *Los Tiempos*, Colección Salamanca
Archivo Histórico de la Prefectura de Cochabamba (AHPC)
Archivo Municipal de Punata
Archivo Municipal de Quillacollo
Archivo Privado de Eduardo Arze Loureiro

LA PAZ, BOLIVIA
Archivo de La Paz (ALP)
Archivo del Servicio Nacional de la Reforma Agraria
Archivo Histórico del Honorable Congreso Nacional de Bolivia
  (AHHCN)

SUCRE, BOLIVIA
Archivo y Biblioteca Nacionales de Bolivia

UNITED STATES
Land Tenure Center Library, University of Wisconsin, Madison
U.S. National Archives (USNA)

Record Group (RG) 59, State Department Records
Record Group 84, Records of Foreign Service Posts, Consular Reports
Record Group 166, Records of the Foreign Agricultural Service

✳ Newspapers and Periodicals

América Indígena. Mexico City
Arte y Trabajo. La Paz
Boletín Indigenista. Mexico City
La Calle. La Paz
El Comercio. Cochabamba
El Diario. La Paz
El Ferrocarril. Cochabamba
Gaceta Municipal. Cochabamba
El Heraldo. Cochabamba
El Imparcial. Cochabamba
El País. Cochabamba
El Republicano. Cochabamba
Los Tiempos. Cochabamba
Revista Jurídica. Cochabamba

✳ Other Sources

Abercrombie, Thomas. "La fiesta del carnaval postcolonial en Oruro: Clase, etnicidad y nacionalismo en la danza folklórica." *Revista Andina* 10.2 (1992): 279–352.
——. *Pathways of Memory and Power: Ethnography and History among an Andean People*. Madison: University of Wisconsin Press, 1998.
Abrams, Philip. "Notes on the Difficulty of Studying the State (1977)." *Journal of Historical Sociology* 1.1 (1988): 58–89.
Aguirre, Nataniel. *Juan de la Rosa*. Cochabamba: Los Tiempos/Los Amigos del Libro, 1987 [1885].
Aguirre, Nataniel, and Fidel Araníbar. *Intereses nacionales*. Cochabamba: Imprenta 14 de setiembre, 1885.
Albó, Xavier. *Achacachi: Medio siglo de lucha campesina*. La Paz: CIPCA, 1979.
——. "From MNRistas to Kataristas to Katari." In Stern, ed. *Resistance, Rebellion, and Consciousness in the Andean Peasant World*, 1987.
——. "Andean People in the Twentieth Century." In Frank Salomon and Stuart B. Schwartz, eds. *The Cambridge History of the Native Peoples of the Americas*, Vol. 3.2. Cambridge: Cambridge University Press, 2000.
Albó, Xavier, and Josep Barnadas. *La cara campesina de nuestra historia*. La Paz: Universo, 1985.
Alexander, Robert. *The Bolivian National Revolution*. New Brunswick, N.J.: Rutgers University Press, 1958.
Aljovín de Losada, Cristóbal. "Representative Government in Peru: Fiction and Reality, 1821–1845." Ph.D. diss., University of Chicago, 1996.

Antezana E., Luis. *Las grandes masacres y levantamientos indígenas en la historia de Bolivia (1850–1975)*. La Paz: Juventud, 1994.

Antezana E., Luis, and Hugo Romero B. *Historia de los sindicatos campesinos: Un proceso de integración nacional en Bolivia*. La Paz: Consejo Nacional de Reforma Agraria, 1973.

Appelbaum, Nancy, Anne Macpherson, and Karin Rosemblatt. "Introduction: Racial Nations." In Appelbaum, Macpherson, and Rosemblatt, eds. *Race and Nation in Modern Latin America*, 2003.

———, eds. *Race and Nation in Modern Latin America*. Chapel Hill: University of North Carolina Press, 2003.

Aramayo, Avelino. *Apuntes sobre el congreso de 1870*. Sucre: Tipografía del Progreso, 1871.

Aranzaes, Nicanor. *Las revoluciones de Bolivia*. La Paz: La Prensa, 1918.

Araoz, Mario C. *Nuevo digesto de legislación boliviana*. Vols. 1–3. La Paz: Editorial "Renacimiento," 1929.

Ardaya, Gloria S. *Política sin rostro: Mujeres en Bolivia*. Caracas: Editorial Nueva Sociedad, 1989.

Arguedas, Alcides. *Pueblo enfermo*. La Paz: Juventud, 1982 [1909, 1937].

Ari, Waskar. "Race and Subaltern Nationalism: AMP Activist-Intellectuals in Bolivia, 1921–1964." Ph.D. diss., Georgetown University, 1996.

Arias, Juan Félix [Waskar Ari]. *Historia de una esperanza: Los apoderados espiritualistas de Chuquisaca 1936–1964*. La Paz: Aruwiyiri, 1994.

———. "La política y sus modelos en la relación con el Estado boliviano y el movimiento indígena del sur de Cochabamba (1936–1947)." In Pablo Regalsky, ed. *Tata Fermín: Llama viva de un Yachaq*. Cochabamba: CENDA, 1995.

Arze Aguirre, René. "El cacicazgo en las postrimerías coloniales." *Avances* 1 (1978): 47–50.

———. *Guerra y conflictos sociales: El caso rural boliviano durante la campaña del chaco*. La Paz: CERES, 1987.

Avila, Federico. *El problema de la unidad nacional (del caudillismo bárbaro a la restauración nacionalista)*. La Paz: Editorial Universo, 1938.

Barcelli S., Agustín. *Medio siglo de luchas sindicales revolucionarias en Bolivia, 1905–1955*. La Paz, 1957.

Barnadas, Josep M. *Apuntes para una historia aymara*. La Paz: CIPCA, 1978.

Barnes de von Marschall, Katherine, and Juan Torrico Angulo. "Cambios socioeconómicos en el Valle Alto de Cochabamba desde 1952: Los pueblos provinciales de Cliza, Arani, Sacaba, Tarata y Mizque." La Paz: Servicio Nacional de Reforma Agraria, 1971.

Barragán, Rossana. "Identidades indias y mestizas: Una intervención al debate." *Autodeterminación* 10 (1992): 17–44.

———. "Entre polleras, lliqllas y ñañacas: Los mestizos y la emergencia de la tercera república." In Silvia Arze et al., eds. *Etnicidad, economía y simbolismo en los Andes*. La Paz: HISBOL/IFEA/SBH-ASUR, 1992.

———. *Indios, mujeres y ciudadanos: Legislación y ejercicio de la ciudadanía en Bolivia (siglo XIX)*. La Paz: Diálogo, 1999.

———. "Los elegidos: En torno a la representación territorial y la re-unión de los poderes en Bolivia entre 1825–1840." In Marta Irurozqui, ed. *La mirada esquiva: Reflexiones históricas sobre la interacción del estado y la ciudadanía en los andes (Bolivia, Ecuador y Perú), siglo XIX*. Madrid: CSIC, 2005.

———. "La representación territorial y la ciudadanía en el sistema directo e indirecto (Bolivia, 1825–1880)." Unpublished manuscript, 2005.

———. *Asambleas Constituyentes: Ciudadanía y elecciones, convenciones y debates (1825–1971)*. La Paz: Muela del Diablo, 2006.

Barragán, Rossana, and Florencia Durán. "El despojo en el marco de la ley." In Taller de Iniciativas en Estudios Rurales y Reforma Agraria, ed. *Collana: Conflicto por la tierra en el Altiplano*. La Paz: Fundación Tierra, 2003.

Beezley, William, Cheryl English Martin, and William French. "Introduction: Constructing Consent, Inciting Conflict." In Beezley, Martin, and French, eds. *Rituals of Rule, Rituals of Resistance*, 1994.

———, eds. *Rituals of Rule, Rituals of Resistance: Public Celebrations and Popular Culture in Mexico*, Wilmington, Del.: Scholarly Resources, 1994.

Bethell, Leslie, ed. *The Cambridge History of Latin America*. Cambridge: Cambridge University Press, 1984–95.

Bethell, Leslie, and Ian Roxborough, "Introduction: The Postwar Conjuncture in Latin America: Democracy, Labor, and the Left." In Bethell and Roxborough, eds. *Latin America between the Second World War and the Cold War*, 1992.

———, eds. *Latin America between the Second World War and the Cold War, 1944–1948*. Cambridge: Cambridge University Press, 1992.

Blanco, Federico. *Diccionario geográfico de la República de Bolivia. Departamento de Cochabamba*, Vol. 2. La Paz: Taller Tipo-Litográfico, 1901.

Blanco, J. *Antonio Alvarez Mamani: Historia de un dirigente campesino*. [La Paz?]: n.p., 1969.

Blasier, Cole. "Studies of Social Revolution: Origins in Mexico, Bolivia, and Cuba." *Latin American Research Review* 2.3 (1967): 28–64.

Bliss, Katherine. *Compromised Positions: Prostitution, Public Health, and Gender Politics in Revolutionary Mexico City*. University Park: Pennsylvania State University Press, 2001.

Bolaños, Néstor Luis. *Prontuario para Jueces parroquiales, corregidores, alcaldes de barrio y alcaldes de campo*. Potosí: Tipografía Artística, 1928.

Bonifaz, Miguel. "El problema agrario-indígena en Bolivia." *Universidad de San Francisco Xavier* 16.37–38 (1950): 137–286.

Bonilla, Heraclio. "Peru and Bolivia from Independence to the War of Pacific." In Bethell, *The Cambridge History of Latin America*. Vol. 3, 1985.

Bourdieu, Pierre. "The Force of Law: Toward a Sociology of the Juridical Field," with an introduction by Richard Terdiman. *Hastings Law Journal* 38 (1987): 805–53.

Brienen, Marten. "The Clamor for Schools: Rural Education and the Development of State-Community Contact in Highland Bolivia, 1930–1952." *Revista de Indias* 62.226 (2002): 615–50.

Bronfman, Alejandra. *Measures of Equality: Social Science, Citizenship, and Race in Cuba, 1902–1940*. Chapel Hill: University of North Carolina Press, 2004.

Bueno, Jael. "La Sociedad 'Hijas del pueblo,' orígenes y desarrollo." *Nosotras/Opinión*.

——. "La mujer cochabambina: En las primeras décadas del siglo XX." *Nosotras/Opinión*.

Bueno, Jael, et al. "Los trabajadores cochabambinos." *Estudios Sociales* 2.10 (1989).

Burbank, Jane. *Russian Peasants Go to Court: Legal Culture in the Countryside, 1905–1917*. Bloomington: Indiana University Press, 2004.

Bustos, Romualdo, and Alejandro Mirones. *Cuestión social jurídica: Indios semi-instruidos atentan la propiedad privada. Las autoridades condescienden en sus pretensiones atentatorias*. Cochabamba: Imprenta la Opinión, 1924.

Cajías, Lupe. *Juan Lechín: Historia de una leyenda*. La Paz: Los Amigos del Libro, 1994.

Cajías de la Vega, Magdalena. "Introducción: Historias y memorias del 52." *Historias* 6 (2003): 5–9.

Capriles, R. Remberto, and Gastón Arduz Eguía. *El problema social en Bolivia: Condiciones de vida y de trabajo*. La Paz: Editorial Fenix, 1941.

Cárdenas, Lázaro. *Primer Congreso Indigenista Interamericano*. Mexico City: Secretaría de Gobernación, 1940.

Cárdenas, Víctor Hugo. "La lucha de un pueblo." In Xavier Albó, ed. *Raíces de América: El mundo aymara*. Madrid: Alianza Editorial, 1988.

Carter, William. *Comunidades aymaras y reforma agraria en Bolivia*. Mexico City: Instituto Indigenista Interamericano, 1967.

——. "Revolution and the Agrarian Sector." In Malloy and Thorn, eds. *Beyond the Revolution*, 1971.

Centeno, Miguel Angel. *Blood and Debt: War and the Nation-State in Latin America*. University Park: Pennsylvania State University Press, 2002.

Chambers, Sarah C. "Little Middle Ground: The Instability of a Mestizo Identity in the Andes, Eighteenth and Nineteenth Centuries." In Appelbaum, Macpherson, and Rosemblatt, eds. *Race and Nation in Modern Latin America*, 2003.

Chartier, Roger. *The Cultural Origins of the French Revolution*. Translated by Lydia G. Cochrane. Durham: Duke University Press, 1991.

——. *On the Edge of the Cliff: History, Language, and Practices*. Translated by Lydia G. Cochrane. Baltimore: Johns Hopkins University Press, 1997.

Chomsky, Aviva, and Aldo Lauria-Santiago, eds. *Identity and Struggle at the Margins of the Nation-State: The Laboring Peoples of Central America and the Hispanic Caribbean*. Durham: Duke University Press, 1998.

Choque Canqui, Roberto. "De la defensa del ayllu a la creación de la República del Qullasuyu." In Encuentro de Estudios Bolivianos, eds. *Historia y evolución del movimiento popular*. Cochabamba: UNRISD/CERES, 1986.

——. *La masacre de Jesús de Machaca*. La Paz: Chitakolla, 1987.

——. "La escuela indigenal: La Paz (1905–1938)." In Choque et al., eds. *Educación indígena*, 1992.

——. "Las rebeliones indígenas de la post-guerra del Chaco." *Data* 3 (1992): 37–53.

——. *Historia de una lucha desigual*. La Paz: UNIH-PAKAXA, 2005.

Choque, Roberto, et al., eds. *Educación indígena: ¿Ciudadanía o colonización?* La Paz: Aruwiyiri, 1992.

Choque, Roberto, and Esteban Ticona. *Sublevación y masacre de 1921 (Jesús de Machaqa: La marka rebelde 2)*. La Paz: CIPCA/CEDOIN, 1996.

———. *Sublevación y masacre de Jesús de Machaqa de 1921*. La Paz: Fundación Diálogo, 1998.

Clagett, Helen L. *Guide to the Law and Legal Literature of Bolivia*. Washington, D.C.: Library of Congress, 1947.

Clark, N. Kim. "Race, 'Cuture,' and Mestizaje: The Statistical Construction of the Ecuadorian Nation, 1930–1950." *Journal of Historical Sociology* 11.2 (1998): 185–211.

———. "Racial Ideologies and the Quest for National Development: Debating the Agrarian Problem in Ecuador (1930–50)." *Journal of Latin American Studies* 30 (1998): 373–93.

Claure, Toribio. *Una escuela rural en Vacas*. La Paz: Universo, 1949.

Cleven, N. Andrew. *The Political Organization of Bolivia*. Washington, D.C.: Carnegie Institution of Washington, 1940.

Coatsworth, John H. "Patterns of Rural Rebellion in Latin America: Mexico in Comparative Perspective." In Katz, ed. *Riot, Rebellion, and Revolution*, 1988.

Comaroff, John L. "Foreword." In Mindie Lazarus-Black and Susan F. Hirsch, eds. *Contested States, Law, Hegemony and Resistance*. New York: Routledge, 1994.

———. "Legality, Modernity, and Ethnicity in Colonial South Africa: An Excursion in the Historical Anthropology of Law." In Richard Rawlings, ed. *Law, Society, and Economy: Centenary Essays for the London School of Economics and Political Science, 1895–1995*. Oxford: Oxford University Press, 1997.

———. "Colonialism, Culture, and the Law: A Foreword." *Law and Social Inquiry* 26.2 (2001): 305–14.

Condarco Morales, Ramiro. *Zárate, El "Temible" Willka: Historia de la rebelión indígena de 1899*. La Paz: Talleres Gráficos, 1965.

Conde Mamani, Ramón. "Lucas Miranda Mamani: Maestro indio Uru-Murato." In Choque et al., eds. *Educación indígena*, 1992.

Condori Chura, Leandro, and Esteban Ticona Alejo. *El escribano de los caciques apoderados: Kasikinakan purirarunakan qillqiripa*. La Paz: HISBOL/THOA, 1992.

Conklin, Alice L. "Colonialism and Human Rights: A Contradiction in Terms? The Case of France and West Africa, 1895–1914." *American Historical Review* 103.2 (1998): 419–42.

Conniff, Michael L. "Introduction: Toward a Comparative Definition of Populism." In Conniff, ed. *Latin American Populism in Comparative Perspective*, 1982.

———, ed. *Latin American Populism in Comparative Perspective*. Albuquerque: University of New Mexico Press, 1982.

Cooper, Frederick, Thomas Holt, and Rebecca Scott, eds. *Beyond Slavery: Explorations of Race, Labor, and Citizenship in Postemancipation Societies*. Chapel Hill: University of North Carolina Press, 2000.

Cooper, Frederick, et al. "Introduction." In Cooper, Holt, and Scott, eds. *Beyond Slavery*, 2000.

Coordinadora de Historia, ed. *Historias bajo la lupa: La Guerra Federal.* La Paz: La Razón, n.d.

Cornejo S., Alberto. *Programas políticos de Bolivia.* Cochabamba: Universitaria, 1949.

Dandler, Jorge. "Politics of Leadership, Brokerage and Patronage in the Campesino Movement of Cochabamba, Bolivia (1935–54)." Ph.D. diss., University of Wisconsin, Madison, 1971.

——. *El sindicalismo campesino en Bolivia: Los cambios estructurales en Ucureña.* Cochabamba: CERES, 1983.

Dandler, Jorge, and Juan Torrico. "From the National Indigenous Congress to the Ayopaya Rebellion: Bolivia 1945–1947." In Stern, ed., *Resistance, Rebellion, and Consciousness in the Andean Peasant World,* 1987.

Davin, Anna. "Imperialism and Motherhood." In Ann Stoler and Frederick Cooper, eds. *Tensions of Empire: Colonial Cultures in a Bourgeois World.* Berkeley: University of California Press, 1997.

Dawson, Alexander. *Indian and Nation in Revolutionary Mexico.* Tucson: University of Arizona Press, 2004.

De Jong, Marianne. "En la sombra de Totora: La historia de una provincia rural en base de testimonios, 1932–1952." Cochabamba: INEDER, 1988.

De la Cadena, Marisol. *Indigenous Mestizos: The Politics of Race and Culture in Cuzco, Peru, 1919–1991.* Durham: Duke University Press, 2000.

——. "Are 'Mestizos' Hybrids?: The Conceptual Politics of Andean Identities." *Journal of Latin American Studies* 37.2 (2005): 259–84.

De la Fuente, Alejandro. *A Nation for All: Race, Inequality, and Politics in Twentieth-Century Cuba.* Chapel Hill: University of North Carolina Press, 2001.

Del Río, Mercedes. "Simbolismo y poder en Tapacarí." *Revista Andina* 8.1 (1990): 77–113.

Delgado, Oscar, and Tomaz Borges, eds. *Reformas agrarias en la América Latina.* Mexico City: Fondo de Cultura Económica, 1965.

Demelas, Marie-Danielle. "Darwinismo a la criolla: El darwinismo social en Bolivia, 1809–1910." *Historia Boliviana* 1.2 (1981): 55–82.

——. "Sobre jefes legítimos y 'vagos': Insurrecciones indias y guerra civil en Bolivia a fines del siglo XIX." *Historia y Cultura* 8 (1985): 51–77.

Díaz Villamil, Antonio. *La niña de sus ojos.* Cochabamba: Los Amigos del Libro, 1988.

Dibbits, Ineke, et al. *Polleras libertarias: Federación Obrera Femenina, 1927–1965.* La Paz: Tahipamu/HISBOL, 1986.

Dorsey, Bruce. "A Case Study of Ex-Hacienda Toralapa in the Tiraque Region of the Upper Cochabamba Valley." University of Wisconsin, Madison, Land Tenure Center, Research Paper No. 65, 1975.

Drake, Paul W. "Conclusion: Requiem for Populism?" In Conniff, ed., *Latin American Populism in Comparative Perspective,* 1982.

——. "Introduction: The Political Economy of Foreign Advisors and Lenders in Latin America." In Paul Drake, ed. *Money Doctors, Foreign Debts, and Economic*

Reforms in Latin America from the 1890s to the Present. Wilmington, Del.: Scholarly Resources, 1994.

Dubois, Laurent. "La République Métissée: Citizenship, Colonialism, and the Borders of French History." *Cultural Studies* 14.1 (2000): 15–34.

——. *A Colony of Citizens: Revolution and Slave Emancipation in the French Caribbean, 1787–1804.* Chapel Hill: University of North Carolina Press, 2004.

Dunkerley, James. *Rebellion in the Veins: Political Struggle in Bolivia, 1952–82.* London: Verso, 1984.

——. *Orígenes del poder militar en Bolivia: Historia del ejército, 1879–1935.* La Paz: Quipus, 1987.

——. "Political Suicide in Latin America." In James Dunkerley, ed., *Political Suicide in Latin America and Other Essays.* London: Verso, 1992.

——. "The Origins of the Bolivian Revolution in the Twentieth Century: Some Reflections." In Grindle and Domingo, eds., *Proclaiming Revolution,* 2003.

Durán Jordán, Florencia, and Ana María Seoane Flores. *El complejo mundo de la mujer durante la Guerra del Chaco.* La Paz: Ministerio de Desarrollo Humano, 1997.

Eckstein, Susan. *The Impact of Revolution: A Comparative Analysis of Mexico and Bolivia.* London: Sage, 1976.

Educación: Revista Mensual de Pedagogía y Orientación Sindical, 4 (June 1940) (Número especial dedicado al Primer Congreso Indigenista Interamericano).

Estrada, Teodomiro. *Pequeña monografía del departamento de Cochabamba.* Oruro, Bolivia: Imprenta de El Tribuno, 1904.

Farcau, Bruce W. *The Chaco War: Bolivia and Paraguay, 1932–1935.* Westport, Conn.: Praeger, 1996.

Federación Rural de Cochabamba. *Memoria de la tercera conferencia nacional de agricultura, ganadería e industrias derivadas realizada en Cochabamba, del 12 al 20 de agosto de 1945.* Cochabamba: Editorial Atlantic, 1946.

Fernández, Marcelo Osco. *La ley del ayllu: Práctica de jach'a justicia y jisk'a justicia (justicia mayor y justicia menor) en comunidades aymaras.* La Paz: PIEB, 2000.

Fernández Terán, Roberto. "Transformaciones y prácticas de poder en el ejército boliviano: Hacia la construcción del ciudadano soldado (1932–1940)." *Análisis político* 3.5 (1999): 51–60.

——. "Prensa, radio e imaginario boliviano durante la guerra del Chaco (1932–1935)." Paper presented at the First Regional Conference of Social Scientists. Catholic University of Bolivia, 2000.

Ferrer, Ada. *Insurgent Cuba: Race, Nation, and Revolution, 1868–1898.* Chapel Hill: University of North Carolina Press, 1999.

Fifer, J. Valerie. *Bolivia: Land, Location, and Politics since 1825.* Cambridge: Cambridge University Press, 1972.

Finot, Enrique. *Sobre el problema del indio.* Mexico City, 1940.

Fitzgibbon, Russell H. *The Constitutions of the Americas.* Chicago: University of Chicago Press, 1948.

Flores C., Gonzalo. "Una indagación sobre movimientos campesinos en Bolivia: 1913–1917." La Paz: CERES, 1979.

——. "Levantamientos campesinos durante el período Liberal (1900–1920)." In Fernando Calderón and Jorge Dandler, eds. *Bolivia: La fuerza histórica del campesinado*. Cochabamba: United Nations-CERES, 1984.

Flores Moncayo, José. *Legislación boliviana del indio*. La Paz: Instituto Indigenista Boliviano, 1953.

Forster, Cindy. *The Time of Freedom: Campesino Workers in Guatemala's October Revolution*. Pittsburgh: University of Pittsburgh Press, 2001.

Fraser, Nancy, and Linda Gordon. "Contract versus Charity: Why Is There No Social Citizenship in the United States?" *Socialist Review* 92/3.22 (1992): 45–67.

Gallego, Ferran. *Los orígenes del reformismo militar en América Latina: La gestión de David Toro en Bolivia*. Barcelona: PPU, 1991.

——. *Ejército, nacionalismo y reformismo en América Latina: La gestión de Germán Busch en Bolivia*. Barcelona: PPU, 1992.

Gallo, Carmenza. *Taxes and State Power: Political Instability in Bolivia, 1900–1950*. Philadelphia: Temple University Press, 1991.

Gamio, Manuel. "La identificación del indio." *América Indígena* 6.2 (1946): 99–104.

García, Antonio. "La reforma agraria y el desarrollo social." In Delgado and Borges, eds. *Reformas Agrarias en la América Latina*, 1965.

García, María Elena, and José Antonio Lucero. "Un País Sin Indígenas?: Rethinking Indigenous Politics in Peru." In Nancy Grey Postero and Leon Zamosc, eds. *The Struggle for Indigenous Rights in Latin America*. Brighton: Sussex Academic Press, 2004.

Gill, Lesley. *Precarious Dependencies: Gender, Class and Domestic Service in Bolivia*. New York: Columbia University Press, 1994.

González Torres, René, and Luis Iriarte Ontiveros. *Villarroel, Mártir de sus ideales, y el atisbo de la Revolución Nacional*. La Paz: Don Bosco, 1983.

Goodrich, Carter. "Bolivia in Time of Revolution." In Malloy and Thorn, eds. *Beyond the Revolution*, 1971.

Goodwin, Jeff. *No Other Way Out: States and Revolutionary Movements, 1945–1991*. Cambridge: Cambridge University Press, 2001.

Gordillo, José M. *Campesinos revolucionarios en Bolivia: Identidad, territorio y sexualidad en el Valle Alto de Cochabamba, 1952–1964*. La Paz: Plural, 2000.

Gordillo, José M., and Robert H. Jackson. "Mestizaje y proceso de parcelación en la estructura agraria de Cochabamba (el caso de Sipe-Sipe en los siglos XVIII–XIX)." *HISLA* 10 (1987): 15–37.

Gotkowitz, Laura. "Education and Race in Early-Twentieth-Century Bolivia." Unpublished manuscript, 1991.

——. " '¡No hay hombres!': Género, nación y las Heroínas de la Coronilla de Cochabamba (1885–1926)." In Rossana Barragán, Dora Cajías, and Seemin Qayum, eds. *El siglo XIX en Bolivia y América Latina*. La Paz, Bolivia: Muela del Diablo, 1997.

——. "Commemorating the *Heroínas*: Gender and Civic Ritual in Early-Twentieth-Century Bolivia." In Elizabeth Dore and Maxine Molyneux, eds. *Hidden Histories of Gender and the State in Latin America*. Durham: Duke University Press, 2000.

——. "Trading Insults: Honor, Violence, and the Gendered Culture of Commerce in Cochabamba, Bolivia, 1870s–1950s." *Hispanic American Historical Review* 83.1 (2003): 83–118.

Gould, Jeffrey L. *To Lead as Equals: Rural Protest and Political Consciousness in Chinandega, Nicaragua, 1912–1979.* Chapel Hill: University of North Carolina Press, 1990.

——. *To Die in This Way: Nicaraguan Indians and the Myth of Mestizaje, 1880–1965.* Durham: Duke University Press, 1998.

——. "Revolutionary Nationalism and Local Memories in El Salvador." In Gilbert M. Joseph, ed. *Reclaiming the Political in Latin American History.* Durham: Duke University Press, 2001.

Gould, Jeffrey, and Aldo Lauria-Santiago. " 'They Call Us Thieves and Steal Our Wage' ": Toward a Reinterpretation of the Salvadoran Rural Mobilization, 1929–1931." *Hispanic American Historical Review* 84.2 (2004): 192–237.

Graham, Richard, ed. *The Idea of Race in Latin America, 1870–1940.* Austin: University of Texas Press, 1990.

Grandin, Greg. *The Blood of Guatemala: A History of Race and Nation.* Durham: Duke University Press, 2000.

——. *The Last Colonial Massacre: Latin America in the Cold War.* Chicago: University of Chicago Press, 2004.

Grieshaber, Erwin P. "Survival of Indian Communities in Nineteenth-Century Bolivia." Ph.D. diss., University of North Carolina, Chapel Hill, 1977.

——. "Fluctuaciones en la definición del indio: Comparación de los censos de 1900 y 1950." *Historia Boliviana* 5.1–2 (1985): 45–65.

——. "Resistencia indígena a la venta de tierras comunales en el departamento de La Paz, 1881–1920." *Data* 1 (1991): 113–44.

Grigoriú Sánchez de Lozada, Raimundo. "Bolivia." In Richard Pattee, ed. *El catolicismo contemporáneo en hispanoamérica.* Buenos Aires: Editorial Fides, 1951.

Grindle, Merilee. *State and Countryside: Development Policy and Agrarian Politics in Latin America.* Baltimore: Johns Hopkins University Press, 1986.

Grindle, Merilee S., and Pilar Domingo, eds. *Proclaiming Revolution: Bolivia in Comparative Perspective.* London: Institute of Latin American Studies, University of London; Cambridge, Mass.: David Rockefeller Center for Latin American Studies, Harvard University, 2003.

Grupo Tupac Amaru. *La victoria o la muerte. Al pueblo boliviano, soldados, estudiantes, obreros. Manifiesto del Grupo Tupac Amaru.* n.pl.: n.p., [1934].

Guardino, Peter. *Peasants, Politics, and the Formation of Mexico's National State: Guerrero, 1800–1857.* Stanford: Stanford University Press, 1996.

Gudmundson, Lowell, and Francisco A. Scarano. "Conclusion: Imagining the Future of the Subaltern Past—Fragments of Race, Class, and Gender in Central America and the Hispanic Caribbean, 1850–1950." In Chomsky and Lauria-Santiago, eds. *Identity and Struggle at the Margins of the Nation-State,* 1998.

Guerrero, Andrés. "The Construction of a Ventriloquist's Image: Liberal Discourse and the 'Miserable Indian Race' in Late 19th-Century Ecuador." *Journal of Latin American Studies* 29.3 (1997): 555–90.

Guevara Arze, Wálter. "Manifiesto de Ayopaya." In Wálter Guevara Arze, ed. *Bases para replantear la Revolución Nacional*. La Paz: Juventud, 1988.

Hale, Charles A. "Political and Social Ideas." In Leslie Bethell, ed. *Latin America: Economy and Society, 1870–1930*. Cambridge: Cambridge University Press, 1989.

———. *The Transformation of Liberalism in Late Nineteenth-Century Mexico*. Princeton: Princeton University Press, 1989.

———. "Frank Tannenbaum and the Mexican Revolution." *Hispanic American Historical Review* 75.2 (1995): 215–46.

Hale, Charles R. "Does Multiculturalism Menace? Governance, Cultural Rights and the Politics of Identity in Guatemala." *Journal of Latin American Studies* 34 (2002): 485–524.

Harris, Olivia. "Ethnic Identity and Market Relations: Indians and Mestizos in the Andes." In Larson and Harris, with Tandeter, eds. *Ethnicity, Markets, and Migration in the Andes*, 1995.

Harris, Olivia, and Javier Albó. *Monteras y guardatojos: Campesinos y mineros en el norte de Potosí*. La Paz: CIPCA, 1984.

Hausen, Karin. "Mother's Day in the Weimar Republic." In R. Bridenthal, A. Grossmann, and M. Kaplan, eds. *When Biology Became Destiny: Women in Weimar and Nazi Germany*. New York: Monthly Review Press, 1984.

———. "Mothers, Sons, and the Sale of Symbols and Goods. The German 'Mother's Day.'" In Hans Medick and David Warren Sabean, eds. *Interest and Emotion: Essays on the Study of Family and Kinship*. Cambridge: Cambridge University Press 1984.

Healy, Kevin. *Llamas, Weavings, and Organic Chocolate: Multicultural Grassroots Development in the Andes and Amazon of Bolivia*. Notre Dame, Ind.: University of Notre Dame Press, 2001.

Heath, Dwight. "Bolivia's Law of Agrarian Reform." In Heath, Erasmus, and Buechler, eds. *Land Reform and Social Revolution in Bolivia*, 1969.

———. "Conclusions and Implications for Action." In Heath, Erasmus, and Buechler, eds. *Land Reform and Social Revolution in Bolivia*, 1969.

———. "Land Reform, Revolution, and Development: A Longitudinal Study of the Case of Bolivia." *Lateinamerika* 24.1 (1989): 52–73.

Heath, Dwight B., Charles Erasmus, and Hans Buechler, eds. *Land Reform and Social Revolution in Bolivia*. New York: Praeger, 1969.

Hertzog, Enrique. *Mensaje al H. Congreso Ordinario de 1947*. La Paz, 1947.

———. *Mensaje al H. Congreso Ordinario de 1948*. La Paz, 1948.

Holt, Thomas C. *The Problem of Freedom: Race, Labor, and Politics in Jamaica and Britain, 1832–1938*. Baltimore: Johns Hopkins University Press, 1992.

———. "The Essence of the Contract: The Articulation of Race, Gender, and Political Economy in British Emancipation Policy, 1838–1866." In Cooper, Holt, and Scott, eds. *Beyond Slavery*, 2000.

———. "The First New Nations." In Appelbaum, Macpherson, and Rosemblatt, eds. *Race and Nation in Modern Latin America*, 2003.

Huacani, Carlos, E. Mamani, and José Subirats. *Warisata "Escuela Ayllu": El por qué de un fracaso*. La Paz: CEBIAE, 1978.

Hylton, Forrest. "Tierra común: Caciques, artesanos e intelectuales radicals y la rebellion de Chayanta." In Hylton et al., eds. *Ya es otro tiempo el presente*, 2003.

——. "El federalismo insurgente: Una aproximación a Juan Lero, los comunarios y la Guerra Federal." *T'inkazos* 7.16 (2004): 99–118.

Hylton, Forrest, Felix Patzi, Sergio Serulnikov, and Sinclair Thomson. *Ya es otro tiempo el presente: Cuatro momentos de insurgencia indígena*. La Paz: Muela del Diablo, 2003.

Hylton, Forrest, and Sinclair Thomson. "Ya es otro tiempo el presente." In Hylton et al., *Ya es otro tiempo el presente*, 2003.

Informe del Prefecto, Superintendente de Hacienda y Minas del Departamento, Cnl. Alberto Arauz. Cochabamba: Editorial América, 1945.

Irurozqui, Marta. "¿Qué hacer con el indio?: Un análisis de las obras de Franz Tamayo y Alcides Arguedas." *Revista de Indias* 52.195/196 (1992): 559–87.

——. "Partidos políticos y golpe de estado en Bolivia: La política nacional-popular de Bautista Saavedra, 1921–1925." *Revista de Indias* 54.200 (1994): 137–56.

——. *La armonía de las desigualdades: Elites y conflictos de poder en Bolivia, 1880–1920*. Madrid: Consejo Superior de Investigaciones Científicas, 1994.

——. *"A bala, piedra y palo": La construcción de la ciudadanía política en Bolivia, 1826–1952*. Seville: Diputación de Sevilla, 2000.

——. "El bautismo de la violencia. Indígenas patriotas en la revolución de 1870 en Bolivia." *Historia y Cultura* 28–29 (2003): 149–78.

Jackson, Robert H. "Evolución y persistencia del colonaje en las haciendas de Cochabamba." *Siglo XIX* 3.6 (1988): 145–62.

——. *Regional Markets and Agrarian Transformation in Bolivia: Cochabamba, 1539–1960*. Albuquerque: University of New Mexico Press, 1994.

——, ed. *Liberals, the Church, and Indian Peasants: Corporate Lands and the Challenge of Reform in Nineteenth-Century Spanish America*. Albuquerque: University of New Mexico Press, 1997.

——. "Community and Hacienda in the Bolivian Highlands: Changing Patterns of Land Tenure in Arque and Vacas." In Jackson, ed. *Liberals, the Church, and Indian Peasants*, 1997.

Jacobsen, Nils. *Mirages of Transition: The Peruvian Altiplano, 1780–1930*. Berkeley: University of California Press, 1993.

——. "Liberalism and Indian Communities in Peru, 1821–1920." In Jackson, ed. *Liberals, the Church, and Indian Peasants*, 1997.

Jacobsen, Nils, and Cristóbal Aljovín, eds. *Political Cultures in the Andes, 1750–1950*. Durham: Duke University Press, 2005.

——. "Concluding Remarks: Andean Inflections of Latin American Political Cultures." In Jacobsen and Aljovín, eds. *Political Cultures in the Andes*, 2005.

Jiménez, Michael F. "Class, Gender, and Peasant Resistance in Central Colombia, 1900–1930." In Forrest D. Colburn, ed. *Everyday Forms of Peasant Resistance*. Armonk, N.Y.: M. E. Sharpe, 1989.

Jordán Pando, Roberto. "Participación y movilización campesinas en el proceso revolucionario boliviano," *América Indígena* 32.3 (1972): 907–34.

Joseph, Gilbert, and Daniel Nugent. "Popular Culture and State Formation in Revolutionary Mexico." In Gilbert Joseph and Daniel Nugent, ed. *Everyday Forms of State Formation: Revolution and the Negotiation of Rule in Modern Mexico*. Durham: Duke University Press, 1994.

Katz, Friedrich, ed. *Riot, Rebellion, and Revolution: Rural Social Conflict in Mexico*. Princeton: Princeton University Press, 1988.

———. "Introduction: Rural Revolts in Mexico." In Katz, ed. *Riot, Rebellion, and Revolution*, 1988.

———. "Rural Rebellions after 1810." In Katz, ed. *Riot, Rebellion, and Revolution*, 1988.

———. "The Liberal Republic and the Porfiriato, 1867–1910." In Leslie Bethell, ed. *Mexico since Independence*. Cambridge: Cambridge University Press, 1991.

———. *The Life and Times of Pancho Villa*. Stanford: Stanford University Press, 1998.

Kerber, Linda. "The Meanings of Citizenship." *Journal of American History* 84.3 (1997): 833–54.

Klein, Herbert. "American Oil Companies in Latin America: The Bolivian Experience." *Inter-American Economic Affairs* 18.2 (1964): 47–72.

———. " 'Social Constitutionalism' in Latin America: The Bolivian Experience of 1938." *The Americas* 22.3 (1966): 258–76.

———. *Parties and Political Change in Bolivia, 1880–1952*. Cambridge: Cambridge University Press, 1969.

———. *Bolivia: The Evolution of a Multi-Ethnic Society*. New York: Oxford University Press, 1992.

———. *Haciendas and Ayllus: Rural Society in the Bolivian Andes in the Eighteenth and Nineteenth Centuries*. Stanford: Stanford University Press, 1993.

Knight, Alan. "Social Revolution: A Latin American Perspective." *Bulletin of Latin American Research* 9.2 (1990): 175–202.

———. "Racism, Revolution, and *Indigenismo*: Mexico, 1910–1940." In Graham, ed. *The Idea of Race in Latin America*, 1990.

———. "Populism and Neo-populism in Latin America, especially Mexico." *Journal of Latin American Studies* 30.2 (1998): 223–48.

———. "The Domestic Dynamics of the Mexican and Bolivian Revolutions." In Grindle and Domingo, eds. *Proclaiming Revolution*, 2003.

———. "Is Political Culture Good to Think?" In Jacobsen and Aljovín, eds. *Political Cultures in the Andes*, 2005.

Knudson, Jerry W. "The Bolivian Immigration Bill of 1942: A Case Study in Latin American Anti-Semitism." *American Jewish Archives* 20.1 (1968): 138–59.

Kohl, James V. "The Role of the Peasant in the Bolivian Revolutionary Cycle, 1952–1964." Ph.D. diss., University of New Mexico, 1969.

———. "Peasant and Revolution in Bolivia, April 9, 1952–August 2, 1953." *Hispanic American Historical Review* 58.2 (1978): 238–59.

Kourí, Emilio. "Interpreting the Expropriation of Indian Pueblo Lands in Porfirian Mexico: The Unexamined Legacies of Andrés Molina Enríquez." *Hispanic American Historical Review* 82.1 (2002): 69–117.

——. *A Pueblo Divided: Business, Property, and Community in Papantla, Mexico.* Stanford: Stanford University Press, 2004.

Kuenzli, Gabriela. "La evolución de la revolución liberal: De aymaras liberales a incas ciudadanos." *Historia y Cultura* 28–29 (2003): 253–72.

Lagos, María. *Autonomy and Power: The Dynamics of Class and Culture in Rural Bolivia.* Philadelphia: University of Pennsylvania Press, 1994.

——. "Livelihood, Citizenship, and the Gender of Politics." In David Nugent, ed. *Locating Capitalism in Time and Space: Global Restructurings, Politics, and Identity.* Stanford: Stanford University Press, 2002.

Langer, Erick D. "Labor Strikes and Reciprocity on Chuquisaca Haciendas." *Hispanic American Historical Review* 65.2 (1985): 255–78.

——. "El liberalismo y la abolición de la comunidad indígena en el siglo XIX." *Historia y Cultura* 14 (1988): 59–95.

——. "Land Struggles, Interethnic Alliances and New Kurakas: A New Perspective on the Chayanta Rebellion of 1927." Paper presented at the forty-sixth Congreso Internacional de Americanistas, Amsterdam, Holland, 1988.

——. *Economic Change and Rural Resistance in Southern Bolivia, 1880–1930.* Stanford: Stanford University Press, 1989.

——. "Andean Rituals of Revolt: The Chayanta Rebellion of 1927." *Ethnohistory* 37.3 (1990): 227–53.

Langer, Erick D., and Robert Jackson. "Liberalism and the Land Question in Bolivia, 1825–1920." In Jackson, ed. *Liberals, the Church, and Indian Peasants*, 1997.

Larson, Brooke. *Explotación agraria y resistencia campesina en Cochabamba.* Cochabamba: CERES, 1983.

——. *Colonialism and Agrarian Transformation in Bolivia: Cochabamba, 1550–1900.* Princeton: Princeton University Press, 1988.

——. "Casta y clase: La formación de un campesinado mestizo y mercantil en la región de Cochabamba." *Allpanchis* 1.35/36 (1990): 187–222.

——. *Cochabamba, 1550–1900: Colonialism and Agrarian Transformation in Bolivia.* Expanded ed. Durham: Duke University Press, 1998.

——. "Andean Highland Indians and the Trials of Nation Making during the Nineteenth Century." In Frank Salomon and Stuart B. Schwartz, eds. *The Cambridge History of the Native Peoples of the Americas*, Vol. 3.2. Cambridge: Cambridge University Press.

——. "Forging the Unlettered Indian: The Pedagogy of Race in the Bolivian Andes." Paper presented at conference on Race, Culture, and Power in Latin America. University of Iowa, Iowa City, 2002.

——. "Capturing Indian Bodies, Hearths and Minds: 'El hogar campesino' and Rural School Reform in Bolivia, 1920s–1940s." In Grindle and Domingo, eds. *Proclaiming Revolution*, 2003.

——. *Trials of Nation Making: Liberalism, Race, and Ethnicity in the Andes, 1810–1910.* Cambridge: Cambridge University Press, 2004.

——. "Redeemed Indians, Barbarianized Cholos: Crafting Neocolonial Modernity in Liberal Bolivia, 1900–1910." In Jacobsen and Aljovín, eds. *Political Cultures in the Andes*, 2005.

Larson, Brooke, and Olivia Harris, with Enrique Tandeter, eds. *Ethnicity, Markets, and Migration in the Andes: At the Crossroads of History and Anthropology*. Durham: Duke University Press, 1995.

Larson, Brooke, and Rosario León. "Markets, Power, and the Politics of Exchange in Tapacarí, c. 1780 and 1980." In Larson and Harris, with Tandeter, eds. *Ethnicity, Markets, and Migration*, 1995.

Lauria-Santiago, Aldo. *An Agrarian Republic: Commercial Agriculture and the Politics of Peasant Communities in El Salvador, 1823–1914*. Pittsburgh: University of Pittsburgh Press, 1999.

Lehm A., Zulema, and Silvia Rivera C. *Los artesanos libertarios y la ética del trabajo*. La Paz: THOA, 1988.

Lehman, Kenneth D. *Bolivia and the United States*. Athens: University of Georgia Press, 1999.

Leonard, Olen. *Canton Chullpas: A Socioeconomic Study in the Cochabamba Valley of Bolivia*. Washington, D.C.: U.S. Office of Foreign Agricultural Relations, 1948.

Léons, Barbara, and William Léons. "Land Reform and Economic Change in the Yungas." In Malloy and Thorn, eds. *Beyond the Revolution*, 1971.

Levine, Robert M. *Father of the Poor?: Vargas and His Era*. Cambridge: Cambridge University Press, 1998.

Lewis, Oscar, and Ernest E. Maes. "Base para una nueva definición práctica del indio." *América Indígena* 5.2 (1945): 107–18.

Lofstrom, William Lee. "The Promise and Problem of Reform: Attempted Social and Economic Change in the First Years of Bolivian Independence." Ph.D. diss., Cornell University, Ithaca, N.Y., 1972.

Lomnitz-Adler, Claudio. *Exits from the Labyrinth: Culture and Ideology in the Mexican National Space*. Berkeley: University of California Press, 1992.

———. *Deep Mexico, Silent Mexico: An Anthropology of Nationalism*. Minneapolis: University of Minneapolis Press, 2001.

Lora, Guillermo. *A History of the Bolivian Labour Movement, 1848–1871*. Cambridge: Cambridge University Press, 1977.

———. *Historia del movimiento obrero boliviano, 1933–1952*. La Paz: Los Amigos del Libro, 1980.

Mallon, Florencia. "Indian Communities, Political Cultures, and the State in Latin America, 1780–1990." *Journal of Latin American Studies* 24 (1992): 35–53.

———. *Peasant and Nation: The Making of Postcolonial Mexico and Peru*. Berkeley: University of California Press, 1995.

———. *Courage Tastes of Blood: The Mapuche Community of Nicolás Ailío and the Chilean State, 1906–2001*. Durham: Duke University Press, 2005.

Malloy, James M. *Bolivia: The Uncompleted Revolution*. Pittsburgh: University of Pittsburgh Press, 1970.

———. "Revolutionary Politics." In Malloy and Thorn, eds. *Beyond the Revolution*, 1971.

Malloy, James M., and Richard Thorn, eds. *Beyond the Revolution: Bolivia Since 1952*. Pittsburgh: University of Pittsburgh Press, 1971.

Mamani Capchiri, Humberto. "La educación india en la visión de la sociedad criolla: 1920–43." In Choque et al., eds. *Educación indígena*, 1992.

Mamani Condori, Carlos B. *Taraqu, 1866–1935: Masacre, guerra y "Renovación" en la biografía de Eduardo L. Nina Qhispi*. La Paz: Aruwiyiri, 1991.

Marof, Tristán. *La tragedia del altiplano*. Buenos Aires: Claridad, 1935.

Martínez, Françoise. "El 'indio' en las representaciones de la elite." In Coordinadora de Historia, *Historias bajo la lupa: La Guerra Federal*, n.d.

Mayorga, Fernando. *El discurso del nacionalismo revolucionario*. Cochabamba: CIDRE, 1985.

McCreery, David. "State Power, Indigenous Communities, and Land in Nineteenth Century Guatemala." In Carol Smith, ed. *Indian Communities and the State: Guatemala, 1540–1988*. Austin: University of Texas Press, 1989.

——. *Rural Guatemala: 1760–1940*. Stanford: Stanford University Press, 1994.

Medinaceli, Carlos. *La Chaskañawi*. La Paz: Los Amigos del Libro, 1982 [1947].

Medinaceli, Ximena. *Alternando la rutina: Mujeres en las ciudades de Bolivia, 1920–1930*. La Paz: CIDEM, 1989.

——. "Redefinición de las comunidades." In Coordinadora de Historia, *Historias bajo la lupa: La Guerra Federal*, n.d.

Mehta, Uday. "Liberal Strategies of Exclusion." *Politics and Society* 18.4 (1990): 427–54.

Mendieta Parada, Pilar. "El movimiento de los apoderados 1880–1889." In Coordinadora de Historia, *Historias bajo la lupa: La Guerra Federal*, n.d.

——. "La revolución federal de 1899." In Coordinadora de Historia, *Historias bajo la lupa: La Guerra Federal*, n.d.

——. "Después de Zárate Willka: Los levantamientos indígenas. Periódo liberal (1900–1921)." In Coordinadora de Historia, *Historias bajo la lupa: La Guerra Federal*, n.d.

——. "Iglesia, mundo rural y política: Jacinto Escobar párroco de Mohoza y su participación en la masacre de 1899." *Estudios bolivianos* 8 (1999): 121–68.

——. "El poder de las montañas y la rebelión indígena." *Historia y Cultura* 27 (2001): 71–92.

Mendoza, Zoila. *Shaping Society through Dance: Mestizo Ritual Performance in the Peruvian Andes*. Chicago: University of Chicago Press, 2000.

Mendoza H., Ruth Marina. "El Mercado 25 de Mayo como espacio comunicacional." Lic. thesis, Universidad Privada del Valle, Cochabamba, 1994.

Mitchell, Christopher. *The Legacy of Populism in Bolivia: From the MNR to Military Rule*. New York: Praeger, 1977.

Mitchell, Timothy. "The Limits of the State: Beyond Statist Approaches and Their Critics." *American Political Science Review* 85.1 (1991): 77–96.

Montenegro, Carlos. *Nacionalismo y colonaje*. La Paz: Juventud, 1990 [1944].

Movimiento Nacionalista Revolucionario (MNR). *Sus bases y principios de acción inmediata*. 1942.

Niño-Murcia, Mercedes. " 'Papelito Manda': La literacidad en una comunidad campesina de Huarochirí." In Virginia Zavala, Mercedes Niño-Murcia, and Patricia Ames, eds. *Escritura y sociedad: Nuevas perspectivas teóricas y etnográficas*. Lima: Red para el Desarrollo de las Ciencias Sociales en el Perú, 2004.

Oblitas Poblete, Enrique. *Recurso de amparo*. La Paz: Popular, 1967.

Ochoa, Enrique C. "The Rapid Expansion of Voter Participation in Latin America: Presidential Elections, 1845–1986." In James W. Wilkie and David Lorey, eds. *Statistical Abstract of Latin America*. Vol. 25. Los Angeles: UCLA, 1987.

Patch, Richard. "Social Implications of the Bolivian Agrarian Reform." Ph.D. diss., Cornell University, Ithaca, N.Y., 1956.

Pearse, Andrew. "Peasant and Revolution: The case of Bolivia, Part I." *Economy and Society* 1.3 (1972): 255–80.

——. "Peasant and Revolution: The case of Bolivia, Part II." *Economy and Society* 1.4 (1972): 399–424.

Peñaloza B., Marco A. "Entrevista a James Dunkerley: Balance historiográfico sobre la revolución de 1952." *Data* 3 (1992): 157–64.

Peñaloza Cordero, Luis. *Historia secreta del Movimiento Nacionalista Revolucionario, 1941–1952*. La Paz: Juventud, 1963.

Pérez, Elizardo. *Warisata, La escuela-ayllu*. La Paz: HISBOL/CERES, 1992 [1962].

Pérez, Louis. *Cuba: Between Reform and Revolution*. New York: Oxford University Press, 1988.

Platt, Tristan. *Estado boliviano y ayllu andino: Tierra y tributo en el norte de Potosí*. Lima: IEP, 1982.

——. "Liberalism and Ethnocide in the Southern Andes." *History Workshop* 17 (1984): 3–18.

——. "The Andean Experience of Bolivian Liberalism, 1825–1900: Roots of Rebellion in 19th-Century Chayanta (Potosí)." In Stern, ed. *Resistance, Rebellion, and Consciousness in the Andean Peasant World*, 1987.

Plotkin, Mariano. *Mañana es San Perón: A Cultural History of Perón's Argentina*. Wilmington, Del.: Scholarly Resources, 2003.

Ponce Arauco, Gabriel. "Los alzamientos campesinos de 1947." *Búsqueda* 1.1 (1989): 107–28.

Poole, Deborah. "Ciencia, peligrosidad y represión en la criminología indigenista peruana." In Carlos Aguirre and Charles Walker, eds. *Bandoleros, abigeos y montoneros: Criminalidad y violencia en el Perú, siglos XVIII-XX*. Lima: Instituto de Apoyo Agrario, 1990.

——. *Vision, Race, and Modernity: A Visual Economy of the Andean Image World*. Princeton: Princeton University Press, 1997.

——. "Mestizaje, Distinction and the Political Language of Culture in Oaxaca." Paper presented at conference on Race, Culture, and Power in Latin America. University of Iowa, Iowa City, 2002.

Primer Congreso Interamericano de Indianistas. *Reglamento, Temario y Agendas*. La Paz: Editorial Fénix, 1939.

Pruden, Hernán. "Separatismo e integracionismo en la post Guerra del Chaco. Santa Cruz de la Sierra (1935–1939)." In Dora Cajías, Magdalena Cajías, Carmen Johnson, and Iris Villegas, eds. *Visiones de fin de siglo: Bolivia y América Latina en el siglo XX*. La Paz: IFEA/Historias, 2001.

Purnell, Jennie. *Popular Movements and State Formation in Revolutionary Mexico:*

The 'Agraristas' and 'Cristeros' of Michoacán. Durham: Duke University Press, 1999.

Qayum, Seemin. "Nationalism, Internal Colonialism and the Spatial Imagination: The Geographic Society of La Paz in Turn-of-the-Century Bolivia." In James Dunkerley, ed. *Studies in the Formation of the Nation State in Latin America.* London: Institute of Latin American Studies, University of London, 2002.

———. "Creole Imaginings: Race, Space and Gender in the Making of Republican Bolivia." Ph.D. diss., Goldsmiths College, University of London, 2002.

Qayum, Seemin, María Luisa Soux, and Rossana Barragán. *De terratenientes a amas de casa: Mujeres de la élite de La Paz en la primera mitad del siglo XX.* La Paz: Ministerio de Desarrollo Humano, 1997.

Quintana, Juan Ramón. *Policía y democracia en Bolivia: Una política institucional pendiente.* La Paz: PIEB, 2005.

Ranaboldo, Claudia. *El camino perdido: Chinkasqa ñan armat thaki.* La Paz: SEMTA, 1987.

Rappaport, Joanne. "Object and Alphabet: Andean Indians and Documents in the Colonial Period." In Elizabeth Boone and Walter Mignolo, eds. *Writing without Words: Alternative Literacies in Mesoamerica and the Andes.* Durham: Duke University Press, 1994.

———. *The Politics of Memory: Native Historical Interpretation in the Colombian Andes.* Durham: Duke University Press, 1998 [1990].

Rasnake, Roger. *Domination and Cultural Resistance: Authority and Power among an Andean People.* Durham: Duke University Press, 1988.

Reinaga, Fausto. *Tierra y libertad: La Revolución Nacional y el Indio.* La Paz: Rumbo Sindical, 1953.

Rénique, Gerardo. "Race, Region, and Nation: Sonora's Anti-Chinese Racism and Mexico's Postrevolutionary Nationalism, 1920s–1930s." In Appelbaum, Macpherson, and Rosemblatt, eds. *Race and Nation in Modern Latin America,* 2003.

República de Bolivia. *Código de las leyes del procedimiento civil boliviano.* Sucre: Imprenta Bolívar, 1890.

———. *Constitución política del estado, Ley de organización política y Reglamento de la ley de organización política. Reimpresión autorizada a Mariano E. Tapia.* La Paz: Imprenta Velarde, 1912.

———. *Redactor de la H. Cámara de Diputados, Legislatura Ordinaria de 1919.* Vol. 4. La Paz: Hugo Heitman.

———. *Proyectos de ley presentados a la H. Cámara de Diputados, 1919.* La Paz.

———. *Informes de comisiones de la H. Cámara de Diputados.* La Paz, 1919.

———. *Proyectos e informes de la H. Cámara de Senadores, 1919.* Vols. 1–2. La Paz.

———. *Redactor de la H. Cámara de Diputados, Legislatura Ordinaria de 1923.* Vols. 1–4. La Paz: Unidas, 1924.

———. *Redactor de la H. Cámara de Diputados, Legislatura Extraordinaria de 1923–24.* Vols. 5–6. La Paz: Unidas, 1924.

———. *Proyectos e informes de la H. Cámara de Senadores, Legislatura Ordinaria de 1923.* La Paz: Unidas, 1923.

———. *Redactor de la H. Cámara de Diputados, Legislatura ordinaria de 1924*. Vols. 1 and 3. La Paz.

———. *Redactor de la H. Cámara de Diputados, Legislatura ordinaria de 1926*. Vol. 2. La Paz.

———. *Redactor de la H. Cámara de Diputados, Legislatura extraordinaria de 1926*. Vol. 4. La Paz.

———. *Redactor de la Convención Nacional del año 1880*. Vol. 1. La Paz: Unidas, 1926.

———. *Redactor de la Asamblea Constituyente del año 1871*. La Paz: Unidas, 1927.

———. *Redactor de la H. Cámara de Diputados, Legislatura ordinaria de 1927*. Vols. 1 and 3. La Paz.

———. *Redactor de la H. Cámara de Diputados, Legislatura extraordinaria de 1927*. Vol. 5. La Paz.

———. *Anuario Administrativo de 1927*. La Paz: Unidas.

———. *Anuario Administrativo de 1939*. Vol. 2. La Paz: Edición Oficial.

———. *Proyectos e informes del H. Senado Nacional, Segundo Congreso Extraordinario de 1931–32*. La Paz: Unidas, 1932.

———. *Proyectos e informes del H. Senado Nacional, Legislatura Ordinaria de 1932*. La Paz: Unidas, 1932.

———. *Proyectos de ley e informes de comisiones de la H. Cámara de Diputados, 1932*. La Paz: La Razón, 1933.

———. *Proyectos de ley e informes de comisiones de la H. Cámara de Diputados, 1933*. La Paz: El Nacional, 1934.

———. *Proyectos e informes del H. Senado Nacional, Legislaturas Ordinarias y Extraordinarias de 1933*. La Paz: Unidas, 1934.

———. *Proyectos e informes del H. Senado Nacional, Legislatura Ordinaria de 1934*. La Paz: Unidas, 1934.

———. *Informes de Comisiones, H. Convención Nacional de 1938*. La Paz: Editorial Trabajo, 1938.

———. *Proyectos de Ley, H. Convención Nacional de 1938*. La Paz: Editorial Trabajo, 1938.

———. *Redactor de la H. Convención Nacional, 1938*. Vols. 1–5. La Paz: Universo, 1938–39.

———. *Anuario Administrativo, 1939*. Vols. 1–2. La Paz.

———. *Proyectos e informes del H. Senado Nacional, 2a. Legislatura Extraordinaria de 1940–1941*. La Paz: Unidas, 1941.

———. *Redactor de la Convención Nacional de 1943, Sesiones extraordinarias*. Vol. 2. La Paz.

———. *Anuario Administrativo de 1944*. La Paz: Edición Oficial.

———. *Proyectos de ley de la H. Convención Nacional de 1944*. La Paz: Editorial La Paz, 1944.

———. *Redactor de la H. Convención Nacional, 1944*. Vols. 1–5. La Paz: Editorial La Paz, 1944.

———. *Proyectos de Ley de la Convención Nacional de 1945*, Vol. 1. La Paz.

——. *Redactor de la Convención Nacional de 1945, Sesiones extraordinarias.* Vols. 1–2. La Paz, 1945.

——. *Redactor de la Convención Nacional de 1945, Sesiones ordinarias.* Vols. 1–5. La Paz, 1945.

——. *Código Busch: Decreto-ley de 24 de mayo de 1939, elevado a rango de Ley general del trabajo en 8 de diciembre de 1942: Edición corregida y aumentada con los últimos decretos y disposiciones del actual gobierno.* La Paz: Popular, 1946.

República de Bolivia, Dirección Nacional de Informaciones. *Bolivia: 10 años de revolución.* La Paz: Burillo y Cía, 1962.

República de Bolivia, Ministerio de Gobierno, Justicia e Inmigración. *Ley Electoral. Con un Apéndice de Disposiciones Legales Modificatorias, Dictadas Posteriormente.* La Paz: Universo, 1946.

República de Bolivia, Ministerio de Instrucción Pública y Agricultura. *Memoria.* La Paz: Artística, 1917.

——. *Memoria.* La Paz, 1918.

——. *Memoria y anexos.* La Paz, 1919.

——. *Anexos a la Memoria.* La Paz, 1925.

——. *Memoria.* La Paz, 1925.

——. *Memoria.* La Paz, 1927.

——. *Anexos a la Memoria.* La Paz, 1929.

——. *Memoria.* La Paz, 1930.

República de Bolivia, Ministerio de Justicia e Instrucción Pública. *Memoria.* La Paz, 1907.

——. *Memoria.* La Paz, 1909.

República de Bolivia, Oficina Nacional de Inmigración, Estadística y Propaganda Geográfica. *Censo general de la población de la República de Bolivia según el empadronamiento de 1 de septiembre de 1900.* 2 vols. 2nd ed. Cochabamba: Canelas, 1973.

Revollo Quiroga, Marcela. *Mujeres bajo prueba: La participación electoral de las mujeres antes del voto universal (1938–1949).* La Paz: Eureka, 2001.

Reyeros, Rafael. *El pongueaje: La servidumbre personal de los indios bolivianos.* La Paz: Universo, 1949.

——. *Historia social del indio boliviano, "El pongueaje."* 2nd rev. ed. La Paz: Editorial Fénix, 1963.

Rivera, Alberto. *Los terratenientes de Cochabamba.* Cochabamba: CERES/FACES, 1992.

Rivera Cusicanqui, Silvia. "La expansión del latifundio en el altiplano boliviano: Elementos para la caracterización de una oligarquía regional." *Avances* 2 (1978): 95–117.

——. *Oprimidos pero no vencidos: Luchas del campesinado aymara y qhechwa de Bolivia, 1900–1980.* La Paz: UNRISD, 1984.

——. "Taller de historia oral andina: Proyecto de investigación sobre el espacio ideológico de las rebeliones andinas a través de la historia oral (1900–1950)." In J. P. Deler and Y. Saint-Geors, eds. *Estados y naciones en los Andes.* Vol. 1. Lima: IEP, 1986.

———. " 'Pedimos la revisión de límites': Un episodio de incomunicación de castas en el movimiento de caciques-apoderados de los Andes Bolivianos, 1919–1921." In Segundo Moreno Y. and Frank Salomon, eds. *Reproducción y transformación de las sociedades andinas, siglos XVI–XX.* Quito: ABYA-YALA and MLAL, 1991.

———. "Reclaiming the Nation." *NACLA Report on the Americas* 38.3 (2004): 19–23.

Rocha, José Antonio. *Con el ojo de adelante y con el ojo de atrás: Ideología étnica, el poder y lo político entre los quechua de los valles y serranías de Cochabamba (1935–1952).* Cochabamba: UCB, 1999.

Rodríguez O., Gustavo. "Expansión del latifundio o supervivencia de las comunidades indígenas? Cambios en la estructura agraria boliviana del siglo XIX." Cochabamba: IESE, Serie Historia No. 1, 1983.

———. "Entre reformas y contrareformas: Las comunidades indígenas en el Valle Bajo cochabambino (1825–1900)." In Heraclio Bonilla, ed. *Los Andes en la encrucijada: Indios, comunidades y estado en el siglo XIX.* Quito: Flacso, 1991.

———. *Poder central y proyecto regional, Cochabamba y Santa Cruz en los siglos XIX y XX.* Cochabamba: ILDIS/IDAES, 1993.

———. "El fuego de la revuelta: Trabajadores y estudiantes en Cochabamba (1900–1932)." In Gustavo Rodríguez, ed. *La construcción de una región: Cochabamba y su historia, siglos XIX–XX.* Cochabamba: UMSS, 1995.

Rodríguez O., Gustavo, and Humberto Solares S. *Sociedad oligárquica, chicha y cultura popular.* Cochabamba: Editorial Serrano, 1990.

Romero Bedregal, Hugo. "Integración y politización en una sociedad compuesta: Los primeros sindicatos agrarios, las huelgas de brazos caídos y el primer congreso nacional indigenal en Bolivia." *Temas Sociales* 4 (1970): 73–92.

Roseberry, William. "Beyond the Agrarian Question in Latin America." In Frederick Cooper, Allen Isaacman, Florencia Mallon, William Roseberry, and Steve Stern, eds. *Confronting Historical Paradigms: Peasants, Labor, and the Capitalist World System in Africa and Latin America.* Madison: University of Wisconsin Press, 1993.

———. "Hegemony and the Language of Contention." In Gilbert Joseph and Daniel Nugent, eds. *Everyday Forms of State Formation: Revolution and the Negotiation of Rule in Modern Mexico.* Durham: Duke University Press, 1994.

Rosemblatt, Karin. *Gendered Compromises: Political Cultures and the State in Chile, 1920–1950.* Chapel Hill: University of North Carolina Press, 2000.

Rouma, Georges. *Las bases científicas de la educación.* Sucre: Bolívar, 1911.

Saavedra, Bautista. "La criminalidad aymara en el proceso Mohoza." In Bautista Saavedra, *El ayllu.* La Paz: Artística, 1903.

———. *La democracia en nuestra historia.* La Paz: Gonzalez y Medina, 1921.

———. *El ayllu: Estudios sociológicos.* La Paz: Juventud, 1987 [1903].

Sábato, Hilda. "On Political Citizenship in Nineteenth-Century Latin America." *American Historical Review* 106.4 (2001): 1290–315.

Safford, Frank. "Race, Integration, and Progress: Elite Attitudes and the Indian in Colombia, 1750–1870." *Hispanic American Historical Review* 71.1 (1991): 1–33.

Salamanca, Octavio. *En defensa de Bolivia: Respuesta a "Pueblo Enfermo."* Cochabamba: Tipografía La ilustración, 1914.

Sánchez, Wálter. "Hacienda, campesinado y estructura agraria en el Valle Alto, 1860–1910." Lic. thesis, Universidad Mayor de San Simón, 1992.

——. "Hacienda, campesinado y estructura agraria en el Valle Alto de Cochabamba, 1860–1910." *Retrospectiva, Boletín del Archivo Histórico Municipal de Cochabamba* 1.1 (1993): 41–54.

Sánchez-Albornoz, Nicolás. *Indios y tributos en el Alto Perú.* Lima: IEP, 1978.

Sanjinés U., Bernardino. *Venta de tierras de comunidad.* La Paz: Imprenta Paceña, 1871. Reprinted in *Illimani* 8–9 (1976): 51–75.

Santivañez, José María. *Rebindicación de los terrenos de comunidad o sea refutación del folleto titulado "Lejitimidad de las compras de tierras realengas."* Cochabamba: Imprenta del Siglo, 1871.

——. *Revindicación de los terrenos de comunidad.* Cochabamba: Imprenta del Siglo, 1871. Reprinted in *Illimani* 8–9 (1976): 99–138.

Schramm, Raimund. "Mosaicos etnohistóricos del valle de Cliza (valle alto cochabambino), siglo XVI." *Historia y Cultura* 18 (1990): 3–41.

Schwartz, Stuart B., and Frank Salomon. "New Peoples and New Kinds of People: Adaptation, Readjustment, and Ethnogenesis in South American Indigenous Societies (Colonial Era)." In Frank Salomon and Stuart B. Schwartz, eds. *The Cambridge History of the Native Peoples of the Americas.* Vol. 3.2. Cambridge: Cambridge University Press, 2000.

Serulnikov, Sergio. "Disputed Images of Colonialism: Spanish Rule and Indian Subversion in Northern Potosí, 1777–1780." *Hispanic American Historical Review* 76 (1996): 189–226.

——. *Subverting Colonial Authority: Challenges to Spanish Rule in Eighteenth-Century Southern Andes.* Durham: Duke University Press, 2003.

——. "Andean Political Imagination in the Late Eighteenth Century." In Jacobsen and Aljovín, eds. *Political Cultures in the Andes,* 2005.

Servicio Nacional de Reforma Agraria (SNRA). *Evaluación de la reforma agraria boliviana: El fermento pre-revolucionario (1932–1952).* Vol 2. La Paz: Servicio Nacional de Reforma Agraria, 1970.

Sider, Gerald. "When Parrots Learn to Talk, and Why They Can't: Domination, Deception, and Self-Deception in Indian-White Relations." *Comparative Studies in Society and History* 29.1 (1987): 3–23.

Silverblatt, Irene. *Moon, Sun, and Witches: Gender Ideologies and Class in Inca and Colonial Peru.* Princeton: Princeton University Press, 1987.

Simmons, Roger A. *Palca and Pucara: A Study of the Effects of Revolution on Two Bolivian Haciendas.* Berkeley: University of California Press, 1971.

Sinkin, Richard. *The Mexican Reform, 1855–1876: A Study in Liberal Nation-Building.* Austin: University of Texas Press, 1979.

Skocpol, Theda. *Social Revolutions in the Modern World.* Cambridge: Cambridge University Press, 1994.

Solares, Humberto. *Historia, espacio y sociedad, Cochabamba 1550–1950: Formación, crisis y desarrollo de su proceso urbano.* 2 vols. Cochabamba: Editorial Serrano, 1990.

Somers, Margaret. "Citizenship and the Place of the Public Sphere: Law, Community, and Political Culture in the Transition to Democracy." *American Sociological Review* 58 (1993): 587–620.

———. "Rights, Relationality, and Membership: Rethinking the Making and Meaning of Citizenship." *Law and Social Inquiry* 19 (1994): 63–112.

Soria Choque, Vitaliano. "Los caciques-apoderados y la lucha por la escuela (1900–1952)." In Choque et al., eds. *Educación indígena*, 1992.

Soux, María Luisa. "Autoridades comunales, coloniales y republicanas: Apuntes para el estudio del poder local en el altiplano paceño. Laja 1810–1850." *Estudios Bolivianos* 6 (1998): 93–123.

Spitzer, Leo. *Hotel Bolivia: The Culture of Memory in a Refuge from Nazism.* New York: Hill and Wang, 1998.

Stepan, Nancy. *"The Hour of Eugenics": Race, Gender, and Nation in Latin America.* Ithaca, N.Y.: Cornell University Press, 1991.

Stephenson, Marcia. *Gender and Modernity in Andean Bolivia.* Austin: University of Texas Press, 1999.

———. "Forging an Indigenous Counterpublic Sphere: The Taller de Historia Oral Andina in Bolivia." *Latin American Research Review* 37.2 (2002): 99–118.

Stern, Alexandra. "Responsible Mothers and Normal Children: Eugenics, Nationalism, and Welfare in Post-revolutionary Mexico, 1920–1940." *Journal of Historical Sociology* 12.4 (1999): 369–97.

———. "From Mestizophilia to Biotypology: Racialization and Science in Mexico, 1920–1960." In Appelbaum, Macpherson, and Rosemblatt, eds. *Race and Nation in Modern Latin America*, 2003.

Stern, Steve J. *Peru's Indian Peoples and the Challenge of Spanish Conquest: Huamanga to 1640.* Madison: University of Wisconsin Press, 1982.

———. "New Approaches to the Study of Peasant Rebellion and Consciousness: Implications of the Andean Experience." In Stern, ed. *Resistance, Rebellion, and Consciousness in the Andean Peasant World*, 1987.

———, ed. *Resistance, Rebellion, and Consciousness in the Andean Peasant World, 18th to 20th Centuries.* Madison: University of Wisconsin Press, 1987.

Stoler, Ann. *Race and the Education of Desire: Foucault's History of Sexuality and the Colonial Order of Things.* Durham: Duke University Press, 1995.

Stoler, Ann, and Frederick Cooper. "Between Metropole and Colony: Rethinking a Research Agenda." In Ann Stoler and Frederick Cooper, eds. *Tensions of Empire: Colonial Cultures in a Bourgeois World.* Berkeley: University of California Press, 1997.

Stoner, Lynn. *From the House to the Streets: The Cuban Woman's Movement for Legal Reform, 1898–1940.* Durham: Duke University Press, 1991.

Suárez Arnez, Cristóbal. *Desarrollo de la educación boliviana.* La Paz: Universo, 1970.

Taller de Historia Oral Andina (THOA). *El indio Santos Marka T'ula, Cacique Principal de los ayllus de Qallapa y apoderado general de la comunidades originarios de la república.* La Paz: THOA, 1984.

———. *La mujer andina en la historia*. Chukiyawu: THOA, 1990.

Taller de Historia Oral Andina/Silvia Rivera. "Indigenous Women and Community Resistance: History and Memory." In Elizabeth Jelin, ed., *Women and Social Change in Latin America*. London: Zed Books, 1990.

Tapia, Luis. "Ciclos políticos del siglo XX boliviano." In Dora Cajías, Magdalena Cajías, Carmen Johnson, and Iris Villegas, eds. *Visiones de fin de siglo: Bolivia y América Latina en el siglo XX*. La Paz: IFEA/Historias, 2001.

Taracena, Arturo. *Etnicidad, estado y nación en Guatemala, 1944–1985*. Vol. 2. Antigua, Guatemala: CIRMA, 2004.

Thiesenhusen, William C. *Broken Promises: Agrarian Reform and the Latin American Campesino*. Boulder: Westview Press, 1995.

Thomson, Guy P. C. "Popular Aspects of Liberalism in Mexico, 1848–1888." *Bulletin of Latin American Research* 10.3 (1991): 265–92.

Thomson, Sinclair. "La cuestión india en Bolivia a principios de siglo." *Autodeterminación* 2.4 (1987–88): 83–116.

———. *We Alone Will Rule: Native Andean Politics in the Age of Insurgency*. Madison: University of Wisconsin Press, 2002.

———. "Revolutionary Memory in Bolivia: Anticolonial and National Projects from 1781 to 1952." In Grindle and Domingo, eds. *Proclaiming Revolution*, 2003.

Thorn, Richard. "The Economic Transformation." In Malloy and Thorn, eds. *Beyond the Revolution*, 1971.

Ticona Alejo, Esteban. "Algunos antecedentes de organización y participación india en la Revolución Federal: Los Apoderados Generales, 1880–1890." *Temas Sociales* 14 (1989): 113–42.

———. "Manuel Chachawayna: El primer candidato aymara a diputado." *Historia y Cultura* 19 (1991): 95–101.

———. "Conceptualización de la educación y alfabetización en Eduardo Leandro Nina Qhispi." In Choque et al., eds. *Educación indígena*, 1992.

Ticona Alejo, Estebán, and Xavier Albó. *La lucha por el poder comunal (Jesús de Machaqa: La marka rebelde 3)*. La Paz: CIPCA/CEDOIN, 1997.

Trigo, Ciro Félix. *Las constituciones de Bolivia*. Madrid: Instituto de Estudios Políticos, 1958.

Turits, Richard. *Foundations of Despotism: Peasants, the Trujillo Regime, and Modernity in Dominican History*. Stanford: Stanford University Press, 2003.

United Nations. *Report of the United Nations Mission of Technical Assistance to Bolivia*. New York: United Nations, 1951.

Urquidi, Guillermo, ed. *Títulos y documentos relativos a la propiedad municipal de Vacas, perteneciente al tesoro de instrucción*. Cochabamba: Editorial López, 1928.

Urquidi, José Macedonio. *La obra histórica de Arguedas: Breves rectificaciones y comentarios*. Cochabamba: Imprenta La Aurora, 1923.

Urquidi Morales, Arturo. *La comunidad indígena: Precedentes sociológicos. Vicisitudes históricas. Cuadernos sobre Derecho y Ciencias Sociales*. No. 11. Cochabamba: Imprenta Universitaria, 1941.

Valdivieso, José. "La igualdad de los hijos ante la ley." *Revista Jurídica* 7.30 (1945): 174–80.

Vallejos, Fermín. *Tata Fermín: Llama viva de un Yachaq*. Cochabamba: CENDA, 1995.

Van Young, Eric. "Conclusion: The State as Vampire—Hegemonic Projects, Public Ritual, and Popular Culture in Mexico, 1600–1990." In Beezley, Martin, and French, eds. *Rituals of Rule, Rituals of Resistance*, 1994.

Viedma, Francisco de. *Descripción geográfica y estadística de la provincia de Santa Cruz de la Sierra*. Cochabamba: Los Amigos del Libro, 1969 [1788].

Villalpando, Abelardo. "La cuestión del indio." In *Primer Congreso Nacional de Facultades de Derecho*. Cochabamba: Imprenta Universitaria, 1940.

Villanueva y Saavdera, Etelvina. *Acción socialista de la mujer en Bolivia*. La Paz, 1970.

Villarroel, Gualberto. *Mensaje a la H. Convención Nacional de 1944*. La Paz, 1944.

——. *Mensaje a la H. Convención Nacional de 1945*. La Paz, 1945.

Wade, Peter. *Race and Ethnicity in Latin America*. London: Pluto Press, 1997.

——. "Afterword: Race and Nation in Latin America: An Anthropological View." In Appelbaum, Macpherson, and Rosemblatt, eds. *Race and Nation in Modern Latin America*, 2003.

Walker, Charles. *Smoldering Ashes: Cuzco and the Creation of Republican Peru, 1780–1840*. Durham: Duke University Press, 1999.

Whitehead, Christine. "Cochabamba Landlords and the Agrarian Reform." B. Phil., Oxford University, 1970.

Whitehead, Laurence. "Miners as Voters: The Electoral Process in Bolívia's Mining Camps." *Journal of Latin American Studies* 13.2 (1981): 313–46.

——. "Bolivia since 1930." In Bethell, ed. *The Cambridge History of Latin America*. Vol. 8, 1991.

——. "Bolivia." In Bethell and Roxborough, eds., *Latin America between the Second World War and the Cold War*, 1992.

——. "State Organization in Latin America since 1930." In Bethell, ed. *The Cambridge History of Latin America*. Vol. 6, 1994.

——. "The Bolivian National Revolution: A Twenty-First Century Perspective." In Grindle and Domingo, eds. *Proclaiming Revolution*, 2003.

Whitney, Robert. *State and Revolution in Cuba: Mass Mobilization and Political Change, 1920–1940*. Chapel Hill: University of North Carolina Press, 2001.

Wilkie, James. *The Bolivian Revolution and U.S. Aid since 1952: Financial Background and Context of Political Decisions*. Los Angeles: UCLA, 1969.

Williams, Derek. "Popular Liberalism and Indian Servitude: The Making and Un-making of Ecuador's Antilandlord State, 1845–1868." *Hispanic American Historical Review* 83.4 (2003): 696–733.

Williams, Patricia J. "Extrajudicial Activism." *The Nation*. 18–25 July 2005: 11.

Yashar, Deborah J. *Demanding Democracy: Reform and Reaction in Costa Rica and Guatemala, 1870s–1950s*. Stanford: Stanford University Press, 1997.

Zabala, Lourdes. "Las Madres de la Política." *Nosotras, Suplemento de Opinión*. 9 and 16 June 1987.

Zambrana, Juan de Dios [Los compradores de terrenos]. *Dos palabras sobre la venta de tierras realengas, a la nación, a la soberana asamblea y al supremo gobierno*. Cochabamba: Gutierrez, 1871. Reprinted in *Illimani* 8–9 (1976): 77–97.

Zavaleta Mercado, René. "Consideraciones generales sobre la historia de Bolivia (1932–1971)." In Pablo González Casanova, ed. *América Latina: Historia de medio siglo*. Vol. 1. Mexico City: Siglo XXI, 1977.

——. *50 años de historia*. Cochabamba: Los Amigos del Libro, 1992.

Zegada, José Antonio. "Declaración judicial de la paternidad." In *Primer Congreso Nacional de Facultades de Derecho*. Cochabamba: Imprenta Universitaria, 1940.

——. "La organización de la familia ante nuestra legislación." *Revista Jurídica* 8.35 (1946).

Zook, David H. *The Conduct of the Chaco War*. New Haven, Conn.: Bookman Associates, 1960.

Zulawski, Ann. "Hygiene and 'the Indian Problem': Ethnicity and Medicine in Bolivia, 1910–1920." *Latin American Research Review* 35.2 (2000): 107–29.

——. *Unequal Cures: Public Health and Political Change in Bolivia, 1900–1950*. Durham: Duke University Press, 2007.

122; constitutional convention of 1938 and, 101–3, 127–29; generation of, 127, 282; indigenous activists' positions on, 50; MNR's roots in, 169; origins of 1952 revolution and, 3, 282, 284–85, 356n.68; political developments following, 111–14; political mobilization of rural laborers and, 146; proposal for "Ministry of Racial Improvement" and, 312n.125; RADEPA and, 163, 167, 169; repression during, 97, 104–7; rural unrest following, 132–34; social mobilization following, 2, 5, 15, 106–11

Chayanta uprising of 1927. See rebellions

chicha, 10, 135, 138–40, 327n.17; protests against taxes on, 108, 157, 263, 330n.58; taxes on, 108, 145, 151, 154, 246

chicheras, 108, 138–39, 263, 328n.30

children's equality, 121–22, 176, 178

Chile: policies concerning "illegitimacy" in, 324–25n.116; War of the Pacific and, 27, 36

Chilina, Desiderio, 214, 344n.80

Chipana Ramos, Francisco, 214–16, 241, 258, 345n.110, 349n.48

Chuquisaca, 24, 53, 103, 154, 161, 234, 261, 297n.25; Alcaldes Mayores Particulares movement and, 152; cacique apoderado networks and, 46, 58; land surveys in, 32. See also Sucre

citizenship, 18–19, 27–30, 87, 273, 283–84, 287, 299n.56, 324n.107; caciques apoderados' invocation of, 56, 71, 90–91; constitutional convention of 1938 and, 103, 117–20, 127–28; definition of, 28–29, 90, 296n.5; gender and, 108, 118–20, 176; Indigenous Congress of 1945 and, 223; military socialism and, 101, 112–13, 118; MNR and, 276–77, 283, 341–42n.34, 354nn.38–39; political elites' views on, 21, 25, 27–30, 38, 44, 63–64; requirements for, 28, 299nn.54–55; work as condition of, 112–13, 118–19

Civil Code, 122, 150, 324n.113

civil rights: caciques apoderados' allusions to, 89–90; Constitution of 1938 and, 102, 149; definition of, 317n.89; Indian and peasant demands for, 284; unrest of 1947 and, 255, 264; Villarroel and, 223; women and, 109–10

civil war of 1899, 35–39

Claure, Toribio, 213, 218

Coca, José María, 236–37

Coca viuda de Coca, Margarita, 236

Cochabamba: agrarian reform of 1953 in, 270–71, 355n.55; Alcaldes Mayores Particulares movement in, 244–45, 332n.97; caciques apoderados in, 46–48, 52, 56, 58, 69–100, 283–84; colonial caciques in, 53–54; Disentailment Law and, 26; geography of, 9–10; hacienda system in, 134–46, 326n.8; Indian communities in, 9, 13, 22, 33–34, 41, 72–73, 82, 92–93, 132, 281, 294n.20; Indigenous Congress of 1945 and, 198–99, 207–8, 214–15; indigenous uprising of 1899 in, 36; landlord class in, 135; land privatization in, 31, 33–34; market women of, 166, 181–91; mestizaje and 12, 171, 174, 180, 183, 185–87, 191; military in, 166–67, 182, 185; Mother's Day in, 180–87; population statistics for, 294nn.18–19; protests by colonos in, 144, 146–59, 261–63; revolution of 1952 in, 269, 281, 286, 353n.7; rural strikes in, 132, 154–59, 210, 224; scholarship on peasantry in, 272–75, 293n.14, 354n.31; smallholding in, 22–23, 33–34, 123; urban population growth after Chaco War in, 107. See also rural unions; rural unrest

Colombia, liberal reforms in, 39

colonaje: in Cochabamba, 134–42, 326n.8; Indigenous Congress and, 216–17, 222; written agreements concerning, 148–51. See also colonos; mitanaje, mitanis; pongueaje

colonialism: impact of, on Indians, 10–11; Indians' invocation of laws and titles dating to, 4, 71, 77–78, 151–52;

revisitas: in Arque, 93; *caciques apode-rados* and, 59–60, 83, 99, 284; constitutional convention of 1938 and, 126; CSTB and, 160; implementation of, 30–34; Indigenous Congress of 1945 and, 209; Liberal Party and, 36, 38–39; mesas de revisita, 26; Primer Congreso Interamericano de Indianistas, 161; resistance to, 35, 97, 100; in Vacas, 71–79

Revolution of 1952, 129, 268, 352n.1; cultural origins and sources of, 283–87; historiography of rural mobilization in, 269, 271–76, 282; legacies of, 287–90; principal reforms of, 276–82; rural roots of, 3–4, 6, 12, 16, 114, 236, 261–64, 281–90, 293n.14, 354n.31; rural unrest following triumph of, 269–71, 281–82, 353n.7

Rivera, Silvia, 273–74, 354n.27

Robertson, William, 23

Rosa, Mariano, 69, 71, 73–79, 93

Rouma, Georges, 311n.112

Royal Dutch Shell, 103

Rumi Maqui movement (Peru), 306n.19

rural strikes, 4, 6, 131–32, 153–59, 162, 184, 210, 242, 247, 251–52, 258, 260–61, 263; following 1945 Indigenous Congress, 224–25; revolution of 1952 and, 269, 285; urban labor's role in 159–60, 199

rural unions, 262, 330n.66, 332n.105; Cochabamba region and, 9, 12, 114, 126, 132, 146, 154, 158, 351n.101; historiography of, 272–76; La Paz region and, 249–50, 254–56; revolution of 1952 and, 277, 280–81, 357n.79; rural strike activities and, 131–32

rural unrest, 3–4, 9, 48, 134, 163; Chaco War and, 106, 320n.28; following Indigenous Congress of 1945, 224–25; from 1948 to 1952, 261–62; revolution of 1952 and, 269–71, 274, 353n.7; in Vacas (1917), 73–74, 76. *See also* rural unrest of 1947

rural unrest of 1947, 2–4, 6, 234–36, 247, 257–60, 263–64, 271, 286, 288; in Anzaldo, 243–46; in Ayopaya, 236–43, 247, 249, 255–56, 258–59, 264–67, 286, 346–47n.3, 347n.10; in La Paz, 247–56, 258–60; in Sacabamba, 243, 246–47

rural–urban migration, 5, 11, 56, 107, 141, 143, 228

Saavedra, Abdón, 58, 312n.125

Saavedra, Bautista, 44, 57–58, 310n.81; *cacique apoderado* networks and, 58–60, 62; educational policies of, 61, 64; Jesús de Machaqa uprising and massacre and, 58–59, 64–65; labor laws and, 59; patronato indígena and, 66; racial ideologies and, 58, 61–62; Uncía mine massacre and, 310n.91

Sacabamba, 159, 243, 246–47

Salamanca, Daniel, 50, 103–6

Salazar, Feliciano, 73–74

Sánchez de Lozada, Gonzalo, 288

Sanjinés, Bernardino, 24–25

Santa Cruz, Andrés de, 296n.8

Santivañez, José María, 22–26

Sanzetenea de Terrazas, Teodosia, 184

Servicio Cooperativo Interamericano de Educación (SCIDE; Inter-American Cooperative Education Service), 213, 343n.76

servitude: ban on, by 1938 Constitution, 127, 330n.65; Indigenous Congress of 1945 and speech on, 216–17; nineteenth-century laws and legislative debates on, 26–28, 298n.50. *See also mitanaje, mitanis; pongueaje*

sharecropping, 141–42, 328n.37, 355n.52

Siles, Hernando, 110, 305n.7

Siles Zuazo, Hernán, 176, 216, 221, 226–28, 283, 346n.129

silver mining, 18–19, 32, 36, 303n.126

Siñani, Fernando, 59, 126, 323n.76

Sindicato de Comerciantes Minoristas, 181

Sindicato de Labradores, 250

Sindicato Gráfico, 112

smallholding, 13, 72, 246; agrarian reform of 1953 and, 279–80, 355n.55; in Cochabamba, 9–10, 12, 23, 33,

Valencia Vega, Alipio, 159
Vallejos, Fermín, 232
Vargas, Getulio, 102, 128
Vargas, Virgilio, 244–46, 262
Vasconcelos, José, 170
Vásquez, Mariano, 74
Vásquez, Martín, 47–48, 55
Vera, Mariano, 242–43
Villalpando, Abelardo, 325n.124
Villarroel, Gualberto, 2, 5–7, 131, 163, 167;
    Bolivian Indigenous Committee and,
    201–6; Indigenous Congress of 1945
    and, 192–97, 208–10, 213–14, 220–21,
    223–24; labor laws of, 175; mestizaje
    and, 165–66, 171, 174–75, 179–80, 187,
    191, 193; MNR alliance with, 164–67,
    276; Mother's Day and, 179–87;
    murder of, 233, 257; overthrow of, 7,
    191, 233–34; revolution of 1952 and
    legacy of, 281–82, 286; rural unrest
    and, 225, 234, 236–37, 239–47, 249,
    255–59, 261–67; social policies of, 175–
    78; urban markets and, 187–88, 190
voting rights. See citizenship

Warisata, indigenista school in, 113, 125,
    215
War of the Pacific, 27–30; formation of
    Liberal and Conservative Parties
    and, 36

women: agrarian reform of 1953 and,
    280; in anti-Villarroel coalition, 191,
    233; as cacicas, 53, 55–56; Chaco
    War and, 108–10; constitutional con-
    vention of 1938 and discussions
    about, 103, 118–20; constitutional
    convention of 1938 and influence of,
    102, 110, 115; hacienda labor system
    and, 136, 138–40, 144; Indigenous
    Congress of 1945 and, 207; labor
    movements and, 108–10, 181–82; as
    large landowners, 32, 151, 251, 300–
    301n.86; as market vendors, 165, 180–
    85, 188–90; revolution of 1952 and,
    268; rural unrest and, 348n.22; Villar-
    roel-MNR policies concerning, 165–
    66, 174–79; violence against, 149,
    240; voting rights and, 118–20,
    176, 276, 283

Yapiticona, Manuel, 88
yatiris, 55–56
Yungas, and unrest of 1947, 251–52

Zamudio, Adela, 181
Zapata, Ignacio, 260
Zapata viuda de Aramayo, María,
    260
Zárate Willka, Pablo, 36–38, 43, 47,
    172, 302n.112

LAURA GOTKOWITZ is an associate professor in the
Department of History at the University of Iowa.

Library of Congress Cataloging-in-Publication Data

Gotkowitz, Laura.
A revolution for our rights : indigenous struggles for land and
justice in Bolivia, 1880–1952 / Laura Gotkowitz.
    p. cm.
Includes bibliographical references and index.
ISBN 978-0-8223-4049-2 (cloth : alk. paper)
ISBN 978-0-8223-4067-6 (pbk. : alk. paper)
1   Bolivia—History—Revolution, 1952—Causes.
2   Indians of South America—Bolivia—
    Cochabamba (Dept.)—Government relations.
3   Indians of South America—Bolivia—
    Cochabamba (Dept.)—Civil rights.
4   Social movements—Bolivia—History—20th century.
    I. Title.
F3326.G68 2007
984.05′2—dc22
2007029317